FULBRIGHT
THE DISSENTER

ALSO BY HAYNES JOHNSON

The Bay of Pigs

FULBRIGHT

THE DISSENTER

Haynes Johnson
and
Bernard M. Gwertzman

HUTCHINSON OF LONDON

HUTCHINSON & CO (*Publishers*) LTD
178–202 Great Portland Street, London W1

London Melbourne Sydney
Auckland Bombay Toronto
Johannesburg New York

First published in Great Britain 1969

*This book has been set in Times, printed offset litho in Great Britain
by Anchor Press on Antique Wove paper, and
bound by Wm. Brendon, both of Tiptree, Essex*

For the Fulbright Fellows,
who are finishing "the great circle."

*"Americans are the western pilgrims,
who are carrying along with them that
great mass of arts, sciences, vigor
and industry, which began long since
in the east; they will finish the great
circle. . . . The American is a new man, who
acts upon new principles; he must therefore
entertain new ideas and form new opinions.
. . . This is an American."*

—Michel-Guillaume Jean de Crèvecoeur,
Letters from an American Farmer, 1782.

AUTHORS' NOTE

While this book is not authorized, or commissioned, Senator Fulbright did make available, without restriction, all of his files, personal and otherwise, going back to 1939. The only limitation was the inevitable one of dealing with still active, and major, political leaders: many letters, memoranda, and official documents cannot, therefore, be printed at this time. Someday, we are certain, the Fulbright correspondence alone will prove a rich and revealing vein to the historian. During the preparation of this book, Senator Fulbright also participated in a number of lengthy tape-recorded sessions. Whenever his words are directly quoted without a footnote citation, they are taken from transcripts of those interviews.

The book itself is the product of the research and thinking of two men, but the actual writing was done by Haynes Johnson.

CONTENTS

PROLOGUE

Power

The Capitol, Friday, January 30, 1959:

Even to senators accustomed to ceremony and theatrical gestures, the circumstances of J. William Fulbright's assumption of power held an element of unusual drama and history. The actual facts of his ascension, as opposed to what the public was told, were as ironic as anything that had happened in his long public career. It was not surprising; that was how Washington really worked.

The senators had been summoned that day, urgently and unexpectedly, by the Majority Leader, Lyndon Johnson of Texas. By noon their business had been completed. When the doors to the committee room finally swung open to admit the crowd of reporters and television cameramen waiting in the marble corridors, even the newsmen were struck by the setting before them.

There, in the mirrored elegance of the ornate committee room, with its crystal chandeliers, exquisitely fashioned fireplaces, and great wall maps of the world, two men were sitting solemnly in front of the oval green baize table where the committee conducted its affairs.

The senator, at 91 the oldest man ever to serve in Congress, small, gray, a slight smile on his face, sat in the high-backed leather chair denoting the chairman, blinking now and then through his glasses as the light from the cameras stung his eyes. On his left was his younger colleague, the Majority Leader, who towered over him in size. As always when it came to Senate business, the Majority Leader dominated the moment. Lyndon Johnson was reading his statement:

"In the whole history of the Senate there have been few careers as distinguished as Senator Green. . . . His love of country is so great that he has decided to resign the chairmanship of the Foreign Relations Committee—an action which I personally advised him against."

The Majority Leader referred to the senator's "alert mind and his vast experience in the field of foreign affairs" and told, with emotion, of the meeting that had just ended: how every member of the committee had urged the old man not to resign; how they had spoken, these leaders of the Senate, each of them in turn.

Fulbright of Arkansas, slated to become chairman by seniority, the system he had criticized so often, spoke first. Among those who followed him were Sparkman of Alabama, his party's candidate for the vice presidency in the last election; Humphrey of Minnesota, who like three others in the room already was planning his campaign to win the presidential nomination the next year; Mansfield of Montana, Johnson's scholarly lieutenant in the Senate; Morse of Oregon, the maverick; Long of Louisiana, Huey's son; and the youngest of them, in age and in service, John F. Kennedy of Massachusetts.

They had not been successful in their arguments, the Majority Leader was saying: they had not persuaded the senator to remain at the head of the most prestigious committee in Congress, the committee some pompously liked to call "the elite of the elite." All in all, Johnson said, it had been one of the "most unpleasant" days of his career.

At last Senator Green had his turn before the cameras.

The newsmen were solicitous. With his pince-nez, his hearing aid, his white moustache, his courtly manners, and his great age, Theodore Francis Green had always been popular. He was resigning, he said, because his hearing and his eyesight were failing. It was difficult for him to carry on his responsibilities as chairman. Still, he hoped to remain in the Senate until he was 100.

The accounts of his extraordinary resignation (Charles L. Watkins, the Senate parliamentarian, could recall no other precedent) were long, laudatory, and laced with sentiment. Everything was said—except what had really happened behind those closed doors.

For despite the accounts of his vigor, Senator Green had not been functioning effectively as the head of what was not only the most important congressional committee, but also the world's most powerful legislative group in the field of foreign affairs. In committee meetings, he dozed or slept. He did not follow the witnesses. He could not reach decisions.

Lyndon Johnson, who knew everything worth knowing in the Senate, was well aware of the problem, but unable or unwilling to do anything about it. Aside from the inviolate requirements of the congressional seniority system, Johnson owed Green a debt: it was Green, six years earlier, who had made the speech nominating Johnson as Majority Leader.

Inevitably, though, in the way of Washington, the story of Green's physical decline began to circulate privately. Finally, on January 29 *The Providence Journal*, the leading paper in the senator's native state, editorially urged him to resign. "A delicate question," the paper said, was being raised about his fitness to continue in such an important post. Green made his own decision and informed Johnson, who hastily called the committee meeting for the next day.

Senators are as used to acting out the required ritual of their office in private as in public. They did so in their meeting that morning when they began to speak words of praise for their chairman. Besides, no matter what they may have thought about Green's performance or capabilities of late, they were genuinely fond of him. He was kind and gentle. He had no enemies.

The old man's eyes filled with tears as they spoke and when, as a formality, they passed a unanimous 14–0 resolution urging him to stay on, Green wavered. His colleagues had done what they really did not intend to: they had, in fact, nearly persuaded him to stay.

"All we were doing," said one senator who was in that room that day, "was being nice to him and trying to flatter him and, by God, it almost made him think that he'd back out. You know how eulogistic we are. In trying to be nice and soften the blow, we almost talked him out of it. We'd overdone the eulogy. Lyndon took the lead in persuading the old man that this ought to be done, that he ought to resign."

With Green visibly undecided, the Majority Leader acted. A recess was called, and Green was given time to reconsider his decision in private. As he walked out, Johnson turned quickly to Carl Marcy, the chief of staff of the Foreign Relations Committee, and said, "This will never do." Marcy and Eddie Higgins, an assistant of Green's, followed the chairman out of the room. "I told him that he'd get a great press, that no one had ever gone out this way," Marcy recalled later, "and Eddie persuaded him that since he had made his decision, he should stick by it."

While they were talking with the chairman outside the room, inside Lyndon Johnson was cautioning the other members of the committee not to be swayed by sentiment. They *did* need a new chairman.

When Green returned, he said he was standing by his decision: he was going to resign. No one spoke up. No one tried to change his mind. His resignation was immediately announced to the press.

In that way, J. William Fulbright became the chairman of the Senate Foreign Relations Committee.

The transfer of power focused new attention on Fulbright's career and led to considerable speculation about his future role. As it was quickly pointed out, his public life had been marked by a number of inconsistencies and incongruities.

His old acquaintance, Arthur Krock, noted one of them when he wrote that Fulbright's name was "perhaps more favorably known in more countries than any American legislator in many decades." And yet, as Krock pointed out, "despite this international fame, the Senator at fifty-three has just attained his first office of direct power in the formulation and conduct of United States foreign policy." Krock's colleague, James Reston, had another interpretation. Fulbright, he said, "has been frustrated and even a little sour in his secondary role under the ninety-one-year-old Chairman Green, but has now a new responsibility and opportunity to create a better atmosphere."

Others saw in the change a hopeful return to a new era in the Senate, and for the Foreign Relations Committee in particular a resumption of its golden age of influence in policy making. As Fulbright's close friend, Walter Lippmann, wrote, "His advent as chairman of the Committee marks a turning point for the better in the conduct of our foreign policy. For the first time since the new era which began with World War II, the administration will have a responsible and articulate and loyal opposition. . . . With Senator Fulbright as chairman of the committee, the windows of the Senate will be open to the fresh air of a new time."

On one point, everyone agreed: under Fulbright, the administration would come under far sharper and more searching criticism, for Fulbright was the most outspoken critic of President Dwight D. Eisenhower's foreign policies. He was even harsher on the administrator of those policies, Secretary of State John Foster Dulles.

In this, Fulbright differed drastically from Theodore Green. During Green's tenure as chairman, he had continued in the pattern set by his predecessors, Walter George, Alexander Wiley, Arthur Vandenberg, and Tom Connally. Unlike the strong chairmen of the past, Clay and Buchanan, Lodge and Borah, the more recent committee leaders could always be counted on to support the administration with hardly a dissent on any given issue. But under Fulbright, it was clear that recent tradition would·pass. Beyond that, no one could say with certainty where Fulbright's leadership might take the committee—or the country.

That both confidence and doubt were expressed about Fulbright was typical of him, for he was an anomaly as a politician.

While his name, through the Fulbright fellowships he had inspired, had become a household term throughout the world, he was aloof and known personally only to a relative few. Although he had few close friends in the Senate, strangely, in view of their different personalities, he admired no one more than the Majority Leader, Lyndon Johnson. Fulbright was solidly behind the Texan for the presidency. Johnson, in his own right, admired Fulbright and seemed to envy him his background of wealth and education. The Majority Leader, as was his nature, let everyone know how he felt: on many occasions Lyndon Johnson would throw his arm around Bill Fulbright and say loudly to all present, "Bill's *my* Secretary of State."

But unlike Johnson and his other colleagues in the Senate, Fulbright was not a member of "the club," that closely knit group of men who by virtue of their elective powers and their accumulated years of seniority set the tenor and the tone for the Congress of the United States. Fulbright was not an insider.

That was not out of character, either, for Fulbright had never been a conventional politician.

There had been a time when no one's political career seemed to hold more promise. In his thirties, as a young Congressman, he had been mentioned seriously for the presidency, or at least the vice presidency. Certainly the position of Secretary of State appeared then to be his for the asking. He was the young man of ideas, the first Rhodes scholar in the Senate, the university president turned politician. But while he was a loyal Democrat, over the years he had alienated himself from his party's leaders by his critical and, even worse for a professional politician, naive comments.

By 1959, after fourteen years in the Senate, his principal contribution consisted of periodic speeches in which he brilliantly analyzed the American character or the American predicament in the Cold War; but their impact was slight. Few heard his words. Most of his speeches were attended by only a handful of senators. The galleries were empty. Still, Fulbright continued to speak out, seeming something of a Henry Adams figure, distant, at times moody, pessimistic, and frustrated by his lack of influence.

He had demonstrated genuine independence and courage, however, and a surprising toughness in a fight. No one had spoken out more forthrightly on foreign affairs or on the McCarthy menace of a few years earlier. At the same time he had compiled a weak record on other issues, particularly civil rights. In fact, he was a strange combination of liberal and conservative. He could be both timid and bold, and thus often left his most loyal supporters perplexed. That his name would become synonymous with dissent throughout the world seemed then an unlikely prospect.

Of one fact there was no question: Fulbright's coming to congressional power at the end of the Eisenhower years held profound implications for the course of America's foreign relations. In that sense, he was in the vanguard of the Democratic senators and political leaders who were destined to place their own stamp on the American and world scene for at least another generation.

Whether Fulbright would be counted among the great ones of that group it was then impossible to say, but he was at least as representative of his country as Kennedy or Johnson or Humphrey or Stevenson or the rest. And, perhaps more than any of them, his life encompassed the diverse strains of America. Fulbright was the Southerner who faced West; the internationalist who represented Arkansas; the liberal who drew for inspiration on the older models, Jefferson and De Tocqueville; the conservative who viewed people in terms of superiority and inferiority; the politician, at once brave and reluctant.

Through Fulbright's life one might be able to perceive more clearly the American ambiguities, those gaps between promise and fulfillment. Where his own future would take him, certainly he could never have foreseen at that time.

BOOK ONE

Student

1

"IN THE MAIN, HONEST, TRUSTWORTHY"

IN 1906, WHEN JAY FULBRIGHT MOVED SOUTH into the Ozark Mountains, Jeff Davis was in his third term as governor of Arkansas. Florid, picturesque, a great stump speaker, Jeff was the most successful politician in the history of the state. He came from the Ozarks himself; he was a man of the people who made the most of his name. When going before his fellow citizens, he always wore a gray frock coat and a black string tie and liked to tell of the time when his clothes had been torn off while crawling under barbed wire fences following his rabbit dogs.[1]

From afar, Jeff was regarded as only another backwoods demagogue, but the people of Arkansas loved him. He was their William Jennings Bryan; indeed, they even called him "The Silver Tongued Orator of Arkansas." The description was typical of the time. Jeff was typical, too. He was representative of his state, and he left his mark on it.

At the turn of the century, Arkansas needed someone like Jeff Davis to cheer. The old jokes about the Arkansas Traveler and the hillbillies had shamed the people—and, with a whoop and a holler for Jeff, they set out to prove the common impression wasn't true. Instead, their actions merely emphasized that, in 1906, Arkansas was still on the frontier. Oklahoma, on the western border, had been opened to white settlers only seventeen years before and was then a territory; and the people of Arkansas themselves were still characterized by that raucous boastfulness which Mark Twain had described thirty years earlier.

"Whoo-oop!" Twain had quoted one of them as saying. "I'm the original iron-jawed, brass-mounted, copper-bellied corpse-maker from the wilds of

Arkansas! Look at me! . . . and lay low and hold your breath, for I'm 'bout to turn myself loose!"

They were, as Twain said, "prodigious braggarts; yet, in the main, honest, trustworthy, faithful to promises and duty, and often picturesquely magnanimous."[2]

Jay Fulbright was not as coarse and unlettered as the corpse-maker from the wilds of Arkansas, but they did have something in common. Jay was hungry for land and money. He was a prodigious worker and, as he came to the Ozarks, he also was prepared to turn himself loose on what was then officially called "The Bear State." (A few years later, the Arkansas lawmakers, realizing that that label led "to a false impression," promptly and unanimously passed a resolution changing the name to "The Wonder State," a fact which, they said, "had been indelibly stamped upon the mind of the world.")[3]

Fulbright was a farmer. He had been born in Rothville, Missouri, a year after the Civil War, and he had worked hard all his life. Although he attended the University of Missouri for a year, he was not an educated man. He cared little for books. Business was his compelling interest.

Long after he had died and his son had become prominent, a genealogist traced the Fulbright line in search of the seeds of greatness. It was a disappointing task. The first American immigrant, a Johan Wilhelm Volprecht, had been born near Berlin, Germany, and had come to Dutch Cove, Pennsylvania, in 1740, but neither he nor his descendants had achieved distinction, or even minor office. With the exception of a cabinetmaker or shoemaker, they had all been farmers. As they headed south and then west, they anglicized their last name and added an American touch to their Christian names: there were George Washington Fulbrights, Andrew Jackson Fulbrights, and Martin Van Buren Fulbrights, as well as the more traditional Jacob, John, and Levi Fulbrights in the family.

Jay's father, William, also was a farmer who had moved his family from Green County, Indiana, to Chariton County in northwest Missouri. The winters were harsh there, and toward the end of his life William Fulbright moved once again—due south into the northwestern corner of Arkansas, not far from the university town of Fayetteville, where, even though it was in the mountains, the climate was more benign.

William Fulbright was an old retired farmer when he came to Arkansas. A family acquaintance of those days, Jack Reed, remembered him as "a strong Republican, and so was Jay. But Jay's father was tougher'n a boot. He liked a bottle of whiskey, and could outcuss a sailor. God, he was tough! His choice of profane language was a wonder." His grandson, the senator, had few memories of him, but he did recall his Grandma Fulbright along similar lines. "She was," he said, "a stern old buzzard, really stern."

Jay Fulbright could be stern and tough, too. He was also ambitious and determined to succeed. By 1893, the year of his wedding, and the year of a great economic depression in the nation, he had accumulated enough money to buy a thousand-acre farm near Rothville. That is where he and his wife began their married life.

Roberta Waugh grew up on a farm near Jay Fulbright. The Waughs originally were of English extraction, and proud of it. They had come to Missouri from Virginia in the 1840s, and like many Virginians who moved west, they fancied themselves a cut above their neighbors—even though they had been poor in Virginia and remained poor in Missouri. Again, like many Virginians, they took comfort in their "good blood." It helped somehow to take their attention away from their lack of money in the bank.

As a child, Roberta heard members of her family ridiculing the thrift, industry, and stinginess of their more prosperous neighbors. She also remembered her mother taking her aside after such a family conversation and saying: "My dear, the rich are not the only ones who love money better than all else. There are some poor ones, near to you, who hold it pretty high. The trouble is they hate rather the industry, the thrift and the frugality of the rich. They prefer to sleep late and long, eat much, and work little." Homely as it was, it was a lesson that Roberta would remember all her life, and which she tried to transmit to her own children.[4]

Financial considerations aside, however, hers was a happy childhood and home. To Roberta, who experienced more than her share of heartbreak, in retrospect they had been bucolic days, and years later she would recall them in detail: her father, up in the early morning splitting kindling and making a fire, first in the kitchen stove, then in the front-room stove; her mother, breaking the ice in the waterbucket, chopping the lard with a butcher knife and a hammer to make hot biscuits, and then grinding the coffee in a mill on the wall; the cooking, churning, sewing, and cleaning that were required of her; the trundle beds, the stile blocks and hitching posts; the long riding skirts and green blouses; the taffy pulls, the spelling bees, the corn huskings.

The hard work taught another kind of lesson. "I am always conscious," she said in middle-age, "of the labor which goes into the things we consume and how calmly we accept them. A pound of butter made by myself created forever within me a respect for butter. . . . The rugs on the floor, the quilts on the bed, the firewood which has taken literally decades to grow and human strength and labor to cut, are all to be respected."

In the early 1890s, Roberta, like Jay Fulbright, went to the University of Missouri at Columbia. She was so homesick at first that she nearly left the campus; then one night she went to the Athenian Society and heard Walter Williams speak. He was small, unprepossessing, and had a high, shrill voice, but for Roberta he had "the quality of martial music." Williams was the founder of Missouri's Journalism School, the first in the world, and, despite his appearance, a vital, commanding figure. He made a convert of Roberta Waugh: he was, as she said, "about the most vivid personality I have ever known." In later years, it was therefore perfectly natural for her to want to take over a daily newspaper, manage it, and also find time to write a daily column.

Roberta did not finish college; instead, she returned home and began teaching in a country school outside of Rothville, Jay Fulbright's home.

Roberta was married in a tweed traveling suit, instead of the white silk bolting dress she had hoped for, and a white stiff collar that "almost cut my throat." Jay's wedding present was a Bible; he had given her *Paradise Lost* the Christmas before. "He knew little of either of them," his wife said later, "but it seemed fitting to him that I should know."

Outside of his own family, those who knew Jay Fulbright well recall him as remote, aloof. The same would be said of his son. "He was an agreeable fellow," said Fenner Stice, who had worked for him, "but there was no fun about him." A university official, T. C. Carlson, put it another way: "You didn't get to know Jay Fulbright very well."

He was self-reliant and thorough; he was also demanding, of his family, his friends, and his business acquaintances. "He always expected the limit of me . . . almost beyond measure," his wife said. The same was true of his children.

After his marriage he worked harder than ever—and required everyone to work along with him. Within two years the mortgage on his thousand-acre farm had been paid off. Then one day he came home with a terse announcement to his wife: "Old woman, I bought the bank." Roberta cried, but they left the farm and moved to Sumner, Missouri, where he had purchased the bank with $10,000 capital. There, Roberta had her second child, also a girl. She would nurse until ten, work at the bank till noon, and return to it after lunch. The bank—and the babies—prospered.

Jay continued to look for new ventures. When the news came that a horseless carriage was making trial runs in New York, Jay said, "if they ever get one of those things, I'm going to have one. I'm tired of mud and horses." But, also typically, when the first car came to the area—an Oldsmobile owned by a banker friend in a nearby town—Jay inspected it and found it wanting. He waited until the machine was better perfected before buying one. When the first telephones were installed in Sumner, he examined them, and pronounced: "I just won't have one of those things; they're no good." Three months later the Fulbrights had their phone installed.

In the meantime, Jay was branching out. He was buying and selling land in western Kansas and the Oklahoma territory, including some of the most valuable acres around what later became the city of Tulsa. Like his bank and his babies (there were three now; the first son, Jack, followed his daughters Lucille and Anna), his businesses were prospering. By April 1905, when his fourth child, James William Fulbright, the future senator, was born, he was ready to move again. He did within a year—to two miles west of Fayetteville, not far from where his father had gone to retire in the Ozarks. Jay had visited there, and had liked it. There the Fulbrights settled, forty miles south of the Missouri-Kansas border and thirty miles east of the Oklahoma Territory.

A family tradition, one that Roberta Fulbright repeated many times to her children, was that they had moved to Arkansas to escape the severe winters in northwest Missouri. That, apparently, was only part of what Jay Fulbright had in mind.

Anxious, as ever, for greater opportunities, he was thinking of moving eventually to Memphis, Tennessee, where he had bought some delta land along the Mississippi. Memphis, he thought, was destined to become the great city of the New South. Naturally, he wanted to be among those to share in that greatness.

As it turned out, though, he found his success in Arkansas and never left.

Once again, Jay started out on a farm, but he also invested in a bank in Fayetteville. He saved and invested, saved and invested, again and again. He had a retail grocery store, and a wholesale grocery store; then a chicken-and-egg business; then a lumber company, a retail lumber and cement company, an ice company, a hotel; then the newspaper, which he bought to help the Republican Party in an area of Democrats; then a partnership in another bank. He was canny and hard-headed, but not all of his ventures were profitable.

During World War I, he lost heavily through an investment in a zinc mine near Joplin, Missouri. He got the lumber company in Fayetteville on a bad note; it paid only one or two dividends in thirty years and, as his son said later, "that goddamn thing has been an albatross around our necks ever since."

But he had an instinct for a good investment. In 1920, when he bought the Coca-Cola franchise for $5,500, the bank's board of directors thought he had lost his mind. Like almost everything he did, it was a smart deal.

Jay expected all of the family to work in one of his enterprises, and they did.

Young Bill Fulbright, who never used his first name, James, worked in the lumber yard, and later in the bottling plant. After he had been in Washington nearly a quarter of a century, he still remembered, with great clarity, the process of washing those bottles with a brush, passing them through a solution of caustic soda, filling them, and then capping them.

When he was older, he delivered them up and down the mountains in a horse and wagon.

In the summers, the Fulbright children were given a choice: they could either work in one of the businesses or go to a summer school which the university was operating for pre-college students. Bill chose school. "I started on the campus of the University of Arkansas in the basement of Old Main and never went to any other school until I graduated," he said, "and I suppose that accounts for my parochial outlook. I spent fifteen years on the campus of the University of Arkansas before I could graduate, which is true." In fact, by going to summer school he was admitted to college before the normal age.

By the time Bill Fulbright began going to summer school, his father was among the three wealthiest men in Fayetteville and probably in that part of Arkansas. The Fulbrights long since had moved into the finest home in Fayetteville, a red-brick, white-columned building atop Mount Nord, which offered a commanding view of the city below and the mountains beyond. Inside, the house was paneled in walnut. It had a spacious formal dining room, a library, and a large stairway winding past a stained glass window of a pastoral scene. Outside, there were lovely gardens, the pride and handiwork of Roberta Fulbright.

Jay Fulbright had put the farm behind him.

2

ALL-AMERICAN FROM ARKANSAS

BILL FULBRIGHT'S BOYHOOD WAS SECURE; he never had any worries that anyone can recall. He loved the physical setting of his youth—the mountains, the streams, and the outdoor life of fishing and swimming. Like his father, whom he greatly admired and whose approval he eagerly sought, he was self-contained and independent. And, again like Jay, Bill was regarded even then as something apart. He did not associate with large numbers of boys. Instead, he found his pleasures in the company of a few close friends, and in the country in which he lived.

One of his earliest triumphs spoke much of his boyhood and of his youthful interests. It was a modest success that came when the Fulbrights still lived on the farm outside Fayetteville: Bill won the annual horse harnessing contest at the Washington County Fair under the eyes of his father, who was chairman of the fair.

"That was a great accomplishment," Bill recalled later. "I thought I was extraordinarily good in taking care of animals. I used to ride horseback. I could ride a horse just like a circus performer, I thought. Bareback. I used to ride to town often bareback when we lived out on the farm. And to harness a horse quicker than anyone else—that was a great accomplishment! It's sort of like riding the Preakness today."

Another of his fondest memories was of loading up a wagon and spending two or three nights camping out with his father on a gravel bar along the White River. That was "extraordinarily thrilling." And when, in the summer of 1918, he went to his first Boy Scout camp on the White River, he found it "the most exhilarating tonic a boy could possibly have. For the first time we were men, away from our mothers, on our own in the wide open spaces. I don't think there is any other pleasure in a man's life quite comparable to that first camp."[1]

To those who met him then, he seemed much like any other boy of that time and place. One of his father's employees remembered seeing him for the first time immediately after World War I. "He crawled out from under an old Chalmers car wearing Indian moccasins, a pair of khaki pants, no shirt, and an old derby hat," said Fenner Stice. "He had grease all over him, and he was grinning from ear to ear."

Yet Bill was not always the smiling stereotype of an American boy of his era, that kind of Tom Sawyer free spirit who beamed down from countless calendars and who was always supposed to be tinkering with cars, roaming the mountains, fishing, and playing innocent pranks. Others remember Bill Fulbright as being "moody at times," as introspective and serious, and as "different." He also had a temper, and knew how to fight: one of his lifelong friends recalled how "Bill beat the hell out of me with his fists" after they quarreled over a girl. Bill was seventeen at the time. Within the Fulbright family itself, there were tensions and strains, particularly between Bill and his brother Jack.

Jack Fulbright was not only the older brother; he was several inches taller, more powerful physically, and a better athlete. Despite these personal advantages, for some reason Jay Fulbright favored his second son, Bill, and the brothers did not always get along. Years later when he was involved in acrimonious disputes in Washington with critics questioning his motivations and even his psychological soundness, Fulbright looked back toward his own family relationships for a bit of self-analysis.

"My father was extremely influential in causing me to do whatever I did," he said. "We hit it off very well. I don't know why. He didn't get along with my older brother and perhaps I was compensating or vice versa. I don't understand all these psychological inspirations. But my father and I got along very well."

Jack followed his father's lead and also went to the University of Missouri, where he played on the football team and was a member of Jay's fraternity. Later, he went to Harvard, while all the time Bill remained at home, the center of attention for his parents and his four sisters (the twins, Helen and Roberta, had been born after the family moved to Arkansas).

Because of their position as leading citizens in Fayetteville, the Fulbright home became a social center. There, on the wide porch overlooking the city, the Fulbright girls served tea to their dates in the afternoons. There, at night, Mrs. Fulbright entertained the university professors and their wives, for, outside of a few business acquaintances, all of the Fulbright family friends came from the university. That was natural: the university dominated the social life of the town; it eclipsed everything in Fayetteville. The Fulbright children grew up in its shadow.

But the University of Arkansas was not a distinguished institution. Like the country in which it was located, it was insular and poor, far removed from the larger educational and national issues. In this, it had much in common with other southern colleges. And Arkansas was the poorest of all the states. In Fulbright's boyhood years, the university still admitted students upon completion of only three years of high school. It wasn't until 1922, when Bill Fulbright was halfway through college, that the University of Arkansas became a member of the American Association of Universities and was fully accredited nationally.

Bill Fulbright did not seem to mind if the university rating was low. He had never considered going anywhere else, and nothing in his years at the university caused him to doubt his choice. On the campus he was something of the boy wonder, the prototype of the all-American boy from Arkansas. He was a fine athlete, the captain of the tennis team and the star football player, a triple threat man, a passer, kicker, and runner. He was president of his fraternity, Sigma Chi; president of the student body; a member of the student senate, and of virtually every other campus organization that counted—Marble Arch, the "A" Club, the Arkansas Boosters' Club, the Glee Club. And he also compiled a straight "B" grade average.

"Hardly a field of student activity has not felt Bill's influence at one time or another," a local paper commented during his college days.[2] Of all those days, the most memorable was in the fall of 1922 when the university scheduled the first homecoming football game in its history. Arkansas already had lost four times that season, and the homecoming game unfortunately pitted them against the conference power, Southern Methodist University. SMU was favored by six touchdowns. But Fulbright, with a display of Dick Merriwell daring, won the game practically single-handedly. He passed for the only touchdown, and later, on fourth down, kicked a perfect field goal. Arkansas was victorious, 9–0. Fulbright was the campus hero. He was only seventeen.

The honors and acclaim were misleading, however, in one respect: Fulbright was not a particularly popular student. "Popular isn't the word," said T. C. Carlson, later the business manager of the university, and then the athletic manager. "Bill was highly respected. Bill was moderately sociable, and not particularly approachable. It somewhat surprised me when he won the student presidency. I didn't think of him as political material."

Neither, apparently, did Fulbright himself. He spoke then vaguely of either teaching or entering the consular service abroad.[3] He was not thinking of a political career. In fact, he did not seem unusually ambitious, nor was he a truly outstanding student. He was not an avid reader; he did not concern himself with ideas and issues; he himself remembered later that he studied more to please his father than out of intellectual curiosity. Jay Fulbright expected him to make good grades; Bill did. If he thought seriously of his own future, he did not indicate it at the time. Indeed, Bill Fulbright had experienced no major problems until the summer of 1923. Then, he and every member of his family underwent a shock that affected all of their lives.

Jay Fulbright had never been sick, that his son could remember. He never smoked; he never drank; he was even something of a health addict, always keeping a bottle of mineral water on his desk at the bank. He was fifty-six years old when, in mid-July of 1923, his mother died of old age. Jay went to her funeral. When he returned home he suddenly became ill. His blood pressure rose alarmingly, he quickly became delirious and, fifty-six hours after he was confined to his bed, he died at his home on Mount Nord. Death was attributed to "high blood pressure and internal complications." In fact, no one ever was certain exactly what caused his death. His wife, Roberta, was convinced, then and later, that he died because he had bad teeth, which he had not cared for. She believed that poison suddenly erupted into his blood stream and killed him. A business associate, Jack Reed, shared her view: "Jay died because he had bad teeth," Reed said later. "He had gold crowns on 'em and he wouldn't take 'em out."

Whatever the cause, his death on July 23, 1923, brought a crisis to the Fulbrights.

His Fayetteville newspaper ran a three-column box with a black border around it on Page One that day, and under it listed all the firms in which Jay had been the owner, director, or major stockholder. In a way, it served as his epitaph. The list read: Arkansas National Bank, Citizens Bank, Democrat Publishing Co., Ozark Wholesale Grocery Co., Fayetteville Lumber and Cement Co., Fayetteville Ice Co., Washington Hotel, Fulbright Wholesale Co., Fayetteville Mercantile Co., the Bank of Winslow, Bank of Elkins, Bank of St. Paul, and the Citizens Bank of Pettigrew. His obituary writer offered words he would have liked: "Fulbright's special genius ran to figures, and to him business was a game, the most fascinating game in the world and in comparison with which all other sports were tame."

At his funeral they sang his favorite hymn, "No Shadows Yonder," and he was buried in a mahogany casket covered with flowers. Within a week the loss of Fayetteville's most prominent businessman was generally forgotten in the dramatic news of President Warren G. Harding's sudden illness, and death. But for the Fulbright family, their personal crisis was just beginning.

"We all had a terrible time," Bill Fulbright said later. "We thought we were going broke and all of us would starve to death and so on. This was where Mother took over. She salvaged enough out of the business to keep going. Mother just carried on."

Roberta Fulbright had had no training in business or any preparation for it. Jay had tried, in his customarily brusque fashion, to make her aware of his business dealings, and once an employee remembered his saying to her: "Old lady, you better start listening about this [the business] because some day you may have to run this." She did not listen.

When her husband died, she thought that his associates would help her. Instead, she was subjected to ruthlessness: The widow with six children and diverse businesses seemed an easy mark. She was forced to fight to survive. She did both successfully, but it left scars on her and on her children, especially on Bill, the future senator.

"I thought that when I began being active in business that the men with whom my husband had labored would extend a helping hand to me," she wrote years later in her newspaper column. "Not so. Resentment and distrust were ever present." She also learned, as she said, "that business has an element of selfish brutality in it. It's difficult to do business with your friends and also difficult to be too friendly in your business. . . . I've learned that a woman has to prove herself over and over again, while men take each other without question. I've learned that everyone is jealous of his or her position, whatever it may be. I've found the common weed of jealousy growing in all sorts of soil, even on rocks and streams. It must be reckoned with in dealing with the human species."[4]

Roberta Fulbright held the family together, and learned to deal with that business world. She never lost, though, a sense of bitterness over her difficulties. In particular, she resented the attacks she suffered because she was a woman forced to compete in a man's world. "Let a woman do well, and she is all but burned at the stake," she said. "I will say for the benefit of those who may be interested, I did not choose business as a career; it was thrust upon me. I did choose it in preference to going broke or dissipating my heritage or that of my children."

Quite naturally, through her earlier interest in journalism, she took special satisfaction in running the family newspaper. She soon found she had an outlet, and a talent, for expressing her thoughts. While she always had been interested in books, now she began to pay increasing attention to public affairs. She spoke out forthrightly about local politics and got in trouble with a judge and a sheriff. She was sued for $100,000, and the judge directed a verdict against her; but the jury refused to return with damages. Enemies founded a rival paper and tried to run her out of business. She lost money, but held on until the opposition paper folded. Over the years she became increasingly interested in public life, and twice nearly ran for Congress herself. She tried to impart the desire for public service to the rest of the family, but especially to her favorite, Bill, upon whom she leaned heavily. She drew even closer to Bill after her oldest child, Lucille, who was married and had a small child, died with equal suddenness of an allergy just a year after Jay.

How much her own thoughts and moods influenced Bill Fulbright is a matter of conjecture. But certainly he later reflected, on a far broader stage, many aspects of her personality and temperament. Through her writings ran an alternating mood of pessimism and self-doubt, with a certain stubborn pride and conviction she was correct. Thus, she would write: "One of my children said to me once: 'Mother, you are cheerful, but you aren't happy,' with the implied meaning that I was a sort of hypocrite. Well, what of it? Have I not beaten the game if I'm cheerful even if I'm not happy?"

And, at times a note of self-pity: "I was born in arrears; I've remained in arrears through a long, heavy lifetime—striving always to catch up but never quite making the grade. No matter what I do, or give, or stand for, I'm still in arrears. So I've about decided to let the matter stand 'in arrears' and let it be graven on my tombstone."

Or, of doubt: "I never write about anything that I'm not possessed of a lurking fear that perhaps I don't know what I'm talking about."

It was a sentiment that Senator J. William Fulbright would express often.

Roberta Fulbright also had a habit of deprecating her abilities. This, too, became familiar in her son. As she wrote once: "It's just plain work to write even an effusion like 'As I See It' [the title of her column]. Someone will say, 'Then why do it?' and I answer 'I must.' "

She did just that, developing the habit of staying up half the night writing her column in longhand on yellow paper, and then giving it to the only compositor on the paper who could decipher her scrawl, a woman named Maude Gold. In business and in personal relations, Roberta became the mainspring of the family, and, as Jay had done, assumed the role of expecting success from her children, Bill the most of all.

Bill had stayed out of school for one semester after his father's death, helping his mother with the multiple businesses. Although he was eighteen years old, he proved to be a shrewd businessman. As one of his friends recalled later, "Bill would trade the pants off you." He became the vice president of a small railroad owned by the family, the Combs, Cass and Eastern Railroad, and a director of several of the local enterprises. Still, he had the feeling then that the Fulbrights were always on the verge of bankruptcy.

Whether that experience affected his outlook or not, he had the reputation—then and years later—of frugality, even stinginess. Within a few years, he also was speaking with contempt of businessmen.

When Fulbright returned to the university he retained his business interests as well as his extra-curricular school commitments. "Bill is conceded to be the busiest boy in Washington County," said a feature story in *The Arkansas Gazette* which hailed him as "a combination of football star, remarkable student, railroad vice president, astute business man, and a possible Rhodes scholar."[5]

The Rhodes scholarship possibility came about casually, almost by chance, as did so many of his later opportunities. Fulbright had never thought of going to Oxford until one day in his last undergraduate semester at Arkansas in the fall of 1924. Professor Clark Jordan, the dean of the graduate school, stopped Bill and told him the applications for the Rhodes scholarships had come in. Wouldn't Bill like to apply? Fulbright asked what it was all about, and what he would have to do. Jordan explained he didn't have to do anything, that the selections were based on the student's record.

Fulbright discussed it with his mother, who urged him to apply. Early in December the candidates were interviewed at Little Rock by a committee headed by President John C. Futrall of the University of Arkansas, a family friend as well as the man Fulbright was to succeed as president years later. In those days the Rhodes scholarships were awarded under a system by which each state was given one scholarship two out of every three years. Later that was changed and the competition became regional.[6] But when Fulbright applied, the competition was not the stiffest; in fact, there was a dearth of candidates.

"I probably never would have gotten one if it had been on the present regional basis," Fulbright was to reminisce. "The competition wasn't too great."

For these various reasons, Bill Fulbright was selected when the Rhodes scholarships were announced on December 14, 1924. He finished his term at Arkansas and was graduated in January at the age of nineteen. Then he stayed on for the next spring semester, working at home and waiting for his scholarship to begin in the fall of 1925.

Again, by chance, his extra semester at Arkansas was profitable. He enrolled in a course in law given by a young professor who had just come to Fayetteville from Harvard. The professor was Claude Pepper, and Bill Fulbright found him fascinating, "the most articulate fellow you ever saw." Pepper was aggressive, ambitious, brilliant, and inspirational. He talked, Fulbright remembered, "about anything and everything." Later, they both served together in the Senate.

Pepper was one of the two men at Arkansas who made the greatest impression on young Fulbright. The other was Julian Waterman, the founder of the Arkansas Law School, and who later became even more important in Fulbright's life. Waterman was compassionate, dignified, widely read, and gentle. He was one of the first men who ever treated Fulbright as an intellectual equal, even though Fulbright knew he was then far inferior. He became a model for Bill. In later years, after having associated with presidents and prime ministers, Fulbright regarded him as one of the greatest men he had ever known. These two men, Pepper and Waterman, helped to prepare him intellectually for Oxford.

In the fall of 1925 Bill Fulbright, accompanied by his mother, took the train to New York on the most eventful journey of his life. He was then twenty years old, more self-possessed than most, not easily intimidated by older or wealthier people and used to handling adult affairs. Still, he was very much a twentieth-century American innocent going abroad. Until then, he had never been east of the Mississippi, had never taken a drink, had never been to any big cities. He had never even seen the sea until he boarded the *Lancastria,* bound for Southampton and Oxford.

3

"IF CONVENIENT, SOME KNOWLEDGE"

CECIL RHODES WAS A CAPITALIST, empire builder, adventurer, and dilettante. He achieved his goals of power and influence through money. It was his common denominator. Diamonds had laid the foundation for his empire; they had given him power and fired his dreams of extending British influence from the Cape to Cairo; they had also permitted him the luxury of fancying himself worthy of attaining Aristotle's precept of excellence. Rhodes, in his own eyes, was the complete man: he had had the whole of the classics especially translated for him, and he liked to carry a well-thumbed copy of Marcus Aurelius. When he died in 1902, his will establishing the Rhodes scholarships for British colonists, Americans, and Germans was regarded as revolutionary.

Rhodes sought not mere bookish scholars for Oxford, but, as he expressed it, "the best men for the world's fight." He wanted men of "moral character," fond of "manly outdoor sports," with "instincts to lead." But particularly, he wanted men who would become public leaders—the future prime ministers, regents, and presidents. In his vision, all these would bear his stamp. They would carry his power, influence, and name to unforeseen destinies for untold generations.[1]

He chose Oxford as their training ground because, as Lord Lothian explained, "he believed that the type of education given there, with its outlook on the civilizations of Greece and Rome, its interest in philosophy, history, law and political science, would develop in his scholars those aptitudes which would specially assist them in the discharge of public duties in after life."[2]

Andrew Carnegie, the tough, canny Scot who also knew something about power and influence, immediately let it be known that the Rhodes Scholarships would never be popular or useful in America. In Carnegie's view, Oxford could not give American boys what they wanted most—dollars.[3] Carnegie's comment strengthened an already widely held opinion among British intellectuals about Americans. To them, Americans were still barbarians. Their colleges were thought of as little better than inferior educational outposts, their curriculum uneven, their professors undistinguished. It was unthinkable to suggest that American students were sufficiently competent to be admitted to Oxford. With perfect English understatement, one of the early administrators of the Rhodes Trust recalled how American academic records aroused in the mind of the normal don "a bewildered, if amused, suspicion."[4]

In the fall of 1925, the same doubts about Americans were still evident when Bill Fulbright arrived and entered the common rooms and quadrangles of Pembroke College at Oxford. "You can't imagine a more complete change in one's life," he said later. He had come to Oxford, he said, seeking as any boy will, "exciting experiences, and if convenient, some knowledge." He immediately found that what helped him most initially was not so much any knowledge he had acquired in Arkansas, but his aptitude for what Rhodes had called manly sports.

At twenty, Fulbright took naturally to the Oxford games. If his manner and his accent made some think him indolent, his ability on the playing fields indicated otherwise. He was a handsome youth, 5 feet 10½ inches tall, 165 pounds, with dark hair, blue eyes, and a cleft chin. Obviously accustomed to the outdoor life, he quickly demonstrated his skills at rugby, tennis, and lacrosse; and, in the fashion of the English university, his athletic talents soon were translated into success in other areas of college life.

Before long, he was receiving invitations to attend clubs and societies, among them the Johnson Literary Society, the namesake of Samuel Johnson, once a member of Pembroke College.

The Johnson Society was composed of fellow students, each of whom was expected to write critical papers which were read and discussed at Society meetings. After attending several, Fulbright came away appalled at his own academic inadequacies.

"My God," he recalled, "I was really impressed! I'd never heard any student anywhere even approach that sort of thing. So when my turn came to give a paper, I worked harder than I'd ever worked in my life. I was embarrassed not to. I really tried to give them a paper."

His first was on Sherwood Anderson, who was then at the peak of his fame. Fulbright's selection of a literary figure for his topic was symptomatic of what was happening to him, for in Arkansas he had demonstrated only slight interest in books, especially his contemporary American writers, Mencken, Fitzgerald, Cabell, Dos Passos, and Wescott. (Hemingway was then known only to a relative few in Paris.) Typically, Fulbright had become interested in Sherwood Anderson through a friend at Oxford, a philosophy student named Ralph Church, who later taught at Cornell. Fulbright's paper on Anderson was, he thought, "the best I'd ever done by a long shot." But, he was also aware, it was by no means the best of his colleagues.

In later years when he looked back on his experience in England, Fulbright realized that he "never became intellectually curious until I got to Oxford."

"I was ashamed of my ignorance and lack of knowledge of literature and other things," he said, "and I began to read just to learn. I never had thought much of that at home—or of reading just to learn. Before, I had studied because it was the thing to do. I was conforming to what was expected of me. I had a minimum of intellectual curiosity from within."

Whether that is an overstatement or not, one cannot say, but it certainly was true that, for him, Oxford accomplished what Cecil Rhodes had hoped for his scholars: it broadened him; it helped him to develop a critical cast of mind; it introduced him to worlds he had never known.

Fulbright read political science and history. As was true of any Rhodes Scholar, he had the advantage of studying under eminent professors. Not all his course work dealt with the classics: in his honors course in modern history, he investigated such subjects as what had happened at the Versailles Peace Conference, and how England had treated her allies during the Napoleonic wars. He never imagined, of course, that one day he, too, would stand at the center of similar historic diplomatic occurrences. Indeed, as a student, Fulbright often felt that he was reading of a world and of events "that never really existed."

"History," he would say in a broadcast in London during World War II, "is somewhat like photographs of a country one will never visit, interesting but of no personal concern. I read about the tyrants; but the tyrants I read of had been dead a long time. I did not look into the world about me to see if new tyrants were growing up. I read of man's fight for liberty throughout the ages and especially of the struggle in England, through many centuries, to establish the power of the people through the Parliament. It was a fight that had, to all appearances, been won; it was finished, and even the shouting had died away. Little did I think that within a very few years this same England would, for a time at least, have to stand alone against the most evil and powerful tyrant the world has ever seen."[5]

Despite his disclaimers, his studies did relate to his present—and directly influenced his future. His reading of British history and politics left him with at least one dominant impression which, as the years progressed, became a major theme in his own public career: the belief in the necessity for government to attract the best qualified men. It was a view that Rhodes would have applauded.

Thus, as Fulbright drew the lesson in a speech in 1940:

"Lesser people have often wondered how England, a tiny, frostbitten island, came to dominate the greatest empire the world has ever seen. The envious seem to think that it was accidental, but such accidents do not happen. Being small, it was perhaps easier for England to organize her manpower and resources, but to my mind the real secret of her success is in the fact that her best brains, her outstanding talent, was always induced to enter politics and to direct the coordination of her every power for the benefit of the country. For centuries the English have honored their politicians above all other citizens, and have supported them, regardless of their personal idiosyncrasies."[6]

It is impossible to say with certainty whether Fulbright was thinking of a political career while he was studying at Oxford; he said later he was then unsure what he wanted to do. However, his reading and his acquaintances did help to shape his interests in that direction. No one at Oxford was more influential in that respect than his tutor (and later the Master) at Pembroke, R. B. McCallum.

McCallum was only two years older than Fulbright, and had just come to Oxford as a don when he became Bill's tutor. He was a vigorous Scotsman with a keen interest in politics, and often drew comparisons between American and English systems: he had held a commonwealth scholarship at Princeton. McCallum was a liberal, and a critical taskmaster. Fulbright admired him.

As a tutor, McCallum was precisely the proper combination of counselor and critic for Fulbright. He could be both challenging and caustic; the two young men complemented each other. For six months of each of the three years Fulbright was at Oxford he and McCallum worked closely together, as was required by the tutorial system. During the remaining six months, Fulbright, like so many Rhodes Scholars, was on the continent.

The Rhodes Scholars were encouraged to take advantage of these periods, to travel and observe, and perhaps to settle down for more serious reading. For a time, Fulbright lived in Paris where his friend Ralph Church introduced him to the Louvre and the Sorbonne, to Montmartre and the sidewalk cafés.

In his own right, Church proved to be a good tutor. Unlike Fulbright, Church had traveled widely throughout the world and had acquired definite tastes. Although he was a thoughtful, introspective person, Church did not shun the more boisterous Parisian society. He had become acquainted with Gertrude Stein and others in her literary salon, and liked to meet at the Brasserie de Lippe on the Boulevard St. Germain to drink beer and talk. He often brought Fulbright along with him. Fulbright had never experienced anything like it.

Fulbright's years at Oxford passed swiftly. By 1928, in his last year, he had become something of a minor celebrity. He had earned his half-blue at lacrosse, and had been a member of the international team that toured the United States playing representative American colleges in the summer of 1926. (That trip had been climaxed by a visit to the White House where the players were briefly received by Calvin Coolidge.) And in his final term, Fulbright had become president of the Johnson Society and the Teasel Club. On a far smaller scale, he was repeating his Arkansas successes. Certainly his mother, Roberta, thought so.

Roberta Fulbright came to Oxford that spring of 1928 to see Bill. She found him an anglicized Arkansan, given to smoking a pipe, wearing tweeds and knickers. In her eyes, he was grander than ever. She saw him taking tea at an estate owned by a relative of Lord Tennyson's, inspecting Norman churches and visiting the palace of the Duke and Duchess of Marlborough, walking in Christ Church Meadows, attending the Pembroke Ball, enjoying dinner at the George Café ("cocktails, wine and everything") and presiding over luncheon at the Teasel Club where Bill "was seated in the wonderful chair at the head of the high table."

Her letters written at that time were revealing, particularly of her relationship with Bill.

"I am now in Oxford [she wrote on April 24, 1928]. This to me was almost a sacred pilgrimage and Oxford, with my boy, my Mecca. I find great content from being near him, which I can scarcely explain; he seems much like his father and is very easy for me to live with; I lean on him intuitively."

Roberta, who loved the Arkansas hills as much as her son, found the English countryside beautiful almost beyond description. "The trees make me cry for the love of them," she wrote. "They are so grand and majestic and there are so many."

As for Oxford, "This wonderful university city . . . there is nothing with which to compare it that I've ever seen."

For the rest of his life, her son would express similar sentiments about Oxford, until years later he would write to a professor there that "I shall look back upon those short years in Pembroke as the happiest of my life, and I get great pleasure in just thinking about them."

Fulbright was graduated from Oxford in June, 1928, with the equivalent of a B-plus average in his honors course; then he, Roberta, a cousin, and a friend set off for their own grand tour across France and Switzerland, into Vienna, and down to Baden. After several weeks there, his mother went home to Arkansas, and Bill began what was, in effect, his personal post-graduate course on the continent. It was to add still another dimension to a boy from the hills of Arkansas.

Fulbright settled in Vienna at the end of that summer of 1928. His experiences were neither startling nor unusual for an American abroad, but they were rewarding: he saw good opera, and loved it; he roamed the city; he read; and, eventually, like the Viennese and everyone else who came to the old imperial capital, he was finally drawn to the cafés.

In Vienna the cafés were unlike any other in the world; everything in the city centered about them. They were the meeting places for writers, painters, poets, and psychoanalysts, the places for social life and reflection, and simply for observing the spectacle of European life as it passed by along the wide boulevards.

For Americans, one of the most exotic and popular of the cafés was the Louvre on Wipplinger Strasse, across the street from the telegraph office. The Café Louvre was the hangout for the American correspondents. There, one could see William L. Shirer and Robert Best (who later collaborated with the Nazis), Walter Duranty, Dorothy Thompson, John Gunther, Frazier Hunt, and there, in October, Fulbright met M. W. Fodor.

Mike Fodor, a stocky, balding and knowledgeable Hungarian, was the correspondent for *The Manchester Guardian* and also for the *N.Y. Evening Post* and the *Philadelphia Public Ledger*. But he was much more than merely another member of that ubiquitous band of journalists who reported from Europe in the '20s. Fodor was scholarly (he had taken his post-graduate work in Zurich after receiving his engineering degree from Budapest University) and patient, a versatile linguist, and he knew everyone worth knowing in central Europe. Although he was fifteen years older than Fulbright, the two became close friends. "I think [Fodor] is one of the best informed and most lovable characters I have ever known," Fulbright once wrote to Dorothy Thompson, who also was a close friend of Fodor's. And later he would remember Fodor as "one of the nicest, kindliest, most decent fellows I've ever known."

The young, impressionable Fulbright was fascinated with Fodor and the workings of a foreign correspondent. He asked Fodor so many questions, with such earnestness, that Fodor took a liking to the young Boswell from Fayetteville.

Through Fodor, Fulbright was introduced to the political currents of Vienna, and to the leading participants of those issues of the day. Fulbright also learned something about how the reporters operated; it hadn't been done that way on the family paper in Fayetteville.

"The correspondents would sit around there in the Café Louvre, 10 and 11 o'clock at night," he recalled, "and old Fodor would tell them what had happened that day. They'd talk to Fodor for over an hour, and they'd all write it down and then send it off at the telegraph office across the street. I remember people would come in there from *The New York Times* and other papers, big papers in the U.S., and have a long conversation with

Fodor. About two weeks later I'd read it all in *The New York Times Magazine.*"

Fulbright remained in Vienna throughout the winter, a constant companion of Fodor's. Then, one day in the spring of 1929 Fodor said:

"I'm going on my annual trip to visit Sofia and Salonika and Athens and Belgrade. Would you like to go? I can put you down as representing one of the papers, *The Ledger* or something, and that will entitle you to go to meetings and interviews."

Fulbright, delighted, accepted instantly. He and Fodor left soon on a memorable trip through the Balkans where they talked to diplomats and high government officials and saw the ancient capitals.

Fodor was a fund of information; he was the perfect guide, for he knew the history of that area intimately, and took pleasure in sharing his knowledge with his young friend. By April they moved on to Greece, where Fodor introduced Fulbright to Athens and the Acropolis. "He wasn't just doing me a favor," Fulbright said. "He liked to show you; he himself was interested. He had a great deal of influence in the sense of inspiring one's interest in these things."

In Athens, however, Fulbright became sick with quinsy, a severe inflammation of the throat. His illness forced him to cut short one of the most rewarding periods of his life. Instead of going to Albania with Fodor, as they had planned, he boarded a boat bound for Marseilles and passage back to the United States. It was a stormy voyage: he lay in his cabin with his inflamed throat, subjected to intense seasickness.

Bill Fulbright, the athlete turned scholar, had never been so sick in his life. In fact, he was sick all the way back to the United States and even on the long train ride en route to Arkansas.

4

THE SQUIRE OF RABBIT'S FOOT LODGE

FROM WHAT HIS FRIENDS IN FAYETTEVILLE could observe, Fulbright appeared to have changed little. While he bore physical reminders of his years in Europe (he wore English shoes and tweeds and had leather patches put on the elbows of his sports jacket, a style distinctly not in vogue in Fayetteville), he seemed, as one man said, "still the same Bill"—friendly and easygoing, but withal rather reserved.

He had come home because it was natural, not because he had formed any definite plans for his future. For Fulbright, Fayetteville and Mount Nord represented security, comfort, and a home base; it gave him something to do, without being particularly taxing or challenging. That seemed to fit nicely with his inclinations then: no one was able to detect any burning ambitions or hidden desires for public life. Although he talked vaguely of teaching at some point, his own ideas for a specific career were, in fact, aimless. As he said later, "I intended to help Mother with the businesses and perhaps on the paper, more or less just what I normally would have done." Then, as was so often the case in his life, circumstances intervened and headed him into a new—and unplanned—direction.

In Paris, Fulbright had become acquainted with a wealthy American dilettante, J. Townsend Russell, Jr., whose father was the Canon of the Washington Cathedral in Washington, D.C. Russell, an archeology enthusiast, had taken Fulbright on a trip to the Dordogne, and they had also explored the Altamira Cave, witnessed the diggings, and learned at first hand about Cro-Magnon. It had all been highly interesting, but essentially inconsequential to Fulbright. Indeed, by the summer of 1929 he nearly had forgotten Russell until he received a telephone call from him in Washington.

Russell was exceedingly agitated. His father had just died, he said, and he was in trouble: there was a plethora of debts, the estate was in disarray, and he was being hounded by creditors. He desperately needed Fulbright's advice and assistance. Could Fulbright come to Washington and help him? Fulbright explained that he could not leave at that time; that he had just begun to work himself, but perhaps Russell could come to Fayetteville where they could discuss his difficulties. Russell came, and stayed for a month.

Fulbright had never encountered anyone quite like him. Here was a very rich, attractive, well-educated young man with a splendid estate in Washington called Beauvoir,* a generous income from a trust fund, and absolutely no knowledge of or capability for business. To Fulbright, the banker's son and boyish businessman, it was incomprehensible that Russell was even intimidated at the thought of going into a bank. He diagnosed Russell's problems quickly. In reality, he said, the solution was simple. All Russell had to do was stop spending so much money a month, and he could easily accomplish that by allocating a fixed amount to pay off his outstanding bills. When Fulbright went to his own bank in Fayetteville and borrowed money to set up a trust arrangement, Russell still was not relieved of his anxieties. He pleaded with Fulbright to come to Washington and complete the necessary transactions so he could then return to Europe.

Finally, prompted partly by curiosity and partly, one suspects, by boredom, Fulbright agreed to go to Washington and stay at Beauvoir with Russell. Within a matter of weeks he had placed the estate in order and had established a trust fund at the Riggs National Bank. Before he went back home, however, he promised to check personally every few months on Russell's financial affairs in Washington. It was during one of those business trips to Washington early in 1930 that chance again intervened for Fulbright.

He came out of the Riggs Bank about two o'clock in the afternoon one day that spring and happened to run into an Oxford classmate and fellow member of the lacrosse team named James Imbrie, who was passing by at that moment. Imbrie was then in Washington as the representative of one of his father's brokerage houses. They stood on the sidewalk chatting about Pembroke, and then Imbrie asked:

"By the way, will you be here Saturday night?"

"Why, yes," Fulbright said, "I'll be here the rest of the week."

"Could you come to dinner? My wife's got a friend and we need a fourth."

The friend was Elizabeth Williams, a tall, slender, attractive brunette

* Later, the site of a private school by the same name.

from the Main Line in Philadelphia. Betty Williams had been raised in a world of wealth and society,* but she was no Lady Bountiful. She was, instead, vivacious, gregarious, sophisticated, and possessed of a down-to-earth manner; Betty was comfortable and assured in any setting.

Their first meeting resulted in an argument at the dinner table. Fulbright teased Betty about coming from Philadelphia. He said he had never met anyone from there he liked. "Don't be an ass," she retorted. He asked her to lunch the next day, and their courtship began.

Neither family favored the relationship. Mrs. Williams did not like the idea of her daughter leaving Philadelphia—and for Arkansas of all places. And Roberta Fulbright feared that a city-bred socialite might not adjust to Arkansas.

Five years after their marriage, on June 15, 1932, Roberta told Betty, however, that among Bill's dates, she had been "the best of the litter."

In the meantime, Fulbright had given up any plans for going back to Arkansas for the foreseeable future. During their courtship, he had enrolled in the George Washington University Law School, primarily, he said, so he could be near her.

That may have been his principal motivation, but he also was enjoying living in Washington and returning to academic work. The Washington world in which he traveled was both restricted and rewarding. Until his wedding, he lived in a small house opposite the GW Law School in Washington's Foggy Bottom section, traditionally the residential area for State Department foreign service officers. A former Rhodes scholar and a Philadelphia socialite were always welcome in their circles.

As a student, Fulbright was working harder than ever during his years at Oxford. No longer did he study merely to conform, or to please his parents, for by the time he entered law school he had become interested in learning for its own sake. His academic efforts reflected his abilities: he was graduated number two in his class of 135.

Yet, it was typical of Fulbright, both then and later, that in a sense he was removed from the main domestic currents of his times. While he was immersed in his books and in his private social life, he seemed scarcely touched by the forces of change so apparent in the early 1930s in Washington. His isolation from the leading issues could not be explained entirely, this time, by his Arkansas heritage. Fulbright had come back to the United States at the peak of the stock market boom, and he was in and out of the nation's capital in the days leading up to the October crash. He had seen the last, bitter months of the Hoover administration, and the bustle and the expectations that came in with the beginnings of the New Deal. Although, he said, he was aware of bank closings and the general state of apprehension and fear throughout the country, the suffering of

* Her father, Robert M. Williams, made his money as a cotton broker, and the family was connected with the prominent Strawbridge-Clothier firm in Philadelphia.

the depression and the weighty arguments about America's future had only slight impact on him.

After he became a celebrated international figure, a number of writers attempted to explain his growth by pointing to his experience in Europe in the '20s and Washington in the early '30s as decisive factors. Fulbright himself always maintained otherwise.

"I hate to be too disappointing [he would say], but I was a very ordinary kind of a fellow. I had no great illusions of playing any great part in the government. I was deeply concerned about my record when I was at George Washington, and then about getting along. And I was very preoccupied both then and later with trying to keep our home base perking, I mean, keeping it solvent. I was scared after the depression began that we were going flat broke. I didn't much like the idea of just being completely penniless, you know. I was deeply concerned about that. I wasn't taken up or involved in the great public issues of the day. I was engaged in what most people are—of finding a place to live and living within their means. I was concerned, as most people are at that age, of making ends meet."

In fact, the Fulbrights were never in danger of going to the poorhouse, but his fears and his basic conservatism were as much a part of him as they were of his father and his mother. Fulbright, after his formal education at Oxford and law school had ended, was something of a liberal Tory.

Bill and Betty Fulbright began their married life in a quiet residential section of Georgetown, where they rented an attached brick row house near the corner of Thirty-first and N Streets for $85 a month. Georgetown then was not as fashionable as it would become in a few years, but it was peaceful and pleasant and, for the Fulbrights, perfect for their mode of life.

After he received his law degree, Fulbright had started to work in the Justice Department's anti-trust division as a special attorney. Again, he did not seek the job out of firm convictions about public service or with thoughts of initiating a government career. A friend, Dwight Savage, whom he respected as a scholarly lawyer and who had taught law at the University of Arkansas, was working there at the time, and persuaded Fulbright to join the department. It sounded interesting; Fulbright decided to try it.

His job matched his expectations for it: it was stimulating, but he never had any sense of rendering important service. Impressive as the title of special attorney was, Fulbright actually began as low as one could, and was paid what he said was "the magnificent sum of $2500 a year." The work consisted chiefly of legal research, which meant Fulbright looked up the law for senior members of the department. But it was not all legal drudgery, for Fulbright had happened to join the department at a vital period in the New Deal, a time when laws were being swiftly enacted—

and swiftly challenged. The Roosevelt revolution, or, more accurately, the Roosevelt reform, made the Justice Department and its attorneys a key part of the process of change. Although he was an insignificant cog in that larger movement, Fulbright did participate in two important cases. One of them was of critical importance to the New Deal.

He had been assigned to work for Walter Rice, a talented and aggressive young lawyer who was to become vice president of Reynolds Metals, but then was on his way up.

Fulbright's first case with Rice involved the Sugar Act, the EWA Plantation Co., and the large operations in Hawaii; but the case that overshadowed those questions dealt with chicken dealers in Brooklyn, N.Y., and the legality of the National Recovery Act codes. In the headline terminology of the day, it became known as the "sick chicken case." To lawyers, it was the Schechter Case.

The government had charged the A. L. A. Schechter Poultry Corp., the Schechter Live Poultry Market, Inc., and the four Schechter brothers who operated them with conspiring to violate provisions of NRA and the fair practices code for the New York metropolitan area. It was a landmark case, the first real test of NRA's constitutionality, and its outcome would be a determining factor in deciding whether the Federal Government had the authority to interfere in a local industry on the grounds that its business affected interstate commerce.

Fulbright assisted Rice in a month-long investigation; then, after indictments were returned, he and Rice went to Brooklyn to try the case in October of 1934.

"It was the only time I'd ever been to Brooklyn," Fulbright said, "and I remember we stayed in the great hotel of St. George. We were there two weeks and in the law court and, oh, I thought this was big stuff, you know. I'd never been to the big city as long as that and there I was participating in a court trial in a courtroom."

The trial attracted national attention, and ended in a legal cliff-hanger. The judge charged the jury on a Wednesday morning, and by 11:30 that night the jurors could not agree on a verdict. They were ordered taken to a hotel, and then returned to their deliberations the next day. A few minutes after noon they brought in their verdict. They had found the defendants guilty on nineteen counts. Rice was ebullient.

"This verdict is a sweeping victory of immense importance," he told reporters that day. "It is particularly significant because Judge [Marcus B.] Campbell charged the jury very definitely on the scope of the NRA and its relation to interstate commerce. He said that the violation of the code, however small, which had effect on the operations of interstate commerce made the defendants amenable to the law."[1]

Fulbright was no less ecstatic. For years after, he would remember that day with a special glow.

"Oh, boy," he would say, "I thought that was a big day. It was like winning the world championship."

As was so often the case, however, the aftermath came as an anticlimax. The case was appealed, and eventually taken to the Supreme Court. "Instead of letting us take it on," Fulbright said, "the Solicitor General took it over. He took it to the Supreme Court and lost it. We would always be in the position of saying, 'Well, if you'd just let us handle it, we'd have won it.'"

It was Fulbright's first—and last—big moment as a lawyer, in or out of the government, for by early 1935 he had left the Justice Department to accept a position as a legal instructor at George Washington University.

Fulbright's year of teaching law at George Washington was enjoyable, but uneventful, except in one respect that was to bear directly on his future. He began telling his students that they should enter public service. It became a basic theme that he would reiterate to young students, particularly law students, until one day a former student who had taken his message literally turned the question around and suggested that Fulbright should practice what he was preaching. In 1935, though, Fulbright found no inconsistency in withdrawing from public life, and yet urging others to participate actively in it. His reading of history and his studies in constitutional law made it perfectly obvious, at least to him, that the effectiveness of the American governmental system was dependent on the quality of people it attracted. The system, as he told his students so often, can operate effectively only if it attracts educated and intelligent men and women.

Implicit in Fulbright's view was a *noblesse oblige* attitude that came naturally to him. His mother, he once said, "always preached this to me: that those who are privileged have to do these things." Still, at that stage in his life, he was content more with enunciating problems and becoming philosophical, rather than personally attempting to do something about them. That, too, would remain a vexing part of his personality when he himself became a public figure.

Fulbright left Washington for Arkansas in 1936 without any compelling reasons. His mother, it is true, had been saying she could use his help in managing the Fulbright businesses, and his old mentor, Julian Waterman, dean of the University of Arkansas Law School, had asked him to consider teaching there in his hometown. But these were not pressing considerations. Fulbright, it would seem, was again drifting. His decision to combine both an academic and a business career in his own backyard initiated one of the happiest periods in his life as a gentleman farmer, resident scholar, entrepreneur, and leading citizen. In Fayetteville, he easily filled all roles.

He was thirty-one years old when he came back to Fayetteville. For three days a week he helped his mother manage the businesses, and discovered that, as in the past, the lumber company was still the sick partner in the Fulbright portfolio. The other three days he taught two courses in constitutional law and equity at the university.

His course schedule was light—he actually taught only on a half-time basis—through an arrangement with Dean Waterman, who was delighted to get Fulbright back any way he could. Another law professor of that time, Robert Leflar, a close adviser to Waterman, recalled that: "When Waterman and I talked about Bill's coming here we thought he was an able man, and we'd be awfully lucky to get him. He was a cut above—maybe several cuts above—anyone else we might get down here."

Fulbright's performance as a teacher fulfilled their hopes. "He was one of our good teachers," Leflar said. "He prepared his materials thoroughly, and was successful with the students. He was interested in academic quality and public affairs. I think he would have been happy being a law teacher, and that, I am sure, is what he thought was going to happen."[2]

Once more, as Leflar indicated, Fulbright began sounding his by then familiar theme of public service, politics, and the law. Often, he drew on his Oxford studies for illustrative points. "The great majority of the successful politicians in England were trained in the law," he said in a typical speech during that period. ". . . It is high time that our good lawyers return to their natural habitat, politics and law."[3]

As might have been expected, his students were impressed because, for them, Fulbright was uniquely qualified: he was the embodiment of the local boy had made good in every field of endeavor, who had been to all the glamorous places, and yet who was too young to be pompous or overbearing. And he had one quality which he never lost. He was entirely free of cant.

From the campus to his business rounds, everything was going well for Fulbright, and, in addition, for the first time he had his own house, in a setting of his own choosing. There, he spent perhaps the most pleasant of all those tranquil days.

Not long after he came home, Fulbright had bought a lodge on a 150-acre plot in the country outside Fayetteville. Originally, it had been built by an architect in an informal, rambling style with chinked logs, shutters, and a wide wrap-around porch. It was situated on the crest of a hill, surrounded by white oaks, magnolias, and catawpa trees. There were stone walls and walks, a big spring down below, and a winding road leading to a fence and main dirt roadway to town.

It was called Rabbit's Foot Lodge after the name of a Sequoia Indian chief who supposedly had ruled over those same hills in the past.

By the time Fulbright purchased it, the property had become run down. It had neither furnace nor plumbing. He and Betty remodeled it completely (one of Betty's touches was to paint the inside a colonial white instead of a somber, lodge-type dark color.) The spring-fed stream was dammed up and a small swimming pool constructed for their young daughters, Betsey and Roberta (called Bosey). More trees were planted, the grounds landscaped, and soon Rabbit's Foot Lodge had been transformed into a country show place, neither grand nor stately, but informal, comfortable, and functional.

With the help of a tenant farmer who lived on the grounds behind the main house, Fulbright raised white-face cattle, chickens, and hogs. Ducks graced the small pond at the base of the hill. They were as serene as life for the Fulbrights. The issues of the late '30s—the Supreme Court packing, the sit-down strikes, the rise of the Bund, Munich and Czechoslovakia—all seemed far away from Rabbit's Foot Lodge.

By the spring of 1939, Fulbright had put aside his business responsibilities and was formally appointed an associate professor of law. He was to begin a full schedule of teaching that September, with every likelihood that he had finally settled on his lifetime career. Then, on the night of September 12, 1939, less than two weeks after World War II began with Germany's invasion of Poland, Dr. John C. Futrall, the president of the University of Arkansas for a quarter of a century, was killed when his car hit a truck at West Fork, Arkansas. Six days later Fulbright was appointed the new president of the university.

He was thirty-four years old, and the youngest university president in the United States.

5

"IT HAS BEEN SUGGESTED I AM TOO YOUNG"

ROBERTA FULBRIGHT WAS A CLOSE FRIEND and political ally of Carl E. Bailey, the governor of Arkansas. Bailey also was the ex-officio chairman of the University of Arkansas' Board of Trustees. It was Bailey's board; he appointed it and controlled it. T. C. Carlson, the secretary of that board and also the university business manager, recalled what happened on September 18, 1939, when the board met to appoint a new president.

"The board meeting was called by Bailey in Futrall's office," he said. "It was a very brief meeting. The governor proposed the name of William Fulbright, lecturer in law, as president of the university. It came as a complete surprise to most of us. One member said, 'Why, Governor, I've never even met the man,' and there was some hesitation about accepting a man the others knew so little. So Bill was called to the meeting.

"One thing you may not associate with Bill is that he was shy, and he came in as if he were being spanked—hesitantly, shyly—and he was introduced to the various members of the board. He was asked to wait, and he was elected without any recorded dissent. And he was elected very perfunctorily, I thought, for such an important position. Among most of us it was popularly thought that Mrs. Fulbright had been responsible for Bill being appointed."[1]

Others who were close to that situation agree that Roberta Fulbright had first suggested to her friend, Carl Bailey, that her son would make an outstanding president of the university, and that Bailey had accepted her views. In fact, the matter had been settled within a day or two after Futrall's death.

Hal Douglas, Fulbright's brother-in-law and later his closest business associate, remembered that Fulbright was called shortly after the accident and told he was the choice to succeed Futrall. Fulbright was astounded, and immediately said no, he couldn't possibly consider it; that Julian Waterman, the law school dean, was by far the best man for the job. He insisted that Waterman be asked. Waterman, then the university vice president as well as law dean, was contacted, but declined for a singular reason: he was a Jew, he pointed out, and, because he would have to be dealing with the Arkansas Legislature, he probably would be leading the university into controversy. Fulbright, according to Douglas, also talked to Waterman and was told essentially the same thing. Then he decided to accept the presidency.

Robert Leflar, of the law school faculty, remembered being asked by Douglas if he would help if Fulbright were named to head the university. He said he would. "A part of my feeling that Fulbright would make a good president," Leflar said later, "was that he would rely on strong advisers until he knew the ropes. Julian Waterman was closer than anyone else to Bill, and he talked over everything with him."

Not surprisingly, Fulbright himself rarely talked about how he had become president of the University of Arkansas. When asked, he usually would brush it aside as if of no importance. In fact, in later years, he would say of his presidency that it had been "a very great strain on me," and refer to those days with a certain distaste, a sense of frustration and failure.

Yet it was a profoundly important period for him. For the first time, he attracted national attention. More important in terms of his future, as president he developed the themes that were to become so familiar in his years of international influence. The role of education and the university, the art of the politician and the legislator, the call for greatness and the American potential, the rejection of the cliché and the questioning of myths, the hopes for peace and the plea for new approaches to old problems, the challenges and the imperfections of democracy—all these he spelled out carefully and fully in less than two years.

For Fulbright, the university presidency was his flowering period. Only in retrospect would that become clear, for in 1939 Fulbright was regarded by many on the faculty and throughout the state as a youthful upstart who had little business heading a large state university.

A newspaper correspondent from Oklahoma City who came to Fayetteville that fall drew a portrait of the young president that would be instantly recognizable to anyone who knew him years later.

"He abhors pose and punditry [the reporter wrote]. He refuses to be dramatized. He balks at crusading. He has no illusions about taking any form of startling leadership. Yet it may be that, just because of the lack of theatricals, this light-hearted, human, extremely likable young man is unconsciously leading the pendulum swing away from the jitterbuggy and frivolous vogue which has flourished as a by-product of so-called modernism. . . . Bill Fulbright . . . is so invincibly young that he isn't afraid or ashamed of having old ideas, such as the desirability of having high grades, or insisting upon a basic education in English, history, and political science."[2]

The reporter found Fulbright modest to a fault, detesting pomposity, and already possessed of a habit that was to be so disarming to opponents, or interviewers: "Just about the time you think he might unguardedly let go a two-ton dictum, which he undoubtedly could if he wished, he disconcertingly asks, 'What do you think?' and clear off balance you go."

Although senior faculty members and university department heads resented his appointment, Fulbright was popular with the student body. In many ways, he seemed one of them: he was studiedly casual, wore sports jackets, drove a station wagon that often contained groceries or sacks of fertilizer and seed for Rabbit's Foot Lodge, smoked a pipe, and looked even younger than he was. Then, too, everyone knew that not so long ago Fulbright had been the boy wonder of the Arkansas campus.

Before long, apocryphal stories were making the rounds about how the new president had been mistaken for a student. The most popular account had Fulbright driving to his first football game as president and trying to park his station wagon in the faculty row. A freshman traffic monitor supposedly spotted him backing in, and shouted: "Back that wreck out of there! That's for the faculty! Can't you read?"[3]

In his first public appearances as president, Fulbright shrewdly capitalized on his youth and the comment his appointment had aroused.

"I realize that to many of you, long accustomed to the formal, dignified and thoroughly competent presence of Dr. Futrall, my appointment came as a shock," he said immediately after taking office. "I confess that it surprises even me."[4]

And, in his first public address in the late fall of 1939, he said, "Many remarks have been made about my youth. I really mean no offense by it and I am confident that definite progress is being made every day to correct it."[5]

Two months later, he was saying, in a more serious vein: "It has been suggested that I am too young to be the president of a great institution, but that is one thing for which I do not apologize. One might be too stupid, but never too young. I find that I am more at home with young people and with those who are interested in young people than some of the more sophisticated of our citizens."[6]

The tone of his remarks grew increasingly serious, and at times defensive, as he found himself confronted with a multitude of complex problems in administering a large university situated in the poorest of the states.

At their Rotary Club weekly meetings and the Chamber of Commerce annual banquets, Arkansas businessmen liked to extoll the blessings of their "Wonder State." Arkansas, they would say, produced great quantities of cotton, rice, oil, and lumber; practically all the aluminum in the United States originated in her bauxite mines, and the only diamond mines in North America were inside her border. There were vast undeveloped deposits of manganese, antimony, mercury, lead, and zinc, while the mountains and streams were the source of potentially unlimited electric power. If those were not blessings enough, some of the state's delta land was among the most productive in the world. The message was designed to please; invariably, it brought forth enthusiastic applause.

And yet, as Fulbright told a group of businessmen in one of his early speeches as president, Arkansas' physical wealth actually counted for little to the people of the state. "With all these resources," Fulbright said, "both natural and human . . . Arkansas has the highest per capita debt and the lowest per capita income of any state in the Union."[7]

In 1940, the per capita income for the state was $250. The per capita cost of the state government was then the lowest of any state. As Fulbright viewed the problems, Arkansas was virtually a conquered territory, an American state controlled by the capitalists of Philadelphia, New York, and Boston.

The fact of absentee ownership was common to all Southern states after the destruction of the Civil War and the Northern-imposed rule of the reconstruction era. Then the depression added another cruel dimension to Arkansas' problems: many of the remaining local businesses were lost on foreclosures and passed into outside ownership.

"The finest land," Fulbright would say, "the oil, the aluminum, the bauxite, and whatever minerals we had—all of the cream of this accrued to somebody out of the state. All we got out of it were a few jobs at a dollar and a half a day. That's about all it amounted to."[8]

Politically and economically, the Arkansas Power and Light Company dominated the state. The Arkansas Legislature was, as Fulbright said, "completely controlled by these kinds of interests." As was true of nearly every Southern state, the State Senate was the main target of the special interests, for the Senate, being a smaller body and holding veto power over the House, was easier to control.

Fulbright's knowledge of these conditions and his experience in attempting to deal with them as a university president directly influenced his future course as a U. S. Senator. He was impressed with the aid the federal government, through the New Deal, was able to give the poorer states, and regarded the federal action as one of the best methods of breaking the old cycle of outside control and poverty within. And that led him, eventually, to become one of the staunchest supporters of the principle of foreign aid. Arkansas, in his view, was not unlike a small, underdeveloped country. If the U.S. government could help it to emerge, then the government could do equally well for economically backward nations, he thought.

In his mind, education always was the key to help build a better society for a poorer state—and, then and later, he looked toward the federal government to provide that aid. Within months after he became president, for instance, he wrote Clyde Ellis, then an Arkansas congressman from his district and formerly Fulbright's pupil, what Ellis described to his colleagues in the House as an "eloquent appeal to restore the reduced [federal educational] appropriations"[9] for the National Youth Administration. The N.Y.A. was a New Deal program to help college-level students. It was the first time Fulbright's name was mentioned in Congress.

"In view of the great concentration of wealth in a few Eastern states," he wrote Ellis, "which enables their many privately endowed universities to give assistance to students, it seems only fair that the students in the poorer states should be given this assistance. Educational opportunities are obviously out of balance in this country when Harvard University can spend $14,000,000 in 1938–39 and many of the state universities of the South and West, serving millions of people, only get $1,000,000 or less. If democracy is to continue in this country, it must be supported by education of the people, and no more efficient way than N.Y.A. has been evolved to accomplish this." He urged Ellis, and through him the Congress, to restore the funds, for "to neglect the education of our youth is the worst thing that can be done for the future of this country."

Fulbright spoke from firsthand knowledge. When he became president for example, more than twenty-five percent of the students came to the campus with only about $15 or $20 in cash. "It is pitiful," Fulbright said, "to see how eager they are for an education, but how often they are not prepared for it. . . . It is a terrific economic and human waste to let our best brains settle down to picking cotton or tending a filling station when, with an investment of $1000 each, they could be made leaders in industry and the professions."[10]

As a young president, Fulbright was confronted with not only formidable economic problems, but the even more difficult one of public attitudes. In Arkansas, education was not regarded as of the greatest importance; he felt it his responsibility to attempt to change that common view. In numerous speeches, he referred to the problems of poverty in Arkansas, and the role a dynamic university could play in alleviating them.

"Man is not naturally a cooperative animal," he said at one point, "and only education can persuade him that progress, in fact, a decent existence, is possible only by intelligent organization and cooperation which is the essence of government. . . . It is of course exceedingly difficult to demonstrate concretely the exact causes of greatness in an individual. We usually call it character. A community likewise has character, and I believe that the educational institutions, especially the universities, have great influence on that character."[11]

But he was also acutely aware that Arkansas had built-in problems of its own. The dust bowls of the Southwest, the migration of the Arkies and Okies, and the jokes about the hillbillies had placed a crippling brand on the state.

One trouble with the people of Arkansas, Fulbright would say, is that they had allowed the "Arkansas Traveler," the slow train, Bob Burns and Lum and Abner to give them a feeling of inferiority. He noticed how many farmers went to Texas or Oklahoma to buy cattle when there were better to be had in Arkansas itself; how rich men sent their sons to schools out of state because they believed the schools couldn't be as good in Arkansas. "We have many things to be proud of in Arkansas and we must cultivate that pride, just as they have in Texas and California," Fulbright said. "Of course, we must also strive to create more things to be proud of."[12]

His speeches were not typical of the garden-variety land-grant college president, that all-too-identifiable figure who was adept at pacifying alumni and legislators and offering platitudes or vaguely sounded warnings about the Challenge of Life. Fulbright addressed himself to broader social issues and problems, and tried to relate them to the function of a state university.

If he had one, Fulbright's educational philosophy was old-fashioned: he favored the classical approach, with emphasis on literature, economics, logic, philosophy, and political history. Although so-called "progressive" education then was at the peak of educational fashion, Fulbright did not favor it.

"I am absolutely convinced," he said, "that in education, as in everyday life, the road to success is, as it has always been, the hard way: a way of laborious, painful, and plugging effort. I trust that you will not think that I am offering this commonplace statement as advice. I mean it merely as a positive disapproval of the excesses of the so-called progressive school of education with its sugar-coated pills labeled 'education.' "[13]

When Robert M. Hutchins of the University of Chicago raised the questions of vocational education versus liberal or cultural education, Fulbright commented, "In my own mind I am unable to accept entirely either view."[14]

Fulbright was convinced that the art of government and politics had been neglected in the United States, and that it was up to the universities to train and inspire its most talented students to enter those fields. That had been a major concern as a teacher; now, as a university president, he expanded on it. The titles of his speeches were illustrative: "Education and Politics"; "The Politician in Society"; "Law and Tradition in Political Life"; "The Need for Lawyers in Government"; and even "Scouting and Political Well-Being."

"It is a mistake to sneer at the word 'politician,'" he said. "In fact, we should accord to the word great respect and honor. We should transfer to the politicians some of the honor and reverence which we have so generously bestowed upon the Lindberghs, the Fords, the Edisons, the Morgans, and the Babe Ruths. . . ."[15]

Over the years, the names in his speeches would change from Ruth to Mantle and Lindbergh to Glenn, but his message was the same: that chemistry, banking, engineering, or manufacturing were "child's play compared to the science or art of government." As he said, scientists can control their methods or subject matter; politicians must deal with personalities, issues, and events they cannot control. With his own background, he naturally looked toward the law school as "the most important" of the professional schools. Well-trained lawyers, he said, made the best politicians—or statesmen.

By the late spring of 1940, as the war in Europe became more ominous to Americans, even those as far removed as in Arkansas, Fulbright broadened his message and began to speak out about foreign affairs. Unlike many on American campuses in 1940, Fulbright was consistently and forcefully on the side of England and the Allies. He was an outspoken interventionist and as sharply critical as any in the country of the isolationists. In a typical reference, he caustically referred to "appeasement idiocy and isolationist dreams."[16]

History, of course, does not literally repeat itself, but the words of its leading actors have a strange way of forcing comparisons between past and present.

Fulbright, in 1940, was cocky, and publicly pugnacious. His speeches about the war were studded with militant phrases ("it is far better to fight for and to lose than meekly to acquiesce" and "this country is soft").[17] He berated and belittled the isolationist United States senators who were fighting to keep us neutral ("too often today we hear the profound pronouncement by an isolationist senator that this country does not want war. . . . The fact is the world has war and the question is what it should do about it" and "Even now, when it is well on the way to becoming a fact, many of your senators are unable to grasp the real significance of the situation").[18]

Some of his comments contained the very clichés that he would later deplore and which would be used against him. "I think every intelligent, clear-thinking American should resent such a statement," he said, in dismissing a statement by Senator Walsh of Massachusetts, an isolationist. And, at another point, "We must not be confused by their false theories [isolationist senators]."[19]

His most vehement attack on the isolationists came in a speech at the

University of Oklahoma in July, 1940. That speech, ironically, led to a personally embarrassing and embittering episode a week later.

The University of Missouri had invited him to speak at the summer-term commencement that month, and Fulbright had accepted with delight, for Missouri and the university had special claim on his affections. As he noted in his prepared introduction for his speech, not only had he been born in Missouri, but his father, mother, brother, a sister, and a brother-in-law all had attended the university.

As a courtesy, Fulbright had sent the university a copy of his speech; it was essentially the same as his Oklahoma speech, and contained one particularly strong passage: "The weasling, timid, and fearful policy of the isolationist senators is one of the greatest dangers to our true interests." Missouri officials, expecting the isolationist Senator Bennett Champ Clark at the ceremonies, asked Fulbright to delete the passage. Stiffly, Fulbright replied that he would deliver it as written, or not at all. Two days before the commencement he received a wire saying he need not come; he did not.

Fulbright's bellicose remarks of those days stemmed partly out of his affection for England and the desperate plight she then faced. He regarded Hitler as an evil force that must be crushed. As Roosevelt maneuvered and improvised in an effort to help Great Britain, so Fulbright made his own small and unnoticed contribution toward aiding the Allies (he was among the group that supported William Allen White's committee of that name). But by the time the American commitment had been made through lend-lease, Fulbright's thoughts about the war turned more toward the future.

Horrible though the war was, he thought we could "turn a barren, ghastly tragedy into a tremendous opportunity, a rare opportunity in the history of the world." Like so many of the time, he looked back to Woodrow Wilson's experience at Versailles and the subsequent wreckage of his dreams for a League of Nations and advocated a new approach. Fulbright did not want himself regarded as idealistic, visionary, or impractical, but he believed in fighting what he came to call "a creative war"—a war that could lead to effective peacetime controls through a world organization.

"America has been the most fortunate of nations," he said, casting a phrase that would reappear in one of his most widely discussed and controversial speeches twenty-five years later.[20] America neither sought colonies nor needed them; the only thing it wanted was the assurance of a peaceful world. That was America's challenge. "The time has arrived for us to make our contribution to civilization. That can be made by creating this organization for all the world. . . ."[21]

His speeches of that pre-Pearl Harbor period were among the finest he would ever deliver, and they served as the foundation for many of his addresses in the years to come. But, by 1941, while the nation was being drawn ever closer into the preparations for war, Fulbright found his attention being forced away from the question of war and peace. In the first months of that year, he was going through a trial of his own at the university.

Because of his youth and the circumstances of his appointment, Fulbright had faced more than the normal problems confronting a new state university president. His lack of experience in college administration was hampering enough, but potentially more harmful, he was not known to all the faculty. Perhaps as a sop to critics, the university board of trustees had fixed his salary at $6000 a year—a cut of $1500 from Futrall's salary —when they named him president. ("For God's sake, Hal, did you vote for that?" Fulbright asked his brother-in-law, Hal Douglas, when he was informed about his pay.) The money itself was not important, except that it underscored what everyone knew: Fulbright was on trial.

Despite these obstacles, Fulbright, in the account of those who worked with him, proved to be a good administrator. He relied on senior advisers, particularly Julian Waterman, and he moved slowly. T. C. Carlson, who had come to the university after World War I, recalled that Fulbright "asked just worlds of questions. He had a very inquisitive mind. He also didn't make the mistake that so many new men make—of trying to remake the institution in a month or two months or a year or even five years."

Carlson remembered one incident from that period which was revealing not only of Fulbright's method of operation, but also of his personal attitude. The university janitors were complaining their pay was too low. Fulbright asked what they were receiving, and Carlson told him. Ever the conservative, Fulbright replied, "Well, we don't pay that much down at our furniture factory." The janitors did not get their pay increase.[22]

Such incidents notwithstanding, Carlson and others agreed that Fulbright was, as one said, on his way to becoming "an excellent president." Yet, Fulbright never was given time to demonstrate his educational leadership because, to all practical purposes, his future at the university was sealed less than a year after he had taken office by the results of the Arkansas governorship race.

In 1940 Carl E. Bailey was running for his third term as governor against Homer M. Adkins, a shrewd and resourceful politician. Adkins beat Bailey —in part, through his campaign slogan of keeping the university out of politics.

When Adkins was elected, Roberta Fulbright, never one to remain silent, wrote in her column that "it seems the people of Arkansas want a hand-shaking governor instead of one who accomplishes something."[23]

To everyone who followed Arkansas politics, Bill Fulbright's job as university president suddenly seemed tenuous. As Robert Leflar of the Law School faculty said, "From the moment that Adkins won, it was apparent that Bill was out, and he served his entire last year on notice."

After Adkins took office in January, 1941, six members of the board of trustees, all of them Bailey appointees, resigned. Adkins immediately appointed his own six men, giving them control of the ten-man board.

Rumors about Fulbright's departure increased daily on the campus that semester. Less than a month before commencement, a mass meeting of students was held in the main auditorium to protest the unofficial reports of his dismissal. Handbills were distributed and speeches were made, but the rally brought no comment from the governor, the board, or from Fulbright.

The denouement came on June 9, 1941. It was commencement day at the university, and, traditionally, the day the board of trustees met.

Again, Carlson recalled the scene:

"The board met and without much ado it was proposed that the president be asked to resign."

As secretary, Carlson was instructed to inform the president, who was in his office in Old Main. ("Imagine me going out and telling Bill a thing like that.")

Carlson, a formal, rather strait-laced man, entered Fulbright's office and said: "Mr. Fulbright, the board has just passed a resolution requesting that you resign."

"For what cause?" Fulbright asked.

"There is no cause stated."

"You may tell the board that I do not wish to resign," Fulbright answered.

Carlson returned with the reply: "Mr. Fulbright declines to resign."

The board then adopted a resolution declaring the post of president vacant at the end of the school year—after the graduation exercises that very night.

Once more, Carlson carried the message.

"Is that all?" Fulbright said.

"Yes."

"Thank you."

As perhaps the final insult, the board voted Fulbright's successor, A. M. Harding, a pay raise of $1500. Everything was back to normal at the university.

The outdoor commencement exercises for the 400 members of the graduating class of 1941 began at 6:45 P.M. in a light rain. News of Fulbright's firing had been announced after the noon meeting, and when he stepped to the lectern to introduce the main speaker, Dr. Edward C. Elliott of Purdue, the students spontaneously rose and applauded for several minutes. They applauded again at one line in his brief remarks: "A tree cannot prosper when its roots are tampered with."[24]

Then, after Elliott's address, Fulbright passed out the diplomas and ended his brief career as president of the University of Arkansas. He never issued a public statement about what had happened, but he shared his mother's feelings.

The lead editorial in her paper the next day was entitled "Der Fuehrer," and began: "It is high time for all the citizens of Arkansas, and especially those of Washington County, to ponder deeply the significance of the most drastic shake-up in the history of the university."

Temperamentally, Roberta Fulbright could not let it go at that. In her column that same day she wrote:

"I would like to make an addition to the statement which seems to have rankled the heart of the present Governor. I repeat. Arkansans prefer a hand-shaker to one who does constructive things. There is a vast and tremendous difference between building and wrecking. Some Arkansans cannot discriminate. All over the state, institutions are feeling the axe of the wrecker."

Once again, Bill Fulbright, then 36, was adrift, if not out of work. Employment was one thing he did not have to worry about. As he had done off and on for literally half his life, he returned to the family businesses, this time as president of the Phipps Lumber Company and president of the Fulbright Investment Company, the parent firm for all the family enterprises. In a way, he had come full circle.

BOOK TWO

Politician

1

A FAMILY AFFAIR

"BUCK" LEWIS, QUIET-SPOKEN AND AMIABLE, one-time sheriff, one-time banker, was drinking a cup of coffee in the Blue Hill Café on the square in Fayetteville one morning in the spring of 1942 when his boyhood friend Bill Fulbright walked in and sat down beside him.

"I'm thinking about running for Congress, Buck. What do you think about it?"

"Hell, I think you're crazy, Bill. You'll never win."[1]

Fulbright, as one might have expected, had not thought of entering politics on his own. He had been approached on Tuesday that week by his friend and former law student, Clyde Ellis, then the congressman from Fayetteville's Third Congressional District. Ellis had decided to resign his seat in the House and run for the U. S. Senate, he told Fulbright. Now was the time for Bill to put his academic ideas about politics into practice. After all, Bill had been the one who said able men should enter government. Well, why didn't Bill run for his House seat? He would have until Saturday to decide whether or not to file for the primary.

"I went to my mother and Betty and we all talked it over," Fulbright recalled. "And Mother said, 'Well, why not? You can afford it. If you don't make it, you still have a job. You can always come back here and work. You might as well do it. You've had unusual opportunities. You've had a good education, and how do you justify a Rhodes Scholarship if you don't intend doing something useful with it?' "

Betty Fulbright was equally persuasive. Although naturally gregarious, she had led an insulated life; the thought of a political campaign and possible career appealed to her all the more.*

Fulbright discussed it with other friends, and quickly visited some of the counties in the Third District. (There were ten of them; Fulbright did not know all their names, and had never even been in six.)

He filed for the race on Saturday, and immediately began a campaign that cost a total of $10,000. "It was all paid by me, my mother, and Betty," he said later. "It was a family affair."

Fulbright's principal opponent was Karl Greenhaw, a State Supreme Court justice with a reputation as a spellbinding stump speaker. Greenhaw was a friend of Governor Adkins, and had the strong backing of Adkins' political machine. Although Greenhaw was the favorite, Fulbright began with three advantageous factors. Even if he had not traveled into all the counties, his name was widely known—and to be running as the political novice and underdog never hurts an able candidate. And, lastly, Fulbright carried with him an undercurrent of sympathy: the method of his firing as university president had created resentment against Adkins and an Adkins-backed man; a vote for Fulbright could right the scales.

Greenhaw portrayed Fulbright as a man above and out of touch with the people; as a wealthy young man who has spent his entire life in higher education; as a gentleman farmer who did his farming from his veranda while admiring his high-priced Herefords and prize-winning Black Angus. These were the kind of political arguments that had been effective since Jeff Davis' days some thirty years before and could be counted on to win support in 1942. In the Ozarks, that year, babies still were born in log cabins and fiddlers still called the square dance sets in many a remote village; and, in the Ozarks, education and money were still highly suspicious commodities. Bill Fulbright, everyone knew, had both.

Despite his academic preoccupation with politics, until he entered the congressional race Fulbright never had participated, directly or indirectly, in any campaign. All he had ever done was vote. Once committed, however, he was determined to campaign aggressively.

In his mind, the best way to win was to start early and maintain a steady pace. His first task, clearly, was to make himself known personally throughout a mountainous, rural district 175 miles long and 50 miles wide. As quickly discovered, in the spring and summer, with the dust rising in a fine choking cloud over the backwoods roads, the mere process of getting to the voters in the Ozarks was a rough and wearying task.

He set out earnestly in an old Ford, his wife always at his side, and traveled into the country stores, farms, barnyards, and blacksmith shops;

* Ellis remembers discussing the matter in a Little Rock hotel with the Fulbrights and says Bill Fulbright was reluctant, but Betty Fulbright was enthusiastic at the prospect.

to city parks and squares, high school auditoriums and community centers; to remote villages and way stations; to picnics, chicken dinners, and rallies where layer cake and homemade jellies were spread beside the mountain streams.

His approach was informal and conversational. He attempted to get across the impression that he, like most of his constituents, was just plain Bill, capable, no matter what the opposition said, of ploughing a straight furrow, milking a cow, pitching hay, and shoveling manure.

With the aid of Douglas Smith, a young man who later worked for the Scripps-Howard Newspapers, the Fulbrights prepared a four-page campaign paper called *The Victory News*. It was edited in the offices of the family paper, *The Northwest Arkansas Times,* set on the *Times'* linotype machines, run off on its presses, and mailed to all boxholders in the Third District. *The Victory News* was homey—and effective. It carried recipes, jokes, and stories about Bill and Betty Fulbright and their girls, Betsey and Bosey. There were pictures of the Fulbrights at Rabbit's Foot Lodge, looking informal and rural, in front of the log house. Bill was shown, wearing a slouch hat, an old pair of pants and shirt, checking for grubs on his Black Angus, chatting with a farmer in a field, and sitting casually with his wife and daughters by the spring at Rabbit's Foot Lodge.

For Fulbright, the hardest part of the campaign was becoming accustomed to making political speeches. He found it was entirely different from his addresses as the dignified, urbane college president.

"This speaking—good Lord!" he would say years after in remembering that first campaign. "The first speech or two I made—it was just awful agony. The embarrassment of it! One of those I remember particularly was out at Elkins, a small town ten miles from Fayetteville. It was about eleven o'clock in the morning, and you have to start somewhere, you know. Had a little loudspeaker and went down on the corner and there wasn't anybody around. I mean there were a couple across the street, and two or three sitting down there, but you couldn't tell whether they were really there to listen or not. They were just around. There wasn't anybody there. And you get up and talk. You know, you feel like such an ass."

One of his worst moments came not long after his Elkins speech in a town north of Rogers, Arkansas. There, he spoke before an audience consisting entirely of one man. After that experience, Fulbright changed his campaign tactics. Instead of trying to speak formally outdoors with a loudspeaker, he began setting up a regular schedule of eight to ten political appearances a day. But the appearances were now informal. He would go into stores and shops and chat quietly. In that way, he managed to get his points across without laboring through a sterile stump speech.

Campaigning, he learned, was more subtle than he had realized. Friendliness or enthusiasm or even a large turnout did not necessarily mean support. They might—but often they might not. The "big" issues, or broad principles of government, did not seem to bring forth any special voter response, either. It was all very well, in the classroom or from the podium, to discuss the values of an intelligent electorate, but going before the people brought a different view of the political process: people were more interested in personalities than in principles. People also had a distressing quality that continually upset the novice politician: in person, they nearly all pledged to support him, even when it was quite apparent they had no such intention, if, indeed, they really planned to vote at all.

In the early days of his campaign, which he had begun nearly four months before the primary, Fulbright found interest in the congressional race flagging. People neither knew nor cared about who was running or on what political planks. His time was not being wasted, though, for he was being assessed and studied and the opinions were then being formed that would prove decisive at the polls. He also was discovering that his own views of politics were changing. The educational process worked both ways.

It was essential, Fulbright immediately found out, to know intimately the state of mind of the prospective constituents; to know what mattered most to them; and to learn how to best appeal to those wishes and reap the advantage on election day.

From his experience, Fulbright would draw a fundamental lesson.

"The ability to compromise and reconcile the differences among people," he would say, "is of the essence of the legislative function, whether it be in Congress or in the midst of a heated political campaign. There are no absolutes in politics and one learns this quickly in a campaign among the voters."[2]

That may not be the noble view, but Fulbright found it the practical one. He seldom deviated from it.

There were other experiences for which he was unprepared. While he was out on the road, his headquarters personnel were struggling with the minor but essential tasks which vex every campaign, and which often make the difference between victory and defeat. And, to his annoyance, no matter how mundane or humble the problem, Fulbright found it had a way of reaching his attention.

As soon as the campaign had begun, a stream of political hangers-on appeared at the Fulbright headquarters in Fayetteville. The handful of students, friends, and members of the family who were manning the headquarters, preparing and distributing the campaign literature, had to take time out to interview them all.

They wanted jobs; they wanted favors; they wanted promises of future support. A number came begging "expenses" to carry certain boxes on election day. Fulbright particularly recalled what he termed "one self-confessed precinct leader" who wanted a fifty-dollar donation from the general campaign fund. In return, he promised to deliver highly tangible rewards. As the time passed and he failed to receive his hoped-for fifty, he kept scaling down his requests. Finally, he broke down and frankly asked for a twenty-five-cent handout to buy lunch.

That incident was a source of amusement; others were not.

Fulbright's nephew, Allan Gilbert, Jr.,* who was working day and night as a volunteer on behalf of his uncle, remembered one bitter moment halfway through the campaign. He had been out for an entire week papering one of the ten counties with Fulbright posters to build up advance notice for the candidate's scheduled appearance there the following week. Gilbert returned, hot, dusty, and tired, but pleased at his efforts, and immediately began preparing advance notices for next week's schedule.

When Fulbright returned and saw Gilbert, he snapped angrily, "What were you doing all last week?"

"Why, I was putting up the posters all over the county," Gilbert replied.

"The hell you were," Fulbright said. "There wasn't a Fulbright poster up in the entire county."[3]

Upon checking, they determined that the state police had followed Gilbert and taken down the posters as rapidly as they were put up. The state police were Adkins' men.

By the last three weeks of the race, the informal appearances were over and Fulbright was deeply engaged in the hardest work of all—the major scheduled political speeches. Now, the voters seemed interested in the race. Now, they turned out in numbers. They always did at the end of a race, but they were as unfathomable as ever.

Fulbright, in his speeches, tried to maintain the low-keyed approach that seemed to be successful so far. He talked about rationing and price controls; about farm labor, REA lines for mountain homesteads, and tick eradication; about education and the Third District's public school system; about winning the war and the need for the United States to take the lead to ensure a lasting peace. But he still was conversational, still striking a casual pose, hands in pockets, suit coat open, tie loosened.

In his earliest speaking efforts Fulbright had been so ill at ease that he had difficulty in getting through a ten-minute speech. By the end of the race all that had changed; he was enjoying campaigning to such an extent that Betty Fulbright was saying she couldn't get him to stop after an hour and a half.

Betty had stayed with him from beginning to end. Afterward, many would say that she, as much as any single factor, had been Fulbright's greatest asset. Before the campaign there had been considerable gossip and speculation about the wealthy Junior League socialite from Philadelphia, the Easterner turned president's lady. Betty's presence quickly

---

* In later years Gilbert became a columnist on the family paper in Fayetteville, thus taking the place of the senator's mother.

convinced the doubters that, although a Yankee, she knew how to sugar-cure a ham, make soup in an outdoor kettle, and worry over her children just as did every other mother in the district.

"Betty had a bundle, but she was plain as an old shoe," said one Fayette-ville resident. "Just another one of the gals. There wasn't anything uppity about her."

She also had the ability, which Bill mainly lacked, of making small talk. "Betty always got to know folks much better than Bill did," said another acquaintance of that time.

Fulbright himself publicly expressed his debt to Betty a few years later when he prepared what he called a "primer for congressional candidates," a document that served as the model for his major speech entitled, "The Legislator."[4]

"It is exceedingly helpful to have a wife who can go into the kitchen and visit with the women of the family while you engage the men in a discussion," he said. "In the conservative rural communities, it is not good manners to discuss politics in the presence of the women. Just why this should be so, I am not quite certain. But in any case, it is an asset to have a wife who likes people."

To his benefit, he did.

He and Betty wound up their campaign at a large rally in Springdale, then actually the Fulbrights' post-office address for Rabbit's Foot Lodge.

Clyde Ellis, who was responsible for Fulbright's entry into politics, lost in his Senate bid while Fulbright won by more than 4000 votes. He won by the largest margin in the Third Congressional District in thirty years.

In Arkansas, victory in the primary assured victory in November. After the August primary, Fulbright acted and spoke like the young congressman with ideas. In September, he attended his first political convention—the State Democratic meeting in Little Rock—and immediately shifted his political emphasis from the local to the national and international. As he had done during his university presidency, once again he was addressing a wider audience.

"During the next two years," he told the Democratic delegates, "I think our party leaders should evolve a daring and an aggressive program for . . . the world organization after this war."[5] Again hearkening back to 1918, he said that "President Wilson had the idea but he and the Democratic Party failed to sell the Congress and the people on that idea."

In the next few weeks he continued speaking in Arkansas on this theme of America's need to fight "a creative war." Then on November 3, 1942, the general election results confirmed what everyone already knew. J. William Fulbright was the representative of the Third Congressional District of Arkansas, and a new member of the 78th Congress.

2

THE MAD CAPITAL OF A MAD WORLD

IT HAD BEEN, *The Evening Star* reported, "a subdued New Year's Eve," and on Friday, New Year's Day 1943, the business of Washington went on as usual. In '43, Washington's business meant the war; the war meant that all government employees had to work that day. They did so with only the expected amount of grumbling, for Washington on New Year's Day was in a state of sustained emotion and nervous tension.

Fulbright found, however, one familiar link with the city he had known so well during the depression and the early New Deal: Society was not being neglected. In war as in peace, hostesses still held sway, still vied foolishly for the famous and the great to grace their lavish private parties. If anything, the war intensified their efforts and brought them new requirements. As an etiquette column that day carefully advised:

"Wartime etiquette demands that you use your own sugar when dining with friends, and to enable you to carry a supply, without trouble, small tube-shaped flasks made of unbreakable plastic material have been placed on the market. The flask will hold approximately two teaspoons of the precious substance, and, thanks to a screw top, there is no danger of sugar spilling into pockets or handbag."[1]

The problems of the hostess and partygoers were indicative, in miniature, of what was happening to Washington. In little more than a year, Washington had been transformed from the placid Southern city of the past to the war capital of the world. Physically and psychologically, the change was dramatic.

Now, at night, the lights no longer were shining on the marble monuments beside the Potomac; now, there were blackouts and dimouts and, in daytime, air-raid drills prefaced by piercing sirens. But by 1943 the drills were being taken less seriously. Indeed, there was far more concern about where to find a place to stay.

Every six months 35,000 more people were crowding into the city. The metropolitan area had gained 366,000; the annual payroll had increased eighty-five percent; living costs were the highest since 1926; and the District of Columbia itself held more people than it would have fourteen years later. A critical shortage of rooms for single women existed, the National Housing Agency was saying, while the government was declaring that an equally critical shortage of office space plagued the war effort. New "temporary" buildings went up on the Mall and near the Lincoln Memorial to stand beside those earlier tempos from Wilson's war—tempos which ever since then had stood as unwelcome reminders that, in Washington, government was capable of moving with both extreme speed and sluggishness.

But there was nothing slow about the government's war effort. Although Pearl Harbor was little more than a year away, the end could be clearly seen—and felt—in Washington. On all fronts, the Allies were moving forward: the Russians had defeated the Germans at Stalingrad; the Americans and British were advancing in North Africa; the Japanese were being beaten on Guadalcanal.

As the new year began, the government pronouncements continued to strike a Spartan note. The veteran warriors, Stimson and Ickes, sounded the official theme. "It is a long, hard road, beset with many obstacles," Stimson said, of the overseas situation. "We are fighting enemies who are strong and who are determined to fight to the end." And Ickes, speaking of the homefront and the need to continue rationing, added: "It may well be that conditions will get much worse before they get better; that the cuts already made will have to be deepened."[2]

Their words were greeted without dismay. It was popular to be patriotic, to have a Victory Garden, to save tin foil and scrap metal (the papers proudly were boasting that in the last six months alone the citizens of the District had collected 60,500,791 pounds of scrap metal), to buy war bonds, and to avoid hoarding. When Marian Anderson sang at Constitution Hall that week,* the press again had words of praise for the manner in which patriotic Washingtonians turned out: only five private cars were seen in the vicinity of the concert and ninety-five percent of the patrons came by public transportation.

Actually, private transportation was something of a moot question, for

---

* Her appearance represented racial progress in Washington. Before the war, she had been barred from singing in Constitution Hall because she was a Negro.

on January 6, just as the 78th Congress convened, the Office of Price Administration (OPA) banned all pleasure driving.

Bill, Betty, Betsey, and Bosey Fulbright had not been affected by the ban. They had driven from Arkansas to Washington, but they had priorities; they were on official government business—congressional government business. They had experienced no housing problems, either. A friend had got them a comfortable apartment on Connecticut Avenue, and although some of their Arkansas neighbors had been distressed about seeing Bill and the family leave the farm, close the house, and lend the grand piano, their move was accomplished smoothly.

They had little time to settle in, though, before Fulbright took his seat in the new Congress on January 7, another day of history on Capitol Hill, as Franklin Roosevelt delivered his State-of-the-Union address in person.

FDR was in fine form, vibrant and jaunty, and the Congress responded in kind. One correspondent noted that the congressmen particularly applauded "when he gave praise to the great fight which the Russians and Chinese are waging."[3]

"The 78th Congress assembles in one of the great moments in the history of this nation," Roosevelt said, in the familiar delivery. "The past year was perhaps the most crucial for modern civilization. The coming year will be filled with violent conflict—yet with a high promise of better things." Within the year, he said, America's armed forces had grown from two to seven million; and they were still growing. "Washington may be a madhouse," he said, "but only in the sense that it is the Capital City of a nation that is fighting mad. And I think that Berlin and Rome and Tokyo, which had such contempt for the obsolete methods of democracy, would now gladly use all they could get of that same brand of madness."[4]

The new thirty-eight-year-old Congressman from Arkansas thought FDR's speech "the highlight of the session so far," and told his constituents so. In his first news letter to them, he also summed up his initial impressions of Washington and the political life.

"The first two weeks in Congress is like going away to college for the first time," he wrote. "The older Members on every hand were congratulating one another on their return and bemoaning the loss of many of their favorite colleagues. Their attitude toward new Members is kindly and helpful, but naturally slightly superior."

Of his colleagues, he said, in a vintage Fulbright passage: "My first impression is that the intelligence of the Member is in inverse ratio to the amount of speaking he does on the floor of the House. The serious and wise Members speak only when they have something to say and do most of their work in the committee. The crackpots jump to their feet at every opportunity to criticize their betters and show off what they think is their clever wit."

Within a matter of days after writing that, Fulbright himself had taken the floor of the House, vigorously and sarcastically criticized another member of Congress, displayed his own caustic wit, and attracted so much attention that his name quickly became known around the country. Suddenly he found himself a national celebrity, quoted, sought after, praised.

3

"I AM FULLY CONSCIOUS OF MY DEFICIENCIES"

EVERY NEW CONGRESS HAS ITS SHARE of celebrities, and the 78th was no exception. Of all its new faces, the two that had attracted the most attention before the session began were, not surprisingly, famous figures from the entertainment field who had turned to politics. Will Rogers, Jr., looked uncannily like his father—the same boyish grin, the same beguiling wise and rustic look, the stray lock of hair, the drawl—and he could even twirl a rope. Whether he would live up to his heritage as a sagebrush philosopher was not yet clear; but he was a principal subject for political speculation. Not far behind him in the public eye was the new Congresswoman from Connecticut, Clare Boothe Luce.

Mrs. Luce came to Congress with the reputation as an acidulous wit, a caustic, clawing beauty adept at evoking applause from the tough New York theater audiences (she had written the Broadway hit *The Women*) and publicly demolishing a foe with a rapierlike phrase. Harold Ickes, she had said, was "a prodigious bureaucrat" with "the soul of a meat axe and the mind of a commissar." In her congressional campaign she had described her unsuccessful opponent, Representative Leroy D. Downs, as "a faceless man who spends a lot of time trying to get his face in the papers."

When Congress convened, it was Clare Boothe Luce, not the son of the Oklahoma cowboy, who immediately demonstrated superior gifts at seizing the center stage.

Although freshmen members of the House traditionally wait a "proper" period before giving their maiden speeches, Mrs. Luce did not stand on any precedents. Before a month of the session had passed, she took the floor to deliver a slashing attack on Vice President Henry A. Wallace. Her speech was an assault not only on Wallace's ideas about the shape of the postwar world, but also on Roosevelt, Churchill, Stalin, the Atlantic Charter, and talk of proposing specific international settlements, including the disposition of national air rights in the ever-growing air age to come. In the midst of her speech, she coined a phrase that brought guffaws from the galleries and became celebrated throughout the world.

"Much of what Mr. Wallace calls his global thinking is, no matter how you slice it, still globaloney," Mrs. Luce said. "Mr. Wallace's warp of sense and his woof of nonsense is very tricky cloth out of which to cut the pattern of a postwar world."

Her ridiculing of "globaloney" stung the Roosevelt administration, and set off a debate in the press. Dorothy Thompson accused Mrs. Luce of advocating imperialism. Eleanor Roosevelt expressed her disapproval, and asked: "Are we going in for a peaceful world, or aren't we?" And, far down the line of public, if not important, figures, the speech highly irritated the new Congressman from Arkansas, J. W. Fulbright. It annoyed him so much that he decided to attempt to answer Mrs. Luce himself.

Fulbright already had demonstrated an unusual degree of independence, or foolhardiness, for a new member by being one of only ninety-four Representatives to vote against continuing the Dies Committee, then the sobriquet of the House Un-American Activities Committee. Asked about his vote, Fulbright had told a reporter with a shrug and then a smile: "I was advised it would be politically unwise to do that. Maybe I'll be around here only for two years."[1]

When Mrs. Luce spoke out, he felt her views represented the opposite of what U.S. policy should be; that her speech would raise suspicion among the allies, and be harmful to the cause of peace later. While he was talking this way with Luther Johnson of Texas, the ranking member of the House Foreign Affairs Committee, Johnson suggested that Fulbright, as a freshman Democrat, should be the one to reply to a freshman Republican. He agreed; then they went to House Majority Leader John McCormack of Massachusetts. McCormack set a time for Fulbright to speak when he would have the widest audience and best prospects of press coverage.

On February 16, one week after Mrs. Luce had spoken, Fulbright delivered his own maiden address while his wife and his entire office staff sat above in the galleries. In a sense, it was the speech that made him. It was entitled, "A Program for Peace—In Reply to Hon. Clare Boothe Luce of Connecticut."

"Mr. Chairman, I rise today for the first time in this House, sooner than I had intended," Fulbright began. "I am fully conscious of my deficiencies in experience, and otherwise, for this task, but nevertheless for all new

Members there must be a first time, so I beg the indulgence of this House for the time at my disposal.

"The reason I am speaking sooner than I had intended is simply this: Although I am not unconscious of the sparkling beauty and suavity of manner of the honorable lady from Connecticut, yet I find that I am not as susceptible to her logic and to her persuasion, at least on the floor of this House, as some of my colleagues appear to have been."

Fulbright then proceeded to give his reply. "The train of her thought is difficult to follow," he said at one point, "so I hope that I may not be held strictly accountable if I should misinterpret certain passages." At another, he slyly dug at "the imperialistic arguments of the gentlewoman." And, he said, "Being unable to follow any serious logic in this reasoning, I am compelled to conclude that the point of this passage [in her speech] was to ridicule the Vice President of the United States." Fulbright defended him. "Her witty and scintillating remarks about Mr. Wallace were quite equal to the sophisticated style of Walter Winchell and *Time* magazine. Not only is Mr. Wallace spasmodically sane, but he is full of 'globaloney,' a wonderful word which convulsed the gallery and will certainly live for many seasons in the folklore of Broadway. There is no denying it, our honorable colleague is a wit."

Fulbright was not merely sarcastic or contemptuous, however. Drawing on his speeches from his university presidency period, he made an appeal for the nation to plan for a postwar period.

"I think it exceedingly unfortunate to assume at this time that nothing whatever can be done about controlling the savage and violent elements of the world, to assume that World War No. 3 is just around the corner," he said. "Such an assumption is a most powerful inducement to that very result. I submit that the only rational policy for this great nation of ours is to assume, what I believe to be true, that the peoples of this earth have learned something by experience, that they earnestly desire to avoid and to prevent another world war, and that they are willing to make reasonable sacrifices to attain this end."

He offered specific proposals: that America's representatives "should begin negotiations at once with our allies to formulate a specific and concrete system for collective security of the nations of the world"; that the American people and their representatives "discard our traditional isolationism, now often disguised under the name of Americanism"; that the Congress, "instead of assuming a defeatist policy with regard to war, immediately authorize and direct its Committee on Foreign Affairs to undertake a thorough study of all proposals for postwar international organizations designed to prevent war"; that the committee report its findings and develop specific recommendations for the consideration of the executive branch.

The speech was greeted enthusiastically, but the highlight came immediately after when Clare Boothe Luce challenged Fulbright on the floor. At several points, she remarked, "the gentleman from Arkansas said I had inferred this or that. I inferred nothing. I implied and the gentleman from Arkansas did the inferring." Fulbright had also "spoken loosely" and carelessly about what she really had said. Would he be good enough to cite specific passages from her speech to back up his interpretations?

The Luce rapier was showing. With all eyes on him, Fulbright stood, bowed slightly in Mrs. Luce's direction, smiled and drawled:

"Would you like me to read your speech again to this audience?"

Loud laughter. Then applause. Fulbright sat down. So did Clare Boothe Luce. The Arkansas freshman had won, even in a direct exchange of *bons mots* with the brittle and brilliant Easterner.

That story went around the country. Fulbright became known as "the man who told off Mrs. Luce," as a *PM* headline put it.[2] He also found himself sought after for speeches, regarded as "a standout new member of Congress," and a hope of the liberals and intellectuals. For Fulbright, this marked the beginning of his adoption by the Eastern liberals. Mail poured into his office from around the country. Several congressmen called to congratulate him. One said it was the best speech he had heard on the floor of the House in ten years.[3]

Flustered and flattered though he was by the attention, Fulbright did not overlook the practical political possibilities of his congressional debut. At the suggestion of Clyde Ellis, whose seat he had taken in Congress, he mailed 25,000 reprints of his speech to voters in his district. (He had already purchased Ellis' addressing machine and mailing list.)

The favorable response encouraged Fulbright to make new efforts in the cause of peace. When Dr. Frank Aydelotte, president of Swarthmore College as well as the American secretary of the Rhodes Scholarship Trust, wrote praising his speech, Fulbright replied, maintaining the pupil-to-professor style:

> "Dear Uncle Frank:
> . . . As you know we have two other Rhodes Scholars in Congress now.* Both of them are very able men and I think will be helpful in the problem of postwar organization."

Fulbright, as a new member of the House Foreign Affairs Committee, was in the appropriate place to work effectively for postwar planning. His appointment to the committee had also been one of his early lessons in the realities of power in Washington for he had come to the Congress hoping, but uncertain, that he would get on the committee. "I didn't think I'd make it," he told Herbert Yahraes of *PM* during an interview that month, "but

---

* Charles R. Clason of Massachusetts and Robert Hale of Maine.

I went gunning for it, and. . . ." Yahraes said Fulbright "grinned like a kid who has finally got the ice skates he'd been praying for."[4]

Actually, to his great surprise, Fulbright had discovered there was little difficulty in being named to the committee. "I remember Wilbur Mills saying to me when I came to the House, 'Well, if you'd like to go on Foreign Affairs there's no problem. There's no competition to get on Foreign Affairs,'" he remembered later. What the knowledgeable congressman should want, Fulbright quickly learned, was a more powerful post—and that meant to the Appropriations, Ways and Means, or Public Works committees. There, the wise politician could best build the kind of important support that might keep him in office.

Fulbright easily got Foreign Affairs.

The chairman was Sol Bloom, the child of penniless Jewish immigrants from Poland whose career had carried him from theater manager to song writer to real-estate operator and finally, after appropriate services for Tammany Hall, to Congress in 1923. Twenty years later, at the age of 73, Sol Bloom was still very much a dandy, given to wearing a pince-nez attached to a broad black ribbon around his neck in the fashion of Theodore Roosevelt, and built-up shoes to compensate for his size. Fulbright thought him "very dictatorial and extremely contemptuous of the junior members."

Fulbright found Bloom's manner of controlling the committee objectionable enough, but he also chafed at being the junior member. The junior member, he discovered, was the last one to have a chance to speak or ask a question—and often Bloom never got down to Fulbright at all.

Bloom's committee had begun daily hearings on lend-lease soon after the session started, and that, at least, was rewarding for Fulbright. The hearings also were interesting from the standpoint of Fulbright's future stance as a critic of foreign affairs. When Edward Stettinius, Jr., white-haired and handsome, but not especially gifted, appeared in his capacity as administrator of the Office of Lend-Lease, Fulbright said:

"Of course you realize that many people in this country are not entirely satisfied with the way foreign relations have been handled in the past and the fact that they may have been handled in the past by a particular agency is not entirely persuasive that they must always continue to be so handled."[5]

That marked Fulbright's first criticism of the State Department, albeit an indirect one. He had also asked if Stettinius had given much thought about postwar planning for peace, and Stettinius, who eventually would become Secretary of State himself, said that was the State Department's job, not his agency's.

The hearings were rewarding, but they were also taxing. In fact, Fulbright was finding the job of being a congressman the most difficult of his life. The hearings, the House sessions, and the office work kept him fully occupied until six or seven every night; then, he would leave to attend meetings, always attempting to keep himself abreast of his primary interest, then and later—foreign affairs. On one night, he would hear General Pat Hurley reporting on events in China; on another, a debate about international organization at the Co-Op forum; on still another, a meeting to discuss possible postwar problems. In his spare moments, Fulbright was reading everything he could about postwar planning, and soon he was expressing his own ideas before audiences throughout the East: in Boston, before the Joint Council for International Cooperation; in New York, before the Commission to Study the Organization of Peace; and in Washington, a sentimental return to the George Washington University Law School, where he had earned his degree and taught, and where, in 1943, as he told students and faculty, he found himself again in Washington "studying much harder than I studied when I sat in this room some ten years ago and listened to Dean Van Vleck and Professor Collier expound the law."[6]

Fulbright's theme was the same he had been developing since his university presidency: the need to fight a "creative war" to lay "the foundations of a warless world."

The lend-lease hearings and his general preoccupation with the postwar subject led Fulbright to attempt to get congressional support for his ideas. His first effort was in February when he offered a resolution urging congressional study and action to develop "a specific plan or system by which peace may be maintained through cooperative international action."

That resolution attracted almost no attention. Fulbright was frustrated but, as a freshman, he was not alone in feeling neglected and ignored. Before long, he was commiserating with other new congressmen. "Most people ignored you then," he would say of that period. "In those days freshmen congressmen couldn't be less important. We were so unimportant we used to sort of gather together, you know, over there and console each other. Walter Judd, Chris Herter [later to be Secretary of State], and that crowd that came in then. We used to meet and talk in an office about how little we could do or talk about what we ought to do, and we would try to think up letters or resolutions, or anything, to attract a little attention or express ourselves. We had a hell of a job to get any attention."

Of all of those congressmen, Fulbright soon had attracted more attention than any one else in the House, new or old. Coming soon after his Luce encounter, his new acclaim solidified his position and assured him fame, at least for the rest of the war. His reputation rested, this time, on what came to be widely known as the Fulbright Resolution.

Fulbright introduced his new resolution on April 5, 1943. Unlike the turgid and flowery passages that filled the Congress every day, the Fulbright Resolution was only one sentence long.

"Resolved: That the House of Representatives hereby expresses itself as favoring the creation of appropriate international machinery with power adequate to prevent future aggression and to maintain lasting peace, and as favoring participation by the United States therein."

Most political seers predicted Fulbright's resolution would be pigeon-holed by Bloom and forgotten. They were mistaken. Fulbright proved himself an able negotiator, and an adept politician. Unlike his first resolution, which was immediately filed and forgotten, he had carefully laid the groundwork for his second, and far broader, postwar planning effort.

First, he enlisted the private support of James W. Wadsworth of New York and Charles A. (Doc) Eaton of New Jersey, both key Republicans on the House Foreign Affairs Committee. Wadsworth, in particular, encouraged Fulbright. The resolution appealed to him on two grounds, one patriotic, the other political and personal; it was simple, direct, and might be effective—and it also would undercut Sol Bloom. "I think it rather tickled old Jim's ego sorta," Fulbright remarked. "I mean, I don't think he really liked Sol."

Fulbright next asked for an appointment with Sumner Welles, then the Acting Secretary of State, and Welles, too, liked the resolution; it fitted in perfectly with the Roosevelt administration's plans for helping to create a strong postwar United Nations. At Fulbright's request, Welles gave the new congressman a letter stating that he and the State Department approved the principles in the resolution. Then Fulbright began a quiet lobbying campaign with other members of the committee—every member, that is, but Sol Bloom. He also took advantage on every possible occasion to boost his own resolution in public.

A speech that May in Constitution Hall about "The U.N. Today and Tomorrow" demonstrated that Fulbright was not afflicted with undue modesty; he also was displaying an increasing trend toward sarcasm.

After praising his own resolution as "the least controversial and the most likely to be acceptable to the Congress now," Fulbright explained why he thought it necessary: "The real significance of the action which we want from the Congress now is the assurance that this country desires to make a genuine and honest effort in cooperation with other nations, to put an end to aggressive warfare. This assurance is absolutely essential before our executive can negotiate effectively with other nations."[7]

Then he voiced his contempt toward congressional colleagues in both houses.

"In view of the historic caution and timidity of our illustrious Senate with regard to foreign affairs," he said, "it is important that it be not frightened with an esoteric or complicated proposal." As for the House of Representatives, it was "so grossly overburdened with wartime legislation, in addition to the usual domestic measures, and so distracted by the struggle for political power in anticipation of 1944, that the members have neither the serenity nor the inclination carefully to analyze and to formulate at this time a detailed plan for international cooperation."

Left unsaid was Fulbright's obvious opinion that he did not suffer that common handicap.

By then, Fulbright had considerable support for his resolution; at committee meetings he firmly continued to bring up his resolution for action. Finally, for three days in June, the full committee met secretly to consider his and all other resolutions, including those introduced in the Senate, about postwar machinery.

Bloom, clearly not relishing being upstaged by a freshman, suggested that the best course might be to meet with subcommittees from the Senate Foreign Relations Committee and his own House committee and thus attempt to agree on "some form of resolution."

"That would seem unendurable if we have to wait until they agree," Fulbright replied.

He was making his point effectively. The laconic New Englander, Foster Stearns of New Hampshire, liked his resolution. "I think its brevity is very strongly in its favor. It is something that can be put on a postcard. . . . Even the readers of the picture papers would be capable of reading that much." Another congressman, Howard J. McMurray of Wisconsin, spoke up, and said privately what he would not say publicly to his constituents: "I come from the heart of isolationism in America. . . . The reason those people there are isolationists is they have never known anything else and they never had the political leaders and never had any political leadership to give them the other side of the picture. They are completely ignorant about it."

The key to the debate came when Bloom was asked if he knew how the State Department felt about the Fulbright resolution.

Fulbright, never the demonstrative man, fairly shouted the answer; he had been waiting for that question to come. "I have a letter," he said. "I have one. I will bring it at the next meeting. It is to the effect that anything of this nature would be helpful. . . . I think the attitude would be if we can get a unanimous report and we feel it would pass the House with a good majority they would like it. That is the way I interpret that letter."

At the next executive session Fulbright produced his letter from Sumner Welles, in which Welles said, in part: "I have discussed the matter with Secretary Hull and he has asked me to let you know that both the President and he are in full accord with the principles contained in your resolution. . . ."

On June 15, the full House Foreign Affairs Committee unanimously reported out the Fulbright Resolution to the floor of the House. It was the first postwar proposal endorsed by that committee, and the first to reach the floor of Congress. Its sudden, and unexpected, emergence in the House after the secret sessions created a sensation. In announcing the vote, Sol Bloom said the committee had studied every proposal for a postwar world organization now pending before either house and decided on the one-sentence resolution introduced by the freshman from Arkansas. "You could write and talk for a week, but you couldn't say any more than that resolution does," he said.[8]

The committee action especially stunned the Senate, a stuffy and ponderous body, filled with prima donnas, and jealously proud of its deliberative procrastinations. No one was galled more than Tom Connally, the leonine old chairman of the Senate Foreign Relations Committee. For months, Connally and a hand-picked subcommittee had been sitting on half a dozen postwar resolutions without a trace of action on any. Now, the House had seized the initiative. To make it worse, a thirty-eight-year-old congressman from Arkansas had stolen the spotlight.

The Fulbright Resolution, Connally commented scornfully, was "cryptic."[9]

But around the country Fulbright's name became firmly linked with the cause of world peace. He became that American phenomenon, the instant celebrity, subjected to all of the pleasures and annoyances of fame in America: His telephone rang constantly; his fan mail increased 100 percent; his company was sought by the noted and by those on the make; his office was filled with reporters and writers seeking interviews for their newspapers and magazines.

An article in *Life* a week after his resolution reached the floor set the tone for them all. The Fulbright Resolution, *Life* said, was the first step in the development of a "truly national foreign policy."[10]

When someone asked Fulbright how long it took him to write his one-sentence resolution, the congressman smiled and said he guessed about fifteen years. "What he meant, of course," *Life* told its readers, "was that he had been studying the problem of United States foreign relations for at least that long."

The writer found a highly pleased Fulbright sitting in his office, deluged with mail and phone calls, and saying: "Everybody assumes that just because a fellow comes from Arkansas he can't read or write. But that's where they're wrong."

The Fulbright Resolution unquestionably would have passed the House with ease had it been voted on shortly after it cleared the Foreign Affairs Committee. Speaker Sam Rayburn, already the undisputed power in the House, favored its adoption, as did Majority Leader John McCormack. They would have brought it up then, had not James Wadsworth shrewdly talked them out of it.

Wadsworth favored the resolution, but he also wanted the Republicans to be able to claim bi-partisan support for its adoption. At a meeting with Bloom, Fulbright, Rayburn, and McCormack, Wadsworth pointed out that if a vote were taken then, at least fifty, and perhaps eighty, Republicans would oppose it on purely partisan grounds. But, he argued, given time he could virtually assure that not over twelve Republicans would vote against it. Action should be postponed until the House reconvened in September, he suggested. In the meantime, he would bring up the matter at a conference of Republican leaders at Mackinac Island, Michigan, later that summer.

The Democrats agreed; the vote was postponed.

At the same time the leading figures of the Roosevelt administration had begun working quietly, but forcefully, behind the scenes on behalf of Fulbright's resolution. Cordell Hull already had called the Speaker in its behalf.

On June 28, FDR wrote Hull about the Fulbright Resolution.

"What do you think of pushing the resolution of the Foreign Affairs Committee of the House?" the President asked. "It seems to me pretty good, and if we can get it through the House it might work in the Senate also. I do not think it can do any harm. Will you talk with me about this? But you had better talk to Connally first."[11]

Hull, and later Harry Hopkins, kept in close contact with congressional leaders that summer, urging, as Hull said, "that Congress begin to align itself behind an international organization, in which the United States would play a dominant part."[12]

Their efforts were successful. Early in September, at the Mackinac Island conference, the Republican leaders went on record as approving U.S. participation in an international cooperative organization following the war. They set the stage for congressional action. On September 20, the debate began in the House over the Fulbright resolution.

The timing seemed auspicious, for the debate began in the midst of the planning sessions for the first meetings of the Allied leaders at Moscow, Cairo, and Tehran. In the midst of the greatest war in history, the House advocates of the resolution felt they had been given a chance to take the lead for peace, to right the wrongs of 1919 and 1920 when the Senate had rejected the League of Nations, and, later, in 1935, turned down participation in the World Court. For the isolationists, the debate marked their final battle. George H. Mahon of Texas spoke for most when he said:

"Mr. Speaker, this is a historic day in the history of our country. Today we propose to pass a resolution which serves notice to the world that when we have won this war we shall try to keep it won. Never before has such action been taken by Congress."

He then read the "resolution known as the Fulbright Resolution."

Speaking in defense of his own resolution, Fulbright said, "I have no illusions that this resolution is the panacea for all international afflictions. It is the first small step in the process of building a foreign policy which I hope may have better results than that which we have followed in the past. . . . We Members of the House have an obligation to see that the children of today's heroes do not have it all to do over again in twenty years."

The principal opposition came from Illinois. "I consider the Fulbright Resolution the most dangerous bill ever presented to an American Congress," said Miss Jessie Sumner. It was dangerous because "it furnishes internationalists with all power they ask to rob Americans of their independence. . . ."

By late in the day, after 48,000 words of debate had been recorded, the House still had not reached a vote. The debate resumed the next day.

The key moment came when Charles A. (Doc) Eaton, the ranking Republican member of the Foreign Affairs Committee, stood to speak. Eaton, white-haired, the former pastor of John D. Rockefeller's Baptist church in Cleveland and later editor of Leslie's weekly, was emotional.

"I have seven sons. One died of war wounds July 30. Another was killed over Nuremberg August 10. By God, I will vote for any measure which carries some hope of the future abolishment of war's wholesale murder." The Fulbright Resolution passed the House by a vote of 360 to 29.

It was a "stupendous majority," Hull said, and "would give me a real advantage in Moscow because it would show Molotov and Eden that the people of the United States, at least through their Representatives in the House, wanted their country to take its full share in an international organization.[13]

With one notable exception, the national press hailed the passage. Col. Robert R. (Bertie) McCormick's *Chicago Tribune,* in an editorial the next day entitled, "The Republic Lives," commented: "The measure was introduced by a first-termer from Arkansas, who in his formative years was sent as a Rhodes Scholar to Oxford to learn to betray his country and deprive it of its independence. In this instance, as no doubt in many others, Mr. Rhodes appears to have got his money's worth."[14]

Harold Ross' *New Yorker* immediately replied, and issued what it called "A Citation" to the twenty-nine congressmen (seven were from Illinois) who voted against the Fulbright Resolution.

"To these twenty-nine unforgettable legislators [the magazine said] whose dim, aloof spirit walks by its wild lone, we now award a special ribbon for density above and beyond the call of duty. The ribbon is made of bloody bandages, and we hope it will forever remind the representatives of the real entanglements of the flesh which belie their quaint and curious theory. Gentlemen, if you do not know that your country is now entangled beyond recall with the rest of the world, what *do* you know?"[15]

Within three weeks the Senate Foreign Relations sub-committee at last reported a resolution of its own to the full committee. It was quickly approved, sent to the Senate for debate and soon passed. That resolution, known as the Connally Resolution, was only seventy-five words long and bore a striking resemblance to Fulbright's. Together, these congressional actions helped significantly to pave the way for the creation of the United Nations.

Fulbright, not Connally, received the greatest public praise and credit. After his resolution was passed, he appeared on an increasing number of influential panels and forums—appearances that were noted with pride back in Arkansas. As the *Arkansas Democrat* in Little Rock remarked:

"Congressman Fulbright, in his first term in Washington, has gained more favorable publicity than any other Representative we have ever sent to the Congress."[16]

Fulbright continued to take every advantage of his ever-widening public arena. In speeches, articles, broadcasts, and even in letters to editors, he spelled out his ideas about America's role in the postwar world.* Fame had come full-bloom to Fulbright, and he was finding the role of a public figure—and potential peacemaker—anything but peaceful. His family was discovering a part of those penalties of fame: Now, it seemed, he was seldom at home.

"It used to be that Bill would drop the children off at school on his way to the office," Betty Fulbright told an Associated Press reporter. "Now he leaves so early I have to get out with them and pound the pavement myself."[17]

After a visit to the Fulbright apartment, the reporter found Fulbright's bookshelf jammed with the latest books on international affairs, and heard Fulbright complain that he didn't have any time to read them. Also unread were several copies of *Mother Goose*. They had been sent to the young congressman after he fumbled the identification of the old woman who lived in a shoe on a radio quiz program.

For Fulbright, it was one of his few mistakes that year.

In retrospect, the fanfare that accompanied the passage of the Fulbright Resolution seemed removed from realistic aspirations, if not misguided commentary on an understanding of world events. But at the height of World War II, with the memories of past mistakes so fresh and the problems of the present so painful, the mere hope—however illusory—of an effective world organization was a beacon in the midst of universal despair.

---

* It was during this period that Fulbright first coined the phrase "arrogance of power" in a letter to the editor of the *N.Y. Herald-Tribune*.

At the center of all the hopes lay the high optimism felt about future relations with Russia. In Churchill's celebrated phrase, Russia may have been "a riddle wrapped in a mystery inside an enigma," but in the United States most people believed the two nations could work together without friction after the war. Fulbright was among them—and he was far from alone.

In '43, everything Russian, from folk songs to Shostakovich's symphonies, was popular. At Madison Square Garden, Donald Nelson, the head of the War Production Board, would share a platform with Paul Robeson and Corliss Lamont and tell a wildly cheering audience that the Russians "understand the meaning of a square deal and a firm agreement." Joseph Davies, the former Ambassador to Moscow, would say that to question Stalin's good faith was "bad Christianity, bad sportsmanship, bad sense." *Collier's* magazine, after studying the Russians at the end of that year, would conclude that the Soviet Union was neither Stalinist nor Communist but rather a "modified capitalist setup" evolving "toward something resembling our own and Great Britain's democracy." *Life* magazine, in the same period, would call the Russians "one hell of a people" who "look like Americans, dress like Americans and think like Americans." Even *Rotarian* magazine was printing highly sympathetic accounts of Russia, while such reactionaries as Captain Eddie Rickenbacker and Congressman John Rankin of Mississippi were voicing more enthusiasm for Stalin's regime. (After a trip to Russia, Rickenbacker expressed his admiration for the "iron discipline" in Russian industry which prevented workers from going on strike.) And at the annual meeting of the DAR, Mrs. Tryphosa Duncan Bates Batchellor, a leading daughter, would describe Stalin as, "a man who, when he sees a great mistake, admits it and corrects it."[18]

Indeed, as Irving Howe and Lewis Coser would conclude in a study later, for a realistic description of the Russian state "one could turn neither to the popular American press nor even to most of the extreme right-wing papers, but to such obscure and harassed weeklies of the anti-Stalinist left as *The New Leader,* the *Socialist Call,* and *Labor Action.*"[19]

Fulbright, therefore, was riding the popular currents, and being applauded for it.

"Either we cooperate with Russia and the other nations in a system to preserve peace," he said, "or we must look forward to the time when, in a chaotic world of warring nations, we may have to compete for survival with an industrialized Russia of 250 millions or a China of 450 millions. It is all very well to be proud of our great achievement and our power, but we must view our strength in its proper relation to the rest of the world and when we do, it is obvious that we are quite a small fraction of that world. I do not think we can possibly depend upon brute strength alone to insure our future. We must use our wits and intelligence if we are to survive."[20]

Fulbright was determined to play a larger role in shaping that future. On January 31, 1944, just one year after he entered Congress, he announced that he would run for the Senate against the diminutive and colorful Hattie Caraway who had held her seat since 1932 when, with the aid of the vigorous barnstorming campaigning of the Kingfish, Huey Long, from neighboring Louisiana, she succeeded her husband, who had died in office.

A young reporter who was covering Capitol Hill for the United Press and had taken to writing a diary at night jotted down his reaction to the news of a Fulbright *vs.* Caraway contest.

"It may well be," Allen Drury wrote, "in fact the press and the Hill in general are sure it will be, that the days of the quiet little grandmother with the bright red fingernails who wanders in, reads a newspaper or sits solemnly in the presiding chair, and then wanders out again, having won nothing, lost nothing, done nothing, are numbered."[21]

4

BRITISH BILLY

FULBRIGHT HAD BEEN THINKING ABOUT RUNNING for the Senate since at least the summer of 1943. One of his acquaintances then, C. F. Byrns, remembered driving along a country road outside Fayetteville with Fulbright that July and discussing the Senate possibility. But, as Byrns recalled, the "idea was new and a little startling to him."[1]

Others continued to try and persuade him. Carl E. Bailey, the former governor and family friend who had been responsible for appointing Fulbright as university president, also sounded him out. Bailey, still a major political figure in Arkansas, first suggested that Fulbright run for governor; but Fulbright was not interested. Then Bailey brought up the Senate: Hattie Caraway was old and ineffectual, he argued, but far more important, Governor Homer E. Adkins, the man who had fired Fulbright, almost certainly would try for Hattie's place—and Adkins, as the leader of the most powerful machine in the state, seemed assured of victory unless he had more vigorous opposition. That prospect of Homer Adkins in the United States Senate finally made up Fulbright's mind.

"I didn't want to be a Congressman with him a Senator," Fulbright said much later. "I had a very graduated idea what a devil he was. A personal grievance, you see. And the idea of his coming in as Senator and me continuing as Congressman didn't appeal to me at all. I'd rather just go on back home than serving with him as Senator."

In fact, Fulbright felt so strongly that he even compared Adkins with Hitler. Adkins reciprocated. While he had never felt any affection for any of the Fulbrights, he particularly resented Bill Fulbright. When Fulbright was running for Congress a year before, for instance, Adkins had told the State Welfare Commission: "I want any of you who have any influence with people in the Third District to do all you can to beat Fulbright. It would be the most humiliating thing that ever happened to me, if he should be elected."[2]

However strong his personal feelings, Fulbright, as usual, moved cautiously before announcing his candidacy. Following the advice of Carl Bailey and others, he traveled throughout the state that fall, meeting privately with leading men and women in every county. The result was encouraging: He was offered substantial support in seventy-three out of the state's seventy-five counties. Heartened, Fulbright announced his candidacy.

His official statement was as stuffy as anything he ever prepared. The response to his inquiries throughout the state had convinced him, he said, that "the people of Arkansas want positive and aggressive representation during the critical years ahead of us." In his view, "my particular qualifications and experience can be of use to Arkansas during these difficult years." He brought up the Fulbright Resolution, for which "I have received praise from the press, from citizens of the forty-eight states, from fellow congressmen, and from many foreign nations," and added: "I believe, as many do, that this action on the part of Congress aided in securing, and contributed to the success of, the first meeting of the allied leaders at Moscow, Cairo, and Tehran." Then, with rather false modesty: "Whether I deserve all the praise and honor for this I do not know and cannot be the judge, but this I do know and offer for your consideration. It has given me recognition and prestige throughout the nation and more especially in Washington, which, if properly and sanely used, can be of great benefit to a U. S. Senator representing the people of Arkansas."

Fulbright's candidacy initiated one of the most bitter and vicious campaigns in Arkansas history. For Fulbright, it was to be the toughest of his political career. When it ended, he would remain unchallenged in Arkansas for eighteen years.

He began as the underdog. Most political observers placed him third behind Adkins and Caraway, but ahead of two other candidates, David Terry, a former congressman from Little Rock, and J. Rosser Venable, a Little Rock World War I veteran. The Fulbright strategists had taken all these factors into consideration; they were counting on resentment against Adkins plus the reputation Fulbright had won to help their cause. What they did not expect was the entrance into the race of still another candidate—this one a candidate with a great deal of money.

T. H. Barton, of El Dorado, Arkansas, was the state's number one industrialist and oil operator. He had made his fortune as the head of the Lion Oil Refining Company, and, at the age of sixty-four, was devoting a large part of his time to promoting such causes as the State Live Stock

Show. Then Barton, popularly known as the "colonel," decided he, too, wanted to be a U. S. Senator.

"This doggone Barton got in there and muddied the waters and created a hell of an uncertainty," Fulbright would say. "He had a lot of money and we didn't expect him to get in. And it worried us because we couldn't estimate what influence he'd have, what he'd take away, where and how."

Scarcely two weeks after Fulbright's announcement, and months before the expected full-scale campaigning for the July 25 Democratic primary, an advertisement, paid for by one of the candidates, Ross Venable, appeared in a Little Rock newspaper. It darkly referred to the threat of Communist and Socialist regimentation. Fulbright was the central target. Venable would speak at a rally, the ad announced, and address "very pointed questions" to "Lord Plushbottom" whose peace resolution held "dangerous implications."[3]

Soon anonymous circulars were being mailed throughout Arkansas attacking Fulbright's record and character. He was called a draft dodger, a "nigger lover," a New Dealer. Invariably, he was referred to as "British Billy."

Fulbright was back at his desk in Washington, planning for his campaign, when he received a boost in his national stature. A conference of the Allied ministers of education from seventeen nations was being planned for London that spring. The conference was regarded as one of the major steppingstones toward creating an effective United Nations; the hope, widely expressed, was that out of the meetings would come a U.N. organization to work for the reconstruction of the war-wrecked educational institutions of the world. On Cordell Hull's recommendation, Fulbright was named chairman of the American delegation.

In London, as the conference opened on April 5, the American delegates found only one overriding concern—the war. Just two months before D-Day, England had been transformed into a burgeoning base of men and munitions, blitzed buildings, airfields, camouflaged trucks, jeeps, and ammunition dumps. Everywhere, everyone talked about the coming invasion.

For Fulbright, the return to England nineteen years after his arrival as a young Rhodes Scholar was especially memorable. He visited old friends, and made new ones, among them the American correspondent Edward R. Murrow; he spent a day and a night at an American Flying Fortress base watching the airmen leave and return from their raids on Germans; he experienced ten German air raids during the month, the closest only three blocks from his hotel. These, though, were all incidental to the business at hand.

As the conference began, Fulbright received yet another honor. On the nomination of the Belgian delegation, he was chosen unanimously as conference chairman. Together, the delegates drafted a tentative plan for a United Nations agency that would accomplish educational and cultural reconstruction. They also discussed what emergency help would be required by the devastated Allied countries before their educational systems could begin again.

The U.S., as expressed in an official statement from Washington, felt the progress made at the London conference had been "another important step in the direction of laying the foundations for international cooperation in the future."[4] By the fall, however, the Dumbarton Oaks conference in Washington had led American officials to put off any such educational organization pending the actual creation of the United Nations. The London conference, however, galvanized Fulbright's thinking in the direction of educational and cultural exchanges. In a way, London in 1944 provided the precedent to the Fulbright fellowship program.

Fulbright's trip ended with two notable experiences—a private luncheon with Winston Churchill and a radio broadcast to the English people over the British Broadcasting Company.

Churchill and his wife, Clemmie, received Fulbright at 10 Downing Street in the midst of one of the Prime Minister's busiest periods. Schedule notwithstanding, Churchill was expansive and lived up to his reputation. Fulbright was struck, among other things, by Churchill's capacity for wine —and later brandy—during and after the luncheon. As always, Churchill dominated the conversation. He asked particular questions about American politics and the presidential elections, and said he understood Fulbright was going to run against Hattie Caraway; then, glancing down the table toward a serving bowl decorated with a large hen on the top, he said: "So, you're trying to unseat the sitting hen." Suddenly, he switched to the war and discussed preparations for the invasion. Recently, he had been intrigued by a great deal of unexplained German activity across the Channel, Churchill said. A number of mysterious explosions also had been heard. "Jerry's got something going on and we don't know what it is." Within weeks, the mystery was solved: the activity had signalled the installation of the buzz bombs; soon London was under siege from rockets.

Fulbright said farewell to wartime England in his BBC broadcast.

"I'll start by telling you about myself," he said. ". . . I live in an old log house, on a small farm with a big spring in the park, and am sometimes called a Hillbilly. [My] constituency is not industrial and the people are ninety-eight percent Anglo-Saxon stock. They are not wealthy, but they are self-reliant, industrious farmers and small businessmen and had created for themselves a decent way of life before this war came along."[5]

Once again, Fulbright turned to his advocacy of an effective United Nations. "We must create something new in this world. No matter how much we have loved the old world before this war, the very fact that we had to fight this war is sufficient proof that something was basically wrong with that world. Call it what you will—fascism, democratic decadence, or general ignorance—the fact remains that something was wrong with that old world or we would not now be killing our finest boys and destroying those natural resources which should be devoted to the welfare of mankind. . . . Some new machinery with adequate powers must be created now, if our fine phrases and noble sentiments are to have substance and meaning for our children."

He closed:

"I am returning home to campaign for a seat in our Senate, and thereby an opportunity to contribute further, perhaps, to our mutual understanding."[6]

While his enemies were quick to capitalize on this new evidence of "British Billy's" anglophilism, Fulbright's London credentials actually further enhanced his prestige in Arkansas. He made certain the citizens were well aware of his international role. In one pamphlet, a letter from Cordell Hull was reprinted. "I continue to receive most favorable reports about the work of yourself and your associates in London," Hull wrote. "I consider the country exceedingly fortunate to have had a man of your statesmanlike qualities to head this delegation."[7]

In the words of his campaign propaganda, Fulbright had "put Arkansas in a favorable light before the Nation." He was a "businessman, farmer, congressman, statesman," and his election would help both "the Man and the State With a Future."

He began his formal campaign in a Saturday night statewide broadcast on July 2. "The real issue in this summer's campaign," he said, "is the ability of the candidate to do something positive and constructive about a sure and lasting peace and to improve the welfare of Arkansas residents."[8]

Yet he found it impossible to maintain the campaign on a high level.

Already, "Colonel" Barton had been stumping the state aided by two groups of fiddlers and banjo players he had hired to drum up enthusiasm for his candidacy. One group—"Uncle Mac" Mackrell accompanied by the Stamps Baxter Melody Boys—was concentrating on the more remote sections, while the Grand Ole Opry troupe of Nashville hit the cities and towns. Fulbright's campaign staff had made light of the Grand Ole Opry, with its performers Minnie Pearl, Jam-Up and Honey, and Uncle Dave Macon, but Barton had turned it into a campaign issue. His groups, he said, "were maintaining morale during these trying times."[9] After his entertainers had warmed up the crowds, Barton, who traveled with his personal barber and masseur, dug needles sharply into Fulbright.

"I submit to you that every sane man and woman in Arkansas favors world peace," he said, "and that a man who has carried the rifle for his country is better qualified to aid in writing the terms of peace than a young man who has never worn his country's uniform."[10]

Barton was troublesome, but Homer Adkins' campaign tactics were more serious and damaging. In a typical broadside aimed at Fulbright, Adkins would begin by raising questions about Fulbright's draft status.

> "Isn't it true that you announced for Congress *AFTER* Pearl Harbor—when you were only 36 years of age, and when draft age was 21 to 45?
>
> "Don't you know that at the time there were thousands of fathers of your age, with two or more children, in the Army, volunteering and being drafted—practically all of them without your wealth?
>
> "Don't you know that there are thousands of fathers of your age NOW in the Army—and NOT ON DESK JOBS BUT ACTUALLY IN COMBAT IN NORMANDY, ITALY AND THE PACIFIC THEATER?"
>
> ". . . On the American Legion poll of attitudes in Congress you are recorded as non-committal and marked with a negative sign."[11]

Disagreeable though it was, Fulbright was forced to respond to charges.* "Little did I realize what my candidacy would let me in for by way of innuendo and whispering campaigns," he said in one speech that July. "Those who favor other candidates, perhaps those instrumental in the effort to elect one of my opponents, have seen fit to charge me with various affiliations, beliefs, and a course of public action calculated to alienate support from different groups of our citizenry."[12]

He summarized the statements against him.

"I am charged with being pro-labor, with voting in Congress as labor dictated, with being endorsed by the C.I.O. You are told that I am a 'New Dealer,' as that term is used in its opprobrious sense. You hear it said that I am pro-British. I am jokingly and sometimes scathingly referred to as 'British Billy.'"[13]

He attempted to show that he was not tainted with such dangerous leanings.

While he firmly believed in the working man's right to organization and collective bargaining, "I do not believe in the radical or racketeering efforts of certain elements within the ranks of organized labor to shackle business, or to deprive industry of the essential function of management."

While he would not do away with much of the recent "beneficial legislation," he was not a New Dealer. "I do not acquiesce in the continuation of unnecessary bureaus, bureaucratic control, and regulation by bureaucratic fiat."

---

* Fulbright, then thirty-six and with two children, did not enlist, and was not drafted in early 1942. By the end of the year, he was in Congress and by law ineligible for the draft.

Further, and even more popular before the electorate, he strongly disapproved of such "noble experiments" as the Fair Employment Practices Committee. As for Negroes and Negro rights, he was outspoken.

"I am not for Negro participation in our primary elections, and I do not approve of social equality."[14]

The U. S. Constitution was a "sacred document, not to be scrapped or changed or perverted to meet every so-called emergency that starry-eyed idealists proclaim." After enunciating that string of clichés, he said:

"I am, after all, like you, a citizen of Arkansas and the South, devoted to Southern traditions and ideals . . . unalterably opposed to the centralization of power in Washington and federal control and regulation of the purely local functions of state government."

In short, with the exception of his international position, he was no different from any other honorable legislator from the South. Fulbright would maintain essentially that public position in years to come.

He objected strenuously, as he said at another point in the campaign, to being labeled under any inclusive names—whether liberal, conservative, or progressive. In business, he said, he was probably a conservative; in international affairs, a progressive. "I know I'm not reactionary. I don't believe in going back to the nineteenth century."[15]

In such a campaign as he was forced to make, the difficulty lay in attempting to discuss anything beyond banalities and the safe chestnuts of local politics. Even these statements, in the Senate campaign, were liable to misinterpretation, for the depth of the bitterness engendered in that 1944 campaign was beyond the memory of most in Arkansas.

"I have been in politics up to my neck since I was twenty years old," a lawyer wrote Fulbright that summer, "and I have seen some mean campaigns, but the Adkins campaign is the worst that I ever saw. Some state officials and state employees drove over the country and flooded it with literature and proclaiming that you: voted for a 'nigger,' would not help pass the Soldier Bill [G.I. Bill of Rights], had the chicken raisers indicted, were endorsed by the C.I.O., by fraud escaped the draft, and everything else they could think of."

A railroad telegrapher wrote with another warning: "They are calling you a 'slacker' and a labor-hater; say that you are in league with every thug and gambler in Hot Springs—anything to slur you, from your alleged repudiation by the American Legion, to being a nigger-lover!"[16]

Since Fulbright had attracted such wide national attention, the campaign was closely followed. The issue, as the *St. Louis Post-Dispatch* saw it, was to see "what kind of representation in the Senate that the people of Arkansas want." Marshall Field's *Chicago Sun* said "Men like him [Fulbright] are needed in the Senate."

Although Fulbright's Senate campaign was, of necessity, immensely larger and more costly than his congressional race, he relied on the same techniques. Once more, a *Victory News* was prepared under Roberta Fulbright's watchful eye in Fayetteville and mailed throughout the state. As was befitting a more important Senate race, however, the *Victory News* was expanded, and added to it was another publication, *Fulbright Facts*, put out by the University Alumni Club. Fulbright Clubs had been organized in every county, and volunteer groups were at work in all sections. But, in the end, the campaign came down, as always, to the personalities.

Once again, Bill and Betty Fulbright set out in a car and crisscrossed Arkansas. And again Betty Fulbright proved an effective vote-getter—as effective in eastern Delta country as she had been in the Ozarks.

"From what I hear when it comes to single-handed mitt-pumping and tub-thumping, in behalf of her old man, Bill Fulbright's ever-loving wife shoots a little better stick than a green hand," wrote a columnist for the *Arkansas Gazette*. "For her to be in politics is just as natural as college boys chasing chorus girls. Regardless of where they are, when Bill stops his hack she jumps out and starts button-holing people with an impassioned plea to the effect that the voters of Arkansas will be unfair to unborn generations if they fail to send her husband to the United States Senate."[17]

He related an incident at Paris, Arkansas.

"Colonel Barton, aided and abetted by his Grand Ole Opry, was in town when Bill and his wife drove through. Bill stopped to contact friends, and his wife, unwilling to let any grass grow under her feet, got out and started telling people that her husband had already forgotten more than all his opponents put together ever knew. Shortly afterwards, a Paris citizen entered a business house and announced: 'You know that Minnie Pearl is the best politician of the bunch. I always have been for Bill Fulbright but, after listening to her for just a few minutes she changed me over and now I'm going to vote for Colonel Barton.' Told that Minnie Pearl wasn't in town yet, this guy pointed out the window to a lady on the street, surrounded by men, and said: 'Oh yes she is. There she is, right now.' Apparently, he had gotten his wires crossed on her 'Go see the Grand Ole Opry and Minnie Pearl and then vote for Bill Fulbright,' because the lady in question was none other than Mrs. Fulbright."

Fulbright closed his campaign with a night rally in Pine Bluff, and awaited the returns. When the ballots were counted the next day, he led Adkins by 16,500. Barton had come in third, and Hattie Caraway was a far distant fourth. The margin was not enough for a clear victory, though, and a run-off between Fulbright and Adkins was set for the following week. Fulbright's lead had been sufficient, however, to set off widespread editorial comment.

To the *Atlanta Journal* it meant that "democracy is gaining. The people, especially we Southern people, are voting more intelligently." To the Scripps-Howard papers, a Fulbright victory at the same time that the notorious Senator "Cotton Ed" Smith of South Carolina was going down to defeat "should raise the level of the U. S. Senate." To Arthur Krock, it meant that a "higher type of legislator than the South has been sending to Washington in recent years" will be a member of the Senate.

In the last days of the run-off, Fulbright confined himself to only two speeches, both addressed to the larger issues of peace and the future. His final speech, the night before the election, over a statewide radio broadcast was the high point of his campaign. He chose his familiar theme: Politics should be on a high plane, attractive and esteemed enough to motivate able young men to enter public life; but they should not have to be confronted with the type of accusations he had faced in his campaign.

Fulbright defeated Adkins by nearly 32,000 votes.

In Fayetteville, Roberta Fulbright could not resist the pleasure of having the final word. Parodying Adkins' ungrammatical style, she wrote:

"Homer Adkins has came and went."

BOOK THREE

Senator

1

"JUST A BOY FROM THE OZARKS"

BY 1945, THE UNITED STATES SENATE had lost its pre-Civil War position of influence in America. It had become a comfortable end of the line for successful local politicians. For the wise politician aspiring to the presidency, an important governorship was the springboard. Since the turn of the century only one man had reached the White House from the Senate —and Warren G. Harding's experience had led only to disgrace and personal tragedy.

The Senate was left with its traditions. Even its employees were a distinct link with the past. John Crockett, the chief clerk who called the Senate roll in a booming voice, had been there thirty-seven years; Paul Johnson, the Senate headwaiter who was proud of his knowledge of which senator liked what to eat, had acquired that knowledge during forty-five years of faithful service; Carl Loeffler, the secretary to the Senate Republicans, had been working for Congress since 1895. From the red-and-gold hallway lavishly decorated with frescoes to the Lobby where the last-minute deals were discussed and even to the spittoons, small wastebaskets, and school-boy desks on the Floor (John Randolph's foxhound had slept under one, a guide would tell the curious), a sense of age hung heavily over the Senate.

Fulbright chafed under the system. His first frustration came over his committee appointments.

"Well, I suppose that you noticed that I did not make the Foreign Relations Committee [he wrote to an old friend in Arkansas]. Needless to say,

I was disappointed, but with eighteen other applicants, all of which [sic] had some seniority, I knew from the start that there was little chance. You know how Senators are about seniority."

He was assigned, instead, to the Banking and Currency, Education, Labor and Immigration, and Public Building and Grounds committees. More than ever, he was determined to beat the system.

In his diary entry for January 8, 1945, Allen Drury shrewdly sized up the new senator from Arkansas.

"J. William Fulbright of Arkansas, 39, is a trim little fellow with an amiable face, little eyes and a little mouth that crinkles up when he smiles, and a great deal of charm of which he is not, perhaps understandably, entirely unaware. A former Rhodes Scholar and President of the University of Arkansas, he has every claim to the brains he exhibits, and the impression he makes on the press is uniformly good. He talked with us for a long time this morning about foreign policy and politics and the ticklish technique of a new man's baptism in the Senate. As a veteran of the House, however, he showed the same disregard as [freshman Senator Warren] Magnuson for the tradition that new senators should be seen and not heard: he was willing to be quoted."[1]

Fulbright, as Drury noted, criticized Roosevelt for saying U.S. foreign policy was being carried out in a "vigorous and forthright" manner. "It doesn't seem that way to me," Fulbright said. "It was sixteen months ago that the House passed the (Fulbright) peace resolution, and nothing has been done." He went on to say, in words other young senators echo, that "we just aren't doing anything" and complained of "delay and delay and delay."[2]

Fulbright's first effort was, once more, a success. Largely on his initiative, the sixteen freshmen senators joined in signing a bipartisan letter to FDR urging vigorous action in creating a United Nations organization. The letter, concisely written in seven paragraphs, also called for quickly concluding treaties for the demilitarization of Germany and Japan.

New Jersey's H. Alexander Smith, a Republican, had worked closely with Fulbright on the letter. They drafted it, called a meeting of all the new senators in Smith's office, and lobbied for agreement.

"I think you boys did a fine job on that," the Majority Leader, Alben W. Barkley of Kentucky, wrote Fulbright, "and I was delighted to see that you were able to secure the statement with reference to the Dumbarton Oaks Program. You, of course, know that this letter has received almost universal approval by the press and others throughout the country."[3]

Encouraged, Fulbright redoubled his efforts. His former law professor from Arkansas, Claude Pepper, then a leading liberal intellectual in the Senate, had drafted a resolution to revoke the Senate's time-honored filibuster privilege during debate on treaties. Even though most Southerners opposed any effort that might lead to an abandonment of the cloture rule, Fulbright supported Pepper's resolution. Then he introduced a resolution of his own calling for ratification of treaties by both houses, a move that would have stripped the Senate of one of its most cherished powers. The resolution failed. It was an impolitic thing to do; Fulbright was demonstrating his independence on international affairs.

Domestic questions were another matter, however, as many of Fulbright's liberal admirers soon discovered when a key vote over a presidential appointment came before the Senate.

Roosevelt had nominated Aubrey Williams, a Southern liberal and protégé of Harry Hopkins, for a ten-year term as head of the Rural Electrification Administration. Williams, who formerly had directed the National Youth Administration, had been forthright in advocating governmental measures to eliminate—by law—racially discriminatory hiring practices. He also had been a good administrator; but his racial views antagonized the Southern conservatives in the Senate. They viewed Williams, a native of Alabama, as an especially opprobrious traitor. Theodore G. Bilbo, the racist from Mississippi, led the fight in the Senate and stated his opinions with his usual frankness. "We do not want this Negro-lover on the job," he said.[4]

Despite the efforts of the Roosevelt administration, the Senate rejected Williams as nineteen Southern Democratic senators voted against him. Fulbright was among them. It was the first time since 1939 that a presidential nominee, other than postmaster, had been rejected by the Senate.

Fulbright's vote, in particular, was regarded with dismay by the liberals, for they had not expected him to act that way. For them, it was to be the first of many disappointments with the junior senator from Arkansas.

From his own vantage point, Fulbright viewed his role more circumspectly. A senator, he would say in a reflective moment, had two courses of action open to him: he could either follow closely what he believed to be the majority opinion of his constituents, or he could make his decisions without regard for what they wanted. In other words, he could be passive, or he could attempt to lead. Throughout his career, he would combine both techniques. On international questions, he would often stand alone and strike unceasingly bold positions; on domestic votes, he would remain largely one of the pack, seldom a boat rocker, nearly always maintaining a politically safe position.

Often, his shifts from cautious to courageous were sudden—and bewildering.

Thus, only four days after his vote against Williams, Fulbright found himself solidly back in favor with the liberal establishment. The occasion was his maiden speech in the Senate on March 28, 1945, and the setting said much about the interest Fulbright's career had aroused.

During the speeches in the Senate, a legislator often addressed his words only to the galleries and to the winds: the chamber, frequently, was occupied by no more than four or five senators. When the word spread that Fulbright was going to deliver his first speech, though, many of the oldtimers gathered to hear him.

As Fulbright adjusted his horn-rimmed glasses to begin reading his lengthy document, more than thirty senators were grouped around him. It was an unusually large audience for any single Senate speech. Vandenberg of Michigan, White of Maine, Saltonstall of Massachusetts, and Ball of Minnesota, Republicans all, crossed the center aisle to listen on the Democratic side of the chamber. Along with them were Taft of Ohio, Austin of Vermont, and the Democratic leaders, Barkley of Kentucky and Hall of Alabama.

Fulbright's opening sentence was arresting, especially in view of his performance in years to come:

"Mr. President, myths are one of the greatest obstacles in the formulation of national policy."

A number of myths were hampering American policies, among them the idea that the Senate was solely responsible for America's failure to join the League of Nations. But the Senate was not free of criticism. Its duty, according to Fulbright, was to advise and consent to U.S. foreign policy. Then, in a passage heavy with irony over his future role: "If it cannot consent to the measures presented by the Executive it seems to me imperative that it offer our Nation and the world an alternative." If the Senate felt inadequate to that task, it should let the House be given a share in the responsibility. At the very least, it was "unbecoming of the Senate to act the part of the dog in the manger."

America also faced these prejudices: many people were still anti-British; even more were anti-Russian. Fear of Communism was particularly harmful to American interests, he felt.

"When one recalls the birth of our own nation—that in 1776 our forefathers were regarded as being quite as radical, by the rest of the world, as Lenin was in 1920—is it not strange that we should be so harsh toward Russia? Since we have been the most successful revolutionary people in history, why are we so critical of others who follow our example? Surely it cannot be because we approved of Czarist Russia with its illiteracy and abject, grinding poverty. As I read history, the Russian experiment in socialism is scarcely more radical, under modern conditions, than the Declaration of Independence was in the days of George III."

While Fulbright firmly believed in capitalism, he said, "we should remember that capitalism is not divine and inviolable. It was not handed down to us by the Almighty; and to question it, or test it, is neither sacrilegious nor treasonable."

As far as the future, "Russia is a great and powerful nation. She can become either a good friend and customer, exerting her influence for peace and stability, or she can become an enemy using every opportunity to thwart us."

As one commentator said: "If you read the *Congressional Record,* through long arid columns of type, that speech will strike you as a new, fresh and dynamic voice." Fulbright's career already was "one of the most remarkable stories of U.S. politics, and where it may lead one can only speculate."[5]

To the new applause that greeted him, Fulbright remained disarming, even diffident. While talking with a reporter in the Senate lobby afterward, Fulbright said, in his soft drawl:

"I am just a boy from the Ozarks, where the hillbillies come from."[6]

Fulbright was well aware he had become a celebrity. He remained in constant demand as a speaker at prestigious forums in New York or Chicago or Boston; and everywhere he went, he called new attention to himself. He was praised, virtually without reservation, and heard himself referred to as a man of unlimited political future. It was during that period when Dorothy Thompson, the columnist, then at the peak of her fame and influence, walked over to Fulbright, touched his shoulder, and said, loudly, in the presence of others: "This man is destined for greatness."

Although he seldom showed it, Fulbright felt the pressure. In the first week in April, while preparing to fill an engagement at the University of North Carolina at Chapel Hill, he wrote out some notes for his speech which summed up his mood at the time. He spoke of living for three years "in the high pressure competitive atmosphere of Washington," of forgetting "all about the real values of life," of struggling for "advantage over one's neighbor or competitor in business or politics"; then, he reflected on the life of a senator.

"The circumstances . . . surrounding a senator are not at all conducive to the making of peace. As I receive the veritable flood of complaints and requests for special favors day after day, I find that I tend to become cynical, to think all people are concerned only with their special advantages. One has to get back to the peace and quiet of a place like Chapel Hill to realize that after all, the percentage of people who are essentially grasping or seekers of special privilege is not so great."

Then, a bit wistfully: "It does one good to participate again in the life of a great institution like this one. It helps restore a sense of perspective."[7]

On April 12, 1945, a soft spring day in Washington, Fulbright drafted a reply to Eleanor Roosevelt, at the White House, about the possibility of

U.S. participation in an international educational and cultural organization; then he went back to his Senate duties.

It was a dull day on the Hill: the Senate was considering a treaty with Mexico over water rights in the Colorado and Rio Grande rivers, an important, but not stirring, issue. Harry Truman of Missouri was presiding, while at the same time unobtrusively writing a letter to "Mamma and Mary" and describing for them how "a windy senator . . . is making a speech with which he is in no way familiar."[8] When the session ended, Truman received the word to go immediately to the White House, and enter through the front gate. Roosevelt had died.

In later years, Fulbright would recall little of those swift and startling events—of his writing Truman and receiving an immediate reply saying "you don't know how very much I appreciated your note"; of seeing Truman briefly with other senators when the new President came to the Capitol the next day: of the long lines in front of the White House; of the look of shock on the faces of so many senators.

On that April 12, no one seemed more stricken than the young Texan, Lyndon B. Johnson. A *New York Times* reporter found Congressman Johnson, suddenly looking very tired, standing in a gloomy Capitol corridor with tears in his eyes. "He was always like a Daddy to me, always," Johnson was saying. "He always talked to me just that way. He was the one person I ever knew—anywhere—who was never afraid. Whatever you talked to him about, whatever you asked him for, like projects for your district, there was just one way to figure it with him! I know some of them called it demagoguery; they can call it anything they want, but you can be damn sure that the only test he had was this: Was it good for the folks? . . . I don't know that I'd ever have come to Congress if it hadn't been for him. But I do know I got my first great desire for public office because of him—and so did thousands of other men all over this country."[9]

Johnson summed up his grief with the words: "God. God, how he could take it for us all."

Fulbright felt no such personal ties toward Roosevelt. "I never did have but one pleasant and rather extended meeting with him," he would recall. "One time is all." That had come during a reception at the White House while Fulbright was still a member of the House. He had been, as he said, "of course greatly impressed by the old boy's personality," but unlike such as Lyndon Johnson he was without any deep attachments to Roosevelt. As Fulbright expressed his feelings to an Arkansas constituent, Roosevelt's death was a loss "particularly to those of us who have been devoting so much of our time to an organization for maintaining the peace."

Fulbright's concern was over the future of a United Nations, and Truman's succession to the presidency had created new doubts about it, especially since he took office less than two weeks before the delegates of fifty nations gathered in San Francisco to draft a U.N. charter.

The creation of the U.N. marked the culmination of Fulbright's principal labors for the past few years; as the final hour of decision neared, he worked harder to create an even more favorable climate for its acceptance. While the San Francisco conference was proceeding, he suggested that athletics should play an important role in future international relations under an educational and cultural program being discussed by the delegates. "It would be one of the best ways to break down existing suspicion and misunderstanding and foster peace."[10] At the same time, he introduced a bill to repeal the act barring credits to nations who had defaulted on their debts to the U.S. The questions growing out of the World War I war debts, Fulbright and many others were convinced, had poisoned the climate of international relations. "I never have thought we should have tried to collect the old war debts," he said. His bill failed.

In those days of 1945 he expressed the conviction that the moment had arrived to change the old methods.

"All of us . . . have for years felt that something is wrong with our society," he said to graduates of Gettysburg (Pennsylvania) College. "In the midst of huge surpluses of all kinds of goods, we have depressions, unemployment, closed banks, soup kitchens, and now a second war that threatens the existence of our way of life. . . . I should like to suggest that the source of our troubles may be found in our failure to recognize what I have called the essential interdependence of all men and of all nations."[11]

Fulbright was finding the Senate a lonely place. As the war against Germany ended, flocks of his colleagues set off on quick European inspection trips. The junkets were so popular that, it was said, only half jokingly, one might be able to find a quorum of senators in Rome or London and Berlin—but not in the chamber of the U. S. Capitol itself. Marquis Childs singled out one incident as typical of the time.

"Last week [he wrote in his column on June 7] Senator La Follette of Wisconsin delivered a long, carefully prepared and carefully reasoned speech on the new league and the issues of power versus democracy. Whether you agreed with his thesis or not, it was a speech that deserved respectful consideration. Yet only three or four senators were on the floor as he spoke. One of them, fortunately, was the conscientious new senator from Arkansas, J. William Fulbright. He interrogated La Follette from time to time. Something like a debate, or at any rate a discussion, took place."

In the midst of such discussions, Fulbright once more found himself at the center of a new flurry of publicity.

For weeks after Truman became President there had been continuing speculation in Washington about Secretary of State Edward R. Stettinius, Jr. Truman, it was widely reported, wanted to replace him. By the end of May, the private speculation had become public. Drew Pearson thought he knew who would get the job. In a radio broadcast, he said flatly that Fulbright was the likely choice.[12]

Fulbright immediately received a flood of letters.

"I only hope that I can be of real benefit to the State and Country," he replied to a former political foe, who now offered his services. "I confess that I do not know that I should like to give up my seat in the Senate for any appointment. I honestly feel that the Senate can be of great importance in the next several years. In any case, we will have to wait developments."

Later, to a friend:

"I am glad to have your comments about the Secretary of State. I hoped that it wouldn't do any harm in the sense that anyone would think I was trying to give up my present office, which I am not. As a matter of fact, I have done nothing and do not intend to do anything toward it and would hesitate like anything if it were offered. Besides, I have a distinct feeling that I had better settle down in one place for a while."[13]

The speculation ended soon after it began when Truman named James F. Byrnes to succeed Stettinius two days after representatives of the fifty nations signed the U.N. Charter in San Francisco. Immediately, the attention switched back to the Senate and the U.N.

Harry Truman returned to the Senate on July 2, 1945, carrying a leatherbound document and accepting the applause from the members and the galleries. (Hattie Caraway, dressed, as always, in black, was seen standing among her former colleagues as the President walked into the chamber.) It was a sentimental scene: the new President, saying in the flat Missouri accent, "You know, I am sure, how much that means to one who served so recently in this Chamber with you"; the senators responding in kind.

Truman had come to urge them to adopt the U.N. Charter, he said, as he briefly sketched the history of its creation. In his recitation, he mentioned the passage of the Fulbright Resolution, causing, as an Arkansas writer noted, Fulbright to stir "with embarrassed pleasure in his seat,"[14] and later the Connally Resolution. "You and the House of Representatives thus had a hand in shaping the Dumbarton Oaks proposals, upon which the Charter has been based," the President said.

Three weeks later the Senate began its debate. Fulbright, never a flowery speaker, always given to qualifications, on that occasion made an unequivocal assertion:

"Mr. President, I rise in support of the Charter. I have no hesitation in saying that I think it is the most important document that has come before this body, or any other body, during the last twenty-five years. In fact, I think it ranks in importance alongside the Declaration of Independence, the Constitution of the United States, the Emancipation Proclamation, and the League of Nations, as one of the most important documents in the history of our country."

By 89–2, the Senate approved the U.N. Charter on July 28. It took effect on October 24, 1945. No one held more hopes for its prospects in achieving world peace than J. William Fulbright. The ratification was a crowning moment for him. Soon after, it became page-one news that Fulbright had been the unanimous choice of a special faculty committee at Columbia University appointed to recommend a successor to President Nicholas Murray Butler.* He had rejected the idea partly because of Arkansas ties, but also, as his office statement pointed out, because he "was already off to a good start in the powerful United States Senate."

Many believed then, however, that eventually Fulbright was destined to rise higher than the Senate. As Bascom Timmons wrote: "Fulbright, now just turning forty, is one of the coming leaders of America and soon to be presidential timber."[15]

---

* Eventually, General Dwight D. Eisenhower succeeded Butler, leading to the intriguing question of what would have happened had Fulbright accepted the Columbia presidency.

2

"A PROFOUND UNEASINESS HAS SPREAD"

WHAT HARRY TRUMAN CALLED "the first 100 days of reconversion" brought as swift and complex changes as America had experienced.[1]

By the end of November, 1945, some three and a half million men had been demobilized from the armed forces and the discharge rate was being stepped up to 50,000 a day, ninety-three percent of all American plants had been converted from war to peacetime use, 27 billion dollars' worth of war contracts had been canceled, all manpower and hundreds of price controls had been lifted, all items except sugar and tires had been removed from rationing. The government was warning of increasing inflationary pressures and pledging to "hold the line," even though it clearly could not. Strikes were threatening to cripple the country and further add to the general state of unrest. Everywhere, labor and management were locked in bitter disputes: Since August alone there had been 1,500 strikes involving 1,500,000 workers.[2]

Although Truman publicly was optimistic about the new postwar scene, he still was forced to warn that "the difficulties we are facing are just as great as they have ever been in the history of the country."[3]

Behind all of the obvious problems—the returning veteran, the rise in prices, the shortages in food and furniture, nylons and suits, electric irons and cars—lay a vague feeling of frustration, nervousness, and tension. Peace had not brought with it the promised land. Fear had not subsided with the end of the shooting. Indeed, in many ways it was more pervasive and universal, for the birth of the atomic age—and the bomb—only three months before had made the weapons of World War II seem as obsolete as the bow and arrow. Already, people were talking about burrowing into underground shelters and migrating to distant hills.

> *"Bongo! Bongo! Bongo!*
> *I don't want to leave the Congo."*

ran the refrain to a popular song that expressed, lightly, the serious mood and desire to escape of so many Americans.

Fulbright felt the frustrations more keenly than most, for in summer he believed he had reason to be highly optimistic. But only weeks later, knowledge of Belsen, Buchenwald, nuclear weapons, advances in rocketry, and the beginning of open quarrels between East and West had made him pessimistic.

"Within a few days of the adoption of the [United Nations] Charter, the atomic bomb not only blasted the Japanese into submission, but it also blasted our confidence in the Charter," he told the influential Foreign Policy Association in New York. "A profound uneasiness has spread over the world, the uneasiness of fear of the unknown."[4]

Gloomily, he spoke of primitive men living in caves, of infinite forces "which threaten to snuff out our lives like one does a candle between the fingers," and went on to say: "We have lost our bearings and we are unsure of our future."

Fulbright's own bearings would never be as secure again. From that time on he became increasingly skeptical; within weeks he began the process of public criticism which, step by step, alienated him from his own party leaders, his Senate colleagues, and eventually the President. In so doing, he virtually lost all chance of moving beyond his position in the Senate, at least for the then foreseeable future.

His speech before the Foreign Policy Association in October began the pattern.

At the heart of his new anxiety was a belief that the U.N. was floundering even before it had been given a chance to prove itself worthy of the dreams it had inspired. Instead of uniting, Fulbright said, "we have already fallen to quarreling with Russia like two dogs chewing on a bone." And the U.N. organization itself, faced with the threat of a veto from any one of five nations, "provides us with only a skeleton machinery without life and vitality." The veto, he said, was "a hopeless principle for any governmental organization."

If these were not disquieting enough, the question of the spread of atomic weapons was graver. Despite a popular opinion then, it was clear to Fulbright and the scientific community that America could not retain exclusive control over the atomic bomb. "Any one of several industrial nations probably can produce bombs in from three to five years," he pointed out, raising the vital questions of disarmament and the effective international control of nuclear weapons. For Fulbright, "the only solution" to these problems would be for all nations to "delegate certain definite powers over armaments" to the U.N.—a distinctly unpopular opinion.

"I for one," he said, "would rather adopt a new idea in politics than risk vaporization by an atomic bomb, or, as some have suggested, spend the remainder of my days in the subterranean recesses of the earth."

One month later he made what was, in effect, a break with the Truman administration's foreign policies and, therefore, with his own party leaders. He did it in dramatic fashion over a nationwide radio address carried by the National Broadcasting Company. He was addressing the country, he began, for the sake of his children, who were facing "fantastic horrors." He did not want them, he explained, "to be blown to bits by an atomic bomb, nor do I want them tortured and exterminated in slave-labor camps by a new dictator."

"I have come to the conclusion that our government has lost its bearings, that it is drifting about in a fog of indecision," he said. As for Truman, he "professes a faith in the United Nations, but his actions and statements are not designed to give life or vitality to that organization." And on foreign policies in general: "Our actions or policies in foreign affairs seem to be improvised on the spur of the moment. We play by ear without the slightest regard for the harmony of the composition. Such a method of dealing with serious questions of government can lead only to disaster. . . . At this critical time in history, when we need, as never before, decision and action in our foreign affairs, we are dangerously irresolute and beset by contradictions."[5]

With customary crispness, Truman replied at his next press conference.

"Mr. President," a reporter asked, "it seems to me Senator Fulbright said the awfullest thing about the administration when he said that your foreign policy was just 'playing by ear'. . . . As a musician—"

Truman cut in: "I think it's playing by music."[6]

Fulbright's pessimistic feeling grew out of more than concern over international developments; he also was reacting to his brief experience in the United States Senate.

Besieged as he was by a multitude of requests for minor services—requests which he felt came "close to destroying the effectiveness of a great many capable representatives"[7]—Fulbright found himself with little time to reflect or study legislation and major issues. His few years in the House and Senate had convinced him that the basic legislative system was becoming moribund. Influence and power were steadily shifting from Congress to the White House and the executive bureaus. Already, the great majority of bills enacted by Congress were drafted in the bureaus. More and more, the senator's role was restricted to merely reviewing—and perhaps criticizing or amending—the bills presented for his consideration by the departments. And even for that task, the senator had too little time to do his job effectively. The volume of legislation alone was overwhelming.

The bureaucrats, protected by civil service, accustomed to seeing presidents, senators, congressmen, and cabinet and agency officials come and go, operated under their own power: They were the constant factor in the kaleidoscope of government in Washington. In truth, they were the government, and often they were noticeably unresponsive to congressional suggestions.

"It is quite irritating to be regarded as a pork-barrel politician who would sacrifice the public good for a favor for a friend," he said, referring to his personal dealings with heads of bureaus in Washington.[8]

Before long he was criticizing presidential appointments. Truman had named Frank C. Walker of Pennsylvania, a former chairman of the National Democratic Committee, as an alternate delegate to the first U.N. session. When his name came before the Senate, Fulbright sarcastically asked whether anyone knew of anything Walker had done to qualify him for an important position dealing with foreign affairs. He also wanted to know if many senators had been present when the Foreign Relations Committee unanimously approved Walker's appointment. Few had been present; no one was able to bring forth any evidence of Walker's expertise in foreign affairs.

"As senators know," Fulbright said, "I have been very much interested in the United Nations Organization. It seems to me that the best way to nullify its effect and to kill it in the long run is to treat it as an opportunity to pass around a few favors or honors to persons who have been fine citizens, and who are still fine citizens, but who do not intend to make this kind of work their career, and do not seriously intend to give it any attention. . . . If that is the attitude with which this organization is to begin, I can see that obviously it is doomed to failure."

His objections had no effect; Fulbright lost the first of what were to be many battles over such presidential appointments. His first fight did not improve his relationships with his colleagues or his party, and by the first of the year they deteriorated altogether, for by then Fulbright had begun to attack the Senate itself—from its sacrosanct seniority rule to the leaders who dictated policies.

"If we don't bring our organization up to date," he said, "the whole legislative body will lose the respect of its constituents and the whole legislative system will bog down. There are eleven members of the Senate past the age of seventy, while sixteen members are between sixty-five and seventy. In their hands lie all the important chairmanships of committees because of the seniority rule. Most businesses that are run efficiently retire their officials when they reach that age, but in the Senate the older men control all important bills."[9]

Fulbright wanted the unlimited debate rule changed, the number of committee assignments lessened, the volume of work reduced; but the heart of his criticism was directed at the handful of old men. "The committee chairman," he said, "has the power of life and death over bills, for under parliamentary procedures now existing he can kill bills by the simple expedient of failing to call a meeting of his committee for a hearing."

Then he added:

"Until you are installed as senator, you think you are a man of some importance, but the party caucus held immediately after the installation ceremonies puts you in your place."

Toward the end of the war, Fulbright had displayed a common ambivalence toward Russia. He hoped that the wartime unity could be continued into the postwar days; but he was angered and perplexed at Soviet actions that made cooperation so difficult to achieve. It was clear, as early as 1944, that Russia was beginning to act out of her own self-interest when she refused to allow free elections in Poland and instead set up a puppet government. Differences at Potsdam in 1945 marked the end of the wartime alliance.

"Russia now thinks that she can do as she pleases," Fulbright was saying in 1946, "that she need not reckon with us. She has become affected by the fervor of expansion and is feeling cocky. We cannot afford to let her go on. If we impress Russia with measures such as extension of the draft, we may be able to maintain stable relations through a breathing period. Then in the next fifteen to twenty years, through the exchange of students, through business relations, we might remove some of the causes of trouble."[10]

America's troubles were complicated by a general lack of confidence in her leaders. By the close of the year, Harry Truman was receiving as much abuse as any President since Andrew Johnson. Whatever he did—or did not do—in his foreign or domestic policies, Truman personally bore the brunt of all public fears and frustrations.

Throughout the year, strikes had continued, piling up a record loss of 107,475,000 man-days of work. Despite all administration efforts, prices had kept climbing until living costs were thirty-three percent higher than the level of Pearl Harbor Day—and the ceiling was by no means in sight. In the face of constant criticism, Truman issued rosy statements, but obviously was wavering. After urging universal military training, he dropped the fight and permitted nearly total demobilization; after backing large loans for European and Asian countries, his administration permitted food shipments to lag far behind to enrage many a former ally. As the congressional elections of 1946 approached, Truman's popularity had dropped to an all-time low as measured by the political polls. At that point, Fulbright climaxed his year of criticism with a sensational suggestion that Truman should resign.

On November 5, 1946, the Republicans enjoyed their best day at the polls since Herbert Hoover's landslide victory in 1928. They gained control of both houses of Congress, and now held twenty-five out of the forty-eight governorships. Nevertheless Fulbright's suggestion that Truman should resign was all the more dramatic because it was so unexpected. The first story was an Associated Press dispatch from Philadelphia, the day after the elections.

> *"Philadelphia,* Nov. 6—Senator J. William Fulbright, D-Ark, said today that since the Republicans had captured both houses of Congress 'President Truman should appoint a Republican Secretary of State and resign from office.'"

At that time, the Secretary of State followed the Vice President in line of presidential succession, and there was, of course, no Vice President in 1946. That first flash was followed by a United Press story quoting Fulbright as naming Senator Arthur H. Vandenberg of Michigan, the Republican leader in the foreign affairs field and the symbol of bipartisanship in the Congress, as the most logical choice to succeed Truman.

Fulbright said he was "only suggesting" that Truman resign because he thought "it would be the best thing for the country as a whole." Truman's resignation, he explained, "will place the responsibility of running the government on one party and prevent a stalemate that is likely to occur. Only one party should control the government. It alone then will have to assume responsibility for all the programs good and bad. Too many times we have had a president from one party and a Congress controlled by another party. . . . It is the biggest defect in our constitutional system. And it has hurt the American people badly."

The next day, Fulbright's proposal received surprising support when Marshall Field's *Chicago Sun,* in a front-page editorial, proposed the same thing—that Truman appoint a Republican Secretary of State and then resign. The *Atlanta Constitution* joined in: The Democratic Party should give "serious consideration" to the idea, the paper commented.

Truman had no official comment, but at the White House reporters were told the idea was "utterly fantastic." Then, in the way of Washington, the grist mills of the gossips began to grind. Some said that Fulbright had made his statement out of personal pique; he already was out of favor with the White House and was venting his jealousy. Others viewed his attack as a move against an unofficial "Arkansas brain trust" in the White House. Truman was surrounded then by a number of men who originally came from Arkansas—Leslie Biffle, Secretary of the Senate and one of Truman's closest friends; John Steelman, a special assistant to the President; John Snyder, the Secretary of the Treasury who had spent all his life as an Arkansas bank teller until moving to Missouri. These men supposedly dispensed patronage favors through Senator John McClellan of Arkansas, not Fulbright, and Fulbright resented it. Fulbright, in this view, was left out by the "in" Arkansas group: he had married a Pennsylvanian, had lived overseas and, as Drew Pearson commented, "just didn't rate as an Arkansan any more."[11]

Alert as ever to the foibles of the famous, the Washington society writers seized on the incident. An account by Betty Hynes of the *Washington Times-Herald* was typical. She was attending a cocktail party and style show given by Mme Monet, wife of the French Ambassador, when she spotted Fulbright: "Others in the fascinated throng—and we mean fascinated—were Senator J. William Fulbright who has turned the political world topsy-turvy the last few days with his suggestion that we adopt the British system of government and change chiefs when the people change their party choice. 'No one could be more surprised when I realized the excitement my remarks seemed to have created,' remarked the senator, shaking his head in honest bewilderment."[12]

As was nearly always the case in Washington, the facts behind Fulbright's statement were different from those portrayed in the press. Fulbright was being neither Machiavellian nor vindictive. In fact, Fulbright's idea had grown out of a serious reflection that he had already expressed on at least two other occasions—in the press and before Congress.* Neither had attracted much attention.

The Truman episode came a week after Fulbright complained in a Chicago speech that nobody "pays much attention to you." He returned to Washington shortly after that speech and was having lunch with his friend, Senator Scott Lucas of Illinois, and one or two other politicians in the public cafeteria of the old Senate Office Building.

"We got to gossiping as all politicians do," Fulbright would recall, "and I was young and inexperienced and probably talked too much about what was going to happen. 'Did you think you'd lose the Senate; did you think you'd lose the House?' You know, how they all do. It's like this numbers game anywhere."

---

* On March 22, 1945, Fulbright had testified before the Joint Committee on the Organization of Congress and warned that dangerous deadlocks could jeopardize world peace and domestic prosperity after the war if the Congress and the President were not working effectively together. He then suggested that the Congress adopt a measure by which "the President could dissolve the government, in cases of deadlock between the two branches, and precipitate a general election." The government should change hands, he thought, whenever the party in power loses the confidence of the country. When the *Washington Post* editorially criticized his suggestion, Fulbright strongly defended his proposal and again warned that changes must be made to meet "the anomalous and dangerous condition which arises when the opposite party from that of the executive controls the Congress." He continued to hold these views from then on, and publicly expressed them on a number of occasions.

While they were talking, two or three reporters gathered around, and the conversation continued. The Democratic politicians were fairly certain their party would lose control of the House, but they did not think they would lose the Senate, too. When someone remarked how difficult it would be if they did lose the Senate, Fulbright spoke up. If that happened, he said, the country would be better off if the government were turned over to the Republicans instead of trying to operate under a divided system. He was thinking of Wilson's experience after World War I, Hoover's after the 1930 election, and Churchill's resignation a year before in England after the Labor Party gained control of Parliament.

Fulbright went back to his office and was visited by Ann Hicks, a reporter who had been present at the lunch. She wanted to quote the senator. Fulbright declined; it was off the record; he wasn't about to make any official prophecy about the election. Besides, he didn't believe the Democrats would lose the Senate anyway. Well, suppose it did happen that way, the reporter asked, could she use it then? Foolishly, Fulbright said yes; then he quickly forgot it.

He gave a speech in Philadelphia just before the election, and spent election night with his wife at the home of an aunt of Betty's. The next morning the phone started ringing.

"My God, she'd released this and it was on the front page," Fulbright said. "I was in terrible shape. Then I had to defend it because it was already printed."

Truman never forgave him. His reaction was in keeping with his celebrated temper (he had called Drew Pearson an "SOB" and written Paul Hume, the *Washington Post*'s music critic, a heated warning after Hume criticized a concert by Margaret Truman).

Not long after the 80th Congress had been elected, Truman appeared at an off-the-record press dinner and addressed some remarks toward Fulbright. His words quickly found their way into the press. Fulbright, Truman was widely quoted as saying, was an "overeducated Oxford SOB."

Years later, on March 14, 1960, after he had left the presidency, Truman wrote Fulbright a letter of explanation, prompted, he said, by doing some background reading of "various things that had happened in the past." "I am sure," he wrote, "that some reporter, as they have a habit of doing, did some misquoting of you and me. This report said I had made the same remark about you as I had about Drew Pearson. Our argument started over what you said about my retiring after the 80th Congress was elected, which I refused to do. If you remember, we had a Press Club dinner at the Statler Hotel and I made the remark that if you had attended a land-grant college in the United States instead of Oxford, you would never have made that statement. I never made any reflection on your personal character nor on your mother." Fulbright, in replying, said "I willingly accept the explanation which you have made," but did have a last sly dig: "Incidentally," Fulbright wrote, "I did attend a land-grant college, the University of Arkansas, in my home town."

3

A COMMON NOUN CALLED FULBRIGHT

IN THE HALCYON DAYS BEFORE WORLD WAR II, American cultural relations with the outside world consisted, as Fulbright would say, largely of the "grand tours" of a handful of citizens who had the money and the cosmopolitan tastes to travel overseas. The Americans fell into a type: they were either as parochial as the characters of Mark Twain's *Innocents Abroad,* as aristocratic as Henry James, or as proudly rebellious as the young expatriates of the '20s.

The Fulbright fellowships sent a new kind of American abroad. For the first time, it meant that many teachers and scholars could study overseas. Although the State Department had arranged a few exchanges with Latin America in 1938, the Fulbright program from its birth immediately involved twenty-two countries around the world as only a start—and it meant that far more money was now available for the uncelebrated but promising student or scholar.

Seldom, if ever, was a government program so clearly the creation of one man. From the Ozarks to Oxford to Washington, Fulbright's life had led him to place the highest values on education, travel, and the exchange of ideas. While he had been thinking along these lines after the war, the catalyst for the fellowship program was a conversation at a garden tea party in Washington.

It was Wednesday, September 26, 1945, a sultry Indian summer day, and Fulbright was attending a party in honor of the daughter of Mrs. Merriweather Post, the wealthiest Washington hostess. As always, the guests were talking about the topics of the day—the burning of a market ;

place and kidnaping of forty Frenchmen by what the press reported was a "revolt of natives" in Saigon; the first meeting of MacArthur and Hirohito in Tokyo; the arrival of the peppery Patrick J. Hurley, who was to report immediately to Truman on his efforts to reconcile Chiang Kaishek's central government and the Communist forces in northern China. Fulbright fell into a conversation with two acquaintances, Oscar Cox, the former counsel for the Lend-Lease Administration, and Herbert Elliston, the editor of the *Washington Post*. They talked about exchange programs and what to do about the postwar debts owed America.

"The result," Fulbright recalled later, "was the birth of an idea that has since had a globe-trotting career."[1]

That next day, September 27, Fulbright rose in the Senate and said:

"Mr. President, I ask unanimous consent to introduce a bill for reference to the Committee on Military Affairs, authorizing the use of credits established through the sale of surplus properties abroad for the promotion of international good will through the exchange of students in the fields of education, culture, and science."

His words meant little to those who heard him; they did not even merit a passing notice in the afternoon press.

Yet those words marked the beginning of a program that in time would be described by the State Department as "the most fabulously profitable investment ever authorized by Congress,"[2] a program that one day would lead Fulbright's tutor at Oxford, R. B. McCallum, to say that his former pupil had been "responsible for the largest and most significant movement of scholars across the earth since the fall of Constantinople in 1453," and to cause a president of the United States, John F. Kennedy, to refer to it as "the classic modern example of beating swords into plowshares."[3]

From idea to final passage, Fulbright's handling of the exchange program legislation illuminated his political personality. He was cautious and quiet; he called on all the political skills he had mastered since coming to Congress: the letter, the private talk, the soliciting of key supporters, the lobbying, the avoidance of controversy.

For some time he had been searching for a way to initiate an exchange program. His interest stemmed not only from his own Rhodes scholarship experience, but also from his participation a year before in the London conference on restoring European educational institutions. Only four days after Roosevelt's death he was saying, in a radio broadcast, that he supported the "exchange of students, the exchange of professors, the translation of books, and the dissemination of books among all the nations . . . to persuade the various nations to treat their own histories in a more truthful manner." He was convinced, he said then, that such an exchange program "can contribute as much to the preservation of peace as the control of violence."

But, as he was well aware, those words sounded visionary, and impractical. How could such a program ever be enacted into law? Fulbright was certain the Congress never would approve a fellowship program financed directly out of the Treasury; and American politicians were noticeably unresponsive to pleas that education and better understanding were important in international relations.

The coupling of the exchange program with American surplus war materials overseas provided a reasonable hope of success. By then, the question of the war debts already had arisen, and congressional leaders were recalling the bitter controversies growing out of the World War I debts. American surplus trucks, jeeps, and bulldozers were rusting away in foreign lands. Those countries would be happy to buy them, but they lacked enough money to do so. If they were permitted to pay for them out of their own currency, Fulbright thought, the proceeds could be used to finance an exchange program. Besides, the surplus equipment really meant the U.S. had a substantial amount of currency frozen abroad; it was doing no good to America. As he explained his idea on the Senate floor:

"Most of the nations desiring to purchase our trucks, railroad equipment and so forth, abroad, do not have American dollars, or even the goods, to pay, and it will, therefore, be necessary for our government to establish credits for this purpose. These debts may never be paid in full and might, like the war debts after World War I, become a source of irritation between nations. . . ."

Fulbright's appeal was couched in practical terms. "The bill was potentially controversial," he would say twenty-one years later, "and I decided not to take the risk of an open appeal to the idealism of my colleagues—deeply idealistic men though they may be. Indeed, it occurred to me that the less attention the matter got the greater would be the chance of victory for idealism."[4] It was a technique Fulbright consistently employed—with varying degrees of success—throughout his years in Washington.

He was not breaking new ground, he argued to any doubters. Why, as far back as 1901 the United States had provided a precedent for a foreign educational exchange program. After the Boxer Rebellion in China in July, 1900, he pointed out, an indemnity of $333 million had been imposed on China, and the U.S. had claimed $25 million as its share. Eventually, through an agreement with the U.S., $16 million was placed in trust by the Chinese government for the education of youth in China and America. That, Fulbright believed, had proved to be "one of the most successful of our international policies."

Treasury officials thought the idea unconstitutional: foreign currencies couldn't be tapped without a specific appropriation bill. At certain levels, the State Department seemed dubious: foreign policy should properly originate within the Department, not in Congress. Besides, with new international tensions already building, such an exchange program could be subverted to allow foreign agents easy entry into the country.

Quietly, Fulbright kept plugging away.

Later in the congressional session, Fulbright introduced another bill to give the Secretary of State greater authority for disbursing funds. In the meantime, he continued his efforts to gain administration and congressional support. As he had done so successfully in securing passage of the Fulbright (Peace) Resolution in 1943, he also sought key bipartisan backing. He approached Herbert Hoover then living in isolation in New York's Waldorf Towers, and received a written endorsement of his bill. "I am indeed glad of such a proposal," the former Republican president wrote, as he recalled his own efforts in establishing the Belgian-American Education Foundation after World War I.[5]

Finally, both bills—Senate 1440 and Senate 1636—were scheduled for a public hearing on February 25, 1946. Fulbright's desire to keep discussion of his proposal to a minimum was successful, for the hearing room and the announced subject matter were a study in obscurity. They were designed, it seemed, for certain congressional oblivion.

Senator Joseph O'Mahoney, the chairman of the Surplus Property Subcommittee of the Senate Military Affairs Committee, called the subcommittee meeting for 10:30 A.M. in Room 224 of the Public Lands and Survey Committee Room. The subject, he said, was a bill introduced by Senator Fulbright of Arkansas amending the Surplus Property Act of 1944.

Of the five senators who were members of the Surplus Property Subcommittee, only O'Mahoney, the chairman, showed up that day.

Fulbright testified, and placed his letter from Herbert Hoover on the record. William Benton, the Assistant Secretary of State, also testified briefly, and endorsed the legislation. Only four other persons appeared; they were all in favor. Three hours after it began, the hearing was over. Two weeks later the full committee, headed by Senator Elbert Thomas, a Democrat of Utah, reported out the consolidated bill, S. 1636, to the Senate floor. On April 12, 1946, still traveling in anonymity, the bill came up for discussion. It passed by unanimous consent without a single word of debate, and without the calling of the roll. On July 25, it passed the House—again, without floor debate—and two days later, the bill, as amended, came up for its final reading in the Senate.

After it had been read, Senator Wallace White, Republican of Maine, stood to ask:

"Mr. President, what is this bill?"

Fulbright spoke. "This is a bill which passed the Senate about three months ago, involving the disposition of surplus property abroad, a part of the proceeds from which is to be used for exchange scholarships. It was unanimously approved by the Committee on Military Affairs, and passed the House."

Then he said quickly:

"I move that the Senate concur in the House amendments."

One other senator arose. William C. Revercomb, Republican of West Virginia, asked "if this is the bill which permits the sale of surplus property abroad, the proceeds to be devoted to an exchange of students?"

"This is the bill," Fulbright answered.

It passed.

On August 1, 1946, as the session was ending, Harry Truman, with Fulbright standing beside him, signed the bill into law as PL 584, 79th Congress, 60 Sta. 754.

The Fulbright Act, as it was called, provided that up to $20 million could be earmarked for educational exchanges with any country that buys surplus property, and that up to $1 million could be spent each year in each country where such an agreement was made. "Thus," as William Benton stated, "tens of millions of dollars should become available under this bill over a period of years."[6] In terms of money and scope, the Fulbright Fellowships dwarfed the Rhodes Scholarships program.

As the bill became law, the State Department announced that it had already completed an agreement with Great Britain to provide $20 million from the sale of surplus property for educational exchanges with the United Kingdom and the British colonies. Similar agreements were being negotiated with more than twenty countries around the globe.

The Fulbright Act provided for a number of educational activities. American students could be given grants to finance the cost of higher education or research in foreign countries. American professors also were covered: They could receive grants enabling them to lecture in foreign institutions. In addition, foreign students could get money to pay for their transportation to the U.S. where they would attend American colleges and universities. Or, if they wished, the foreign students were eligible for scholarships to study at such American non-denominational institutions overseas as the American University at Beirut, Lebanon, and Robert College at Istanbul, Turkey.

Although the Fulbright Act made the State Department the disposal agency for surplus property located outside the U.S. and gave the Secretary of State authority to enter into executive agreements for exchanges with foreign governments, it also had been carefully drafted to ensure that the program would be free of governmental or partisan political domination. Supervision of the program would come from distinguished citizens appointed by the President from the academic and cultural world to serve on a Board of Foreign Scholarships. Creation of the board was the first step in insulating the programs from political control. The board set the general policy of the exchange programs, and ultimately approved the selection of the grantees. For its own part, the board relied heavily on the assistance of such private organizations as the Institute of International Education and the Conference Board of Associated Research Councils—thus again underscoring the desire to maintain the program's independence.

As soon as the Fulbright Act became effective, the exchange program awakened immediate interest and enthusiasm. The State Department received numerous requests for information on grants and programs. Foreign governments also were eager to conclude exchange agreements. For them, particularly, the Fulbright program was a popular vehicle: It meant instead of paying their debts in dollars they could pay in scholarships and thus cancel their obligations to the U.S. without sending a penny outside their borders.

The sudden attention brought an inevitable counterreaction at home. For the first time, some congressmen realized the implications of what they had enacted into law.

"An influential senator told me later that he would have killed the bill instantly if he had grasped the contents," Fulbright said later, and quoted that critical senator as adding "I don't want our impressionable American youths to be infected with foreign isms."

His opposition was too late. In 1948 the first Fulbright exchanges took place; thirty-five students and one professor came to the U.S. and sixty-five Americans went overseas. Within twenty years educational exchanges were being carried out with 110 countries and geographical areas, with forty-nine having formal exchange agreements. The program itself had cost the U.S. about $400 million, mostly in foreign currency. During that period 82,585 persons—47,950 of them students—received Fulbright Fellowships, nearly 12 million school children in the U.S. and abroad were taught by exchange teachers, and 88,500 American and nearly 12,500 foreign schools participated by receiving teachers or sending them abroad. The impact was even greater. In 1960 Michigan State University made a study of 5,300 American Fulbright fellows who had returned home. While they were overseas, those Americans had spoken before more than a quarter of a million people. After they came home, they spoke before 2,700,000 Americans. As a group, they wrote more than 4,000 books, monographs, and articles, compiled more than 2,100 professional papers; and in writing only about their foreign experiences, they introduced nearly 500 academic articles into their home educational institutions.[7]

As the years passed the Fulbright program was expanded several times. In 1948, the Smith-Mundt Act made possible exchanges to countries that had not signed agreements. That law also permitted Fulbright fellows to receive additional financial support. In both 1953 and 1954, the Congress doubled the number of countries eligible to enter into formal exchange agreements and substantially increased the money available. Finally, in 1961, the Fulbright-Hays Act brought together the various pieces of legislation affecting educational exchanges.

But the real significance of the Fulbright program never could be measured by dollars or statistics. Even Fulbright hardly dreamed of the effects his program would achieve. Even by 1945, almost no university in Europe taught American history except as an appendage to the history of Europe. Oxford and the University of London had endowed chairs in American history by that time, but they were the exception. Elsewhere the situation was the same: although after World War II America had clearly emerged as the most powerful nation in history, it was a nation about which little was known and even less was taught.

The Fulbright program directly changed that. Within a generation after the war, every country in Western Europe offered American studies, and many universities had established chairs in American history, literature, or civilization. A tally made in 1964 listed 116 chairs, 338 courses, and 70 seminars in American studies.

"The exchange program," Fulbright would say, "is the thing that reconciles me to all the difficulties of political life. It's the only activity that gives me some hope that the human race won't commit suicide, though I still wouldn't count on it."[8] And, in the same philosophic vein, one day he would look back on the program and say:

"Americans and Europeans are prone to thinking of their own societies as the center and source of world civilization, forgetting that the West is only one of the world's great cultures, and forgetting also that some of the most barbarous physical and intellectual slaughters of all history have taken place in the West within our lifetime. It follows, I believe, that man's struggle to be rational about himself, about his relationship to his own society and to other peoples and nations, involves a constant search for understanding among all peoples and all cultures—a search that can only be effective when learning is pursued on a worldwide basis. The educational exchange program is built on this premise, which stated in another way, holds that America has much to teach in the world but also much to learn and that the greater our intellectual involvement with the world beyond our frontiers, the greater the gain for both America and the world. . . .

"There is nothing obscure about the objective of educational exchange. Its purpose is to acquaint Americans with the world as it is and to acquaint students and scholars from many lands with America as it is—not as we wish it were or as we might wish foreigners to see it, but exactly as it is— which by my reckoning is an 'image' of which no American need be ashamed. The program further aims to make the benefits of American culture and technology available to the world and to enrich American life by exposing it to the science and art of many societies. Finally, the program aims, through these means, to bring a little more knowledge, a little more reason, and a little more compassion into world affairs and thereby to increase the chance that nations will learn at last to live in peace and friendship."[9]

Over the years a number of distinguished men and women have received Fulbright Fellowships. From the American side, the list includes:

Gardner Ackley, U. S. Ambassador to Italy, former Chairman, President's Council of Economic Advisers, research scholar grantee in economics at the University of Rome, 1956.

Felix Bloch, professor of physics, Stanford, and Nobel Prize winner, 1952, lecturer grantee in 1959 at Hebrew University, Jerusalem.

Irene Dalis, mezzo-soprano with Metropolitan Opera, student grantee in Milan, 1951.

Carl Kaysen, director, Institute for Advanced Study, Princeton, economics research scholar grantee in London, 1955.

Alfred Kazin, lecturer grantee in American studies at the University of Aix-Marseille, 1956.

Arthur Mizener, professor of English, Cornell (Fitzgerald scholar), lecturer grantee in American studies at King's College and Bedford College, University of London, 1955.

Allen Tate, critic, poet, professor of English, University of Minnesota, lecturer grantee, Oxford University, 1953.

From abroad:

Alfred A. Alvarez, book critic of *The Observer* and drama critic of the New Statesman, student grantee at Princeton, 1954.

Dr. Martin Noel, professor of Spanish-American Literature, University of Buenos Aires, lecturer grantee to Western Reserve University in 1959.

Luigi Broglio, dean of school of aeronautical engineering, University of Rome, and vice president of European Committee for Space Research, lecturer grantee at Purdue, 1951.

Solly Cohen, dean of faculty of science, Hebrew University, lecturer grantee at Princeton, 1959.

Dr. Shafik Ali El Khishen, minister of agriculture of the United Arab Republic, research scholar grantee in insecticides, University of California at Riverside and Berkeley, 1962.

Dr. Alfonso Ortega Urbina, Nicaraguan Minister of Foreign Affairs, student grantee in comparative law, Southern Methodist University, 1953.

Impressive as any such compilation of names was, the heart of the program centered around the unknowns. Many of them, in turn, felt a special bond with the man they regarded as their sponsor. As the program accelerated, Fulbright began receiving letters from all over the world. Some of them were touching, others thoughtful, still others impulsive. A student from Chicago summed up much of the feeling in a telegram to Fulbright.

"BECAUSE OF YOUR INTEREST IN US THE EARNEST STUDENTS
OF AMERICA I AM ENABLED TO STUDY FURTHER IN FRANCE
I COULD NOT LEAVE ON THE QUEEN MARY WEDNESDAY WITH-
OUT EXPRESSING TO YOU WHOSE EFFORTS HAD MADE THIS
WONDERFUL HAPPINESS POSSIBLE MY GREAT APPRECIATION
AND AFFECTION FOR YOU A FRIEND INDEED."[10]

By the end of the 1940s, people were referring to themselves as "Ful-
brighters" and talking of getting "a Fulbright." James W. Silver, then the
chairman of the history department of the University of Mississippi (and
later the author of a book about that state) was in Aberdeen, Scotland, in
December of 1949, during his fellowship period. It wasn't until he saw the
windows of the Southampton–London boat train plastered with the word
FULBRIGHT that he became conscious, as he said, "of the size of the
movement with which I had become connected."

Silver ventured a prediction: "My guess is that one of these days the
word will find its way into the dictionary. For the Fulbright program is
undoubtedly the most comprehensive experiment of its kind yet undertaken. It is one of the few great things that have come out of the war and
should be a great force for making American democracy more completely
understood by people we like to call our friends."[11]

Webster's Third International Dictionary now carries the entry:

> *ful-bright.* . . . n -s usu cap [after James William *Fulbright*
> b1905 U.S. senator]: a grant awarded under the Ful-
> bright Act that makes U.S. surplus property in foreign
> countries available to finance lectures or research abroad
> by American students and professors.

4

THE DETERIORATION OF DEMOCRACY

DEAN RUSK, the little-known Assistant Secretary of State for Far Eastern Affairs, was having dinner with Frank Pace, the Secretary of the Army, at Joseph Alsop's on a hot and drowsy Saturday late in June, 1950.[1] In Washington, the pace of the government reflected the weather: the city and its officials slumbered. In Sandy Spring, Maryland, Rusk's superior, Secretary of State Dean Acheson, was spending the weekend at his old farm, "Harewood." And in Independence, Missouri, Harry Truman was attending a family reunion.

Then, as is so often the case, a crisis broke. At 9:26 P.M. the first cable began arriving at the State Department. Rusk was telephoned immediately.

"NORTH KOREAN FORCES INVADED REPUBLIC OF KOREA TERRITORY AT SEVERAL PLACES THIS MORNING [*John J. Muccio, the American Ambassador to the Republic of Korea had wired*]. . . . IT WOULD APPEAR FROM THE NATURE OF THE ATTACK AND THE MANNER IN WHICH IT WAS LAUNCHED THAT IT CONSTITUTES AN ALL-OUT OFFENSIVE AGAINST THE REPUBLIC OF KOREA."[2]

Rusk left instantly for the State Department, Pace for the Pentagon. It was Rusk who called Acheson, who in turn informed Truman that the Korean War had begun. It had come less than five years after the end of World War II and only three years since waging the Cold War had become official U.S. policy through the Truman Doctrine of giving military aid to Greece and Turkey and the Marshall Plan pledging to rebuild Western Europe.*

That the actual armed conflict, when it came, occurred in the Far East was a surprise to all concerned, for the problems of Asia were considered secondary to those of Europe. Virtually every major American policy maker thought the central threat to peace rested in the Kremlin; and the Kremlin's targets, it seemed, were on the continent. The danger spots already had been clearly defined: Berlin, where the blockade and the airlift had raised the real possibility of a direct war with Russia and where Fulbright, among others, had gone at the height of the crisis in 1948 for a personal inspection; Yugoslavia, where Washington had received constant reports that Soviet allies were about to attack the first defector from the Russian orbit; Greece or Turkey.

Instead, it was Korea, a waif of a country in a wayward part of the world.

Still, no matter where the fighting centered, American officials remained convinced that the signals were being called by Moscow. Korea, in their thinking, was evidence of Russia's lust for power through expansion. It was inconceivable that Korea, or its powerful northern neighbor, China, which only recently had been taken over by the Communists, could act independently of Moscow.

Such an interpretation—and an American response based on such an analysis—held profound implications for the course of U.S.-Asian diplomacy. In a real sense, Korea in the early 1950s foreshadowed Vietnam a decade later. From the American side, a vital question in Korea, as it was to be in Vietnam, was the nature of the conflict—whether, in fact, it might have been primarily a nationalist battle, a largely Asian-oriented struggle, or part of a worldwide Communist campaign of conquest. The question was scarcely debated; the answer seemed evident. And, for the first few months following Truman's immediate commitment of American troops on June 27, the question was moot: Military necessities dictated actions.

In those first four months, the war had moved from moments of despair and near defeat to high elation and conviction that victory was assured. The summer had brought disaster, with the ill-prepared, ill-trained American and Republic of Korea forces hanging grimly to a last, desperate perimeter about the port of Pusan. Then, after a military buildup and a slow push forward, General Douglas MacArthur, in a lightning stroke, had carried out a successful amphibious landing at Inchon below the 38th Parallel dividing

---

* Fulbright had supported both, although he was less enthusiastic in his endorsement for the harsher Truman Doctrine. He had been an immediate and vociferous backer of the Marshall Plan, not only because of its humanitarian aspects, but because he saw it as a way to further his idea of a United States of Europe. He already had introduced a Senate resolution urging U.S. backing for an economic-political federation of the Western European nations. But he was ahead of his time; his resolution languished for lack of administration support.

North and South Korea. Soon, under the authority of a vague United Nations resolution, MacArthur's forces were plunging far into North Korea. By October, they were nearing the Yalu River and the Chinese border. The war seemed over.

But as the U.N. troops pushed north, the Chinese began warning ominously that they would not "supinely tolerate seeing their neighbors being savagely invaded by the imperialists."³ Truman was concerned. That "moot" question concerning Chinese (or Russian) intentions, the nature of the war, and the merits of expanding the struggle or holding the line then came up for review.

In a celebrated meeting, the President, accompanied by Rusk, Pace, Harriman, and others flew to Wake Island and conferred with General MacArthur on October 15, 1950. Truman asked MacArthur about the possibilities of Chinese intervention.

"We are no longer fearful of their intervention," the imperious old general replied. "We no longer stand hat in hand. The Chinese have 300,000 men in Manchuria. Of these probably not more than 100 to 125,000 are distributed along the Yalu River. Only 50 to 60 . . . could be gotten across the Yalu River. They have no air force. Now that we have bases for our Air Force in Korea, if the Chinese tried to get down to Pyongyang there would be the greatest slaughter."⁴

MacArthur predicted:

"I believe that formal resistance will end throughout North and South Korea by Thanksgiving."⁵

A month later, on November 26, just at Thanksgiving time, thirty-three full Chinese divisions hit the U.N. lines with devastating force. Once more, the Americans were in danger of being driven from their farthest advance into South Korea, and the lines had become stabilized in a scene reminiscent of World War I trench-warfare conditions. It had become a war neither side could win, given the forces then deployed.

The question of expanding the war and fighting on to a total victory suddenly had become nothing less than a question about beginning World War III. To bomb Chinese bases, as advocated by some in the military, was, in the eyes of many key policy makers, a strike against the real master, Russia. Thus, such an attack would be inviting instant Russian retaliation.

Dean Rusk spelled out a common opinion in a speech that years later would be cited by his critics as evidence he was uninformed and unreliable about Asia—and particularly about China:

"The Peiping regime may be a colonial Russian government—a Slavic Manchuko on a larger scale," the Assistant Secretary said. "It is not the government of China. It does not pass the first test. It is not China."⁶

Fulbright had sat on the sidelines through all the early phases of the Korean War, strangely silent for a senator so deeply involved in foreign affairs. Indeed, in 1950 he does not seem to have issued a single public comment on the war. Although after the massive Chinese attack his private correspondence reflected an intense pessimism, he still did not comment publicly on the war.

When he finally did speak out, he had a startling suggestion—that the United States pull out of Korea altogether rather than risk a larger war. China's intervention had changed "the entire character of the struggle," he said; it had made the military situation untenable.* He warned of the dangers in becoming involved in a major land war with China and went on to say, in a passage which sounded much like Rusk: "If this is the beginning of World War III, we must not forget that the Kremlin is the primary enemy and China merely a satellite." Then he added:

"It is far wiser to recognize the hard military facts of the situation and to withdraw from Korea than to persist in an undertaking which is now quite a different one from that which we began in June. In spite of the valid principle which we sought to support, we should not jeopardize our military security by pursuing an impracticable undertaking."

A few weeks later, influenced by more favorable military communiqués, his convictions were weakened. Then, stepping back, he remarked that recent military victories had changed the situation somewhat. "However," he said, typically, "I still doubt the feasibility of this military venture."[7]

Fulbright had fluctuated. He had been indecisive, and was clearly swayed by day-to-day events. Having waited so long to comment at all, he virtually had negated any influence his opinions might have had. His views on Korea attracted little attention.

In fact, at that point Fulbright was being paid only slight attention on foreign-policy questions. Even more unusual for him, his major interest then did not lie with foreign affairs. Concerned though he was about Korea, his deepest worry was with what he called "the moral deterioration of democracy" at home.

Fulbright, in the closing years of the Truman administration, had become one of the President's foremost domestic critics. For the first time in his public life, he was addressing himself primarily to the state of the nation at home. In a day of cynicism, corruption, and general disillusionment, Fulbright's career had taken on a new gloss as an investigator of dubious ethical practices in—and out—of government. He was hailed, justly, as a scholarly moralist who was attempting to redress some old evils. In the end, Fulbright would contribute greatly, though unintentionally, to the failure of his party to maintain control of the White House, and the subsequent beginning of the Eisenhower era.

As he had done so often before, Fulbright came onto the center stage casually, almost by chance.

* Fulbright spoke on Korea at Christian College in Columbia, Missouri, January 18, 1951.

In the summer of 1949 Fulbright was presiding, as chairman, over a routine hearing of the Senate Banking and Currency subcommittee. During the questioning, it was developed that one witness, John Haggerty, the Boston loan agency manager for the Reconstruction Finance Corporation, had accepted a $30,000-a-year job with the Waltham Watch Co. Earlier, the Waltham Co., then bankrupt, had borrowed $6 million from the RFC.

Fulbright thought Haggerty's action was unethical, and questioned the five RFC directors about its propriety. He learned that another RFC employee had gone to work for a company that also had borrowed money from the agency. In addition, the RFC directors seemed evasive when questioned closely about practices within their agency. Fulbright felt the entire agency needed further examination. He requested—and on February 8, 1950, received—Senate approval to conduct a full investigation of the RFC.

The RFC, a government agency established by Congress in the waning days of the Hoover administration as an emergency measure to try and forestall the epidemic of bankruptcies sweeping the nation, had been a useful endeavor—especially in such a poor state as Arkansas. By providing money with less collateral terms than normal banks required, it had been able to pump needed dollars into smaller financial institutions and help them meet their commitments. Although it had been set up as an independent agency not subject to political control, by the late 1940s the RFC had become an outlet for other government agencies. Through the RFC, they could obtain funds without going through the regular congressional appropriations committees. The seeds of corruption had been sown.

What began early in 1950 as an unheralded congressional investigation led within a year to sensational disclosures of influence peddling, of gifts of mink coats and all-expenses-paid trips to Florida, of irregularities, official indifference, of deep involvement with the White House—and ultimately a bitter public dispute with Harry Truman.

As the story unfolded, one dramatic disclosure led to another. In the end, Fulbright's subcommittee uncovered a tangled web of political manipulations and named, among others, Donald S. Dawson, a presidential assistant, as the man who tried to dominate the RFC from his post in the White House; Democratic National Chairman William M. Boyle, Jr., and his assistants, who, from party headquarters, dispatched a number of attorneys to RFC offices seeking favors and "special attention"; E. Merl Young, an "expediter" or go-between, whose friends included a lawyer who once boasted that he had two of the RFC directors "in his hip pocket"; and a host of lesser figures, in and out of government.[8] It all added up to bad news for the Democrats.

Fulbright's investigation did more than affect the political climate. For the first time the public was introduced to the image of a drawling, at times indolent, smiling and courteous senator with a wry sense of humor who had a habit of peering quizzically over his glasses at witnesses. He seldom raised his voice; he never lost his temper; and, unlike other politicians of that period, he did not obviously play to the press.

"He has a quiet manner with almost an impish grin [a reporter for the *Buffalo Evening News* wrote] that leads witnesses on until they become entangled in their own efforts to avoid a flat answer. He frequently sums up the apparent meaning and significance of a whole series of answers in one statement and asks the witness if that is the impression he wants to leave with the committee.

"Thus brow-beating tactics which so infuriate witnesses and lead them to the belief they have been made the 'goat' of congressional enquiries have been eliminated. The new system seems sure to leave a much better taste in the mouth of the public."[9]

Fulbright's hearings were a model of judicious questioning, of careful staff work headed by a persistent investigator, Theodore Herz, and, most important, of fairness. As Walter Lippmann commented at the time, "Senator Fulbright has set an example, all the more impressive because its sincerity has been so effortless, of how a good senator can behave."[10]

What did not come through to the public as clearly then—or later—was a more vital aspect of Fulbright's personality. Even though he had been involved in a series of controversies since coming to Washington, Fulbright temperamentally did not welcome conflict. To borrow the words from one shrewd assessment of him, he was "the Capitol's reluctant gladiator"*—a man who preferred the privacy of his office and hours of peaceful contemplation to the turmoil of the arena. "He's a child of the eighteenth century," said his friend, Senator Paul Douglas who served with him on the RFC subcommittee. "He's a throwback to that age of enlightenment, trust in reason, temperate argument and slightly aristocratic tendencies. That, I think, explains why he seems a little aloof, a little different from the rest."[11]

Fulbright's method of handling the RFC investigation typified the manner in which he conducted subsequent and even more significant hearings. Instead of pressing his advantage, or attempting to lay out all the problems in public, he sought to achieve reforms and changes by quiet persuasion and private conferences.

After his investigation had convinced him and other members of his subcommittee that a basic RFC reorganization was needed, including a change of the top directors, Fulbright privately informed the White House of his thinking and preliminary findings in September, 1950. Truman ignored him. By December, while the press was clamoring for a subcommittee report, Fulbright again tried a private approach. He asked for an off-the-record meeting with Truman. On December 12, accompanied by

---

* The phrase is taken from a *Harper's* magazine article, "Fulbright: the Arkansas Paradox" by Charles B. Seib and Alan L. Otten, published June, 1956.

Senators Douglas and Charles Tobey of New Hampshire, a Republican, Fulbright went to the White House.

"We went in the back door," he would recall later, "and I thought this was big stuff. I think that was the first time I'd ever done it. We went in the southwest gate and saw no reporters or anybody. The President was very congenial and more or less made us feel that he appreciated our telling him about it, and about our recommendations."

The senators outlined their findings and asked the President to submit an RFC reorganization plan along the lines recommended in their report. That could be accomplished with little embarrassment, they said; it could then be announced as a move to strengthen the RFC administration. The meeting ended on a friendly note. The senators were pleased.

On December 28, Truman, without a prior hint to the senators, announced he was resubmitting the names of all the present RFC directors. Since Fulbright's subcommittee still had not issued its report, it came under criticism for suppressing the findings. Still, Fulbright held back. In early January, he called the White House to try and find out what other actions the President was going to take. The information was not forthcoming.

After much delay, the subcommittee report was released on February 2, 1951. It was titled, provocatively, "Favoritism and Influence," and laid bare a story of shocking revelations.

Truman responded in expected fashion—with bare knuckles. The report, he told reporters, "was asinine." "You know," he said, "I spent ten years in the Senate and I wrote a lot of reports, but I am happy to say I never wrote one like this." He stood firmly by the RFC and its directors, and personally accused Fulbright of ducking him—"he left town when he found out I wanted to see him."[12] It was not one of Harry Truman's better moments.

From Florida, where he was giving a long-scheduled speech, Fulbright replied:

"As to whether the report is asinine, I am willing to let the report speak for itself. According to the press dispatches, the President states that I left town when I found out he wanted to see me. I do not want to seem disrespectful to the President but this statement of the President is not true."

Later that month, the RFC hearings resumed to extensive press coverage. But Fulbright, despite further dramatic and damaging testimony to the RFC, announced that he hoped to wind up the hearings by the middle of March.

"This is a day when it might be expected that stars will shine at noon and rivers run uphill," the *Detroit News* commented editorially. "A United States Senator wants to retire from the headlines. It is also a day for the people to say 'no' and insist that Senator Fulbright, Arkansas Democrat with a nonpartisan moral sense, continue to explore the cesspools of government."[13]

In April, Truman capitulated. He submitted an RFC reorganization plan similar to one proposed by Fulbright's subcommittee. In time, it passed the Congress, and W. Stuart Symington of Missouri was appointed the new administrator. The Fulbright hearings ended quietly—amidst criticism that Fulbright had pulled his punches and failed to pursue the final end aggressively.

For Fulbright, the RFC was symptomatic of a more serious malaise—a cancer threatening the very fiber of democracy in the United States.

As the RFC hearings were concluding, the nation sat affixed before the enthralling and repelling televised spectacle of the big-time criminals testifying contemptuously—or refusing to testify at all—before the Kefauver crime committee in New York. Corruption and criminality seemed the hallmark of the times. Deep freezes and five percenters and Harry Vaughan became political slogans. In Kansas City, a hoodlum, Charlie Binaggio, was found murdered before a huge portrait of Harry Truman. In New York, the City College fans were dismayed to learn that their heroes, the brilliant national basketball champions, had been involved in taking bribes of up to $1500 to rig scores. Soon similar bribery cases were revealed at Long Island University, N.Y.U., Bradley University, the University of Kentucky. In the big cities, parents were concerned about their teen-agers and juvenile delinquency, and police were warning of the dangers of marijuana. As a capstone, an even greater scandal broke at West Point. Ninety cadets were dismissed for cheating on examinations, including the son of the football coach, an All-American quarterback, eight other students on the Army first team, and varsity members from most other sports.

"God help this country if we didn't play football," said the Army coach, Earl Blaik, in a choking voice at a New York press conference. ". . . General Eisenhower came to West Point with his greatest desire to play football."[14]

In the midst of such turmoil, and while his own subcommittee was completing its tasks, Fulbright rose on the floor of the Senate and delivered a searching speech on "the moral deterioration of American democracy."

"When confronted with an evil, we Americans are prone to say, 'There ought to be a law.' But the law does not and cannot apply effectively over wide fields of men's activities. It cannot reach those evils which are subtle and impalpable. . . . The law cannot prevent gossip. It cannot prevent men from bearing false witness against their neighbors. It cannot restrain a man from betraying his friends. In short, it cannot prevent much of the evil to which men are, unfortunately, too prone."

Then he asked his questions:

"What should be done about men who do not directly and blatantly sell the favors of their offices for money and so place themselves within the penalties of the law? How do we deal with those who, under the guise of friendship, accept favors which offend the spirit of the law but do not violate its letter? What of the men outside the government who suborn those inside it? . . . . Who is more at fault, the bribed or the bribers? The bribed have been false to their oaths and betrayers of their trust. But they are often relatively simple men—men of small fortune or no fortune at all—and they weaken before the temptations held out to them by the unscrupulous. Who are the bribers? They are often men who walk the earth lordly and secure; members of good families; respected figures in their communities; graduates of universities. They are, in short, the privileged minority, and I submit that it is not unreasonable to ask of them that high standard of conduct which their training ought to have engendered."

As far as he was concerned, the questions affected everything America stood for—where it had been and where it was going.

"I wonder whether in recent years we have unwittingly come to accept the totalitarian concept that the end justifies the means, a concept which is fundamentally and completely antagonistic to a true democratic society?" he asked. "Democracy is, I believe, more likely to be destroyed by the perversion of, or abandonment of, its true moral principles than by armed attack from Russia."

He recommended that Congress appoint a commission of eminent citizens to consider the problem of ethical conduct of public affairs. It would serve as a catalytic agent to draw forth meaning "from the mass of data revealed by the current investigations."

"In making this suggestion," he went on, "I am quite prepared to be dubbed naïve. It will not be the first time. As I look back on our history or upon my own experience, nearly every progressive or fruitful move has been considered naïve. To expect, or even hope, for an improvement in the moral climate of Washington is, in the eyes of the boys who know, I am sure, thoroughly utopian."

Aside from stimulating discussion in intellectual circles, Fulbright's suggestion came to naught. But his efforts had focused new attention on his own political future. Senator Paul Douglas said publicly he favored Fulbright as the Democratic choice for President, assuming Truman would not seek re-election at the 1952 convention in Chicago.[15] Sid McMath, the liberal governor of Arkansas and Truman's friend, was saying that Fulbright's candidacy was more serious than the routine "favorite son." "Anything can happen at Chicago and Fulbright's nomination is possible," the governor said.[16]

There never was a possibility, and Fulbright knew it. The Democratic professionals, from Truman down, would have nothing to do with him; he had lost their support forever by his RFC investigation and by his earlier critical comments, including the unforgivable suggestion in 1946 that Truman resign in favor of a Republican. For his own part, Fulbright was at best only a lukewarm political supporter of the President in 1952.*

Fulbright's name was placed in nomination in Chicago as Arkansas' favorite son in circumstances befitting the man. The senator had requested there be no demonstrations, no pins, pamphlets, or banners. After the speech nominating him, the delegation from Arkansas applauded for exactly two minutes.

Then Fulbright watched as his friend, Adlai E. Stevenson of Illinois was nominated.

Stevenson and Fulbright had known each other since the early New Deal days when both were young government lawyers, Stevenson for the Agricultural Adjustment Administration and Fulbright for the Justice Department. Intellectually and philosophically, they were much alike: they both had a gift of expression, both were keen students of politics, both were inclined to take the long view, and both were liberal in the broad sense of that word.

But they did have important differences. Fulbright, despite a common opinion of him as an idealistic, intellectual senator, was more the practical politician. He also was inclined to be more pragmatic generally. And, again contrary to wide impression, Fulbright could be as tough as the situation demanded. Stevenson, as Fulbright would say of him years later, "really was kindly, sort of a sweet character, you know."

Although there had been a time during Fulbright's most disenchanted period with Harry Truman when he, like many Democrats, had leaned toward Eisenhower as the Democratic nominee, despite his opposition to the principle of a professional military man in the White House (the return of MacArthur and the divisive debate it engendered reinforced his distrust of the military), the campaign changed his view.

"As a candidate for President, the general has fumbled and faltered every time he sought to go beyond the safe limits of campaign platitudes," he said. ". . . the general's awkwardness, I am convinced, reflected his deep uncertainty. He has moved into unfamiliar territory."[17]

---

* Yet at Truman's lowest point, when he removed General MacArthur from command in Korea on April 11, 1951, Fulbright had taken the floor of the Senate to deliver one of the strongest endorsements ever given the President during his administration. "I do not know what the verdict of history upon Mr. Truman will be," Fulbright said. "His contemporaries, such being the frailty of human nature, are more likely to exaggerate his faults than to enumerate his virtues, while he, as most men, has a full quota of both. I am not in his good graces. I have spoken with him only once in several years. This, however, does not blind me to the fact that he has made decisions on a number of occasions that equal in imagination, courage, and effectiveness any ever taken by an American President. Nearly all of these decisions are without precedent in our history." He cited such decisions as dropping the atomic bomb, aiding Greece and Turkey, the Marshall Plan, the North Atlantic Treaty, the Berlin airlift, sending troops to Europe in peacetime and later to Korea.

At the same time, it was quite clear that no matter how eloquent his speeches, Stevenson's campaign was going badly. In late September, Fulbright himself was brought into the Stevenson headquarters in Springfield, Illinois, to play a leading role as a strategist for the remainder of the campaign. Fulbright, in Springfield, was in some ways a lonely professional in a group of dedicated amateurs.

The Stevenson campaign was flagging on a number of fronts. Although many reporters were attracted to the governor, press relations were bad: texts of speeches invariably were late; good news photographs were missed or ignored; the candidate was seldom available. In addition, the absolutely essential political advance work was not functioning effectively.

Fulbright long since had mastered the art of political compromise, and by then he knew something about political organization. In Springfield, he took over as principal liaison man with the Democratic organizations across the country.

Within a day after he moved into the Executive Mansion, Fulbright, with Stevenson's approval, had dispatched telegrams over the governor's name to every national committeeman, committeewoman, state chairman, Democratic governors, and key congressional candidates asking their advice and assistance. Within a week, he had talked to more than 200 leading Democrats across the country, getting suggestions, trying to generate enthusiasm, plan future trips, and raise money. He urged Stevenson to consider bringing a top political leader to Springfield—recommending among others, Speaker Sam Rayburn and Senator Richard B. Russell of Georgia—to help with the regular party organization. He also dealt with Lyndon Johnson of Texas, in an attempt to keep the South Democratic.

But neither he nor the rest of the Springfield team—among them were Wilson Wyatt, Clayton Fritchey, William M. Blair, Philip Stern, and George Ball, later the Undersecretary of State—could alter the downward direction of the Stevenson effort. Probably nothing could have changed the final outcome, but Stevenson did make a number of serious political errors.

Truman, Fulbright, and others were critical of Stevenson's failure to coordinate and utilize the existing party organization in the major population centers. Stevenson thus alienated important political leaders and, as Truman remarked, "needlessly sacrificed basic political backing and perhaps millions of votes."[18]

Part of the problem lay within Stevenson himself. As Fulbright would recall:

"The Governor just ran everybody crazy, including me, over what we called his perfectionism. We thought he did as well impromptu, particularly on those short speeches about anything, but he insisted on having something prepared and he would work—well, he would work until three or four o'clock in the morning changing a word. And he was always late. The texts were never available. And the reason they weren't is he wanted to go over them and change a word. He rewrote or reworked no matter what it was."

In November, Adlai Stevenson carried only eight states, all of them in the South.

The Stevenson-Fulbright relationship continued to be close from then until Stevenson's death in the summer of 1965. They saw each other frequently, in good times and bad times for them both, and one day Fulbright would reminisce of Stevenson that:

"He was a curious fellow, you know. He was such an eloquent man on the stump and then, privately, when he was talking to you at lunch or something, he had such self-doubts. He always was haunted with the idea what a fool he was to have run in '52; that his timing was absolutely bad; that he should have stayed on as governor.

"With better timing, the whole thing might have been different. I don't know if he ever got over that. I think it created doubt in his mind as to his own judgment, because he used to consult me about things that people don't normally consult anybody about.

". . . Professionally, he was unhappy. I think it all goes back to 1952. We never know the alternatives, but I can imagine him thinking, 'Well, if I had stood my ground'—and I don't think he really wanted to run—'resisted the call, let them put up some nonentity to sacrifice, why then in '56, I again would judge whether to run or still have another term.'

"Then he would have been President. That's what I think he thought. And he probably was right because he had a great gift of eloquence."

On the final question of whether Stevenson would have been an effective President, Fulbright came to have serious doubts.

"I'm not sure what kind of President he would have made," the senator said. "I know his motives and his intentions would have been, in my view, right. Whether or not he would have been able to maneuver properly and manage this kind of lions' den, snake pit sort of situation we have here, I don't know. This is a pretty tough government. There are some pretty tough people in it—in all areas of it. Adlai was a gentleman. I don't know whether a gentleman can make this government really operate or not."

5

"SENATOR HALFBRIGHT"

*Governments, like clocks, go from the motion men
give them, and as governments are made and moved
by men, so by them they are ruined too.*

William Penn

IN THE SENATE, employing the art of compromise is often an act of wisdom.
The senator yields a point or extends a favor; he stands silent on a controversial issue, or quietly supports a measure with which he does not
agree; he often speaks in platitudes because they, too, are the safe course.
In time, his debts are repaid and he gains credit for actions that aid his
constituents, and maintain him in power.

While the public likes to think in terms of boldness and strength, of
profiles of courage and points of honor, the practical politician sees hero-
ism and duty in different perspective. His first task is to be elected. Eventually he hopes to accumulate enough power to influence events. He knows
that no matter how soaring his words, a rash speech often leads to disastrous political effects. After all, that ambitious young politician, Abra-
ham Lincoln, lost his seat in Congress after only one term because of his
importunate criticism of President Polk's handling of the Mexican War.

As a general rule, the longer the legislator serves in the Senate, the
more cautious he becomes. And the longer a man stays, the more he en-
joys the comforts and privileges of being a senator. His sense of survival
sharpens with years and teaches elemental lessons. Only the foolish or
the young stick their necks out.

Fulbright is no different from the ordinary senator. By nature, he does not seek a fight. His public disputes normally grow out of differences over policy questions. If they become personal, it is only through happenstance, for Fulbright nearly always tries to avoid a direct encounter.

Yet it is to his everlasting credit that in the midst of almost universal political timidity and a climate of fear unparalleled in American history he stood virtually alone among his colleagues and subjected himself to vicious personal abuse and the possible end of his senatorial career by opposing Joseph R. McCarthy.

The McCarthy era—or "McCarthyism," as Herbert Block (Herblock), the brilliant cartoonist and social commentator for the *Washington Post,* named it*—officially lasted from 1950 to 1954, but its corrosive after effects lingered over the country for more than a decade. At its peak, McCarthyism aroused fears and suspicions and created hatreds and bitterness that still have not been entirely quenched. For a time, it damaged almost beyond repair America's reputation as a fair and responsible democratic nation capable of exerting effective international leadership.

McCarthyism distracted America, nearly immobilized America. It destroyed confidence in America's institutions, its schools, churches, press, military forces, private and political leaders. It stifled debate and dissent; it came close to paralyzing America's ability to deal intelligently with the vital questions of the day. Its hallmarks were character assassination, guilt by association, and trial by publicity. Its techniques were the innuendo, the reckless charge, the big lie. Its targets were nothing less than the highest officials of the country. Its basic weapon was an all-encompassing and largely spurious threat of domestic Communism.

What is most remarkable—and most disturbing in retrospect—is how few public leaders spoke out on a menace that was poisoning democracy at home. In itself, the official silence helped to explain the strength of McCarthyism, for McCarthyism always stood for something far greater than the man for whom it was named.

By himself, Joe McCarthy, the freshman senator, was an unlikely candidate for the title of supreme demagogue. He was a poor speaker, given to outrageously inaccurate statements, a heavy drinker, and personally lacking in the grace and charm that usually lead to general public support. His bushy eyebrows, glowering looks, and slouching figure made a perfect foil for the caricaturist. He also had an unattractive habit of suddenly giggling or stammering, and, clearly, he was a bully who relished the role of publicly browbeating a weaker man—or woman. He was not subtle; he

* Herblock had sketched a Republican elephant being prodded, rather unwillingly, by G.O.P. Senate leaders toward a stack of buckets of tar. On the largest and highest bucket, he printed the letters McCARTHYISM.

was not even original. Indeed, he was not especially gifted in any way. But he was powerful.

McCarthy drew his support from fear—essentially, fear of Russia, Communism, and the bomb. In the early '50s, these fears were based on a solid enough foundation to give him wider backing than he would have received at any other time. An aggressive international Communism was a fact. The Korean War was a fact. Alger Hiss was a fact. Klaus Fuchs, the British atomic scientist who betrayed his country by giving secrets to Russia, was a fact. So were the Rosenbergs, Julius and Ethel, Morton Sobell, and Harry Gold—Americans all, who all stood convicted of conspiring with the Soviet Union.

But the threat of subversive Communism was not McCarthy's only source of strength. He capitalized on the decline in public morality, with the subsequent disgust and lack of confidence in the government and its leaders. By promising to clean out both the corrupted and the corruptors, McCarthy attracted the mid-twentieth century Puritans. Incongruous though it seemed at the time, it was entirely logical that the surface soil of Wisconsin that had produced the great progressives and liberals, the La Follettes, also produced McCarthy, the La Follettes' successor in the Senate.

In addition, McCarthy was assisted by an old and still powerful American tradition—of distrust of foreigners, Easterners, sophisticates, diplomats, the powerful, and government itself. McCarthy became the inheritor of the viewpoint of the modern Know-Nothings—of what Fulbright, in a speech at the height of the McCarthy era, would call the "swinish blight so common in our time—the blight of anti-intellectualism."[1]

Formidable and wide-ranging though his support was, McCarthy never would have achieved such prominence had he not received the encouragement of his own party, including the Republican leaders of the Senate. Their tacit approval, and even outright advocacy of his tactics, was a shabby chapter in the history of the Republican Party. In part, their backing grew out of extreme frustration and political impotence: the Democrats had been in power for nearly a generation, and then, when the Republican chances of recapturing the White House seemed greatest, the G.O.P. had been defeated in stunning fashion by Truman in 1948. Dispirited and disillusioned, as well as deeply convinced that the Democrats were bringing ruin to the country, the Republicans struck back bitterly. McCarthy became one of their vehicles.

In fact, the speech that launched the McCarthy era—before the Women's Republican Club of Wheeling, West Virginia, on February 9, 1950—had been assigned to the Wisconsin senator by the Senate Republican Campaign Committee. McCarthy's assigned topic was "Communism in the State Department." He more than lived up to his billing. From that first day, when he charged that the State Department was "thoroughly infested with Communists" and waved a list that he claimed contained the names of 205 known Communists then shaping the department's policy, he proceeded to even more sensational accusations.[2] The charges made the headlines; the denials were lost in the resulting sound and fury.

McCarthy was not the only man to raise the cry of treason in high places. In 1950, in the aftermath of Alger Hiss' conviction, Congressman (and soon to be senator) Richard M. Nixon lashed out at those who "permit the enemy to guide and shape our policy," and went on to warn darkly that "traitors in the high councils of our own government make sure that the deck is stacked on the Soviet side of the diplomatic table."[3]

And in the Senate, the most distinguished of Republicans, Robert A. Taft of Ohio, was being quoted as saying "McCarthy should keep talking and if one case doesn't work out he should proceed with another." Taft also said: "Whether Senator McCarthy has legal evidence, whether he has overstated or understated his case, is of lesser importance. The question is whether the Communist influence in the State Department still exists."[*]

As McCarthy and McCarthyism began to permeate the American consciousness, few men in public life dared to confront the Wisconsin senator, including leading Democrats in Washington. Fulbright was one who did. Their encounters became increasingly vitriolic. For his part, McCarthy, then at the peak of his power, was contemptuous and insulting. Fulbright, he would say with a sneer, was misnamed. He dubbed him "Senator Halfbright," or just plain "Halfbright," an expression he repeated at every chance. Fulbright was not intimidated. Time and again, he spoke out about the McCarthy menace. In doing so, he laid himself open to an obloquy that increased in venom, and from which he would never be entirely free. From that time on, Fulbright became a special target of the extremists. For a man who tried to shun conflict, he had thrust himself into the center of the ring.

Fulbright's first impression of McCarthy had been unfavorable. While he was presiding over the RFC subcommittee investigations, the inquiry had turned briefly to certain activities involving the Lustron Corp., which was financed with government money. It turned out that McCarthy had accepted $10,000 from Lustron for compiling a pamphlet on housing. It was a clear case of conflict of interest, because McCarthy then was a member of the Banking and Currency Committee, the body that had over-all jurisdiction over the affairs of Lustron. Fulbright had been shocked; it made him believe, as he remarked later, that McCarthy "was a boodler." Noth-

* Long after McCarthyism had become only an ugly epithet, with both Taft and McCarthy dead, Fulbright would say: "I think it was one of the most cynical things Bob [Taft] ever did. I think he did it because he thought he was destroying the Democrats. . . . I think the election in '48 was such a bitter disappointment that it created a background that made McCarthyism possible."

ing, however, came of the incident at that time. The senator had not violated the law, and he, directly, was not the subject of the investigation.[4]

The next encounter, in October of 1951, was more serious. It involved Truman's nomination of Philip C. Jessup to be a U.S. delegate to the United Nations.

Jessup was a distinguished professor of international law at Columbia University who earlier had served with honor at the American delegation to the U.N. and still later as Ambassador-at-Large and roving personal negotiator for the Secretary of State. He had represented the U.S. at a number of major conferences, including stormy confrontations with the Russians. But McCarthy singled out Jessup as one of the cardinal examples of Communists in government. Jessup, McCarthy had charged publicly, had "an unusual affinity for Communist cases."[5] The senator failed to document his charges.

Truman's nomination routinely went to the Senate Foreign Relations Committee, where Tom Connally, the chairman, appointed a five-man subcommittee for the hearings. Fulbright, then a junior member of the committee, having been first appointed in 1949, was named to the subcommittee. (In controversial and potentially damaging matters politically, it was common practice to assign junior members to bear the heat and take the responsibility for making what might become unpopular decisions.)

McCarthy himself asked to testify against Jessup's nomination. On October 1, as the hearing began, McCarthy showed up as the first witness. He brought with him a series of documents, which he had prepared to discredit Jessup. They had been placed inside small folders. With a flourish, McCarthy distributed folders to each senator. The folders had been carefully tinted a lively pink color, denoting McCarthy's assessment of Jessup's political leanings.

"This was the first time I realized that there was just no limit to what he'd say and insinuate," Fulbright would say. "As the hearings proceeded, it suddenly occurred to me that this fellow would do anything to deceive you to get his way. I was deeply repulsed, repelled, offended by his conduct in those hearings."

From the first moment, Fulbright and McCarthy tangled sharply. At one point, after pressing McCarthy for specific proof of his charges, Fulbright interrupted tartly to say: "You shift your position every time." During another exchange that day, McCarthy said: "Men of little minds are trying to make this a political issue." With heavy sarcasm, Fulbright replied: "You wouldn't try to do anything like that, would you?"

The hearings soon developed into acrimonious encounters marked by shouts, pounding of gavels, and bitter exchanges between Fulbright and McCarthy. When McCarthy attempted to tarnish Jessup by listing various organizations he or his wife had joined, Fulbright asked McCarthy: "Don't you think it's hard on a man to hold him responsible for all the organizations his wife may have joined?" Then he asked whether McCarthy considered him to be a subversive because Mrs. Fulbright had joined the Red Cross during the time it was headed by General George C. Marshall, "that well-known subversive and conspirator, according to your presentation?"

McCarthy sneered and made no reply.

Even though his documentation failed to substantiate in any particular his charges, McCarthy was winning his fight.

On October 19, 1951, the subcommittee, by three to two, voted against Jessup's nomination. The three Republicans—Owen Brewster of Maine, H. Alexander Smith of New Jersey, and Guy Gillette of Iowa—voted against him. Fulbright and Sparkman were for him.

"This is a great day for America and a bad day for the Communists," McCarthy told reporters.[6]

The subcommittee action was a demonstration that McCarthy's power was growing. With another presidential election year approaching, there appeared to be no limit to his disruptive influence. And the campaign itself, with Eisenhower declining to be drawn into the controversy and Nixon talking of Communists in government and pledging to fight "until we drive the crooks and the Communists and those that defend them out of Washington,"[7] added still more muscle to Joseph R. McCarthy.

As the Republicans swept the country, regaining control of the Congress and the White House, McCarthy became the new chairman of the Government Operations Committee in January, 1953. Immediately, as the head of this permanent Investigating Subcommittee, he launched an investigation of Communists in government that earned him a lasting place in American history. Soon he, his young chief counsel, Roy M. Cohn, and a wealthy young dilettante, G. David Schine, who claimed to have expert knowledge of Communist subversion, were making headlines throughout the world. Their first target was the International Information Administration, then a part of the State Department but scheduled soon to become a separate agency, the U. S. Information Agency.

That attack particularly struck home to Fulbright, for at that time the IIA included educational exchange programs. The Fulbright Fellowship program, the senator's most cherished endeavor, was in danger.

Fulbright did not confine himself to criticizing McCarthyism from within the sanctuary of the Senate. In speeches and television appearances, he attempted to raise a general alarm. An address at Dickinson College, in Carlisle, Pennsylvania, on February 24, 1953, was typical.

"If I were a genuine Communist agency," he said, "I can think of no more effective way to injure this country than the promiscuous accusation of good Americans. Last year I expected the more violent attacks upon our government, because it was an election year. Now, however, the election is over and it is high time we begin to settle our differences and try to pull together. . . . [But] instead of rebuilding the Department of State, they continue to tear it down."

He warned that if "the present trial by headline" and the spectacular attacks upon the State Department and the schools continued they could lead toward "the very thing we are fighting—the police state." In other speeches, he was even more foreboding: ". . . Something ominous has happened to our community. A bitterness, a suspicion, a kind of primitive ruthlessness quite alien to our traditions, has taken root and is spreading."[8]

His remarks set the stage for a personal encounter with McCarthy that summer enacted before the television cameras in the old Supreme Court chamber in the Capitol—the same chamber where, before the Civil War, the Senate had listened to the debates of Webster and Hayne, Clay and Calhoun.

The Senate Appropriations Committee, of which McCarthy was a member, had scheduled a hearing on the annual appropriation for McCarthy's target, the IIA. At stake, thus, was the future of the Fulbright Fellowship program, for the exchange funds were included among the IIA appropriation requests. It was a situation made to order for McCarthy.

The hearing came at a time when public attention had been drawn recently to Fulbright's close connection with student exchanges: Only a month before, he had been among six men honored at Oxford during the fiftieth anniversary ceremonies of the Rhodes Scholarships.

When Fulbright appeared to testify in the afternoon of July 24, McCarthy displayed his customary tactics. He was loud, abusive, tried to interrupt the proceedings again and again, called Fulbright "Halfbright," and at one remarkable point, even though he was not the chairman, he grabbed the gavel as if to take over the committee anyway.

Fulbright maintained his poise and gave a strong endorsement of the program. It was McCarthy who became rattled.[9]

After McCarthy made a series of attempts to break into Fulbright's prepared remarks, Fulbright replied:

"Mr. Chairman, I do not know what the procedure in this committee is. I would be perfectly willing to answer questions from all the members except . . . the senator from Wisconsin, who I am clear is determined to destroy my testimony. I will answer his questions after I am through."

McCarthy broke in: "Mr. Chairman, may I ask this witness—"

"Go ahead," said the chairman, Homer Ferguson of Michigan.

"May I say this to the chair," McCarthy continued, "that he allow this witness to do that with the understanding that I have to go to the Senate floor for a short period of time on a bill involving the Menominee Indian claims. I do not want the witness to disappear while I am gone. He is reluctant to answer questions."

Both senators and spectators appeared astounded at McCarthy's effrontery. Although Fulbright laughed, Ferguson was angered. Turning toward McCarthy, the chairman said sharply: "Mr. McCarthy . . . there is no justification for saying the witness might disappear."

McCarthy's voice rang out in the chamber: "Mr. Chairman . . . Mr. Chairman . . . Mr. Chairman." But McCarthy did not gain control of the moment.

Later, McCarthy's questioning turned to loyalty and security checks, with the implication that Fulbright Fellows were subversive, or worse.

The line of questioning was revealing:

McCarthy: One other question, Senator. Do you know whether the board that selected the students receives a security check?

Fulbright: It does.

McCarthy: Not what you heard. Do you know of your own knowledge?

Fulbright: I have not made the check myself, but on the best authority I know of, it does.

Then, minutes later:

McCarthy: You say they get State Department security clearance?

Fulbright: It is my understanding they also are checked by the FBI—that is, the members of the Board of Foreign Scholarships [which administered the program]. There are just ten of them.

McCarthy: Do you know whether the policy is not to give Communists or Communist sympathizers scholarships or appoint them as lecturers or professors?

Fulbright: I think one of the leading members of the board is Dean McGuire of Catholic University here, who is an original member.

McCarthy: Can you answer the question?

Fulbright: I cannot believe that he is interested in giving Communists scholarships. Another is Colonel Anderson of the Veterans Department . . .

McCarthy: Could you answer the question?

Fulbright: [continuing] . . . who has been on it since the beginning, and I do not believe he is interested in doing it.

McCarthy tried again:

McCarthy: Could you answer the question?

Fulbright: It is an answer. They do not in my opinion for a moment countenance giving scholarships to Communists if they know it.

At still another point, McCarthy tried to deprecate the board's integrity and independence. "I ask you these questions," McCarthy said to Fulbright, "because the program bearing your name—and I assume the board pays some attention to what you say—"

This time it was Fulbright who interrupted.

"Your assumption is entirely incorrect. The board does not pay any attention to what I say. I do not tell the board what to do and I would not think of telling the board about anything. It would be the best way I know of to destroy it."

McCarthy made one last attempt to discredit the program. He said he wanted to insert into the record statements made by some Fulbright students "condemning the American way of life and praising the Communist form of government."

Fulbright quickly countered. If McCarthy was permitted to do that, he said, he also should be allowed to insert "other kinds of statements that have been received." As he made clear, he had come prepared to submit thousands of names and many statements by and about former Fulbright Fellows. When Chairman Ferguson ruled that "if we receive one, we will receive the other," McCarthy dropped his line of attack. He never again attacked the exchange program.

In the opinion of Walter Johnson, the historian, and Francis J. Colligan, a high official of the State Department, both of whom had served in administrative roles for the exchange program:

"Senator Fulbright's counteroffensive [in the hearing] represented the first successful resistance to McCarthy within the government since his premier appearance on the national scene in 1950."[10]

Within six months, Fulbright faced another major decision involving McCarthy. Early in 1954, the question of whether to appropriate more money for McCarthy's Permanent Investigations Subcommittee came to the floor of the Senate for a vote.

McCarthy was regarded as nearly impregnable. By then, he had created fear even within the confines of the Senate. In the beginning, many senators had been inclined to believe the old adage that where there is smoke there had to be some fire; that no senator could be foolish or reckless enough to make wholly unfounded charges; that he *had* to have *something* to his case. But as McCarthy's power increased, and the country seethed with discord and suspicion, the question became more practical: to cross McCarthy was to lay oneself open to charges of being soft on Communism, to being destroyed personally and politically. For by early 1954, when McCarthy was at the pinnacle of his power, the political evidence was unmistakable: McCarthy was no ordinary opponent. In 1952, he had been re-elected to his second term by 140,000 votes. No less than eight senators owed their seats to his efforts on their behalf. Those who had dared to counter him—such as William Benton of Connecticut and Millard Tydings of Maryland—had gone down in defeat. Even President Eisenhower withheld commenting on McCarthy's ever bolder assaults (although privately he could not stomach the senator).

In that context, the Senate deliberated over continuing support for McCarthy. In the single most courageous act of his career, Fulbright voted "nay." He was the only senator to oppose McCarthy.[11]

The immediate reaction of his colleagues, as he would recall, was that

"I was a very foolish young fellow who's not going to be around here very long." One senator told him he had just made a "very improvident" act. A day or two after the vote, Herbert Lehman, the distinguished senator from New York, came to Fulbright's office. Lehman said he admired Fulbright's action, and wanted him to know that he was sorry he had not voted with him. It had been a lapse; it would not happen again.

Privately, others felt the same way. While his colleagues were searching their souls, Fulbright was receiving a torrent of insulting mail, both from Arkansas and throughout the country. He was accused of being a Communist, a fellow traveler, an atheist, a man beneath contempt. The reaction was symptomatic of the prevailing national mood of hysteria. Although it seemed then as if there was no way to stop McCarthy and McCarthyism, McCarthy had already begun the process of self-destruction. Before the year was out, he had been discredited and finally censured by his colleagues in the Senate. One of the leaders of that censure movement was "Halfbright" of Arkansas.

The McCarthy censure on December 1, 1954, was the final seal on the era. The vote itself was an anticlimax: the tide had obviously turned against McCarthy long before. Sixty-seven senators voted to condemn McCarthy's conduct; twenty-two stood by him. Of the seven who did not vote, only two never announced how they stood. One was Alexander Wiley, McCarthy's Republican colleague from Wisconsin. The other was John Fitzgerald Kennedy of Massachusetts.*

More than any other factor, McCarthy himself was responsible for his own decline. He had gone too far; he had been too reckless; he had offended too many. Where he had survived with his cries of twenty years of treason under the Democrats, he began to disintegrate when he started speaking, after Eisenhower was inaugurated, of twenty-one years of treason. Now, it was a Republican State Department, a Republican President, a Republican government that he was attacking. At this point he made his greatest blunder. He assaulted the Army, bullied a hero, and outraged the elite West Point officer corps.

Finally, the country itself saw what McCarthyism meant. For thirty-six days, from April 22 to June 16, 1954, millions of Americans watched McCarthy in action through 188 hours of exposure during the televised Army-McCarthy hearings. Those were days without parallel in contempo-

* At the peak of the McCarthy period Kennedy indicated to Arthur M. Schlesinger, Jr., that, although he disliked McCarthy's techniques, "he showed no interest in saying so publicly." Schlesinger quotes Kennedy as saying then: "Hell, half my voters in Massachusetts look on McCarthy as a hero." Schlesinger also says, in *A Thousand Days,* that Kennedy had prepared a speech in August, 1954, explaining that he would vote for McCarthy's censure, but when the vote finally occurred he was awaiting his critical back operation in a hospital. Still, he never publicly announced his stand. The Schlesinger citations are found on pages 12–13 of his Kennedy history.

rary American life. Out of two million words of testimony, one moment stood out. It came when the gentle Boston lawyer, Joseph N. Welch, with tears in his eyes, spoke up in defense of the honor of a young law assistant whom McCarthy had viciously attacked:

"Until this moment, Senator, I think I never really gauged your cruelty or your recklessness. . . . Let us not assassinate this lad further, Senator. You've done enough. Have you no sense of decency, sir, at long last? Have you left no sense of decency?"[12]

For all practical purposes, Joe McCarthy was finished as a political power at that moment. The Senate merely made it official. Still, the Senate action was essential, not only to uphold its dignity and reputation, but to show that responsible American leaders officially disapproved and disassociated themselves from everything McCarthy represented. Getting the Senate to act in unison on any question was difficult; on McCarthy, for a time, it seemed impossible.

Fulbright's role in the censure was vital. Senator Ralph Flanders of Vermont, who had introduced the censure resolution, readily conceded later that "I could not have accomplished censure"[13] without Fulbright's support.

The censure movement grew out of the aftermath of the Army-McCarthy hearings. Because McCarthy had alienated so many important Republicans, Fulbright thought the timing was right for Senate action against him. Recognizing that it would be best for a member of McCarthy's own party to take the lead, he approached Flanders, a Republican, and helped him prepare his resolution. Fulbright himself did the bulk of the research on the historical and legal precedents for a censure action. He also carried out the delicate negotiations with the Democratic leadership, and with key individual senators. He met privately with, among others, Carl Hayden of Arizona, Richard Russell of Georgia, Lyndon Johnson of Texas, and frequently with Flanders.

Fulbright was employing the same methods he had used in gaining passage of his peace resolution of 1943 and his fellowship act three years later. He asked for guidance and solicited advice; he showed various drafts and proposals for possible forms of action; he listened to criticism. What he wanted was agreement on the most effective approach. Only one thing really mattered: that the Senate condemn McCarthy.

Most senators with whom he spoke agreed that the censure approach was the best. Stripped of its verbiage, it said simply that McCarthy had brought discredit on the Senate. Mild though it was, nevertheless, it remained difficult to enlist senatorial support. Senators, as Fulbright would recall, "were very touchy about any public talk."

When the debate on Flanders' censure resolution began in July, it quickly became apparent that many senators on both sides of the aisle were trying to avoid a vote on the resolution. Some, such as Everett Dirksen of Illinois, boldly defended McCarthy. "Thou shalt not follow a multitude to do evil," Dirksen said, after pointing out that the Communist Party, the *Daily Worker,* and a host of liberal groups favored censuring McCarthy.

The resolution seemed too general for Senate support. On August 1, Fulbright then amended it with a bill of particulars charging McCarthy with specific acts of misconduct.

In the ensuing debate, McCarthy demonstrated his greatest skill—of raw intimidation.

After Ralph Flanders had read a long list of thirty-three charges against him, McCarthy rose.

"We have a number of senators—Flanders, Cooper, Lehman, Morse, Monroney, Hennings, and 'Halfbright'—who made charges on the Senate floor which [sic] were not under oath. This resolution will not allow the committee to subpoena those senators. . . . Those who have made the scurrilous, false charges on the floor should not object to being subpoenaed."

McCarthy demanded not only that they be subpoenaed but that he be given the right to cross-examine them.

"I assure the American people that the senators who have made the charges will either indict themselves for perjury, or will prove what consummate liars they are, by showing the difference between their statements on the floor of the Senate and their testimony in the hearing," McCarthy said.

By calling out the senators' names, one by one, McCarthy forced them to say they would submit to his cross-examination. When the list had dropped to two, Fulbright took the floor.

"Mr. President," he said, "we have already had a very slight example of what we can expect. I think the junior senator from Wisconsin is a great genius. He has the most extraordinary talent for disrupting and causing confusion in any orderly process of any body of men that I have ever seen. . . . I am interested in that kind of character as a psychological study. But I think it is doing incalculable harm to the work of the Senate. I know it has already done tremendous harm to the relations of the United States with all the rest of the world, because the people of the other countries think we have lost our minds if we are willing to follow such a leader."[14]

Eventually a select committee of the Senate, headed by Arthur V. Watkins of Utah, a Republican, after rigorous hearings, recommended censuring McCarthy. When the final debate began at the end of November, Fulbright again took the floor.

From August to November he had received literally thousands of hate letters. Some were profane, some illiterate, some vile. As Fulbright told the Senate, they were examples of McCarthyism. "By his reckless charges

[McCarthy] has so preyed upon the fears and hatred of uninformed and credulous people that he has started a prairie fire, which neither he nor anyone else may be able to control. If there are ten million people in this country similar to the authors of these letters, I believe it is something about which all of us ought to be deeply concerned."

He read some of the milder ones that day.

From the president of an oil company in Texas: "we have asked Mr. McCarthy to help get you in insane asylum. . . ." From Philadelphia: "you are one of the phony pinko punks." From Buffalo: "You refused to vote one dollar to the McCarthy committee. A fine dirty red rat are you." From a postcard: "Tie hyena Morse and jackal Lehman around your foul coyote neck and jump into the Potomac." From Brooklyn, New York: "You dirty, low-down, evil-minded traitor. . . ."

They evidenced, as Fulbright said, "a great sickness among our people, and that sickness has been greatly enhanced and increased during the course of the past year." He hoped that censuring McCarthy might help to put a stop to "the reckless incitement of the hatreds and fears of people who are suffering from a lack of information or a lack of understanding."

Joe McCarthy died on May 2, 1957. The doctors said he died of acute hepatic failure; it was well known that he had been drinking extremely heavily. In some respects, he became a pathetic figure in his last days. Ignored by his Senate colleagues and by the press, he already was regarded as something of an anachronism, a musty footnote to a troubled era. Even worse for one who flourished under bright lights, publicity, and the attention of the crowds, he was not being recognized by the public.

During the Christmas holidays before his death, and not long before he entered the hospital, McCarthy got in an elevator in the Senate with Fulbright's assistant, Lee Williams. Williams was accompanied by his wife and some of Fulbright's Arkansas constituents. McCarthy, who was carrying an armful of Christmas presents, seemed lonely and eager to talk. "I'm Joe McCarthy," he said to those who had never met him. The presents, he explained, were for his wife and newly adopted daughter. He was going to mail them that day to where they were staying in Arizona. As he talked, he put the presents down on the floor. Then he reached inside his overcoat to a suit pocket and took out a large oval picture in a gold frame. It was a photograph of his daughter. McCarthy was still showing it around when the Arkansans got off the elevator. The doors closed and McCarthy rode on alone.

His sudden death while still in his forties, and a certain feeling of pity for his long fall from the pinnacle, prompted people to say in later years in Washington that Joe McCarthy hadn't been such a bad fellow after all; that despite all his bluster, he was gregarious and friendly; that, no matter what his offenses, his intentions were good.

Fulbright never changed his own views. He would never think of McCarthy in any kindly light. In the closing hours of the censure debate, he had described McCarthy as "having the greatest contempt for the human personality of anyone I have ever seen"; years later, in recalling him, he would say he was "a very ugly fellow. . . . I never saw him exhibit any humor, particularly about himself."

Whatever McCarthy's own personal qualities, McCarthyism, in one form or another, outlived the man to further pollute the democratic process. From the very beginning of the menace, Fulbright had served splendidly. It was easy to forget, later, who had been brave and who had been timid in the Senate—in a Senate that then contained two future presidents and two vice presidents of the United States.*

---

* Lyndon B. Johnson, John F. Kennedy, Hubert H. Humphrey, and Richard M. Nixon.

6

"OH, NO, SENATOR, NOT YOU!"

LIKE EVERY SOUTHERN POLITICIAN, Fulbright is a captive of his region. The South's prejudices and unrealized potential have caused him anguish; they also have deeply affected his political career. The civil rights question has been a crucial thread in his political life, and, in time, has diminished his stature nationally, lessened his influence, and cost him an opportunity to serve as Secretary of State. It has caused some of his earliest admirers to regard him as a tragic figure. As Reinhold Niebuhr once said, patronizingly, "Many of us are inclined both to pity and to admire Senator Fulbright rather than castigate him."[1]

With Fulbright, as with many talented Southerners, the dilemma represents more than a question of personal philosophy. It is a trap from which there seems no escape. He is no bigot, no racist. Neither is he a liberal—nor a conservative. For him, those terms are meaningless. In the shrewdest analysis ever given of him, Fulbright was aptly placed as a twentieth-century Whig.[2] As his years in Washington lengthened, the civil rights question became increasingly a personal burden, until one day a very high government official who has known him intimately for years would say privately:

"Bill's always been intensely uneasy about civil rights. He's always considered it vital to stick by the Southerners, that it would be an act of betrayal to do otherwise. But it's torn him to pieces in the process."[3]

History may not always offer a choice, but there are times when a wiser course is clear. For Fulbright, such a moment came in 1956 not long after his encounters with McCarthy. It provided him an opportunity to break away from the common pattern. Some would say it gave him a chance for greatness.

On Monday, March 12, 1956, nineteen senators and seventy-seven congressmen, all from the eleven states of the old Confederacy, joined in attacking the Supreme Court of the United States. Their "Southern Manifesto" bristled with angry words. The Supreme Court, they said, had substituted "naked power for established law," had abused its judicial power, had created chaos and confusion, and had planted racial hatred and suspicion where there had been friendship and understanding. They pledged to resist integration. Although they added the qualifying phrase "by any lawful means," their statement was taken as a call to arms.

Their action lent official endorsement to the words of the demagogues then being heard across the South. At a time when Negroes were beginning their own move toward freedom in the Deep South and white citizens' councils were rising in opposition to them, the South's political leaders had failed dismally in allaying tensions and burying the hatreds of a bitter past. By advocating defiance instead of accommodation they made conflict inevitable and gave impetus to an accelerating racial revolution in America.

The names of only three senators normally associated with the Southern bloc were missing from the Manifesto: Albert Gore and Estes Kefauver, both from the border state of Tennessee, and Lyndon Johnson of Texas. Gore and Kefauver had refused to sign as a matter of principle. Because of his important political position as Majority Leader, Johnson had not been asked to sign at all, and neither had his Texas counterpart, Speaker Sam Rayburn.

Of all those who did sign, no one's name caused more dismay than Fulbright's.

As soon as news of the Manifesto was announced, Fulbright began receiving an extraordinary response from all over the world. Students, teachers, ministers, rabbis, college presidents, Rhodes Scholars, Fulbright Fellows, bankers, housewives, and an unusually large number of Southerners dispatched long and searching letters. These were not the normal letters a politician receives in an emotional moment—pejorative, demanding, or insulting. They were thoughtful, often eloquent, and generally written in a tone of disbelief. With more literary polish but no less emotion, they reflected the words of the tearful boy who saw his hero, Shoeless Joe Jackson, after the "Black Sox" baseball scandal: "Say it ain't so, Joe."

Fulbright's correspondents could not understand how the author of a celebrated exchange program, a humanitarian, a man who had stood alone against McCarthy, could have, as one wrote, "repudiated your earlier splendid work."

"You might wonder that I am aggrieved by you in particular," another said. "The answer is that it is natural to single out certain leaders in any field, to follow their careers, to admire and be grateful for them. This was my attitude toward you. And, reasonable or not, I feel hurt."

A native of Selma, Alabama, spoke for many in the South:

"I do not think I can describe to you adequately the sickening shock I felt on the morning I heard the newscast of the Southern Manifesto, and learned that you were one of the signers. . . . When men of your calibre, education, intelligence—nationally and internationally known and re-spected—issue such statements in disregard of American principles and ideals, to whom can we of the South turn for responsible and morally sound leadership?"

The common reaction came from a woman in Kansas who began, "Oh, no, Senator Fulbright, not you, oh please no, not you!" and went on to write:

"If, in this little Kansas town of less than ten thousand people, eight people today have said to me, 'Can you believe that Senator Fulbright signed that thing?' with such amazed disappointment in their voices, what will the people of the world ask when they see your name?

"Forgive me, Senator. I have no right to rebuke you, but I am so sorry!"

Race was not the only tie that held together the Southerners in Congress. They were bound by history, economics, traditions, and, most important, by reasons of self-interest. Standing shoulder to shoulder, they controlled the Congress. With one-fourth of the members of Congress in their bloc, they exercised the balance of power. By swinging with the Republican minority, they could defeat any President on any issue. Through seniority and their one-party status, they held the key committee chairmanships, and thus controlled the legislation. What the Confederate legions had failed to accomplish in war, they had achieved in peace: They ruled Washington.

Unanimity was the key to their strength. If the alliance cracked, their power was gone. Their leaders made certain there were few defectors. If a Southerner didn't go along with his group, he became an outcast. When he needed the votes for a bill important to him, his colleagues held the power of political life or death over him. It made true independence a rare, and often foolhardy, act. The result was a continual process of legis-lative backscratching: Vote for me, and I will vote for you. That was the system; and for the Southerners, the system worked with superb success.

By virtue of their more exalted position and longer tenure, the Southern-ers in the Senate formed the most exclusive club of all, a club that met regularly, dispensed favors and plaudits, and planned new forays.

Their undisputed leader was the aloof patrician bachelor, Richard B. Russell of Georgia, the best parliamentarian and potentially one of the foremost statesmen of the country. Harry Truman thought Russell might well have been President if he had been able to escape the Southern trap.[4] But as the years passed, Russell became ever more involved with the civil rights issue, until there were those who felt he was obsessed by it.

Second in power and influence among the Southerners was Harry Flood Byrd of Virginia, the fatherly clan leader who gave the small parties to celebrate a victory and further strengthen Southern solidarity. He praised the faithful, and icily turned on the occasional dissenters. There were few mavericks.

Thus, after a successful filibuster in 1949, Byrd would write a "My dear Bill" letter to Fulbright saying:

> "My purpose in writing you is to say how much I have enjoyed being associated with you in this fight. I shall always recall this as one of the finest experiences in my career. The more I come in contact with representatives of the South, the closer I feel to them."[5]

Then he added in a sly underlined note of disapproval: *"with one or two exceptions."*

Throughout the 1940s and early 1950s the Southerners stood together, increased their strength, beat back occasional attacks, and showered economic benefits on their region. But by the middle of the decade the situation was rapidly changing.

The Supreme Court school desegregation decision of May 17, 1954, had struck at one of the cornerstones of segregation—but it was only one part of the attack. Despite all the public talk of "outside agitators" fomenting racial strife, it was apparent to any observant Southerner that Negroes —Southern Negroes—were stirring in most unlikely and disturbing ways.

In 1955, in Montgomery, Alabama, the old capital of the Confederacy, a Negro woman named Rosa Parks had been arrested when she refused to move to the back of the bus. When Negro ministers there met to discuss what action to take, and the discussion bogged down in generalities, one man asked, "Am I to tell our people that you are cowards?" From the crowd came the raised arm of a young man in his twenties. He was signalling that he was not afraid. His name was Martin Luther King, Jr., and his church stood only a stone's throw from the steps of the Capitol where Jefferson Davis had taken his oath of office. Before that meeting of ministers had ended, King had been nominated, seconded, and elected president of something called the Montgomery Improvement Association. On December 5, 1955, King led 42,000 Montgomery Negroes in what was to become a successful year-long boycott of the city's buses and the beginning of a movement that would alter the face of America.[6]

Early in 1956, the Southerners on Capitol Hill began meeting continuously in private. Once again, Russell led them.

Those were stormy meetings. Tempers and passions had been aroused. Now the issue was not economics, or even politics; it was emotional. Already, mob violence had stained the South when the Negro, Autherine Lucy, had tried to enter the University of Alabama.

And from Oxford, Mississippi, had come a long, impassioned open letter to the people of the Northern States. William Faulkner, writing of his belief that discrimination was immoral, nevertheless warned the North to stop, go slow, delay, or else reap the consequences of disorder.[7]

Aside from their own personal feelings, the Southerners were being pushed by extremists at home to stand up for Dixie, to show the North that white Southerners would not be intimidated. The pressure to conform was immense.

A case in point was Georgia. There, the former governor, Herman Talmadge, the son of "Ole Gene," the suspenders snapper, was running hard for the Senate against Walter George, the chairman of the Foreign Relations Committee. Talmadge was advocating all-out measures against desegregation. George, a moderate, was in danger.*

The subject of "saving Walter George" came up often at those Southern strategy meetings in Washington. It was deemed important for all the senators to join in some form of declaration that would safeguard their political positions at home. In addition, many of the Southerners felt inflamed themselves.

Out of those meetings came a number of suggested drafts for signing. The early ones incorporated the old doctrine of nullification, of resistance at any price, by any means—in or out of the law.

At one of the meetings where such a document came up for discussion two men flatly opposed it. One was Price Daniel, later the governor of Texas. The other was Fulbright.

Fulbright had strong feelings about the question. Although he was willing to go along with a general statement deploring threats to use the federal government's police powers, the usurpation of the role of the states, and the belief that the Supreme Court decision had created grave problems in the South, he refused to subscribe to any statement that would countenance illegal action. The Supreme Court ruling was the law; the only way to oppose it would be through legal means.

The issue became so central that at one point he was planning to go against his colleagues in public. He prepared a draft explaining why he could not conscientiously subscribe to the Manifesto as then written. It was a splendid statement—but one which he never made public.

"I fear the statement [Manifesto] will not appeal to the good sense, understanding and, indeed, compassion of non-Southerners—with whom

---

* He subsequently withdrew from the race and was appointed an Ambassador to NATO by Eisenhower.

we have lived in relative peace since Reconstruction days," the draft had said. ". . . I fear the statement holds out the false illusion to our own Southern people that there is some means by which we can overturn the Supreme Court's decision. Our duty to our people in their hour of travail is one of candor and realism. It is not realistic to say that a decision of the Supreme Court is 'illegal and unconstitutional,' and to imply, thereby, that it can be overturned by some higher tribunal.

". . . There also appear in the statement expressions which I fear may be interpreted as approving or encouraging actions which certain states have taken to avoid the impact of the decision, and assurances that we shall support such measures. I do not wish to be in the position of giving any such blanket endorsement and commitment, particularly since my own state has taken no such action."

Finally, he said, addressing himself to his fellow Southerners:

"It is a false assumption that the nation will support us in defiance or castigation of the Supreme Court.

"In the end this problem will be solved by the good will, tolerance, understanding, and moderation of all the people—North and South.

"I fear the statement will give aid and comfort to agitators and trouble-makers within and without the South."[8]

With both Fulbright and Daniel in opposition, the Southern bloc agreed to moderate the harsher statements. As always, it was a question of politics: On this one issue, unanimity was essential. In exchange for the two opposing signatures, the Manifesto was rewritten, stricken of its most provocative language, and based on the principle of opposition through "all lawful means" and "by any lawful means." It remained inflammatory.

Fulbright never publicly said a word of disapproval of his colleagues. He had made his decision; he stood by the Manifesto.

He had a choice: He could have left his Southern colleagues and gone on his own, or stayed with them and be assured of remaining in the Senate (he was coming up for his third term that summer). He was convinced he could not possibly survive if he stood apart. He chose to stay in the Senate, follow what he presumed were the wishes of his constituents, and continue to serve his country from within the government. He won his election. But in another sense he lost far more than he had gained.

Fulbright had not come to his decision easily. Neither had he lacked contrary advice. Sid McMath, who had been the liberal governor of Arkansas and a strong supporter of Fulbright, recalls that during that period he called the senator on several occasions urging him to issue a statement calling for moderation. He suggested that Fulbright come back to Arkansas, go on television, speak about the need for wisdom and caution. It was a chance, McMath argued, for Fulbright to take the lead for a truly New South, to become the unchallenged leader in a new Southern era.

Fulbright declined. According to McMath, he said that his position in the Senate was such that he had no other choice.*

McMath and other Arkansas liberals were frankly disillusioned. So were others throughout the United States.

But if Fulbright had been disappointing, he did not stand alone. Far more disturbing in the long perspective was the spectacle of an entire group of Southern politicians turning toward the past instead of the future. At a moment when the Deep South desperately needed the wisdom of its statesmen of the past—indeed, Fulbright's own heroes, Washington, Jefferson, Lee—not one major figure dared to challenge a stultifying present. Leadership would come, but not at first from the South's politicians. It would be the ministers, teachers, students, editors, reporters, lawyers, judges, and businessmen—to say nothing of the South's own Negroes—who would begin to lead their section out of the past.

Fulbright's apologists often say his positions on civil rights are dictated by harsh political necessities—that he participates only grudgingly in the debates. Not surprisingly, they want the senator to conform to their own ideas of virtue. They do him a disservice on at least two grounds: They fail to understand both him and the section he represents.

The senator's political record is clear. Although compromise is involved, as it is on any major issue, Fulbright's stands on civil rights are matters of conviction. And far from refraining from the heat of debate, he has been an active participant.

From 1946 when the Senate first dealt with Harry Truman's proposed Fair Employment Practices Commission (F.E.P.C.) and on through a series of filibusters and bitter civil rights contests, Fulbright has been prominent among the Southern bloc. He has been a leader in debate and strategy; he has spoken out as strongly and frequently as any other Southerner.

That doesn't mean he shares the views of the more extreme Southerners —of the Strom Thurmonds and Jim Eastlands. Fulbright, on race, is a moderate, a gradualist, an evolutionist. He never waves the bloody shirt, never descends to demagoguery. More than most, he has addressed himself to the South's unique problems—poverty, ignorance, disease, lack of economic opportunities. He has tried to place these problems in historical perspective, and in that sense can he himself best be understood.

The historical facts of slavery, the Civil War, Reconstruction and its

* An indication of Fulbright's private feelings came in a letter he wrote at that time to Will L. Clayton of Houston, the former Undersecretary of State and influential Democrat: "The rising tension in the South threatens to weaken the educational system in the various Southern states. Senator Byrd is asserting very strong leadership in stirring up the resistance of the South, which as you know, is sometimes difficult to control once it is underway. The statement which has just been issued was reluctantly signed by a number of senators, but the alternative was unacceptable. All in all it is not an encouraging picture."

bitter aftermath, crippled the South. The South *was* treated like a conquered territory; it *was* exploited; it *did* become ever more insulated and removed from the mainstream of American life. Its fears, frustrations, and antagonisms are without parallel in the American experience.

In common with other able Southern politicians, Fulbright has been frustrated in attempting to effect change. With his own business background and intimate knowledge of financial conditions in Arkansas, he particularly has resented the domination of outside economic interests —Northern economic interests.

Once, while opposing the routine appointment of a Philadelphia banker to the Federal Reserve Board, he gave a revealing glimpse into his own attitudes.

"The people of the North are extremely solicitous of our welfare and progress," he said. "They assure us that if we will furnish better schools and abolish poll taxes and segregation that strife will cease and happiness reign. They are critical of our relative poverty, our industrial and social backwardness, and they are generous in their advice about our conduct. Their condescension in these matters is not appreciated . . . because these people . . . have for more than half a century done everything they could to retard the economic development of the South. It is no secret that the South was considered like a conquered territory after 1865. Since that time, the tariff policy and the freight rate structure were designed by the North to prevent industrial development in the South; to keep that area in the status of a raw material producing colony. Above and beyond these direct restrictions, the most insidious of all, the most difficult to put your finger on, is the all-pervading influence of the great financial institutions and industrial monopolies. These influences are so subtle and so powerful that they have in many instances been able to dominate the political and economic life of the South and West from within those states as well as from Washington."[9]

His domestic voting record reflects these views. He strongly supports the economic interests within the South, and especially within his state. Thus, Fulbright led a long fight in Congress to repeal sixty-four-year-old federal taxes and license fees on margarine (made almost entirely from soybeans and cottonseed)—a fight that saw such liberals as Hubert Humphrey of Minnesota, a dairy state with a vested interest in butter, racing to the side of the conservative Republicans. He staunchly supported the Dixon-Yates power combine, and alienated still more liberals across the country. He sponsored the 1955 natural gas bill, which led to a scandal when a lawyer representing an oil company contributed $2500 as an "inducement" to Senator Francis Case of South Dakota.* He op-

* Case himself brought the matter to public attention on the floor of the Senate when he told of the contribution and said that even though he had been for the bill he was voting against it. Although personally in favor of the bill, Eisenhower cou-

posed a minimum-wage bill and incurred the displeasure of the unions.

In short, on these basic economic matters Fulbright differs little from the conservatives. His record, therefore, lays him open to another complaint by the liberals. When stripped of his fine phrases and idealistic speeches on international affairs, they will say, Fulbright is merely another "tool of the interests."

Fulbright does differ significantly from the conventional conservatives, however. Where they fear the government, wish to restrict it, and generally are opposed to federal programs designed to redress social wrongs, Fulbright takes the opposite position. From his first moment in Congress, for instance, he has fought for passage of a federal aid to education bill. He has been an enthusiastic supporter of such endeavors as federal housing, job training, and anti-poverty programs. These, he believes, are the best methods to get at the basic problems breeding social unrest.

Consistently, he has said the federal government must do far more than it has; that the government's scale of values has been misapplied; that allocating money for highways, defense, or space at the expense of social-economic programs in the end only creates more problems. Genuine equality, he thinks, will never be achieved in the North or the South without such fundamental and aggressive government support. And his central theme, enunciated in countless speeches over a score of years, is that the best hope for amicable race relations lies in improving education.

To Fulbright, inadequate learning opportunities are the most tragic discrimination of all; they are the true barrier to progress, the breeder of ignorance, the perpetuator of prejudice.

"It is paradoxical," he said once, "that Southern educational systems should be expected to produce well-rounded, broad-minded, and wholly dispassionate individuals whose well-developed intellects can suddenly reject lifelong patterns of conduct. This is a high standard to expect for schools without adequate facilities—stemming from a tax base incapable of producing sufficient revenue. Southern states—and particularly my own—have made valiant efforts in recent years to devote greater portions of their resources to education, but . . . only since the 1930s has the South begun to share in the prosperity and affluence of America. It has only been during recent years that we have begun to be drawn into the political, economic, and cultural mainstreams of the nation."[10]

Fulbright would remain convinced that much of the racial violence which tore at the South and the nation from the mid-1950s on could have been avoided had the nation been willing to pay the price of raising educational standards and facilities for all races.

But even if the Congress had adopted more progressive measures, the finest school system in the world would not have undone the past. Nor

rageously vetoed it when it was passed. Fulbright's sponsorship of the bill also led to a break with his old friend, Senator Paul Douglas.

would it have resolved an elemental conflict. In the end, the question really wasn't just one of education, or of economics. It was moral. That awareness weighed heaviest on white Southerners. Fulbright, the most enlightened and civilized of men, hardly could escape this in his own private thoughts.

He seldom discussed the race question on any personal terms. Usually, he skirted it: he talked of the law, of history, of economics, of traditions, of unmet needs and unfulfilled hopes. Once, however, he did speak out, in sorrowful tones, about the legacy of slavery that rested uniquely on the South.

"The whites and Negroes of Arkansas and the South are equally prisoners of their environment," he said, "and no one knows what either of them might have been in a different environment or under other circumstances. Certainly, no one of them has ever been free with respect to racial relationships to the degree that the Vermonter or the Minnesotan has been free. The society of each is conditioned by the presence of the other. Each carries a catalogue of things not to be mentioned. Each moves through an intricate ritual of evasions, of make-believe, and suppressions. In the South one finds a relationship among men without counterpart on this continent."[11]

That came as close to being a cry for racial understanding as Fulbright ever made. For the rest of the time, Fulbright tried to remain silent on the subject. Even that, as he discovered, carried its own high price.

The inevitable civil rights confrontation between the federal government and the South took place in September of 1957—not in Mississippi, Louisiana, Alabama, or Georgia, as one might have expected, but in the heart of Fulbright's own state. Arkansas, the border state, the moderate state, the state where integration had begun years before in the university, became the historic battleground. Around the world, Little Rock and Arkansas became symbols of segregation, of bayonets and mobs and white adults shouting obscenities at Negro children.

Arkansas had been making progress, and there seemed no likelihood of racial trouble. Little Rock itself, the state capital, was far from a hotbed of reactionaries. The city's school board already had perfected a plan for integrating the schools gradually. While it was not an aggressive plan, it was nonetheless acceptable to the Arkansas branch of the National Association for the Advancement of Colored People. And the Arkansas governor himself was regarded as one of the most progressive in the South, and particularly as a man with a good record in race relations. Indeed, Orval Faubus was considered so liberal in some quarters that at the height of the McCarthy hysteria, Westbrook Pegler, the columnist, had linked him with Communism. Faubus, Pegler had written, was elected governor "notwithstanding his attendance at a Communist college known as Commonwealth."[12]

Faubus was a poor boy from the Ozarks who took pride in being regarded as a man of the people. His father, Sam Faubus, was an even more outspoken liberal. Between them, the Faubuses were the inheritors of the old radical populist tradition. Although Faubus came from the same part of the state as Fulbright and had been a supporter of his, he always had been suspicious of the senator. Fulbright represented wealth and the advantages that flowed from it. "If I had been in Fayetteville, the Fulbrights wouldn't have let me in the country club," he once said.[13] But no matter what their personal differences, neither Fulbright nor anyone else expected Faubus to act as he did.

Before the fall of 1957, Fulbright had been optimistic about his state. Only that spring, he had sounded a hopeful note while addressing an education conference in Little Rock. "The difficulties ahead are not insurmountable if we tackle them with confidence and imagination," he remarked then. "The federal government has an important role to play in the development of the South; indeed, it is in the interest of the entire nation that it do so . . . [but] the greater portion of the effort must . . . be made by the South itself. We have the potentialities."[14] Later, before the Senate session ended, he noted with pride on the floor that Little Rock had just been named to receive one of *Look* magazine's "All American City" citations. "I wish to take this opportunity," he said, "to congratulate the energetic and civic-minded citizens of Little Rock, whose activities made this award possible."

After adjournment, Fulbright left on a scheduled trip to Europe. He was in London when the Little Rock crisis began that September.

Faubus, for what were widely considered to be political motives, had chosen to thwart plans to integrate seventeen Negro students into Little Rock's Central High School. On September 3, on the eve of the opening of classes, Faubus suddenly acted. He placed armed Arkansas National Guard units around the school. The next day the troops forcibly barred nine of the Negro students who tried to enter the school. The situation rapidly deteriorated. In an effort to avert possible bloodshed, Eisenhower and Faubus met vainly in Newport.

Finally, reluctantly, on September 24, 1957, Eisenhower ordered federal troops to Little Rock. Faubus added more fuel. In a nationally televised speech, he portrayed Arkansas as under "military occupation," and spoke of "the warm red blood of patriotic citizens staining the cold, naked, unsheathed knives."[15]

Lyndon Johnson, the leader of the Senate, said he thought "there should be no troops from either side patrolling our school campuses." Senator Olin Johnston of South Carolina was belligerent. "I'd never go down without a fight. I'd proclaim a state of insurrection and I'd call out the national guard and then we'd find out who's going to run things in my state." Governor LeRoy Collins of Florida said the South should abandon its "Confederate blanket" and "stop consuming itself in racial furor."[16]

Little Rock's *Arkansas Gazette,* spoke out forthrightly.

> "We in Little Rock had perfected a plan to meet the Supreme Court's new racial requirements in education gradually and largely on our own terms [the paper commented]. The Federal Courts had sustained us. But now Mr. Faubus and the angry, violent and thoughtless band of agitators who rallied to his call may well have undone the patient work of responsible local officials. . . . Unhappy though it may be, the action of the President in using Federal troops to restore order will in time also restore the calm that is essential to an orderly approach to any problem."[17]

But from England there was no comment from Senator Fulbright. Although questioned repeatedly by newsmen, he would not comment. After his return home, he still had nothing to say publicly. One month after Eisenhower called in the troops, he issued his only statement. It was three sentences long:

"It is regrettable and it is tragic that Federal troops are in Little Rock. The people of Little Rock and of Arkansas do not deserve this treatment. The citizens of Arkansas are, and have always been, law abiding people."

That was all he had to say until two years later, while appearing on the CBS-TV program "Face the Nation," he was asked by another former Rhodes Scholar, Howard K. Smith, if he thought Faubus had mishandled the Little Rock situation. "I do," Fulbright answered. "There is no doubt about that. I mean it's perfectly evident."[18]

Fulbright's silence helped him with neither side. Faubus criticized him for failing to defend his—and therefore Arkansas'—official position when the state was being subjected to "federal interference." The liberals, within and without Arkansas, were inclined to write him off as unworthy of respect. "Why does he have to sell his soul and his people like that?" said Mrs. L. C. (Daisy) Bates, the NAACP's leader in Little Rock at the time of the crisis. ". . . I'll listen to Faubus more than I'll listen to Fulbright."[19]

What would always be hard for them to understand was how a man who could express so eloquently the aspirations of humanity, who could challenge America to think unthinkable thoughts, could reconcile his lofty principles with his public position on such a vital issue.

It would be one thing if Fulbright lacked compassion or integrity—or if he were cautiously playing a most cynical game of politics. No one who knows him could ever believe that. The answer lay deep within him. As a reflective man full of doubts, he tends to agonize over every major question. None is greater than the complex one of civil rights. One can only guess at the inner turmoil.

In the aftermath of Little Rock, when a boyhood friend wrote urging him to seize the chance to "achieve glorious fame" by denouncing Faubus and the White Citizens Council, Fulbright rejected the idea; then, in a handwritten postscript, added, in an air of resignation:

"I think there is sufficient blame to go around to everybody. If I knew the solution to Little Rock, I would truly be a Solomon."

The blame, he seems to have recognized, lay at least in part on his own shoulders as a representative of the South.

7

"THE AGE OF THE AMATEUR IS OVER"

THE SENATORS WERE RESTLESS. They had been up until 11:30 the night before in interminable deliberation over court legislation, and from the news tickers that morning had come reports of another crisis in the making. Once more, Eisenhower and Faubus were exchanging long-distance threats. In a few days school would be opening again in Little Rock, and although a year had passed since the confrontation of 1957, the situation seemed to have improved little. The senators were anxious to leave. Outside, it was as stifling as ever in late August;* everyone agreed it had been a long, acrimonious, and exhausting session. Lyndon Johnson was promising they stood within hours of adjournment—*if* there were no filibuster, *if* the Middle East situation did not suddenly flare up again, *if* the President and the Governor could resolve their differences.

Senator Fulbright took the floor. From the gallery above the speaker's well, his words came through as a hoarse whisper. He shouldn't have been speaking at all: he had ruptured a blood vessel in his throat earlier in the summer and his doctor had told him to save his voice. Only two weeks before, he was unable to utter a word; then the Senate legislative clerk had read his speech warning of the "drift to disaster" if the Eisenhower foreign policies were pursued. That speech had precipitated a partisan debate. A few days later John F. Kennedy of Massachusetts added a new warning: "A nuclear gap" had developed between the Russians and the

* That month Fulbright personally had filed an *amicus curiae* brief with the U. S. Supreme Court against the federal government in connection with the pace of integration in Little Rock, an act that did not further endear him to civil libertarians.

United States. Two other senators, Lyndon Johnson and Stuart Symington, presidential aspirants all, soon were making the same attack on the Senate floor. The theme for the 1960 presidential election had been discovered.

Now, in the closing hours of the 85th Congress, Fulbright was pronouncing an indictment of the entire Eisenhower era of the 1950s. It had been an era, he said, when the people got what they wanted, when "they were at liberty to stop thinking any more . . . [when] they could bask in the artificial sunlight of a government which did not bother them with serious things." It had been a time of "luxurious torpor."

"Can anyone here deny that the distinguishing feature of American society during much of the decade of the 1950s was its weakness for the easy way?" he asked.

"What show of reflection and choice was there in much of the decade of the 1950s when the word 'egghead' became a word of abuse; when education was neglected; when intellectual excellence became a cause for suspicion; when the man in public life, or the writer, or the teacher, who dared articulate an original thought risked being accused of subversion? What show of reflection and choice was there in this period when the man of distinction was the man who had a station wagon, a second car plated with chrome, a swimming pool, a tax-free expense account, and a twenty-one-inch color television set with the thirty-six-inch star on the screen?"

America had endured similar periods before, both in the 1920s and the 1870s. "In each case, we eventually came to our senses, went to work, and corrected a good deal of what had been wrong." But now, at the end of the Eisenhower era, it was more serious.

"It is time," Fulbright said, "to cease going along as usual. . . . The age of the amateur is over."[1]

Later, when the young Lochinvars came, it would be seen that it had not been that bad—that, indeed, Eisenhower had been done a disservice. But there was enough substance, enough of an undercurrent of displeasure and unease, to lay the administration open to serious attack. Fulbright was among the leaders of that opposition. To a man who had expounded the theme of politics as being worthy of the highest professional training, the sight of the businessman's administration was disheartening. As he put it:

"In this, the most critical period of our history, when the full reserve of American political activity should be at the disposal of the national community, hardly ten percent of the chief posts of government are now filled by men with any previous experience in political affairs. The rest are amateurs, pitted in a worldwide contest against adversaries who are carefully trained political professionals."

Ironically, the one true professional on the Eisenhower team—Secretary of State John Foster Dulles—was to receive Fulbright's sharpest criticism.

By the late 1950s, Fulbright had become the ranking man—and soon to be the chairman—on the Senate Foreign Relations Committee. Although from the beginning he had been closely identified with foreign affairs, his rise to a position of influence was unusually swift, for he had not been appointed to the committee until 1949. Through deaths, departures, and defeats, and through the seniority system he had once deplored, he moved upward rapidly. Within seven years he had become the number two man. Tom Connally, the chairman when Fulbright joined the committee, had left the Senate in 1952 at the age of seventy-five. Alexander Wiley of Wisconsin, who became the Republican chairman under Eisenhower, was sixty-nine and seventy during the two years he held the post. When the Democrats regained control of the Senate in 1954, Walter George assumed the reins at the age of seventy-seven. When Talmadge took George's Senate seat, the aged Theodore Francis Green became the chairman.

Fulbright, already regarded as the best equipped man on foreign affairs in the Senate, became the Democrat's leading spokesman on international issues.

He had been among that small group of congressional leaders who sometimes conferred informally with the President in his oval office between five P.M. and dinner. There, over a drink and a canapé, he and such men as Lyndon Johnson, Everett Dirksen, Sam Rayburn, and William Knowland would discuss issues with Eisenhower. At other times, in the moments of crisis, he was always among the group of leaders who gathered at what often were tense meetings in the Executive Mansion.[2]

In Fulbright's opinion, the failure of the Eisenhower administration lay in the frequency of those crises. It wasn't enough to extricate the nation from the brink; the true test of leadership was deciding in advance what measures to take before events reached a crisis stage. Too often, he thought, the U.S. was on the defensive (as it would remain, in his opinion, throughout most of the 1960s).

The Eisenhower-Dulles policies were a continuation and an expansion of the Truman-Acheson policies. The Southeast Asia Treaty in 1954 and Eisenhower's subsequent talk of the falling dominoes theory centered about Indo-China; the Formosa Resolutions of 1955; the Suez Canal controversy of 1956 leading to the Eisenhower Doctrine of 1957; the dispatching of Marines to Lebanon in 1958—all these were essentially defensive and, to Fulbright, negative. They maintained the peace and security of the West, but they did not gain the initiative for the U.S.

Fulbright took on the State Department whenever the occasion demanded. Debate over those issues seldom commanded the headlines; the clash of powerful personalities did. Thus, Fulbright received most attention during the Eisenhower period for his opposition to John Foster Dulles. As James Reston commented, "these two highly intelligent men have established a relationship roughly equivalent to the chemical reaction of dogs and cats. When Mr. Dulles talks, Mr. Fulbright growls, and when the Senator talks, the Secretary arches his back."[3] Actually it was not one Dulles, but two, with whom he dealt. During his two terms Eisenhower relied heavily on John Foster and Allen Dulles, the sons of a Presbyterian minister and scions of diplomats. They had his total confidence. Together, they fashioned, directed, and implemented U.S. foreign policy. What Secretary of State Dulles could not achieve publicly through treaty or alliance or conference, Central Intelligence Agency Director Dulles could accomplish under the table.

The CIA, with practically unlimited and unchecked resources, fomented revolutions, organized coups, trained guerrillas, led insurrections, financed students, and organized massive propaganda activities in such disparate places as Burma, Formosa, Iran, Egypt, Suez, Costa Rica, and Guatemala.[4]

None of that became clear until years later.*

Fulbright would become a severe critic of the CIA and in turn the object of personal attack by the Agency. But in the early years of the Eisenhower administration, he regarded the CIA leaders and their work highly. The senator passed on material he thought might be of interest to the CIA, including lengthy memoranda written from Europe by his old friend and European tutor, M. W. (Mike) Fodor. And Fulbright, in his private comments to Allen Dulles, expressed as much concern about the Russian menace and the need to strengthen Western defenses as any high-level member of the Eisenhower administration.[5] Years later, many of his most vocal admirers would regard him as a pacificist. Fulbright never has been. Where he differed with Eisenhower and Dulles was over the implementation of policies aimed at countering Communist aggression.

He had known John Foster Dulles since 1943, had served with him in the Senate six years later, and always, no matter how strong their public disputes, regarded him as an outstanding lawyer, and a person one could deal with privately. What bothered him while Dulles was Secretary of State was his rigidity, his seeming refusal to seek new methods, his moralizing, and his stubborn conviction that he was always right. Once convinced of a course, Fulbright himself could be as stubborn as any man. But of the two, Fulbright was the more flexible.

One of their earliest direct encounters came in 1956 while the Communist Party was holding its 20th Party Congress in Moscow. Dulles, then testifying before the Senate Foreign Relations Committee, gave this assessment:

* In January, 1954, for instance, Americans were still so innocent and their legislators so naïve that most believed the State Department's denials after President Jacobo Arbenz Guzman of Guatemala publicly accused the U.S. of plotting to overthrow his regime. He was correct. Six months later, the CIA, with the approval of the President, led the coup that overthrew his regime—an operation accomplished with such ease that it became the model for the Bay of Pigs invasion seven years later.

". . . I think they made very little progress in the last few days and the proof of it is that at this very moment in Moscow they are having to revise their whole program. If we had to go through such a revision and change our whole program as they are undergoing, it would be advertised all over the world that we failed.

"The fact is they have failed and they have got to devise new policies."[6]

Fulbright led the questioning. Did Dulles mean that speeches by Nikita Khrushchev and others at the party Congress indicated an admission of failure? Did he mean that the Russians were losing?

"Absolutely," Dulles answered.

Dulles had given what appeared to be a singularly inaccurate evaluation, one that Fulbright never forgot. As later events demonstrated, far from having to "undo the teachings of many years," the Russians continued to keep the U.S. on the defensive and gave the appearance of gaining strength while America was losing. Such overoptimistic assertions also caused Fulbright to doubt the intelligence reports on which judgments were made. Within a few years he had become dubious of both Dulles brothers—a state of mind that helped him make the only sound and outspoken evaluation of Allen Dulles', and the CIA's, most ambitious and disastrous venture at the Bay of Pigs.

John Foster Dulles' rashest action was also the most costly.

The United States and Egypt had been discussing American financing of the huge High Dam, planned as the largest in the world, at Aswan on the Nile. Although the U.S. government already had offered a loan to Egypt in December, 1955, by the following summer the American proposal had become controversial. Egyptian President Gamal Abdel Nasser was then under attack in the U.S. both from Jewish and anti-Communist groups who feared he was threatening Israel and aligning himself too closely with the Russians. At the same time Dulles was receiving urgent pleas from British Ambassador Sir Roger Makins, Prime Minister Anthony Eden, and Foreign Secretary Selwyn Lloyd and French Ambassador Couve de Murville "not to be precipitate" over the dam.[7] The crucial moment came on July 19, 1956.

At eleven o'clock that morning Dulles met the Egyptian Ambassador, Ahmed Hussein in his office. Dulles, sitting in an armchair, his legs propped on a coffee table, slowly, and in rather "sad and firm" tones lectured the Ambassador about the difficulties in granting the loan. Hussein became agitated. Finally, waving his arms, Hussein leaned over the table and blurted out, "Don't please say you are going to withdraw the offer, because . . . we have the Russian offer to finance the dam right here in my pocket."

Dulles, feeling challenged, instantly retorted: "Well, as you have the money already, you don't need any from us. My offer is withdrawn!"[8]

Dulles' precipitate action led to the gravest continuing crisis of the Eisenhower presidency. One week later Egypt seized and nationalized the Suez Canal. By October open warfare had broken out. Israel invaded Egypt's Sinai Peninsula; France and Britain supported her—and their interest in the canal—and jointly attacked Egypt; Eisenhower threw his support behind Russia against our closest allies and secured, under pressure, a ceasefire through the United Nations; the English, French, and Israelis withdrew. When the dust had settled, a power vacuum resulted in the Middle East.

Dulles proposed an alternative. His idea, which became known as the Eisenhower Doctrine, was to guarantee the safety of any independent Arab nation against a Communist takeover. To secure the fullest backing, congressional endorsement would be asked and the use of American force authorized. Some two hundred million dollars in American economic-military aid also would be provided for those Middle Eastern countries.

Fulbright had been following the developing Middle East crisis closely. He was convinced that Dulles had blundered over the Aswan Dam incident, and that the subsequent American responses had been improvident. Even though news of the Eisenhower Doctrine already had been leaked to the press at the end of the year, the senators had not been officially informed of what would be requested. Without warning, Dulles urgently requested a secret meeting with the Foreign Relations Committee at six P.M. on January 2, 1957. His timing was unfortunate: not all the members had returned from the Christmas holidays, and Green, the chairman, could not even be located.

When the senators who were available arrived at the committee room, Dulles briefed them. The Middle East crisis was getting worse, he said; action was imperative. He read the proposed resolution which he hoped Congress would adopt. The President, he said, would address the Congress three days later to urge its passage.

Mike Mansfield spoke up first. He didn't believe any resolution was necessary. Further, the President already could dispatch troops if he wanted.

Fulbright was angered at Dulles. "I cannot see any emergency for it. It wasn't so long ago that the Secretary was assuring the Committee that things are in good condition in the Middle East. I do not think at this hour we can go into this subject."

After Eisenhower delivered his speech, Fulbright argued that the President, under the cover of a call to patriotism, was seeking to eliminate debate, force senators to sign a blank-check, and endorse an unwise policy. Fulbright was reacting exactly as he would in another crisis within a decade.

His response to the Eisenhower Doctrine also led to his only sharp personal difference with Lyndon Johnson as Majority Leader. Fulbright told Johnson he was going to oppose it; he thought all the Democrats should. Johnson disagreed. Since the President had asked for support, Johnson felt it was his duty to give it. Congressional disunity would create an impression of weakness around the world, and might inspire the Communists to further foolish adventures, Johnson argued. Neither senator influenced the other.

At that point other Democratic leaders were urging key congressional members to unite in opposing the Eisenhower-Dulles policies. On January 24, 1957, for instance, Adlai Stevenson was drafting a letter to Fulbright from his Chicago law office bewailing the lack of leadership among the Democrats and wishing they could agree on a course of action "to give us some initiative in foreign policy and invite public attention to the Administration's failures—including the fact that the world has lost confidence in Dulles."

Unknown to Stevenson, that same day Fulbright delivered a stinging personal rebuke to Dulles as the Secretary of State sat before him in a witness chair, flushed with anger. The clash occurred during a joint meeting of the Foreign Relations Committee and the Armed Services Committee hearing on the proposed Eisenhower Middle East resolution.

"Not since the turn of the century," Fulbright said, "have our relations with the other people of the free world been so strained—so unsatisfactory. Nations in whose behalf we have spent billions of our treasure are now indifferent, if not hostile, to our policies.

"This disastrous and remarkable collapse of our relations with our closest allies has taken place under the direction of our present Secretary of State, and apparently within the relatively short space of a few months. . . . I regard the policies which he has been following as harmful to our interests, as being calculated to weaken the influence of the free world in the Middle East, disastrous to the NATO organization and as damaging to our friendship with Great Britain and France."[9]

When Stevenson heard the news, he immediately scrawled a note:

"Bill—I apologize for bothering *my hero* the other day! Adlai. P. S. May your *tribe* increase!"

And from Florida, where he was enjoying "perfect happiness, remorseless laziness," Dean Acheson also offered his congratulations: "I am proud to know you and wish you every success in future broadsides."

For the remainder of the Eisenhower years, Fulbright urged new approaches to old problems. He questioned "the fear of the deviltry of Communism," and called for removing "this comforting belief that the Soviet Union is the sole source of our troubles." He favored admitting Red China into the United Nations, and spending more on economic development and technical assistance than on military aid. He challenged the assumption that sole reliance on massive nuclear strength would ensure America's liberty; that military alliances with underdeveloped nations were as valuable as we thought; that the two great powers, Russia and the U.S., between them could keep the peace around the globe. In 1958, for instance, he anticipated future troubles in such remarks as:

> "War can begin in many parts of the globe between nations which may not be amenable to restraints by the Soviet Union or by the United States. Is anyone . . . prepared to say, for example, that war has become an impossibility even among the Arab states themselves? Is war in Indonesia a complete unlikelihood? Have we seen the end of a possibility of conflict between the two segments of Viet Nam, of China, of Korea?"

> "We have grossly overestimated the value of military alliances with underdeveloped Asian countries. . . . As an example, Pakistan is receiving a lot of foreign military aid and defense support money from us. Pakistan, because we have provided the equipment, has diverted far too many of its own men into uniform. . . . Because we have armed and are arming the Pakistanis, the Indian government feels that it must spend a large proportion of its national income on armament in order to protect itself against a possible Pakistani attack."[10]

On January 30, 1959, he became chairman of the Foreign Relations Committee. He was nearly fifty-four years old then. His sixteen years in Congress had changed him. He was more cautious, more skilled; he had learned all the maneuvers; he knew when to stand and when to withdraw. No one could place him properly. He was at once the most traditional and the most unlikely senator in Washington. When reporters were clamoring and the big headlines beckoned, he would not hold press conferences. He would turn down opportunities to go on national television—but then talk for two hours in the most revealing terms to a young reporter whose work he admired. At times he was petty, querulous, and pessimistic; at others magnanimous, witty, charming. He was vain and polite, wise and foolhardy, intense and forgetful. Despite his drawling exterior, he was not free of stress: some who knew him well said he was obsessed with his health, that his father's early and sudden death haunted him. He was, in fact, a health addict, ate only certain foods, watched his weight and rest, took his exercise. While he seldom showed anger and tried to hide his emotions, he brooded so much and became so upset during the McCarthy period that he would leave his house and walk out alone into the night. Certain senators said he was lazy. It was a common opinion; he knew it and resented it strongly. There was substance to the criticism: He did not

bother himself with all the burdensome committee and congressional duties. But no one worked harder on specific issues, and he was capable
of turning out the most polished and literate senatorial prose in the soli-
tude of his office without the customary platoon of ghost writers—page
after page of handwritten drafts and revisions of revisions. His best ranked
at the top of his times and came as close as any to equaling his favorite,
De Tocqueville. Strangely, for all his experience, he was not a good
speaker: He slurred his words, he mumbled. Yet he was capable of sum-
moning such eloquence that he once brought a tough, sophisticated New
York audience of intellectuals to its feet in a spontaneous rising ovation
never granted Nobel Prize winners speaking before that group.* His enemies thought him a fraud, a poser, a fencesitter, a pseudo-intellectual.
"Which does he think he is, Moses or Martin Luther?" jeered old Kenneth
McKellar of Tennessee in the Senate cloakroom after Fulbright had urged
Congress to appoint an ethics committee in the aftermath of the RFC
scandals.[11] No one really knew him. But he had as good a grasp as anyone of what the Senate could achieve and what it could not. He had studied
the issues carefully. It was another reason why he was called "the professor."

On any day in the Senate, Fulbright could look around him and see future
presidents and presidential candidates at work. No one was more notice-
able than the tall Majority Leader. Lyndon Johnson dominated the Senate.
He was ruthless, driving, absorbed, egotistical, sensitive, proud, and he
had a special talent for mastering the nearly unmanageable legislative
process. Until he came on the scene in 1949 (after congressional appren-
ticeship going back to 1937 and personal tutelage of Franklin Roosevelt)
no one had been able to make the Senate work.

"Lyndon was a great operator," Fulbright would say. "He made the
Senate function better than anyone. He pushed things around; he got
things done. He was a hell of an operator."

He also would say: "He was one of the greatest political animals I have
ever seen, in the best sense of that word. He had an instinct for politics.
He was as dedicated to the practice of politics as any man I have ever seen.
It was remarkable the attention he used to give to every bill—big and
little—small and unimportant as they may be."[12]

Johnson drove himself—and he drove others equally hard.

For Fulbright, it became normal for the phone to ring at seven in the
morning—or eleven at night. "Bill? Lyndon." Johnson wanted this or that
done; and he outlined how he wanted it handled, and when.

His system brought success, but it was not without strains. His vaunted
skill at bringing people together, at reconciling differences, at juggling ap-

* The speech, "The Mummification of Opinion," was delivered at the National
Book Awards dinner in New York, January 25, 1955, during the McCarthy period.

ples and oranges and producing pears, also meant that the substance or principle of an issue often became lost in the legislative dealing. But the two men understood each other. Their respect was based on something more solid than sectional loyalties. They were professionals; they had definite ideas about the country, where it should be headed, what it should be doing. Johnson, for his part, admired Fulbright's intellect, his scholarship, his ideas on policies. In his exuberant style, he let everyone know: "Bill's *my* Secretary of State." Fulbright, while never so demonstrative, always made clear his own admiration. By 1959, he was publicly on record as backing Johnson for the presidency.

Still, at times, he could not resist a wry jest about the Texan's larger-than-life style and desire to be loved and recognized. One day he happened to notice Walt Kelly's comic strip, "Pogo."

Pogo was talking to another character, Albert the Alligator.

"Doggone, Albert, I'm givin' out ideas and *you* claims they's yours! Don't you think of nothin' alone ever?" Pogo said.

"I thinks of nothin' alone constantly, friend," Albert replied.

To Fulbright, Kelly had captured a perfect characterization of Lyndon (Pogo) Johnson and Dwight (Albert) Eisenhower.[13]

If he could not resist a laugh every now and then at the Majority Leader's expense, he also shrewdly understood his strivings and had a genuine sympathy for his feelings. "I do hope you have a rest that you deserve so much," he wrote Johnson consolingly at the close of the lengthy 1959 session, "and that you will not let the unfairness of our political life disturb you too much."

Of the other leading contender for the Democratic presidential nomination, John F. Kennedy, Fulbright at that time had an unfavorable impression. Since 1956, Kennedy had been running hard for the presidency and his attendance record in the Senate was poor. He was the junior member of Fulbright's Foreign Relations Committee but spent little time there. When he was in town, he devoted most of his time to the more widely publicized Senate racket hearings.

"I knew Jack very little indeed," Fulbright would say. "I don't think he attended more than two or three meetings for a few minutes. And I'd never really had a conversation with Jack to be frank about it—never had occasion. He traveled in a different world."

In appearance, they were opposites—Kennedy, flashing good looks, aggressive, driving; Fulbright, reserved, tweedy, ungregarious. Yet they had much in common. They were attracted by words and ideas, they relished the apropos quote, they were reflective and appreciative of originality and learning, they tolerated mistakes of others, and they inspired loyalty and affection. They also detested sham and took a wry amusement in deflating their more overblown political colleagues.

Once, during Nikita Khrushchev's visit to the United States, Fulbright was presiding over a coffee in the Soviet Premier's honor. After the session, Khrushchev's interpreter carefully gathered up each place card bearing the name of every senator there and gave it to the Russian. With a flourish, Khrushchev autographed them all. Then he ordered the interpreter to present them to Fulbright as if they were priceless gifts. The next morning Fulbright mailed Kennedy his autographed card with a note saying:

> Dear Jack:
> . . . Maybe this will enable you to get out of jail when the revolution comes, but it may have some other value that I do not now recognize.

But at that time and throughout much of 1960 the Kennedy-Fulbright relationship was still distant. As the time approached to pick a presidential candidate, it appeared that Fulbright, like many old Stevenson supporters, had a last, secret yearning to see "the Governor" nominated once again.

On the eve of the Democratic National Convention in Los Angeles, where John F. Kennedy soon would mount an open-air platform, face west, and pledge to lead a "new frontier," Fulbright sent Stevenson a note:

"I am not wise enough to advise you except that I hope you will find some way to get a little more positively into the picture before long."

In the same letter, he said: ". . . It is becoming apparent that it will be a tragedy if there is no reasonable alternative to the gentleman from Massachusetts. I believe there is deep concern in many responsible quarters at the prospect of the country having to choose between Kennedy and Nixon." Despite these private reservations, Fulbright backed Kennedy aggressively in the campaign.

After the election, Fulbright prepared to leave for Europe to attend the NATO Parliamentarians' Conference. He was in high spirits. He felt Kennedy had handled himself superbly during the campaign and gave bright promise of becoming an outstanding President. From his own standpoint, the future appeared equally promising. After years of frustration, he would be exercising congressional power and influence in an administration with which he was in harmony. His days of sharpest dissent seemed behind him—his most creative period ahead.

BOOK FOUR

Critic

1

JFK: "HE MADE ME PROUD OF MY COUNTRY"

London, November, 1960: Lyndon Johnson was exhilarated. The NATO Parliamentarians' Conference was over, and only hours before their London departure, the key American delegates had dined with Prime Minister Harold Macmillan. As their jet climbed through a thick layer of clouds, leveled off, and began the long trip across the Atlantic, Johnson settled down next to Bill Fulbright and started a conversation about politics and politicians that lasted most of the way back to the United States. It was an awe-inspiring performance.

"He remembers verbatim conversations from twenty years ago," Fulbright told his assistant, John Erickson, on his return. "I never saw anything like it. With his knowledge and understanding of Congress, he can be of great help to Kennedy's legislative program."

Erickson asked what kind of President he thought Kennedy would be. Fulbright instantly replied:

"He'll be as good a President as he makes use of Lyndon Johnson's political genius."

Fulbright then went home to Arkansas to await the start of the Kennedy Administration.

The senator was well aware that he was being considered as Kennedy's Secretary of State, but he had not heard from any of the Kennedy intimates. Lack of information heightened newspaper speculation, which had begun during the campaign. As November wore on, the rumors increased.

Fulbright's own personal wishes have always been a matter of conjecture. As in anything so important and so intimate, there are conflicting versions and interpretations. On at least several occasions, though, Fulbright did make clear his own views about becoming Secretary of State.

Early on the morning after the election Fulbright had called John Erickson to discuss the matter. As Erickson entered the Little Rock hotel room, he found the senator in a talkative mood, sitting up in bed in his pajamas.

"I'd be the worst possible Secretary of State," Erickson recalls Fulbright as saying. "I'd be a lousy one. Can't you see me at those ceremonial affairs—meeting dignitaries at the airport and all that?"

After that, Fulbright left for the NATO conference. Before returning to Arkansas, he asked Senator Richard Russell to convey to Kennedy his personal feelings about being Secretary of State. Temperamentally and ideologically, he told Russell, he was unsuited for the job. He did not want it and would appreciate it if Russell would pass on that message to the President-elect. Russell demurred and said he thought Fulbright should be Secretary of State.

Later that month Fulbright received a telephone call in Fayetteville from an acquaintance, Gene Farmer of *Life* magazine. It was definite, Farmer said. He had heard directly from the Kennedy camp that Fulbright was going to be appointed Secretary of State. He wanted to come down to Fayetteville immediately to begin preparing a profile.

"Well, I've had no word of anything from anyone," Fulbright said. It was entirely too premature for any article.

That call set off a Fulbright family conference. Hal Douglas, the senator's brother-in-law, remembers sitting around the living room in Fayetteville weighing the possibilities. Douglas also recalls Fulbright saying emphatically that he didn't want the job—but, of course, if the President offered it, he would have to accept.

At that point, Fulbright's chances did appear favorable. Later, Kennedy's close friend, Charles Bartlett, would say that "Fulbright was the preferred candidate."[1] Kennedy already had considered and rejected Adlai Stevenson, Chester Bowles, and McGeorge Bundy. None of them had been Kennedy's personal choices. Then, for a time, he settled on Fulbright.

"When I talked to Kennedy on December 1," Arthur M. Schlesinger, Jr., wrote, "it was clear that his thoughts were turning more and more to Fulbright. He liked Fulbright, the play of his civilized mind, the bite of his language, and the direction of his thinking on foreign affairs. Moreover, as chairman of the Senate Foreign Relations Committee, Fulbright had considerable influence on the Hill."[2]

Yet, as Schlesinger noted, "there were problems too."

Fulbright's civil rights record had antagonized the NAACP. His position on Nasser and Israel had alienated Zionist groups.* His lack of administrative experience since his university presidency days and the recurring stories about his lackadaisical working habits as a senator had created doubts among important Kennedy advisers. Beyond that, as Secretary of State, Fulbright might become embarrassing to the administration if he were forced to take a strong stand against an African nation. He then would be liable to attack on grounds of personal prejudice rather than reasoned belief. In addition, Kennedy's closest confidant, his brother, Robert, never had been too impressed with Fulbright.

"Kennedy had almost decided on Fulbright," Schlesinger recalled, "but finally, after heated arguments, the President-elect yielded and struck Fulbright's name from the list."[3]

He chose instead a man he had never met until December 8, 1960. Dean Rusk had the strong support of his former superior, Dean Acheson, and from Robert A. Lovett, the New York financier and former Secretary of Defense. Rusk, although like Fulbright a Southerner and former Rhodes Scholar, already had made it clear to Kennedy before they met that his views on race would pose no problem. On November 30, he had written Kennedy a long and unsolicited letter which began:

"As a Georgia-born citizen who believes that the Supreme Court decision on integration was long overdue, I feel inclined to offer a comment on the pressures arising from the threat of certain delegations to disregard the popular votes in their states in casting their ballots in the Electoral College in December."[4]

If it became necessary for Kennedy to issue a statement, Rusk suggested that he stress "long-range historical and constitutional traditions of the country rather than upon the immediate issues now involved."

Rusk's appointment as Secretary of State was announced December 12, four days after his first meeting with Kennedy.

A few days later Fulbright, then in Little Rock, received his first word from the Kennedy group. Kennedy himself called from Florida and asked Fulbright to visit him in Palm Beach after the Christmas holidays.

"The whole purpose was to try to soften the blow," Fulbright would recall of that meeting with Kennedy in Florida. "He thought it was a terrible blow, I guess. He more or less apologized for the publicity, which he regretted, he said, but he couldn't help it. He was being nice and pleasant and agreeable and that was it."

Whatever reservations Fulbright had had earlier about Kennedy were removed by the manner in which Kennedy handled that Palm Beach visit.

---

* Fulbright in 1946–47 supported the creation of the State of Israel, but he had been critical from time to time of lobbying tactics carried on by American Jewish groups on behalf of Israel. He particularly resented efforts by U.S. labor unions to boycott Egyptian ships in retaliation for Egypt's closing of the Suez Canal to Israeli bound ships. His attitude, unsurprisingly, did not endear him to many organized Jewish groups.

"I don't think I've ever seen a man of such importance, with more consideration, more sympathy for another politician than this man was," he said later. ". . . I think he was the most tolerant and sympathetic person I've ever known."[5]

During his stay at Palm Beach, Kennedy's father, the "Ambassador," Joseph P. Kennedy, took Fulbright aside and told him the liberals, the NAACP, and the Zionists "just raised hell" when they heard about the possibility of his becoming Secretary of State.

When Fulbright returned to Washington, he found a case of scotch at his house, compliments of Joe Kennedy.

From then on, Fulbright and his closest friends would maintain that he never really wanted to be Secretary of State. Certainly, he knew it was politically unfeasible and, as he would say, "it wasn't in the cards anyway." Others felt Fulbright was deeply disappointed, that secretly he had hoped Kennedy would appoint him in spite of his political liabilities.

Lyndon Johnson was one who had been a staunch supporter of Fulbright for Secretary of State, and who seemed puzzled by Fulbright's behavior. Not long before the inauguration, Johnson happened to pass the Foreign Relations Committee Room in the Capitol. When he saw Carl Marcy, the committee chief of staff, standing in the doorway, Johnson stopped, wheeled, and strode over to him.

"What's the matter with your boss?" Johnson said. "He could have been Secretary of State. I was for him all the way. I got Jack to agree to take him, and then he turned it down. What the hell's the matter with him?"

In the days before the official beginning of the New Frontier, Fulbright had more on his mind than his own personal situation. As the chairman of the Foreign Relations Committee, a leading Democrat, and someone whom the next President obviously regarded highly, he himself was active in helping to perfect the Kennedy team. He was responsible for the appointment of George Ball, Adlai Stevenson's former campaign adviser, as Undersecretary of State. He was among those who urged Kennedy to appoint Edwin O. Reischauer as Ambassador to Japan, a position which he told Kennedy was perhaps "the most difficult, the most sensitive, and one where an inadequate representative would result in the greatest harm to our prestige and influence." He championed the cause of William Benton as Ambassador to the Court of St. James, a post which went to David Bruce; he supported Philip Stern, another Stevensonian from the '52 campaign, as Assistant Secretary for Congressional Relations; he recommended his former law student and predecessor in Congress, Clyde Ellis, as Secretary of the Interior.[6]

By the time of the inauguration, he had established a close relationship with Kennedy, and he had every reason to expect to become even more influential in the days ahead.

The New Frontier began with a glow that everyone connected with it would always remember. The bareheaded young President, his breath vaporizing in the icy air, the sparkling skies, the exuberant crowds, the challenging theme of the address, the spirit of change in the '60s and the sense of renewal with the past—all merged to become an enduring American legend.

After the speech, the youngest man ever elected to the presidency turned and shook hands with the oldest man to hold the office; then he and his wife walked through the crowds into the Capitol for an hour's interlude in the glittering Foreign Relations Committee Room. There, as chairman, Fulbright presided over a small luncheon group in honor of the President. At exactly 2:25 o'clock the President left to review his inaugural parade and begin his term in the White House.

The glow ended abruptly and disastrously three months later at the Bay of Pigs. That crisis not only marked an end to innocence, but it affected American foreign policies throughout the Kennedy administration and beyond. It taught harsh lessons and brought basic changes. Some of the changes were necessary and useful; others would plague U.S. policy makers for the rest of the decade.

Fulbright's part in the Bay of Pigs was small. He was not privy to the planning. At the last moment, however, he was brought into the fateful and highly secret deliberations that determined the go-ahead. His dissent and his forceful opposition expressed to the President earned him a special place in the history of the Kennedy administration. Had his advice been followed, the course of contemporary events would have been altered. Fulbright had become involved by chance; but, as on other occasions, he demonstrated a talent for capitalizing on an unsought opportunity.

On March 23, 1961, President Kennedy gave a coffee hour at the White House for thirty-three members of Congress, Fulbright among them. Although Kennedy had called Fulbright frequently, it was the first time the senator had been with the new President since the inauguration. During the coffee hour, the President and the senator fell to chatting. The Easter holidays were coming up shortly, and Kennedy asked:

"Where are you going for Easter?"

"We're going to Delray Beach [just below Palm Beach, Florida] to stay with Betty's aunt," Fulbright said.

"Well, I'm going to Palm Beach. How'd you like a ride?"

Fulbright accepted.

As soon as he got back to his office, he called Pat Holt, the Foreign Relations Committee's staff expert on Latin America. He and Holt already had been talking about rumors of an impending U.S.-sponsored invasion of Cuba. It was an open secret. In Miami talkative Cubans were boasting of the forthcoming action, and the "secret" training camps in Guatemala were public knowledge throughout the world. American reporters, among them Richard Dudman of the *St. Louis Post-Dispatch,* had filed on-the-scene dispatches about the camps, and Fidel Castro himself was well aware of the training progress. For months, Fidel had been preparing for the invasion.[7]

Realizing that he would shortly have an unusual opportunity to talk privately with the President, Fulbright and Holt discussed what approach to take in regard to Cuba. The Committee's chief of staff, Carl Marcy, also was brought into those discussions. They decided to draft a formal memorandum to the President, a typical course for Fulbright, who prefers to give advice privately—and to put his thoughts on paper.

Holt drafted the memorandum, and Fulbright then reworked it. Together they achieved a prophetic document.

First, it began with the assumption the invasion would succeed. Because of the common knowledge that the U.S. was backing Cuban exiles in the adventure, the memo said, the American government will be blamed for the intervention even though it tries to disclaim it. "Such an action would be denounced from the Rio Grande to Patagonia as an example of imperialism and as the conclusive answer to those who felt that the 1960 elections presaged a change in U.S. policy. We would undoubtedly also confront a serious situation in the U.N. . . . Thus, so far as insulating the rest of the Hemisphere is concerned, the United States would not find the overthrow of Castro, in the manner described above, a pure gain. It might even find it a net loss."

The memo questioned the Cuban exiles' political leadership, and doubted that it could arouse popular support. Once Castro was overthrown, a vacuum probably would result and the U.S. would be faced with the long, expensive, and arduous job of coping with a bankrupt country in an advanced state of disorder. The U.S. would be forced to try and put together the pieces without any assurance of success.

The memo warned:

"The prospect must also be faced that an invasion of Cuba by exiles would encounter formidable resistance which the exiles, by themselves, might not be able to overcome. The question would then arise of whether the United States would be willing to let the enterprise fail (in the probably futile hope of concealing the U.S. role) or whether the United States would respond with progressive assistance as necessary to insure success. This would include ultimately the use of armed force; and if we came to that, even under the paper cover of legitimacy, we would have undone the work of thirty years in trying to live down earlier interventions. We would also have assumed the responsibility for public order in Cuba, and in the circumstances this would unquestionably be an endless can of worms.

"One further point must be made about even covert support of a Castro overthrow; it is in violation of the spirit, and probably the letter as well, of treaties to which the United States is a party and of U.S. domestic legislation. . . . To give this activity even covert support is of a piece with the hypocrisy and cynicism for which the United States is constantly denouncing the Soviet Union in the United Nations and elsewhere. This point will not be lost on the rest of the world—nor on our own consciences for that matter."

In the end, the memo suggested, Castro would become an expensive liability to the Soviet Union; his government would not be able to compete within the inter-American system. Therefore, if the U.S. had faith in its own system and leadership, "there is no need to fear competition from an unshaven megalomaniac." A policy of isolating and insulating Castro's Cuba from the rest of the hemisphere in time could even strengthen the cause of democracy. The question was: "Can we afford the time? The answer is yes . . . provided that the Soviet Union uses Cuba only as a political and not as a military base ('military' is used here to mean missiles and nuclear weapons, not small conventional arms).

"Remembering always this proviso, the Castro regime is a thorn in the flesh; but it is not a dagger in the heart."*

On March 30, the day after the final memo was completed, Fulbright boarded Kennedy's plane to fly to Palm Beach.

Halfway down the coast, after a pleasant and light conversation with the President, Fulbright said he had something he wanted Kennedy to see. He drew out the memo from his coat pocket, handed it to the President and said, "I'd like you to read this." Kennedy quickly did.

"What do you think of it?" Fulbright asked, when the President had finished.

Briefly, they discussed the enterprise, Fulbright saying he thought "it would be a great mistake," Kennedy remaining noncommittal. At that point some other people aboard joined them, and their discussion of Cuba ended. Minutes later, the plane landed and Bill and Betty Fulbright left for Delray. The senator thought his memo had been a failure; Kennedy seemed to have dismissed it as of no consequence.

The Fulbrights were planning to return by commercial airline when the phone rang Easter Sunday. The President wanted Fulbright to go back on the plane with him that Tuesday, April 4. Nothing more was said about Cuba on the way back until shortly before Air Force One was about to land in Washington. Then Kennedy spoke casually to Fulbright.

"I'm having a meeting to discuss the subject of your memorandum at five o'clock this afternoon on the seventh floor of the State Department, and I'd like you to come along. I'm going to the White House first, then over to the [State Department] Auditorium for a press conference and

---

* Fulbright would remember that proviso and when the Russians secretly attempted to install missiles in Cuba, he was among the small group who advocated an American military response.

from there I'll go on upstairs to join you. You can go to the press conference if you like."

Fulbright stood in the back of the room while Kennedy handled the press with his usual grace; then he went up to the seventh floor and entered a room where he received the shock of his life.

From what Kennedy had said, Fulbright thought it would be a small, perhaps informal meeting. Instead, he found as intimidating an array of key American officials as would be assembled in one place. Three members of the Joint Chiefs of Staff, resplendent in their uniforms and campaign ribbons, Generals Lyman Lemnitzer and Thomas D. White, and Admiral Arleigh Burke, were there. So were Allen Dulles, the CIA chief, smoking his inevitable pipe, and Dulles' principal aide, Richard Bissell. The Secretary of Defense, Robert McNamara, and his assistant, Paul Nitze; the Secretary of State, Dean Rusk, and his Latin American assistant, Thomas Mann; the Secretary of the Treasury, Douglas Dillon; Adolph Berle, the old Latin American expert, and two other presidential assistants, Richard Goodwin and Arthur M. Schlesinger, Jr., from the White House—all sitting around a long table surrounded by maps and charts.

"God, it was tense," Fulbright would remember. "I didn't know quite what I was getting into."

It was, in fact, the full-dress and final major policy review for the Bay of Pigs.

Kennedy waved Fulbright to a seat near him and directly in front of Dulles. Seated next to Dulles was a heavy-set man in civilian clothes who had just returned from the secret training camp in Guatemala. Dulles introduced him and said he was there to give "the very latest" word on the CIA operation. The CIA emissary spoke in glowing terms of the combat readiness of the Cuban soldiers, Brigade 2506, of their zeal and determination, and of the American belief that everything was ready for the successful invasion.

"Then Dulles took it up and made his pitch," Fulbright said. "He told what would happen in Havana and all over Cuba after the landing. After the landing their source in Havana believed there would be a sympathy uprising."

Both Dulles and Bissell argued forcefully that the invasion could not be abandoned at that late date. What would the President do with all those emotional Cubans the United States had trained and implicitly promised to support? They would be disillusioned and embittered, and certainly would accuse the U.S. of going back on its pledge, of being weak and perhaps even soft on Communism.

"I remember also their discussing at considerable length that if anything unexpected happened to thwart them from moving on toward Havana, they could easily escape to the Escambray Mountains.* So it couldn't fail."

After the CIA briefing on the invasion plan, the President pointed around the table calling on specific people for assessments—feasible or unfeasible.

"I must give the military credit," Fulbright said later. "They weren't enthusiastic, but they said that given the conditions as outlined 'We think it's militarily feasible.' They were very solemn."

Although it was the first time he had heard any details of the invasion plan, Fulbright had been singularly unimpressed with the arguments advanced by the CIA. The point that the U.S. would be in a terrible dilemma if it called off the invasion "didn't appeal to me a damn bit," he said. Besides, because of his experiences in the 1950s with John Foster and Allen Dulles, he was highly dubious of such advice.

Kennedy did not call on everyone—Rusk, Goodwin, Schlesinger, and Dillon did not speak. No one opposed the invasion until the President pointed to Fulbright.

Excited, unprepared for such an occasion, and faced with overwhelming contrary views from the experts, but with the points and language of his memorandum still fresh in his mind, Fulbright spoke up strongly. He denounced the entire undertaking.

It would be a mistake no matter how one looked at it, he said. It would be a mistake if the military invasion succeeded, because without question the United States would be left with the task of rebuilding Cuba in our own image. Cuba would become an American puppet, an American Hungary, and the U.S. would be branded an imperialist. It was a mistake, obviously, if it failed, and despite what he had heard he was unconvinced the plan was so foolproof. Beyond that, it was the kind of undertaking that went against the very grain of the American character. It was a violation of our principles and our treaty obligations. No matter what the final outcome, it would clearly compromise America's moral position in the world.

"He gave a brave, old-fashioned American speech," Schlesinger remembered, "honorable, sensible and strong; and he left everyone in the room, except me and perhaps the President, wholly unmoved."[9]

After Fulbright spoke up, the CIA officials redoubled their efforts to get the President to give the green light. Kennedy, however, closed the meeting by saying:

"Well, gentlemen, I think we better sleep on this."

* That was the CIA's alternative plan which, the agency had repeatedly stressed to Kennedy, would ensure that a disaster could not occur. The Cubans, they said, had been trained to take such alternative action and also had been trained to fight on as guerrillas. Both statements were false. The CIA deliberately had refrained from informing the Cubans of the alternative plan. Neither did they tell Kennedy that such a plan was not a part of the operation. The Cubans also had *not* been trained as guerrillas, but as a conventional Army unit using World War II infantry tactics.[8]

At sunset, ten days later, the men of the Cuban Brigade steamed out of the harbor at Puerto Cabezas, Nicaragua, waving their colored combat scarves and singing their national anthem. In less than seventy hours after their landing those that were left had been consigned to prison, or were crawling through the vast *Cienega de Zapata* swamps surrounding the Bay of Pigs, and in Washington John F. Kennedy was wrestling with the most serious defeat of his life—and for the nation, one of its most humiliating.

On April 19, only hours after the final flash of defeat had come from the beachhead, Kennedy was host, in white tie and tails, at the White House reception for his Cabinet and the members of Congress and their wives. For an hour and a half the President and his beautiful wife whirled around the ballroom, the picture of youth and confidence, as the Marine Band played such numbers as *Mr. Wonderful*. At 11:58 P.M., he slipped away to meet privately in the Cabinet Room with top officials. Present were his brother Robert, Dulles, Lemnitzer, Burke, McNamara, Rusk, Lyndon Johnson, and such congressional leaders as Mansfield, Dirksen, Russell, Rayburn, McCormack, Vinson, Bridges, Saltonstall, Halleck, Arends, and J. W. Fulbright.[10]

Kennedy grimly reported on the failure. Half an hour later he stood up to leave. As he passed Fulbright, he turned and said clearly enough for those present to hear:

"Well, you're the only one who can say I told you so."

Fulbright always believed that the Bay of Pigs accounted for many of the ills that afflicted America throughout most of the 1960s. He and others felt that Kennedy's poor handling of that situation caused Khrushchev to misjudge the young President as inexperienced, unsure, and perhaps weak. Conversely, the shock of defeat strengthened Kennedy's determination to prove that he could be as tough as any leader. Subsequently, Kennedy moved to bolster American forces in Berlin and in Saigon. The emphasis of the administration switched to paramilitary operations, and a harder line was manifested. Now, one heard expressions of desire to beat the Communists at their own game.

Although Kennedy's performance had created doubt at home and abroad, Fulbright was not among the President's critics. Privately and publicly, he was urging the President's detractors to give him time, for he was convinced Kennedy would become an outstanding President who would lead America toward a more mature handling of world events.

Fulbright's counsel on the Bay of Pigs had elevated his stature in Kennedy's eyes, and the senator attempted to take advantage of an opportunity to exert more influence. He urged Kennedy to eliminate his less essential ceremonial duties and thus free himself for more vital problems. When a new Berlin crisis arose, he submitted another private memorandum. Before Kennedy left for a forbidding meeting with Khrushchev in Vienna that June, Fulbright urged him to reconsider the nature of American policies in Southeast Asia, specifically U.S. programs in Korea, Taiwan, South Vietnam, Laos, and Thailand.[11]

On June 29, in a major address, he posed questions that would bear on American foreign commitments. Should the United States attempt to impose its will on an alien land involved in an essentially nationalistic—if leftist—struggle? What were the wise uses of power available to a great democracy? What damage would result to that power if its own people lost faith in its government's credibility?

He cited as an example the little-noted country of Vietnam.

"The French spent eight years trying to defeat the Vietminh guerrilla army," he said. "They invested $7 billion in this war, which cost the lives of 100,000 French and Vietnamese soldiers. At one stage, the French committed a force of half a million men to the fighting. But France bore the heavy burden of its colonial record and its unconcern with political and social reform. Inevitably, France lost."[12]

As for what America was doing in Vietnam in 1961 with a small group of advisers, the best that might be said then was: "qualified success." The problem, as he saw it then, was our emphasis: The American stress in Vietnam was on military rather than economic needs. As long as that emphasis continued we, too, were doomed to failure.

He predicted that the tempo of Communist subversion in Southeast Asia would continue to step up in the months ahead, and warned that "the pressure will be relentless." At the same time, the United States realistically had to face the knowledge that no amount of guns, tanks, jeeps—or even dollars—would guarantee that Communism would be eliminated from any underdeveloped country.*

In that same speech, Fulbright also questioned whether a Communist regime in Cuba was intolerable to the United States. "I know it is embarrassing and annoying and potentially dangerous, but is it really intolerable?" he asked.

Yes, answered Barry Goldwater.

The U.S. should "*win* the Cold War, not merely wage it." Goldwater advocated resuming nuclear testing and then going on "to chart a positive course aimed at total victory. . . ."[13]

Fulbright replied sarcastically.

"The Senator says that our fundamental objective must be 'total victory' over international Communism. I must confess to some difficulty in understanding precisely what 'total victory' means in this age of ideological conflict and nuclear weapons. Certainly the term is a stirring one. It

* The administration never claimed for itself, however, such a mission. Both Kennedy, and later, Johnson, saw the United States acting as it had done since the 1940s —coming to the aid of a friendly country threatened with aggression.

has a romantic ring. It quickens the blood like a clarion call to arms, and stimulates the imagination with a vision of brave and gallant deeds."

Fulbright and Goldwater had foreshadowed the campaign to come.

On the weekend of the Bay of Pigs invasion three unheralded conferences were held in Arkansas—in Little Rock, in Fort Smith, and in Fulbright's own home town, Fayetteville. Called "strategy for survival" conferences, they were intended to promote discussion of the threat of Communism. The discussions, as Fulbright learned, were loaded. He was particularly incensed to learn that a speaker at the Fort Smith meeting had denounced the conservative and mild congressman, James W. Trimble, as one who "has voted eighty percent of the time to aid and abet the Communist Party."[14]

Fulbright began a private investigation. Before long he had discovered a national pattern: Similar meetings were being held across the country, and in every case the seminars were being promoted and sponsored by professional military men. Their authority rested on an obscure National Security Council directive of 1958 stating "It was the policy of the U.S. government to make use of military personnel and facilities to arouse the public to the menace of the cold war."[15] The military and the radical right wing were joining in an obviously political undertaking.

Instead of taking his case to the country, Fulbright wrote another memorandum, this time to Secretary of Defense Robert S. McNamara (with copies to Kennedy and Rusk).

The seminar programs, he said, by using "extremely radical right-wing speakers and/or materials," were leading to public condemnation of the administration's foreign and domestic policies. He recommended that the Defense Department issue general directives to stop military men from letting their official positions be used to oppose government policies.

McNamara issued such a directive and the military, enlisting major support on Capitol Hill, struck back. In an episode recalling McCarthy, J. Strom Thurmond, the ultra-conservative senator from South Carolina (and a reserve major general), burst into Fulbright's office and angrily demanded a copy of his military memorandum. Fulbright was out of the office. His assistant, Lee Williams told Thurmond he would be happy to give him a copy, but there was none available. Thurmond ordered the memo placed on his desk "within the next hour."

Two weeks later Thurmond got his "memo" when Fulbright told of the incident on the Senate floor.

"I was unaware that it was the custom, the practice, or the right of senators to demand access to the private correspondence of their colleagues," he said. "Although I should not have thought it my duty to open my private files, I would have been quite willing to show the memorandum in question to any senator who courteously requested to see. I was not willing, however, to comply with an ultimatum such as I received from the junior senator from South Carolina."

Fulbright then made public the entire memorandum by placing it in the *Congressional Record*.[16] Now Fulbright's enemies were convinced he was hopelessly un-American. Lee Williams soon drafted a private memo to him which described the opposition the senator was encountering.

"As a result of your Senate speeches, press conferences, television appearances and other public utterances in the past two weeks," Williams wrote, "you have succeeded in arousing the ire of practically every organized segment of world public opinion. This is reflected in the mail you have received during this period. The following is a list of the groups from which you have had messages indicating their displeasure with your expressed opinions:

"John Birchers, McCarthyites, Goldwaterites, Thurmondites, Dixiecrats, militarists, isolationists, Zionists, Germans, Catholics, Chinese Nationalists, Koreans, N.A.A.C.P.-ers, A.D.A.-ers, Communists, private powerists, veterans, farmers' cooperativites."

Right-wing spokesmen made it clear they placed the highest priority on removing Fulbright from his position of influence when he came up for his fourth term in 1962. For the first time in eighteen years, Fulbright had serious political opposition at home. And before the primary campaigning began, Senators Goldwater and John Tower, the Texas conservative, had announced they were going into Arkansas to campaign against Fulbright.

Both Governor Orval Faubus and the Dixiecrat Congressman, Dale Alford, planned to run against the senator. Faubus appeared to have a good chance, but after weighing his prospects, chose not to oppose Fulbright.* The senator won the Democratic primary handily. That fall of 1962, however, he faced his first serious challenge. On September 9, 1962, he left Washington to open his campaign headquarters in Little Rock, confident he would be returned to the Senate.

In the closing days of his campaign, Fulbright was summoned back to Washington aboard a special presidential jet for an urgent conference with the President.

At five o'clock on the afternoon of October 22 some twenty congressional leaders were shown into the President's oval office. While the President listened somberly, McNamara, Rusk, and CIA Director John McCone briefed them on the discovery of Russian missile installations inside Cuba. Kennedy told them that he had decided to institute a naval blockade of the island. He asked for their comments. Russell spoke first and argued against the blockade. He was supported by Fulbright. They counseled an American invasion of Cuba.

* Instead, he won an unprecedented fifth term as governor.

Fulbright argued that since blockade could lead to a forcible confrontation with Russian ships, it was more likely to provoke a nuclear war than an invasion pitting Americans only against Cubans.

His views particularly surprised—indeed, angered—Kennedy, for the senator had seemingly taken a totally different stance on the Bay of Pigs. (Fulbright's position was consistent with his memorandum. In it he had warned of the dangers that would result if the Soviet Union used Cuba as a military base for missiles and nuclear weapons.)

The meeting dragged on until after six o'clock. Kennedy, irritated, under enormous pressure, then rushed upstairs to change his clothes for his famous nationwide television address at seven o'clock initiating the Cuban missile crisis. As he walked out of his office, the President muttered to his assistant, Theodore C. Sorensen, "If they want this job, they can have it—it's no great joy to me."[17]

Later, Fulbright would view his part in that hurried meeting with distaste—not over his advice, but over the unsatisfactory role of the Senate in advising a President.

The senators had not really been called to give advice; they had been summoned to be told of fateful decisions already made in advance. In such a setting, with no prior knowledge or time for questioning and fact-finding, they were limited in reaching sound judgments.

"Had I been able to formulate my views on the basis of facts since made public rather than on a guess as to the nature of the situation, I might have made a different recommendation," he would say. "In any case, the recommendation which I made represented my best judgment at the time and I thought it my duty to offer it."[18]

It was an example, he would remark, of the "extraordinary difficulty a senator has in trying to discharge his responsibility to render useful advice and to grant or withhold his consent with adequate knowledge and sound judgment." In the future, he would be still more doubtful of the power and wisdom of presidential decisions reached in secrecy. Later, when he became the leader of the disparate forces of dissent, Fulbright made this a public issue in 1967–68. He insisted, then, that the Senate be consulted before any decision was made to involve the United States militarily anywhere in the world. This issue was to become a keystone of his opposition to increasing American participation in Vietnam.

When the missile crisis ended, Fulbright returned to Arkansas to complete his Senate campaign. He carried every county in Arkansas and received about seventy percent of the total vote.

Following the Russian withdrawal from Cuba, tensions eased. In 1963, Kennedy was moving forward with surer grasp. Abroad, the cold war was becoming a term of the past—the new operative words were "thaw" and "détente." At home, the non-violent "Negro Revolution" was bringing whites and blacks together in common cause. But for the world in general, the most glittering hope of all was the signing in August of the limited Test Ban Treaty: a small, but significant step toward slowing down the arms race by eliminating atmospheric testing.

Fulbright led the fight for ratification of the Test Ban Treaty, and during the year delivered a number of major addresses. At the end of the Eisenhower era his words had been urgent; now they were philosophical. He spoke of the eighteenth century and the prospects for a new age of reason; of the *Pax Brittanica,* and its lesson: Peace rested not only on military and economic power, but on the political uses of that power. For a great nation, the touchstone was restraint. He resumed his questioning of national priorities. One of his themes was new: The space race to place a man on the moon, costing billions of dollars, "was an astonishing distortion of priorities" for a society that had "shamefully starved and neglected its public education," unemployment, and urban renewal. As he examined the sums for space and defense, he turned to foreign aid and questioned some of its uses, though not its basic intent.

On September 24, 1963, by a vote of 80–19, the Senate gave its consent to ratification of the Test Ban Treaty. As Kennedy expressed it, "A journey of a thousand miles must begin with a single step." The step had been taken; the climate had improved noticeably.

The administration was uniformly optimistic. On October 10 and 11, the Foreign Relations Committee was briefed privately on two principal areas of concern—Vietnam and the Dominican Republic. After listening for three hours and fifteen minutes behind closed doors to Defense Secretary McNamara and General Maxwell D. Taylor, both of whom had recently returned from Vietnam, Fulbright emerged to tell reporters those experts had reported "impressive progress" in South Vietnam's military situation. They were both sanguine about meeting the goal of ending the Communist threat there by the end of 1965, although what they called "political unrest" conceivably might delay that prospect.

The following day, after a two-hour session with Undersecretary of State George Ball, Fulbright again stepped before the television cameras to say that Ball was "considerably more optimistic" about prospects for the new U.S.-backed regime in the Dominican Republic.

That same month Fulbright left on a trip to Arkansas with Kennedy. The President, in effect, was opening his 1964 campaign with trips into the South and Southwest. As they traveled across Arkansas, Kennedy ignored protocol and local dignitaries to plunge again and again into the crowds, once becoming separated from the Secret Service men accompanying him. Fulbright saw him one more time at a small White House luncheon for Marshal Josip Tito. Then the President was off again.

The Foreign Relations Committee met at 9:30 o'clock in the morning of

November 22 in a routine executive session on amending the Foreign Assistance Act of 1961. Later in the day Fulbright met his close friend, Eugene Black of the World Bank, at the F Street Club. There, during lunch, they received the news of the President's assassination.

"He had an unusual courtesy in small ways with people," Fulbright said that weekend in a radio interview. "I never saw any example of arrogance on his part; he never exhibited it to me. He was the most approachable President. I never had the slightest hesitancy in saying anything I thought to him. I never thought he might take offense at any idea I might have contrary to his own. He had an unusual combination of really profound understanding together with personal consideration and understanding of people.

"I think he set a tone about our government that I thought was somewhat unique. In every meeting that I attended with foreign people he always seemed to articulate exactly the right way. I never heard him say a gauche thing, never an insulting thing. I think he had a sensitiveness to foreign people that no other President had. We're a rather conceited people, rightly so in many respects. But he did not throw this at them; and I think he created an understanding among other people—that we are a civilized people, and he was a civilized man. Every time I went to a White House dinner, or any kind of ceremony, I was very proud of the way he represented me and my country."[19]

At 6:45 o'clock on the evening of November 22, 1963, President Lyndon B. Johnson arrived at his old office in the Executive Office Building adjoining the White House. For more than two hours he met and conferred with intimates and leaders. The first person he talked with was his old friend, J. William Fulbright of Arkansas.

2

LBJ: "ON THE VERGE OF THE GOLDEN AGE"

Air Force One. The presidential compartment.
Breakfast. The two men, face-to-face, leaning toward
each other, smiling. The photographer taking their pic-
ture. Afterward, the autographing: "To J. William Ful-
bright, than whom there is no better. Lyndon B.
Johnson."

THE PICTURE AND THE INSCRIPTION accurately expressed their relationship in December 1963. The senator already had said publicly that his old friend and colleague probably would become a great President; the Texan had reciprocated by bringing the senator into his closest confidences. They conferred, met frequently. The President was always friendly, always willing to talk; the senator felt himself a valued counselor, an important part of the administration.

When their break came, Fulbright would be inclined to think that the President actually had regarded him as a backbencher, a junior senator from Arkansas who willingly and unquestioningly would do anything the leader requested. But that was later—much later in terms of history and personal equations. Then, in early '64, there were no doubts.

The President's leadership was sure and firm. Better than Kennedy, he understood the Congress and knew how to make it work. On a series of fronts, the President moved swiftly and smoothly to attack the old problems of poverty, health, education, old age, the cities, race relations, conservation, national beauty. He was building what he began calling a "great society." To Fulbright, who had been urging such programs for so long and whose speeches in the '50s and early '60s had sounded the call for creating a "good society" in America,* Lyndon Johnson's presidency appeared the answer to dreams.

"I thought," the senator would say, "we were on the verge of entering our golden age. We had the opportunity: unlimited wealth, technical know-how, intelligent, energetic people—people not yet worn out, not too stratified by old and ancient traditions. We were doing almost everything I thought ought to be done. It was really a tremendous opportunity."

That was how he expressed it later. At the time, in a penciled note to Will Clayton in Houston at the end of January 1964, he said simply:

"The Texas President is doing a fine job under difficult circumstances. . . . He will come out all right, I think."

The setting was familiar: a nearly empty Senate chamber, a handful of tourists in the gallery, a few reporters glancing idly down toward the speaker's well. Fulbright adjusted his glasses and began speaking in tones that scarcely carried to the onlookers. It was the pattern he had followed before.

He was speaking, he explained, because it appeared as if profound changes were occurring in the character of East-West relations. Since the Cuban missile crisis and the Test Ban Treaty, both the United States and the Soviet Union had implicitly repudiated the insanity of a "total victory" goal. Responsibility and restraint had replaced the earlier reliance on massive retaliation and maintaining order through a balance of terror. Peaceful co-existence was more than a controversial phrase; it was a necessity if men were to survive.

Such changes from the earlier, harsh cold-war attitudes had been unsettling in the U.S. because, Fulbright believed, Americans were accustomed to view events in moralistic terms. "We are predisposed to regard any conflict as a clash between good and evil," he said, "rather than as simply a clash between conflicting interests." Then, in a celebrated passage, he remarked:

". . . It is within our ability, and unquestionably our interest, to cut loose from established myths and to start thinking some 'unthinkable thoughts'—about the cold war and East-West relations, about the underdeveloped countries and particularly those in Latin America, about the changing nature of the Chinese Communist threat in Asia and about the festering war in Vietnam."

Fulbright didn't think he was saying anything revolutionary. Since his maiden speech in the Senate, when his opening words had been "myths are one of the greatest obstacles in the formulation of national policy,"

* The title of a book in 1937 by Fulbright's friend, Walter Lippmann.

he had spoken time and again on such themes. Now, only four months after Lyndon Johnson became President, he was speaking of myths again. But this time, he touched chords that had been unresponsive in the past.

Within seven days he had received more than fifteen thousand letters. Among them were expressions of praise from eminent world leaders, statesmen, liberal politicians, and conservative businessmen.[1] Twice, in successive press conferences, the President had to deny any connection with Fulbright's views and specifically state that the administration disagreed with him on at least two points. Secretary of State Rusk also disassociated the administration from Fulbright's positions; and from the radical right came a new torrent of abuse.

He had intended his "Old Myths and New Realities" speech as a review of American foreign policy. The starting point—"the master myth of the cold war"—involved the Communist bloc of nations, he said. Contrary to popular opinion, they were not monolithic powers; they did not always act together, but contained variations. Neither was it still true that the Soviet Union was "totally and implacably hostile to the West." If Americans persisted in believing that all Communist regimes were equally threatening and equally hostile, and that the only way to oppose them was through a policy of overthrowing captive nations, then the U.S. was falling into the same trap Stalin had set for himself.

In the early postwar years the specter of an evil Stalin had frightened the West into a unity it undoubtedly never would have achieved without his menacing shadow. By the same reasoning, "the West may enforce upon the Communist bloc a degree of unity which the Soviet Union has shown itself to be quite incapable of imposing." The test was whether America would be wise enough to keep the Communist world divided.

"The myth is that every Communist state is an unmitigated evil and relentless enemy of the free world; the reality is that some Communist regimes pose a threat to the free world while others pose little or none, and that if we recognize these distinctions, we ourselves will be able to influence events in the Communist bloc in a way favorable to the security of the free world."

Through treaties, promotion of trade, and joining in other peaceful endeavors, cold-war tensions could be allayed. Fulbright had no illusions, however, that any specific act or series of acts "will lead to a grand reconciliation that will end the cold war and usher in the brotherhood of man." The most that might be expected would be to lessen extreme animosities heightening the threat of nuclear war. No matter what course we followed, it was unrealistic to think the cold war could be won or ended immediately and completely.

The part of his speech that attracted the most attention dealt with Cuba. Fulbright observed that U.S. policies aimed at overthrowing or blocking Castro had been failures. Neither military invasion nor an American trade ban had—or would—succeed in the future. The U.S. therefore should learn to accept the reality that the Castro regime was "a distasteful nuisance but not an intolerable danger" and stop flattering "a noisy but minor demagogue by treating him as if he were a Napoleonic menace."

When Fulbright turned to Vietnam he gave an analysis that placed him one full year ahead of the positions then held by the highest American officials but which he himself would reject two years later.

"The situation in Vietnam poses a far more pressing need for a reevaluation of American policy," he said. "Other than withdrawal, which I do not think can be realistically considered under present circumstances, three options are open to us in Vietnam."

These were: to continue the U.S. supported military effort against the South Vietnamese guerrillas; to try and end the war through negotiations and an eventual neutralization of North and South Vietnam; to expand the scale of the war "either by the direct commitment of large numbers of American troops or by equipping the South Vietnamese Army to attack North Vietnam territory, possibly by means of commando-type operations from the sea or the air."

At that time, Fulbright ruled out negotiations because of the military situation. He then expressed the thought that later became the Johnson administration's private justification for continuing the war: "It is extremely difficult for a party to a negotiation to achieve by diplomacy objectives which it has conspicuously failed to win by warfare. The hard fact of the matter is that our bargaining position is at present a weak one; and until the equation of advantages between the two sides has been substantially altered in our favor, there can be little prospect of a negotiated settlement which would secure the independence of a non-Communist South Vietnam."

He concluded: Until [U.S. officials] have had an opportunity to evaluate the contingencies and feasibilities of the options open to us, it seems to me that we have no choice but to support the South Vietnamese government and Army by the most effective means available. Whatever specific policy decisions are made, it should be clear to all concerned that the United States will continue to meet its obligations and fulfill its commitments with respect to Vietnam."

Senator Fulbright had anticipated the conclusions U.S. policy makers eventually would reach. He, not the President, not the Secretary of State, was performing a service that the administration was failing to do—to educate Americans to problems ahead, and to discuss the situation candidly. The administration's near silence on problems and policies would contribute considerably to difficulties in the future.

As had been the case so often in his career, the headlines seized on the current controversy and ignored the broader issues involved.

"He says what he believes is true rather than what is supposed at the moment to be popular," wrote Walter Lippmann. "He is not listened to on the floor of the Congress until he has been heard around the world. He has become the leading witness to the present truth, but it is not a fatal mistake to be right too soon."[2]

Ten days later Fulbright spoke out again, but in a different arena. His theme at the University of North Carolina, in Chapel Hill, was "The Cold War in American Life." There, on a rainy night in the college town, he was greeted with the most enthusiastic response of his life.

A capacity audience of students, townspeople, and faculty members turned out to hear him. When he finished, they crowded around him. The unpretentious, retiring politician had become a hero—and a hero of youth at that.

He told them how the cold war had consumed money, time, and talent, and had diverted attention away from the unmet needs at home, the "schools and homes and hospitals . . . the blight of ugliness that is spreading over the cities and highways of America . . . the poverty and hopelessness that afflict the lives of one-fifth of the people in an otherwise affluent society." In a perverse way, as he said, "we have grown rather attached to the cold war. It occupies us with a stirring and seemingly clear and simple challenge from outside and diverts us from problems here at home which many Americans would rather not try to solve. . . ." He spoke of "the mindless trivia of television," of "the gaudy and chaotic architecture that clutters the central areas of our great cities," of "the festering slums that surround them."

His goal, he said, was to raise the quality of American life by turning "our creative energies away from the cold war that has engaged them for so long back in on America itself.

"If we do this, and then let nature take its course, we may find that the most vital resources of our nation, for its public happiness and its own security as well, remain locked within our own frontiers, in our cities and in our countryside, in our work and in our leisure, in the hearts and minds of our people."[3]

The emotional response to his words was puzzling. Some saw in it a yearning among youth to find someone to fill John F. Kennedy's place. Indeed, before long another Kennedy would draw more fervent response with similar speeches. Lyndon Johnson addressed himself to such questions with as much ardor and conviction as any man. With the possible exception of Andrew Johnson, no one since Lincoln had come to the presidency with a background so deeply rooted in the problems of the people. But fate, the temper of his times, and his own personality led people to misunderstand and distrust him.

What Johnson thought privately of Fulbright's performance during his "old myths" speech and its sequel is a matter of conjecture. Publicly, he indicated annoyance. Within a month, however, he had taken steps to quell any speculation about friction between the administration and the senator by asking Fulbright to undertake a personal diplomatic mission. New clashes had broken out between Greek and Turkish Cypriots; the President wanted Fulbright to express America's concern to the Greek and Turkish governments. The senator, who had been planning a long trip to Europe, added Athens and Ankara to his itinerary.

When he came back, Americans had only one compelling interest—the national political conventions.

In San Francisco, in July, the Republicans convened in an evangelical atmosphere unmatched since Theodore Roosevelt led the Bull Moosers on a vain crusade. In '64, they chose Barry Goldwater to lead them.

In Atlantic City, in August, the Democrats made the obvious choice of their candidate official. On Lyndon Johnson's fifty-sixth birthday he was nominated in his own right.

The lines were drawn; the issues were as basic as in any campaign of the century.

Barry Goldwater was the intuitive, shoot-from-the-hip candidate. His philosophy was so oblivious to the complexities of the 1960s that meaningful debate was compromised. Communism was an evil; there could be no compromise with it. The struggle was inevitable; we must not shrink from it. Atomic bombs were a weapon; they should be used. His comments were so startling that, it seemed, he must have been misquoted. He was not.

When asked what he would do about Vietnam, he said blithely:

"I would turn to my Joint Chiefs of Staff and say, 'fellows, we made the decision to win, now it's your problem.' "[4]

In the same loose style, he would drop remarks about "defoliating" the trees over the jungle trails in Vietnam with "low-yield atomic weapons." When he spoke, also, of carrying the war to North Vietnam by bombing that country, interdicting supply routes, and knocking out bridges and roads leading into the south, he sounded equally menacing—and impossible to support.

For Fulbright, the prospect of Barry Goldwater as President was so unthinkable that it brought out his sharpest tongue and strongest emotions. Goldwater *had* to be defeated, and defeated decisively.

It was Fulbright who gave the first full-length administration response to Goldwater's views.

"The foreign policy issue in this campaign is as profound as any that has ever arisen between the two great American political parties. The Goldwater Republicans propose a radical new policy or relentless ideological conflict aimed at the elimination of Communism and the imposition of American concepts of freedom on the entire world. The Democrats under President Johnson propose a conservative policy of opposing and preventing Communist expansion while working for limited agreements that will reduce the danger of nuclear war."[5]

At that time Fulbright believed those words so strongly that he never once doubted Lyndon Johnson's prudent nature. (Within a year he would doubt not only the President's nature but the motives of his administration.) Earlier, at Atlantic City, in his speech seconding Johnson's nomination, he said:

"I know him well. . . . He has a genius for reconciling the irreconcilable, for resolving differences among men of deep conviction. . . . The same understanding of human nature which enabled him to lead the Senate so effectively during a difficult period in our history will enable him to find a way to resolve differences which exist among nations.

"I commend Lyndon Johnson to this convention and to all our people as a man of understanding with the wisdom to use the great power of our nation in the cause of peace."

Johnson's campaign emphasized his restraint, patience, and talent for persuasion. He talked of the "awesome burden" of the presidency, and liked to tell of being awakened with news from Vietnam.

". . . I never send a reconnaissance mission out about eleven o'clock with our planes and our boys guiding them to take a look at what is developing and realize they have to be back at three-thirty in the morning, but what promptly at three twenty-five I wake up without an alarm clock, because I want to be sure my boys get back. And sometimes they don't get back. . . ."[6]

Of the Southern senators, it was Fulbright who worked the hardest for Lyndon Johnson. He was primarily responsible for keeping Arkansas in the Democratic column while five other Southern states went Republican. Indeed, Fulbright was so totally committed to Johnson that some felt he worked harder for the President than on any of his own recent campaigns. He even spoke out directly for the first time about the need to bury the civil rights issue in the South and move on to more important business. In contrast, Senator Richard Russell went to Europe, and Georgia went Republican for the first time in a hundred years.*

When the verdict was in, the Fulbrights wired the Johnsons:

"WHAT A TEAM YOU ARE!! HEARTFELT CONGRATULATIONS
TO BOTH OF YOU FROM BOTH OF US, AND ALL BEST WISHES
FOR HAPPY AND FULFILLING YEARS AHEAD."

Once again, on the day after the election, Fulbright left for the annual NATO Parliamentarians' Conference in Europe. Also he was to witness

---

* After the election Johnson singled out Russell for a three-day visit at the LBJ ranch while other senators, including Fulbright, were not invited.

Yugoslavia's becoming the first Communist nation to join the Fulbright fellowship program. He departed with even more assurance than in 1960 that the country was in the best possible hands. When he returned, after conferring with Tito, he spoke optimistically of "building bridges" between East and West and of the hopes for further lessening of world tensions.

What he did not know—and would have found it hard to believe—was that highly secret contingent decisions already had been made to expand the war in Vietnam. Soon the very proposals that the militant Goldwater had been advocating would be put into practice by the moderate Johnson. And J. William Fulbright would discover that unwittingly he had helped to give the President the official congressional authorization he had lacked to carry the war in Vietnam to the North.

3

THE BREAK: PRELUDE

LYNDON JOHNSON BROUGHT to the presidency unusual political talents. To the public, he was the model of the politician—the politician who, like all such since Machiavelli, measured his steps, cautiously chose his alternatives, and never made a mistake. False as the impression was, the myth grew and, for many, became reality. For Johnson, it added to his problems as his administration became enmeshed in embittering and frustrating situations, most not of his making.

Basic to his problems was his failure in political leadership. Try though he did, he failed to educate; he failed to inform. As a result, the public—and other important politicians—often did not believe him. His penchant for secrecy sowed its own confusion and, ultimately, doubt.

It is too easy to rely on hindsight, but one fact seems clear: Lyndon Johnson could have forestalled much of the divisiveness that poisoned the political atmosphere in Washington and subsequently spread through the country by the simple device of being more candid with his political intimates and with the general public. His relationship with Fulbright was an example. Fulbright became an outright dissenter only after prolonged soul-searching and a long series of events which, piece by piece, chipped away at his natural inclination to work from within, rather than noisily and ineffectively from without.

The first link in the ultimate break was forged in the summer of 1964 as the presidential campaign was just beginning. It boiled down to a crisis of confidence in the President of the United States.

On Sunday, August 2, 1964, Lyndon Johnson was awakened early in the morning at the White House with a report that the U.S. destroyer *Maddox,* on routine patrol in the Gulf of Tonkin off the coast of North Vietnam, had been attacked by three North Vietnamese torpedo boats. The *Maddox,* aided by airplanes from the nearby carrier *Ticonderoga,* had sunk one ship and damaged two others.

Johnson reacted vigorously. Throughout the day he was in close contact with his principal advisers, Secretary of State Rusk and Defense Secretary McNamara. He wanted the answers to several vital questions. Why had North Vietnam's small navy directly engaged U.S. naval power? Why had it openly entered the Vietnam war? Did the action indicate a change in North Vietnam's military strategy? For up to then, North Vietnam's role in the war had been clandestine—the sending of cadres and supplies down through Laos and into South Vietnam to support the Viet Cong, the military arm of the National Liberation Front which for more than five years had been trying to seize power and unite the two Vietnams under the Hanoi regime.

Out of the discussions that day came two decisions. The first was not to retaliate. As McNamara's deputy, Cyrus Vance, said: "We assumed the attack was brought about by mistake." The second was less military and more political. Johnson decided to use the incident to warn the North Vietnamese that the United States, with its long history of defending the freedom of the seas, would not permit a second attack to go unanswered.

The President made that announcement himself. He called the White House reporters into his oval office the next day, Monday, August 3, and read a brief statement saying he had ordered the Navy "to attack any force which attacks them in international water, and to attack with the objective not only of driving off the force but of destroying it."[1]

Dean Rusk added his comment. "The other side got a sting out of this," he told reporters that day. "If they do it again, they'll get another sting."[2]

Within twenty-four hours the State Department had issued a formal note warning North Vietnam of "grave consequences" if U.S. ships were attacked again. In the Gulf of Tonkin, the *Maddox,* now joined by the destroyer *C. Turner Joy,* resumed its patrolling.

The next—and what was to become the suspect—part of the drama took place late in the night of August 4, again in the Gulf of Tonkin.

As the administration reported, sometime before midnight the *Maddox* made radar contact with unidentified surface craft and with three unidentified planes. The message was flashed back through the military communications channels to Washington. An hour later the *Maddox* and the *Joy* were reporting they were under continuous torpedo attack; they were firing back. According to McNamara's Senate testimony later, the vessels relayed messages saying they were avoiding "a number of torpedoes" and that "they had sunk two of the attacking craft."

In Washington, Johnson began one of his rare National Security Council meetings. The recommendation was swift: retaliate. Later, at lunch with McNamara, Rusk, and McGeorge Bundy, Johnson discussed the matter further. He had no choice but to hit back, he told them.

By late that afternoon the Joint Chiefs of Staff, at Johnson's request, had submitted targets of torpedo bases along the coast, Rusk and McNamara had crossed out bases on the border with China, and the President had given orders for the first American attack on North Vietnamese soil. Then, Johnson summoned the congressional leaders to tell them of his decision and ask for their approval.

Mansfield, Dirksen, Fulbright, Russell, and McCormack, among others, filed into the President's office and heard him report gravely on the situation. Rusk and McNamara, John McCone of CIA, and General Earle G. Wheeler of the Joint Chiefs also briefed the congressional leaders. After they had finished, Johnson said he wanted a resolution passed immediately "making it clear that our Government is united in its determination to take all necessary measures in support of freedom."

Unlike the Cuban missile crisis, there were no dissenters in that room. By nightfall, Lyndon Johnson was telling the American people on television that he had been given "encouraging assurance" that such a resolution "will be promptly introduced . . . and passed with overwhelming support." He was grim and tense as he told of the "renewed aggressive actions" against American ships, and of the orders he had given to retaliate.[3]

That was the public face of crisis the American people had become accustomed to in the 1960s. What the public did not see was another face of Washington in an hour of crisis.

While the President went before the nation to report on developments, private meetings were held on two sides of the Potomac River. On the seventh floor of the State Department, Dean Rusk met privately with the dozen or so correspondents who regularly covered his department. In his office at the Pentagon, McNamara did the same with reporters there. The Cabinet officers were not identified by name in the stories written later, but only as "U.S. officials."

Those were the "background" meetings. The sessions were "backgrounders," an important and in some respects questionable method of informing the public, for the intimate relationships and the sense of confidences shared and stories yet to be written could impose subtle restraint on the press's vital role of challenging information and determining facts, as opposed to what the government wanted the public to believe.

At his background session during the Tonkin Gulf crisis, held while the American air raids were in progress, Rusk appeared unperturbed. The presidential decision had been easy, he said, not nearly as fraught with danger as during the Cuban missile crisis. When Rusk was asked whether he thought the Vietnamese conflict might be expanded into a wider war, he said that decision was out of American hands. The North Vietnamese, the Secretary said, "are writing the scenario."

The next day, Thursday, August 6, Lyndon Johnson briefly hit the campaign trail with a speech at Syracuse University. There, before thousands and to thunderous applause, he uttered the phrase that would be his theme in the days ahead: "Aggression unchallenged is aggression unleashed."[4]

On that same day the President held a private meeting that was to become one of the most controversial of his administration. In Washington, he and U Thant, the United Nations Secretary General, discussed the Vietnamese situation. After his meeting with the President and other officials, U Thant left with the feeling that he had been given the go-ahead to try and bring about diplomatic contact, and possibly negotiations, between the U.S. and Hanoi.

And on that same August 6, in Washington, J. William Fulbright experienced what he would come to regard as his most humiliating moment in public life. It fell to Fulbright that day to introduce to the Senate the resolution the President had requested after it had been quickly reported to the floor from a joint Foreign Relations and Armed Services Committee meeting.

The resolution was five hundred words long. Calling the attacks in the Gulf of Tonkin "part of a deliberate and systematic campaign of aggression that the Communist regime in North Vietnam has been waging," it gave the President the authority:

> "TO TAKE ALL NECESSARY MEASURES TO REPEL ANY ARMED ATTACK AGAINST THE FORCES OF THE UNITED STATES AND TO PREVENT FURTHER AGGRESSION. . . .
>
> "THE UNITED STATES IS THEREFORE PREPARED, AS THE PRESIDENT DETERMINES, TO TAKE ALL NECESSARY STEPS, INCLUDING THE USE OF ARMED FORCE, TO ASSIST ANY MEMBER OR PROTOCOL STATE OF THE SOUTHEAST ASIA COLLECTIVE DEFENSE TREATY REQUESTING ASSISTANCE IN DEFENSE OF ITS FREEDOM."[5]

In the House of Representatives, the resolution passed swiftly by a vote of 416 to 0. In that entire chamber only one man expressed doubt. Adam Clayton Powell of New York voted "present."

In the Senate, in a chamber more crowded than usual, Fulbright stood to say, "Mr. President, I recommend the prompt and overwhelming endorsement of the resolution now before the Senate."

Then, in language that would embarrass him later, he said:

"The action taken by the United States in retaliation for the North Vietnamese torpedo boat attacks must be understood both in terms of the immediate situation and in terms of the broader pattern of Communist military and subversive activities in Southeast Asia over the past ten years. On both levels the North Vietnamese regime is patently guilty of military aggression and demonstrably in contempt of international law."

Only two senators—Morse of Oregon and Gruening of Alaska—voted against the resolution. But it was Gaylord Nelson of Wisconsin who asked Fulbright the most searching questions.

Nelson was concerned that the resolution would lead to a much greater involvement in Vietnam and "concerned about the Congress appearing to tell the executive branch or the public that we would endorse a complete change in our mission."

Fulbright did not share his fears. "As I understand it," he replied, ". . . the joint resolution is quite consistent with our existing mission and our understanding of what we have been doing in South Vietnam for the past ten years."

Then, in response to another question about whether the resolution could lead to the landing of large American armies in Vietnam or China, Fulbright gave his own interpretation of what the resolution meant—an interpretation that incorrectly forecast the events of the next three years.

"Everyone I have heard," Fulbright remarked, "has said that the last thing we want to do is to become involved in a land war in Asia; that our power is sea and air and that this is what we hope will deter the Chinese Communists and the North Vietnamese from spreading the war."

Senator Nelson still was not satisfied. He offered an amendment which said "our continuing policy is to limit our role" in Vietnam, and went on to state: "Except when provoked to a greater response, we should continue to attempt to avoid a direct military involvement in the Southeast Asian conflict."

Fulbright would not accept the amendment; it would delay passage by Congress, and time was short. But he did say, significantly in view of future difficulties, that he thought Nelson's amendment "is an accurate reflection of what I believe is the President's policy."

The Tonkin Gulf resolution gave the President the power he wanted. Within six months the resolution became the legal justification for further action. By then, the war that Nelson feared and Fulbright doubted had taken place.

In the bitter aftermath, Fulbright believed he and the entire Congress had been deceived. The resolution, he would say publicly two years later, was "a blank check signed by the Congress in an atmosphere of urgency that seemed at the time to preclude debate."

"I myself as chairman of the Foreign Relations Committee, served as floor manager of the Southeast Asia resolution, and did all I could to bring about its prompt and overwhelming adoption," he said. "I did so because I was confident that President Johnson would use our endorsement with wisdom and restraint. I was also influenced by partisanship: an election campaign was in progress and I had no wish to make any difficulties for the President in his race against a Republican candidate whose election I thought would be a disaster for the country."[6]

Later, when he examined the available information, he would conclude that the announced second attack of the torpedo boats on the American vessels was, at the least, shrouded in doubt. He was left with an extremely uneasy feeling that it had been deliberately staged or set up by the Americans to gain public support for military action. After all, he had not sat in on the Bay of Pigs deliberations for nothing. Some of his disquiet stemmed from an unsolicited letter from a retired admiral, Arnold E. True, who questioned whether the incident ever could have happened as reported in the press. Rear Admiral True, an expert on destroyer duty from his World War II Pacific service, wrote that it would have been extremely difficult for the *Maddox* to have determined whether the PT boats were in an attack formation at their reported distance. He also stated that the *Maddox* itself, by opening fire, had created "an act of provocation." The administration to this day insists that its version of the Tonkin Gulf incident was accurate and rejects categorically any insinuation that the crisis was staged. Because of his doubts, Fulbright asked for and received a "top secret" briefing from the Pentagon in 1966 and again in 1967 on the Tonkin Gulf affair. One machine gun shell, said to have been fired from the North Vietnam vessels, was produced, but Fulbright remained unconvinced.

A part of Fulbright's future anguish over his role in the resolution concerned what he felt was his own blindness at the time. Fulbright was so deeply involved in the Goldwater-Johnson campaign that he lost his critical detachment. He was so opposed to Goldwater, so certain Goldwater was rash and improvident, that he could not believe Johnson capable of aggressive military actions.

As he would say in private later, placing himself in the context of those early days of August when the campaign between Goldwater and Johnson was beginning in earnest and he himself was taking a leading part in it:

"It just seemed sort of really treasonable to question that damn Tonkin Gulf resolution at that time. But looking back on it now, there's just no excuse for it. I mean, in the first place, it's obviously questionable on its face as to whether it was unprovoked or not. I mean, from what I know now and what I knew then—it would look to me that the whole damn thing was provoked, that it was planned that way."

He would add:

"This sort of thing leaves you very, very doubtful."

The doubt came later.* In August, 1964, the Tonkin Gulf crisis, the Ameri-

* In the fall of 1967, Fulbright authorized the staff of the Foreign Relations Committee to investigate the Tonkin Gulf incidents. The staff produced a secret report,

can attacks, and the conflict in Vietnam itself were all secondary to the political campaign. And in that campaign Lyndon Johnson was by far the more decorous and prudent candidate. At every occasion, he stressed the need for caution. He particularly played down the possibility of military escalation in Vietnam.

His words were clear.

In September: "There are those that say I ought to go north and drop bombs, to try to wipe out the supply lines, and they think that would escalate the war. But we don't want to get involved in a nation with seven hundred million people and get tied down in a land war in Asia."[7]

That same month: "As far as I am concerned, I want to be very cautious and careful, and use it [escalation] only as a last resort, when I start dropping bombs around that are likely to involve American boys in a war in Asia with seven hundred million Chinese. So just for the moment, I have not thought that we were ready for American boys to do the fighting for Asian boys."[8]

In October: "Sometimes our folks get a little impatient. Sometimes they rattle their rockets some, and they bluff about their bombs. But we are not about to send American boys nine or ten thousand miles away from home to do what Asian boys ought to be doing for themselves."[9]

His words were reassuring. Fulbright, among others, believed them.

Neither Fulbright nor the American public was aware of what was taking place in the highest councils of the Johnson administration during those summer and fall months of 1964. Despite the constant public attempt to minimize Vietnam, the problems there were becoming critical. As Goldwater was pointing out, a time of decision was clearly at hand.

In contrast to his public utterances, in private Lyndon Johnson talked with his advisers of increasing the military pressure, of pressing for quick results. Roger Hilsman, Assistant Secretary of State for Far Eastern Affairs and a central figure charged with the problem of Vietnam under both Kennedy and, briefly, Johnson, offered inside testimony. Not long after the assassination, Hilsman wrote later, Johnson began pushing for action.

One of Johnson's first instructions, Hilsman said, "had been for everyone in the administration to ask himself each day what he had done toward victory there and to remind everyone that Vietnam was 'the only war we've got.' He appointed (at McNamara's recommendation) an interdepartmental committee to develop a list of bombing targets, a committee which in February [1964] became the new Vietnam task force."[10]

---

based on official Navy logs, that proved the two destroyers were on an intelligence-gathering mission—not the "routine patrol" as claimed by the administration. Within the Senate demands for a full and public airing became so intense that outgoing Defense Secretary Robert S. McNamara appeared before Fulbright's committee on February 20, 1968. Although the hearing was held privately, a "sanitized" transcript was quickly made public. McNamara, unconvincingly to his critics, stood by the administration's version. The Tonkin Gulf issue became a prime "credibility" issue, and was used by presidential candidates in 1968.

In the months after South Vietnamese President Ngo Dinh Diem's assassination, a succession of coups and countercoups brought only more instability in Saigon and weakened military morale. By the time of the U.S. presidential campaign, Johnson was receiving top secret reports telling him that the war was not going well. In late summer, an analysis by the Central Intelligence Agency gave the Saigon regime then in power only four months before it might be taken over by the Viet Cong.

From Maxwell Taylor, the former chairman of the Joint Chiefs, and then the ambassador in Saigon, came further alarming reports: For the first time, North Vietnam was sending regular army units into South Vietnam through Laos along the so-called Ho Chi Minh trail. From American intelligence came the word that the 325th North Vietnam division had begun operating in the South. And from the American generals at home came increasing pressure to expand the war. From the Joint Chiefs to the President came the opinion that only a major U.S. military role could turn the tide in South Vietnam. From General Curtis LeMay, the tough bomber pilot from World War II, came the blunt remark, in advocating bomber strikes on North Vietnam: "We are swatting flies, when we should be going after the manure pile."[11]

In the midst of such urgent problems, Lyndon Johnson continued to stress his patience and desire for peace. He gave every impression of being opposed to escalation of the war. Barry Goldwater, in that abused term, was the "hawk." While he chose to do nothing dramatic, Johnson was helped in the waning days of the campaign by other international events that focused public attention away from Vietnam. In Russia, Nikita Khrushchev was forced out; in Sinkiang Province, the Chinese exploded their first nuclear device.

Even after his smashing victory at the polls, Johnson continued to refrain from public discussion of the problems in Vietnam. Yet privately he set in motion the steps that led inevitably to the major commitment. In November, unknown to Fulbright, he appointed William P. Bundy, Hilsman's successor (and McGeorge Bundy's brother), to head an interagency committee to study the question of bombing North Vietnam on a regular basis. There is some evidence that Johnson himself already had decided upon such a step during the campaign.*

By early December, Bundy recalled, a "contingent decision" to bomb had been made secretly by the President.[12] If the military situation did not improve, bombing the North and increasing the American forces probably would be necessary.

Through all of that critical period, Johnson kept his own counsel and bound his advisers to the tightest secrecy. Although stories kept appear-

---

* Charles Roberts says in his book *L.B.J.'s Inner Circle* that the President personally told him he had "made the decision to bomb . . . at the height of the presidential election campaign."

ing about the inevitability of military escalation, of top-level discussion, of the highest deliberations, the President and his aides consistently denied that any major change was imminent.

Even those officials who ventured a candid appraisal of the situation refused to be quoted. Thus, Maxwell Taylor, on his return to Washington from Saigon in late November for an urgent conference with Johnson, privately conceded in a briefing with newsmen at the State Department that conditions in Vietnam were deteriorating, but offered the public nothing but cautiously optimistic words.

In Washington, political leaders still placed faith in Lyndon Johnson. They seemed united in the belief that Johnson, somehow, would find a way out of the dilemma. This impression was fortified by the private appearances of top men in the administration. Dean Rusk was central among them.

In those days, Rusk was arguing with what appeared to be great personal conviction that it would serve no useful purpose to bomb North Vietnam or to send in American fighting men. In his "bottle club" sessions,* with newsmen on the eighth floor of the State Department, Rusk would say that white men should not fight an Asian nation's war; that large numbers of U.S. troops would only lead to future and serious hostility with Vietnamese. On the question of bombing, Rusk always would say "the war must be won in the South." When pressed to be more specific, he would beg the question, for, as he would remark, the President had said he was not "going North" but was undecided about what action he might take to counter specific situations.

His public appearances backed up his private remarks. On January 3, 1965, for instance, when interviewed on a television program, he said that an expansion of the Vietnam war would lead to a multiplication of casualties and subject the people to devastation.[13]

Such remarks contributed to what came to be known in Washington as a "credibility gap" between the government and its citizens. No one spelled out the frustrating prospects of Vietnam better than Rusk himself at that time. To expand the war, he said in the same January television show, would lead down the trail "the end of which no one in any country could possibly see with assurance."[14]

Fulbright, himself, had no sure opinions about what to do in Vietnam. As his private correspondence indicated:

January 14, to a friend:
"Like everyone else I am more than a little disturbed by the situation in Southeast Asia, and more than a little perplexed as to what our proper course should be."

* The "bottle club" was the affectionate name newsmen gave to Rusk's frequent "background briefings" held at five P.M. on Fridays in one of the State Department's social rooms. Drinks were always served.

January 21, to Frank Stanton, president of the Columbia Broadcasting System:

"I have just read the report [a transcript of a CBS show on Vietnam]. A classic dilemma if I ever saw one. I confess I have not been able to arrive at a conclusion."

January 28, to a constituent in Little Rock:

"I am glad to have your comments about your son's experience in South Vietnam. It certainly is a distressing situation and seems to get worse every day. We have had many meetings trying to understand the situation, but so far no one has come up with any hopeful solution. I agree with your son's idea that we are trying to do the right thing, but the difficulties seem to be beyond our capacity to handle."

He concluded that letter with words that pointed toward his future position:

"I have been perfectly willing to go along with the efforts of the past, but I am not willing to enlarge this into a full-scale war."

Still, publicly Fulbright remained silent. While such leading senators as Mike Mansfield began warning against escalation because "in the end we might find ourselves in a full-scale war all over Asia," while scholars voiced fears that expansion of the war might drive Russia and China together in common defense of North Vietnam, while George Ball, the No. 2 man in the State Department, argued eloquently and forcefully in the private councils of the Johnson administration against bombing North Vietnam and thereby risking war with China, Fulbright, the man whose name would become synonymous with opposition and dissent, stood silently aside.

He was clearly unhappy, as he demonstrated at the end of January in answer to a hypothetical question from a *Time* newsman. Asked which road he would follow given the choice of escalation or withdrawing through negotiations, Fulbright was specific—he would negotiate. He also said he was strongly opposed to escalation and bombing. As he said, "You can't selectively do a little bombing," but he did not seem to think the choice was imminent.[15]

Then, and for months to come, he kept hoping that he would be able to persuade the President. He was still seeing the President often, and he was expressing himself. Those meetings had their frustrations, however; often Johnson either would do all the talking, or, while Fulbright would be speaking, obviously be preoccupied with other concerns.

Johnson, for his part, clearly wanted Fulbright's continuing support, although his method of operating was hardly flattering. When he perceived that Fulbright was disturbed over policy, the President told Rusk to "go and see Bill Fulbright and have breakfast with him." When Johnson noticed that Fulbright's views had not changed, he again urged Rusk to spend time with Fulbright. After the Secretary told of the times he had met or talked with the senator, Johnson said: "Go and see him some more."[16]

The technique of bringing together men with differing positions had worked for Johnson in the Senate. It was not as successful in the White House. The Johnson-Fulbright relationship remained cordial, however, and Fulbright remained convinced that, as he would say, "if there was any way of influencing him, it had to be by persuasion and he'd take the lead." Also he knew that supporting Johnson publicly strengthened his chances of exerting influence.

Nothing in Johnson's manner gave any hints of the imminent military escalation in Vietnam. His State-of-the-Union message barely mentioned the war. That same month he secretly authorized U.S. fighter bombers to begin attacking the supply trails in Laos. The next—and decisive—step followed quickly.

Early in February, Johnson sent his special assistant, McGeorge Bundy, to make an on-the-spot recommendation from South Vietnam on whether to bomb North Vietnam. Bundy's decision was made easier for him when, on February 6, Viet Cong forces mounted four early morning attacks, two of them at U.S. bases in Pleiku. Eight Americans had been killed and more than a hundred wounded. Those, however, were not sudden and unexpected Pearl Harbor-variety attacks, but merely the latest in a long series of terroristic assaults. Two days before the presidential election, a mortar barrage at Bien Hoa airfield had left five dead, seventy-six wounded, and six B-57 bombers destroyed; on Christmas Eve, a plastic charge had demolished Saigon's Brink Hotel, an American officer's billet, killing two and wounding ninety-eight. On those occasions no retaliatory action had been taken. In February, Johnson responded differently.

Within hours after he learned of the Pleiku attacks, Johnson was speaking before the National Security Council. The question, he said, was not what to do. The question was where to bomb.

That next morning it was announced that U.S. bombers had attacked North Vietnam in retaliation for the Pleiku incidents.

At first, the raids continued on the same tit-for-tat basis. But on February 17, the President inserted four paragraphs into a speech before a group of businessmen which fundamentally altered American policy.

"We must all understand," he said, "that we will persist in the defense of freedom, and our continuing actions will be those which are justified and those that are made necessary by the continuing aggression of others. These actions will be measured and fitting and adequate."[17]

This meant from then on, as long as Hanoi continued the war in South Vietnam, the United States would carry the war to the North. The U.S. would not wait for a specific attack before retaliation. Although this represented a clear shift, Johnson refused—then or later—to concede that any policy change had taken place.

On March 13, with obvious irritation, he said:

"I would say that our policy there is the policy that was established by President Eisenhower, as I have stated since I have been President, forty-six times, the policy carried on by President Kennedy, and the policy that we are now carrying on. Although the incidents have changed, in some instances the equipment has changed, in some instances the tactics, and perhaps the strategy in a decision or two has changed."[18]

The expansion was clearly a desperate step by the administration to halt the downward trend of the war. Johnson's hope was that North Vietnam would stop its war in the South to escape further aerial devastation. Until the military balance shifted more toward the U.S.-South Vietnam side, Johnson thought negotiations would be futile. Thus, in late February, Rusk told a news conference that negotiations would be pointless because Hanoi is not ready "to stop what it is doing." He saw little likelihood of talks succeeding and said: "A negotiation which simply ends in bitterness and hostility merely adds to the danger."

The air war immediately caused great concern in Washington and around the country. Many prominent Americans, recalling Red China's entry into the Korean war, feared the once insignificant Vietnam conflict might widen into a major war with China—or even Russia. The new bellicosity of the Johnson administration was underscored when U Thant reported from the United Nations that the United States had spurned a chance to meet secretly with North Vietnam in the fall of 1964. Rusk would say later that such talks would have had only one agenda topic: "Our surrender." This, he said, was unacceptable.

Fulbright reflected the apprehension. His next scheduled speech was a major appearance at Johns Hopkins University on March 12. Perhaps, he wondered, he should address himself to Vietnam? He chose not to, although in an oblique way he made a critical observation.

"I think we ought to ask ourselves hypothetically whether a Communist regime that leans away from China is worse or better from the viewpoint of our political and strategic interests than a non-Communist state, such as Indonesia or Cambodia, that leans toward China."

In other words, he was suggesting that a Communist—but basically nationalistic—Vietnam might serve as a buffer to China, an Asian version of a Titoist buffer state. The point would run through the debates to come. To him, the essential test was: How nationalistic was the struggle? In Vietnam, as in Cuba, he believed, the evidence was compelling. The revolution was from within; it concerned Vietnamese, not Chinese or Americans.

Fulbright's comments drew no attention. By the end of March, the war was not improving. Instead of ending the war, the only apparent result of the daily bombing raids was increased Viet Cong activity. To counter that action, Johnson ordered two U.S. Marine battalions to South Vietnam for "limited duty." By April 2, Johnson was announcing his intention to dispatch "several thousand" more troops.

Inch by inch the United States kept climbing toward the war that no one wanted and toward the end that no one could foresee.

Fulbright worried not so much about the specific military action, but about the long-range implications. There were two immediate fears: the possibility of another dangerous and direct confrontation with the Soviet Union over Vietnam, and the erosion of the hopes for an East-West *détente*.

Nevertheless, at the end of March, Fulbright believed the U.S. still had not become irretrievably involved in the Asian land war. And he thought, even though many of their meetings had been frustrating, the President might be receptive to his views. One day at the end of March, Johnson asked Fulbright to see him in the White House on his way to work the next morning. At 9:30 A.M. Fulbright was shown into the oval office, where he and the President conferred alone and at length.

This time, Johnson listened closely. Fulbright left feeling he was getting through.

When he returned to his office, he discussed the general Vietnamese situation with Seth Tillman, one of his principal foreign policy advisers and his chief speech writer. Fulbright wanted to draft a policy memorandum on Vietnam, along the lines of his earlier memoranda on the military and the Bay of Pigs. It was sent to Johnson on April 5. Fulbright also took a copy of the memorandum to a two-hour session with McNamara on a Sunday morning.

The senator's Vietnam memo made these general points:

1. It would be a disaster for the United States to try to engage in a massive ground and air war in Southeast Asia. Not only would it be extremely costly, but it would also revive and intensify the cold war, which had begun to ease following the missile crisis in Cuba.

2. The threat to Asia was not Communism, as such, but rather Chinese imperialism.

3. The smaller nations of Asia were historically afraid of—and independent of—China. Thus, a Communist regime in Vietnam independent of China, as Tito was independent of Russia, would be of greater value to world security than weak anti-Communist regimes dependent primarily on U.S. manpower and money.

4. As a way of finding an end to the war, the United States should declare a moratorium in the bombing, make clear its aims, and begin a campaign to persuade the people of Vietnam, north and south, of the economic and political advantages of a free and independent regime.

5. The United States might make its wishes known through Great Britain or Russia that it would accept an independent regime, regardless of its political makeup, and that we would at the same time join in guarantees

of the independence of the country and the rights of minorities, and that the regime not be a pawn or satellite of any great power.

6. It would be advantageous to world stability to have a regime in Vietnam oriented to Russia, rather than exclusively to China, since, at least at this point, China was in a belligerent and resentful mood.

Fulbright's Vietnam memorandum stands up well. Later, when the situation had changed drastically, he would look back on the memorandum and believe he had been right. He was more than willing to be judged by the advice he gave then.

On April 6, the day after the memorandum had been sent to the White House, the President asked Fulbright and Mansfield to come by and read a speech he was preparing for delivery the next night in Baltimore at Johns Hopkins. The newsworthy part of the speech was buried in a section devoted to peace talks.

"We will never be second in the search for a peaceful settlement in Vietnam.

"There may be many ways to this kind of peace: in discussion or negotiation with the governments concerned; in large groups or in small ones; in the reaffirmation of old agreements or their strengthening with new ones.

"We have stated this position over and over again fifty times—and more —to friends and foe alike. And we remain ready—with this purpose—for *unconditional discussions.*"[19] [Italics added.]

Despite a disclaimer by Johnson, the line about unconditional discussions represented another switch by the administration, and the principal reason the White House went to such unusual lengths to publicize the speech in advance.

Fulbright was pleased at the "affirmative tone" of Johnson's Baltimore speech. He thought his views had carried weight. A few days later, in an interview with Jack Bell of the Associated Press, he expressed approval of Johnson's Vietnam policies and offered two tentative suggestions. Before the escalation goes too far, the senator said, a temporary cease-fire might be advisable "just to give opportunity for reflection and possibly to go to discussions as proposed by the President." He also suggested that "the prospects for discussions might be enhanced by a temporary cessation of the bombings."[20]

His friendly words about Johnson's policies were lost in the many stories of protests—particularly on college campuses where the word "teach-in" had become a new term of dissent, something of an educated man's "sit-in" against the war in Vietnam.

Then, suddenly, at the end of April, 1965, the Vietnam war was eclipsed by trouble in the eastern half of the small impoverished Caribbean island of Hispaniola, the Dominican Republic. There, within a few days, more American troops would be involved than in all of Vietnam. And there Lyndon Johnson faced another crisis in political leadership, a crisis that led to the break with Fulbright.

4

THE BREAK: DENOUEMENT

IN FEBRUARY OF 1965, FULBRIGHT was quoting Pope John's blessing for Khrushchev's grandchildren and saying, optimistically, at the *Pacem in Terris* conference that "the world may well be on its way toward fulfilling the most vital condition of coexistence." In June of 1965, he was quoting Mark Twain's bitter "War Prayer" urging the Lord, in the spirit of love, to "stain the white snow with the blood of their wounded feet," and saying, pessimistically, that "the nations are sliding back into the self-righteous and crusading spirit of the cold war."[1]

He had evolved that swiftly from friendly critic to dissenter. In two corners of the world—in Saigon and in Santo Domingo—American policy seemed to him to have become jingoistic. From his earlier talk of "building bridges" between East and West, he began warning of the tyranny of the Puritan strain in American life; of dogmatic ideology, of false patriotism, of a resurgence of manifest destiny.

Part of Fulbright's uneasiness was due to the President's singular style. Under attack for his dispatch of troops to foreign lands, Johnson would become evangelically patriotic.

"I have seen the glory of art and architecture," he said in May, recalling a declamation from his youth. "I have seen the sun rise on Mont Blanc. But the most beautiful vision that these eyes ever beheld was the flag of my country in a foreign land."[2]

Once again, Lyndon Johnson was creating problems for himself. In an effort to prove a point, he often made statements at variance with the facts. His supporters attributed his occasional misstatements to his exuberant nature. It was his style, they would say: He was indulging in a bit of "Texas hyperbole." His detractors were less generous. In time, the Dominican crisis brought all of the elements of doubt and dissension into the open. It led directly to the debates over American involvement in Southeast Asia and, eventually, to Fulbright's questioning of U.S. foreign policy in the mid-1960s.

On Wednesday, April 28, 1965, the President had been conferring on Vietnam for forty-five minutes in the White House with McGeorge Bundy, Rusk, and Undersecretary George W. Ball, when, at 5:30 P.M., he was handed a cable sent fourteen minutes earlier by Ambassador W. Tapley Bennett in Santo Domingo. Bennett's cable was marked "critic"—the highest priority.[3]

During the past four days, a rebellion had swept the Dominican Republic. Donald Reid Cabral's pro-U.S. government had been overthrown, and the country was caught in a struggle between supporters of Juan Bosch, the former president, and the regular military leaders trying to restore order. Now, Bennett was cabling, the police no longer could protect the ordered evacuation of American citizens (a thousand already had been evacuated without incident the day before). American lives were in danger. Bennett reported that the military junta was dejected, several top members were weeping, and one was hysterically urging retreat. He said the time had come to land the Marines.

A few minutes later another cable from Bennett was handed to Johnson. Serious thought, he said, should be given to "armed intervention which goes beyond the mere protection of Americans." The question was not only to establish order, but to prevent "another Cuba" if the military junta's forces collapsed, as seemed likely.

From the beginning of the rebellion, American officials had been concerned about the possibility of a Communist take-over. The government had been well informed in advance about the attempt to overthrow Reid. In fact, the U.S. had tipped off Reid that a coup was imminent (but the CIA believed it would not occur before June 1). Bennett himself had been called back to the U.S. for urgent consultations about the CIA reports on the coup; he had stopped off in Georgia to see his parents before heading on to Washington when the actual revolt began on April 24. He immediately proceeded to Washington and then back to Santo Domingo.

In the first days of the revolt, the CIA began receiving reports from its fourteen agents in the Dominican Republic that known leftists and Communist-trained Dominicans were taking an active part in the rebel camp. During that period an increasing number of reports of Communist support for the Bosch cause began to bother Washington—particularly Undersecretary of State Thomas C. Mann, the top Latin American specialist in the administration and a "hard-liner" on Communism. By Monday, April 26, the Dominican military leaders, headed by the militant anti-

Communist General Wessin y Wessin, had asked for U.S. troops to quell the rebellion. They warned of the serious threat of a Communist take-over. As the revolt spread, the military leaders maintained their pressure for American intervention, and stepped up their warning of the Communist menace.

Wednesday, April 28, was the fateful day. Colonel Pedro Bartolone Benoit, who had been appointed head of the Dominican junta that morning, formally sent a written message asking the U.S. government for "unlimited and immediate military assistance." He added, ominously, that "the present revolutionary movement against democratic institutions . . . is directed by Communists." If successful, he said, it "will convert this country into another Cuba."

Thus, by the time Bennett had dispatched his "critic" cable, the question of Communist control already had become a vital factor in Washington decisions.

Johnson, after briefly discussing the situation with Mann, ordered McNamara to send in the Marines. It was the first U.S. military intervention in Latin America since 1927.

While orders were going out to Navy Task Force 44.9 on duty off the southwest coast of the Dominican Republic, Johnson summoned the congressional leaders for a seven P.M. meeting.

The President stressed the threat to American lives. Nothing was said about the threat of a Communist take-over.

At a briefing later, Fulbright raised a question. He asked Admiral William F. Raborn, who had just been appointed to succeed John McCone as head of CIA, how many Communists the agency had identified as taking part in the rebellion.

"Well, we identified three," he remembered Raborn replying.

At 8:40 o'clock that night the President spoke to the country. He said the congressional leaders had given him their support in his decision to land the Marines. They had been sent to "give protection to hundreds of Americans who are still in the Dominican Republic and to escort them safely back to this country."

Again, he said nothing about Communism.

Within twenty-four hours, Rusk and McNamara were in contact with Bennett. Did the Ambassador agree that a rebel victory probably would lead to a pro-Communist government? He did. Was direct military action necessary to prevent the installation of a pro-Communist government? He believed it was. When told not to hesitate in recommending whatever action he thought necessary, Bennett said, "Now that we are in this, we must do the full job as needed."

Out of such conversations, evolved the decision to send additional American forces. They established an international safety zone separating the two opposing sides and sealing off the rebels in downtown Santo Domingo.

Before long, more than 21,000 American troops—both Army and Marines —were active in Santo Domingo.

When the new landings were announced, Dean Rusk called in reporters at two o'clock on the morning of April 30. Santo Domingo news reports had been quoting anonymous U.S. officials as saying fifty-eight Communists were in charge of the rebel movement. Although Rusk acknowledged that extremists posed a danger, he discouraged reporters from emphasizing what he called "the ideological aspects of this thing." Major papers thus reported that U.S. officials had denied American troops were being sent to Santo Domingo to prevent Communist take-over.

On the same day that Rusk cautioned against the importance of the "ideological aspects," the President met with McNamara and General Earle G. Wheeler, the chairman of the Joint Chiefs of Staff. He asked them, John Bartlow Martin wrote later, "what they would need to take the republic." One or two divisions, they replied. Martin, a former Ambassador to the Dominican Republic who had been called back to Washington by Johnson, also recalled:

"The President said he foresaw two dangers—very soon we would witness a Castro/Communist-dominated government in the Dominican Republic, or we would find ourselves in the Republic alone without any support in the hemisphere. He didn't want either to happen."

Johnson went on to say, Martin reported, he did not "intend to sit here with my hands tied and let Castro take that island. What can we do in Vietnam if we can't clean up the Dominican Republic? I know what the editorials will say but it would be a hell of a lot worse if we sit here and don't do anything and the Communists take that country."[4]

Despite the public denials of the Communist threat, critical articles questioning administration motives began appearing in the *New York Times, N.Y. Herald-Tribune,* and *Washington Post.* The list of fifty-eight Communists was the source of the most controversy. It contained a number of inconsistencies and mistakes. In addition, the idea that fifty-eight Communists represented a massive threat in any Latin country was ridiculed.

Johnson reacted sharply. He began exaggerating: He described scenes that never took place, misquoted cables for dramatic effect, spoke contemptuously of his critics.

Throughout Sunday, May 2, Johnson briefed congressional leaders and railed against his critics. More troops were going into Santo Domingo; the issue was now greater even than the loss of American lives. Now the Dominican Republic must be saved from "other evil forces." On TV that night, he said fervently:

"The American nation cannot, and must not, and will not permit the establishment of another Communist government in the Western Hemisphere. . . . Our goal, in keeping with the great principles of the inter-

American system, is to help prevent another Communist state in this hemisphere."

Thus, the action to protect American lives had become a crusade to prevent Communism in the Caribbean. In language that evoked the cold-war period of the '50s, he closed:

"I want you to know and I want the world to know that as long as I am President of this country, we are going to defend ourselves. We will defend our soldiers against attackers. We will honor our treaties. We will keep our commitments. We will defend our Nation against all those who seek to destroy not only the United States but every free country of this hemisphere. We do not want to bury anyone as I have said so many times before. But we do not intend to be buried."

The next afternoon at a union convention in Washington he told how he had received Bennett's "critic" cable. He quoted it as saying: "You must land troops immediately or blood will run in the streets, American blood will run in the streets." (The night before, on television, he had quoted the same cable as saying, "Mr. President, if you don't send forces immediately, men and women—Americans and those of other lands—will die in the streets.") Then, in a veiled reference to John F. Kennedy's handling of the Bay of Pigs, he said:

"What is important . . . in this hemisphere . . . [is] that we know, and that they know, and that everybody knows, that we don't propose to sit here in our rocking chair with our hands folded and let the Communists set up any government in the Western Hemisphere."

By June 17, after an unsteady peace had been established in the Dominican Republic and criticism of his actions had increased, the President again went to extraordinary lengths to justify his position. In a press conference in his office, away from the television cameras, he was unforgettable. He shouted and snapped his fingers under the noses of reporters, thumped on his desk, pulled what he said were secret documents from his pockets. As an example of his style that day, he gave a new—and macabre —version of the dead in Santo Domingo.

". . . In this particular instance, a fact that has been emphasized all too little, I think," he said "[is that] some 1500 innocent people were murdered and shot, and their heads cut off. . . ."

He also said, in that press conference, that on April 28 Tapley Bennett "was talking to us from under a desk while bullets were going through his windows and he had a thousand American men, women, and children assembled in the hotel who were pleading with their President for help to preserve their lives."

These accounts mystified Johnson's aides, for they never reported such facts to him. In fact, they did not happen. Fulbright, in time, would seize on the story of the "1500 beheaded people" and use it as an example of the administration's deception. Johnson's friends would view these accounts as an example of his use of hyperbole to make a point.

On April 30, Secretary Rusk privately briefed the Senate Foreign Relations Committee—but carefully omitted mentioning administration fears about a Communist take-over. He stressed that the overriding reason for the intervention was to save lives. The senators were told no more than the reporters had been.

Thus, two days later when Johnson announced that the U.S. was acting to halt the establishment of a Communist regime, members of the committee immediately registered private annoyance. They felt the administration had treated them cavalierly. Wayne Morse called for another private briefing the next day.

Fulbright was not present at that executive session which saw Senator John Sparkman of Alabama in the chair and Morse doing most of the questioning. In the witness chair was Thomas Mann. He more than lived up to his reputation as a strong anti-Communist. As Mann put it, the Dominican situation started off as a normal rebellion in which known Communists went into the streets, organized mobs, and passed out submachine guns and rifles to people of all ages. He said the tone and tenor of the radio messages had a "strong Communist Castro tinge to them."

His response bothered Senator Morse, the committee's top specialist on Latin America. Since Friday, Morse said, there seemed to have been a change in the President's policy. While, as he said, he didn't want to see a Communist stronghold develop in the Dominican Republic, he had "grievous doubts" as to whether or not the United States had any right to take sides. Morse went on to say the issues involved were going "to be the debate in this country for some time unless we can get it clarified very quickly."

In his long testimony before the committee, Mann appeared ambivalent. At one point he told Morse that the U.S. was not taking sides. Then, minutes later, he said he did not want to leave the committee with the impression that he thought the Communist threat was very small. Castro, he remarked, started out with twelve people; and the Dominican Republic was then in a situation of chaos without law and order, thus open prey to a Communist take-over.

His black-and-white terminology annoyed some of the senators. For instance, in justifying the intervention, Mann went far beyond the reasons given by the President, and bluntly remarked:

"If we had to, we could say that this is justified on the grounds of self-defense. This has certainly occurred to us many times."

He said he himself had been thinking of such a defense for intervention for two years. But the administration hesitated to take that position publicly right then because it would raise other questions. Mann talked of the prospect of another Russian missile base there and flatly predicted that "if that half of the island were Communist, Haiti would fall within thirty minutes." The dangers, as he spelled them out, did not rest solely within the Dominican Republic. They were directly linked to difficulties in such countries as Venezuela, Colombia, or Panama.

Far from reassuring the committee or gaining its support, Mann's views created more concern. Eighteen days later, with Fulbright presiding, the committee heard another private report from Rusk. By then the U.S. intervention had made it impossible for the rebels to win. But the *junta* also was unable to win. Because of the new doubts over the U.S. intervention, the small executive hearing room on the first floor of the Capitol was crowded with other senators that day. They had been invited by Fulbright to sit in on the closed-door session.

Rusk told the senators that although there had been reports about extremists moving in, the decision to send in the troops on the twenty-eighth "was ninety-nine percent the problem of protecting American and foreign nationals." He also stated that the administration at that time was not "involved in all of these possible ramifications." Once the troops were ashore, though, he said, the administration became increasingly aware of the role "that was being played by these hard-core, extreme-left people."

Fulbright, who for so long had criticized American policy makers for failing to make meaningful distinctions between leftist revolutions and Communist-dominated ones, asked Rusk:

"Do you consider it now a struggle against Communism?"

Rusk sidestepped that question. After Senator Clifford Case of New Jersey noted that many influential men in Washington were now expressing disapproval of the decision to intervene, Fulbright attempted another line of questioning.

In the beginning, he said, he was certain most senators approved of an evacuation operation. Then he asked: When did it cease to be an evacuation and then an occupation? Was there any point?

Rusk never directly answered.

Throughout the months ahead, that question gnawed at Fulbright as his committee took a long, hard, and thorough look at the complex Dominican situation—a crisis in which honest men had honest differences on what had happened, what should have happened, and what would result from the American intervention.

From Fulbright's standpoint and that of his committee, enough questions had been raised to justify an extensive investigation. While the committee staff, headed by Carl Marcy and Pat Holt, began a six-week period of research based on State Department cables and memoranda preparatory to private hearings, Fulbright left for Europe to attend the Council of Europe meeting in Strasbourg, France. When he returned, it was not the question of the Dominican Republic that commanded his immediate attention. He found himself involved again with Vietnam.

The war was not going well in June when the President called Fulbright to the White House. The President was under heavy pressure to commit larger numbers of American troops. In addition, he was frustrated by the failure of Hanoi to respond and by the reluctance of his critics to applaud his willingness to hold negotiations.

At the White House, Johnson told Fulbright that McNamara would soon announce the dispatch of six new combat battalions, plus additional logistical support to South Vietnam. Few were aware of the pressures he was under to escalate the war, he complained. As they walked together in the Rose Garden, the President said it would be helpful if the senator gave a speech stressing the administration's attempts and desire to end the conflict by negotiation. The President clearly was seeking his help, and Fulbright responded: He agreed to deliver a speech on Vietnam. It was Fulbright's first major address on that subject.

His Senate speech on June 15, 1965, backed the administration, praised Johnson personally for resisting pressures to expand the war "with steadfastness and statesmanship," and said the President "remains committed to the goal of ending the war at the earliest possible time by negotiations without pre-conditions. In so doing, he is providing the leadership appropriate to a great nation."

Although the speech contained some slight criticism of the policies today, its tone was favorable and it stressed—as Johnson had asked—the number of times the U.S. had attempted "to reach reasonable settlements in Southeast Asia." Before giving it, Fulbright showed it to the President. It was the only time he ever had done that.

Fulbright had given the speech in an attempt to encourage the President's peace efforts. But later it would seem oddly out of key. It would lay Fulbright open to criticism that he was indecisive and ambiguous; that his future critical views grew, perhaps, out of personal pique.

"I am opposed to an unconditional American withdrawal from South Vietnam," Fulbright said then, "because such action would betray our obligation to people we have promised to defend, because it would weaken or destroy the credibility of American guarantees to other countries, and because such a withdrawal would encourage the view in Peiping and elsewhere that guerrilla wars supported from outside are a relatively safe and inexpensive way of expanding Communist power."

Neither Johnson nor Rusk ever stated that side of the argument better.

The Dominican crisis would have passed into history, merely another footnote to a troubled era, had it not been for the Senate Foreign Relations Committee. The committee, at the insistence of Fulbright and Senator

Eugene McCarthy of Minnesota, decided to hold full—and private—hearings on the crisis. The purpose, as McCarthy expressed it, was to find out "why the administration found it necessary to dispatch a strong force of Marines and paratroopers to the Dominican Republic to protect lives."

Facts were not the main issue. Judgment was. Through all the hearings that were to take place, the Johnson administration attempted to convince the senators that it had acted prudently, wisely, and appropriately, given the situation that existed. But the more he heard, the more disenchanted Fulbright became.

The date was July 14, 1965, the time 10:15 A.M., the place the committee's private room in the Capitol, S-116. The witnesses were Tom Mann and Cyrus Vance, McNamara's chief deputy. Besides Fulbright, Senators Lausche, Hickenlooper, Aiken, and Carlson were present. As the hearing proceeded, Senators Clark, McCarthy, Williams, and Case came into the room.

At this writing, the transcripts of the Dominican hearings have not been officially released. This is unfortunate, for they offered an intimate look at the decision-making process in Washington, with close examples of the working of the Pentagon, State Department, Executive Branch, and the CIA. The central question of the hearings involved the nature of Communism, how much of a threat it represented, and what American reaction to it should be.

In the case of the Dominican Republic, administration spokesmen indicated that a potential military dictatorship was preferable to a Communist regime. Tom Mann was specific. Any popular front which gives respectability to Communists by making them a part of an alliance is "per se a dangerous thing," he said. Mann placed Juan Bosch, the former Dominican president who had enjoyed strong American backing under Kennedy, in that category. Although he did not think Bosch was a Communist, Mann felt he was "a poet professor type" who could be controlled by the leftists. He also disclosed that the U.S. had seriously considered intervening against the rebels.

If we were so concerned about the Communists, Fulbright countered, why didn't we back the Reid regime or the non-Communists in the rebel group? Mann's answer did not satisfy Fulbright.

The testimony indicated that Ambassador Bennett may have missed an opportunity to resolve the strife before America intervened. At a meeting with Bennett on April 27, three days after the revolt began, a group of non-Communist rebels had indicated they were about ready to give up if the U.S. would back them. Bennett said the rebels "wanted us to negotiate for them a victory which they hadn't won." He also said the rebels were asking him to take their side, and he didn't feel he should.

Yet, having said that, Bennett readily admitted under questioning that he had orders to try and get the military to form a provisional government.

Admiral Raborn, the CIA director, produced a CIA document placing the Dominican involvement in the context of a larger threat throughout Latin America. The CIA felt that at any moment, with little warning, the following countries could be overthrown by a coup: Bolivia, Haiti, Panama, Guatemala, Ecuador, Honduras, Uruguay, Colombia, Venezuela, Argentina, and British Guiana.

The effect of this, Fulbright said, is that the United States would oppose any movement that the Communists support; this would narrow the choice for all of Latin America either to one of Communists or a military *junta*.

Moments later, Fulbright summed up what he called "the real guts of this."

What is important for the future, he said, is to be very discriminative in the application of American force. If the U.S. is going to intervene whenever there is even a small Communist influence present, the final result will be an increase in Communist influence all over Latin America.

Many people are dissatisfied with the status quo in these countries, Fulbright pointed out, and a lot of them ought to be dissatisfied and are seeking ways to change. If the U.S. maintains too harsh an attitude and makes too many mistakes, they are going to conclude that the only solution is to become Communists. He hoped the administration would encourage changes within a non-Communist context.

The Dominican hearings ended as they began: with distrust and a certain amount of ill will on both sides. On that last day, both Mann and his assistant, Jack Vaughn, said they couldn't believe that President Johnson had said 1500 people had been beheaded in the Dominican Republic. Even when Fulbright waved the official State Department bulletin with a reprint of the President's June 17 press conference, Mann still refused to believe it.

Committee members were divided on what they had accomplished, or what they should do. It was quickly apparent that a majority would not be able to agree on any report and none was ever written.

Fulbright was dejected. The hearings themselves had begun at a bad moment: On the first day his friend, Adlai Stevenson, had died of a heart attack on a London street. The day before Stevenson's death, Fulbright had written him a last note, passing on a routine request for a summer job from a constituent. As an afterthought, Fulbright wrote, in hand, a brief postscript.

"Now you see in action the major function of a senator."

In the first week of August, Fulbright left for Brazil at the personal request of Lyndon Johnson. Although the ostensible purpose was to examine U.S. foreign aid programs there, some Fulbright intimates believed

Johnson was thinking of casting Fulbright in a new role—a liberal foreign affairs emissary who could go places and do things that were inconvenient or impracticable for Rusk. If that were true (and there is no firm evidence to back the belief), the events of the next few weeks dispelled the possibility of such a role.

While Fulbright was away, Pat Holt, the committee's Latin American specialist who had helped write the Bay of Pigs memorandum, had begun drafting a speech about the Dominican Republic. His version was also worked on by Seth Tillman.

Carl Marcy, the veteran staff director of the committee, added his counsel. In a memo to Fulbright dated August 17, Marcy asked: "Has the time come for a speech on foreign policy that would review and comment on the developments of the last twenty-four months?"

"What has happened in the last two years to thrust the hopes of the world for peace, into the abyss of fear of world war? What has happened to turn the liberal supporters of President Kennedy into opponents of the policies of President Johnson? What has happened to turn the right wing opponents of Eisenhower and Kennedy into avid supporters of the policies of the present administration? Perhaps it is the Russians who have changed; perhaps the Chinese; perhaps the Viet Cong; perhaps Hanoi.

"I suggest, however, that most of the change has come within this nation itself. We have tried to force upon the rest of the world a righteous American point of view which we maintain is the consensus that others must accept. Most of the tragedies of the world have come from such righteousness. . . ."

After such provocative language, however, Marcy said he was not sure Fulbright should give such a speech. It "would break you with the administration," he said, "and make Borah and Hiram Johnson and Cabot Lodge, Sr., look like pikers."

At about that time, Lee Williams, Fulbright's principal personal staff assistant, learned of the draft Dominican speech. Williams, who had come to Fulbright ten years before as a young Arkansas lawyer, was devoted to the senator and particularly watchful of political implications. He strongly urged the senator against speaking out in opposition to the Dominican policy. He was convinced it would cause an "irreparable break" with Johnson, and thus ruin Fulbright's hopes for playing an influential role within the administration. Williams immediately telephoned Marcy and conveyed his fears. After discussing the possibilities, Marcy, too, came to a decision: He agreed that such a speech would cause more political damage than it was worth.

Late in August, Fulbright called a meeting in his private Senate office. It was the key moment. Pat Holt and Seth Tillman argued strongly for giving the Dominican speech. The administration had deceived the public, they said, and the intervention had led to great resentment in Latin America. For Fulbright to speak out would clear the air and also serve U.S. interests by letting liberals in Latin America know that not everyone shared Johnson's policy. They also believed Fulbright's speech was important to preserve the integrity and independence of the Foreign Relations Committee.

Williams was equally firm in arguing against making the speech. "You're just going to ruin yourself with the President."

The senator asked Marcy for his opinion. Marcy said it would cause a break with Johnson.

"That's a political decision I'll have to make," Fulbright observed. "I want to know if the speech is accurate."

It was accurate, Marcy said.

Fulbright said he was going to deliver it.

Not since Borah had criticized the sending of the Marines into Nicaragua in the 1920s had the chairman of the Foreign Relations Committee directly challenged an administration of his own party. But the circumstances were hardly comparable. In addition, Fulbright had closer personal ties with the President than any of his predecessors. As much as any other factor in his decision to dissent was a belief that he was getting nowhere with Johnson.

On the morning of September 15, 1965, he sent a copy of his speech to the President with a letter explaining his reason for making it. He gave it that afternoon in the Senate.

"As you will note," he wrote the President, "I believe that important mistakes were made. I further believe that a public discussion of recent events in the Dominican Republic, even though it brings forth viewpoints which are critical of actions taken by your administration, will be of long term benefit in correcting past errors, helping to prevent their repetition in the future, and thereby advancing the broader purposes of your policy in Latin America. It is the hope of assisting you toward these ends, and for this reason only, that I have prepared my remarks."

He made it clear that he was not criticizing the President personally but the "faulty advice that was given to you." He ended with the words:

"Public—and I trust, constructive—criticism is one of the services that a senator is uniquely able to perform. There are many things that members of your administration, for quite proper reasons of consistency and organization, cannot say, even though it is in the long term of interests of the administration that they be said. A senator, as you well know, is under no such restrictions. It is in the sincere hope of assisting your administration in this way, and of advancing the objective of your policy in Latin America, that I offer the enclosed remarks."[5]

The speech itself was sharply critical. "U.S. policy in the Dominican crisis was characterized initially by over-timidity and subsequently by over-reaction," he began. "Throughout the whole affair it has also been characterized by a lack of candor." He commented on "exaggerated estimates of Communist influence," of "a general tendency on the part of our policy makers not to look beyond a Latin American politician's anti-Communism," and of the administration's cardinal mistake: "The administration acted on the premise that the revolution was controlled by Communists—a premise which it failed to establish at the time and has not established since."[6]

The reaction was quick, cutting, and more personal than Fulbright had anticipated.

In the Senate, the rebuttal was left to Thomas Dodd of Connecticut, the President's friend and member of the Foreign Relations Committee. Dodd rarely attended committee meetings; in fact, he sat in on only one session of the Dominican inquiry; but he had a reputation of being willing to deliver administration speeches as his own. Fulbright, he said, suffers from "an indiscriminating infatuation with revolutions of all kinds—national, democratic, or Communist."[7]

In the press, William S. White, the President's long-time intimate, said Fulbright's criticism "had created a poignant crisis for the orderly conduct of American foreign policy." White took Fulbright to task not only for breaking with Johnson and Rusk, but for committing perhaps a graver offense: He had "also broken the unwritten rule of the game, a code which demands of those holding high committee chairmanships—and uniquely the chairmanship of foreign relations—a degree of self-restraint and personal responsibility not demanded of the rank and file."[8]

White was entirely correct. Fulbright had broken the rules of the game, but it was precisely those very rules that had contributed so much toward the erosion of the influence of Congress and the continuing shift of power to the White House.

While he never heard directly from the White House, Fulbright knew from friends that Johnson was displeased. In the following weeks, Fulbright realized how far apart they had drawn.

On October 8, the President suddenly announced he would have to enter Bethesda Naval Hospital for a gall-bladder operation. Because of his massive heart attack years before and the pace at which he drove himself, the news was greeted with alarm.

Fulbright composed a sensitive letter to the President and went to unusual lengths to see that Johnson received it before entering the hospital. He sent a note to Jack Valenti, then Johnson's closest personal aide, saying: "You told me sometime ago that if I wished to be sure the President received a communication to send it to you. I am, therefore, enclosing a letter which I hope you can deliver to the President before he goes to the hospital."

The letter set forth both Fulbright's admiration for Johnson and also his conviction that he could be of most value to him by remaining independent. The senator hoped his letter would fall on receptive eyes.

"I am very sorry to read that you must have an operation for the removal of your gall-bladder," he wrote. "Betty had hers out nearly thirty years ago, and she says to tell you that she has never missed it for a minute. So apparently its removal creates no great sense of loss! Nevertheless, I am truly sorry that you have to have any kind of operation.

"I sense from various sources that you were displeased by my recent speech. I regret this. I sincerely believe that in the long run it will help you in your relations with the countries of Latin America. I admit, of course, that my judgment could be wrong, but there is already a very considerable response from here and abroad which supports my basic premise.

"Regardless of the validity of my judgment in this instance, I have done in the past, and shall continue to do in the future, what I can to help you to the best of my ability. I make no secret of the fact that I think you were the best Majority Leader the Senate has ever had, and that I believe you are and will continue to be a great President. It does not seem to me that I can be of any help to you by always agreeing with every decision or every opinion of your Administration. These are necessarily, in many cases, collective opinions, and like all others may sometimes be in error. As I understand the function of a senator, especially one who is deeply interested in the success of his President, it is his duty whenever there is any question about a policy to raise the matter for clarification and for correction if the resulting discussion reveals the need therefor. Subservience cannot, as I see it, help develop new policies or perfect old ones.

"As you know, I have been in the Congress a long time. I desire no other office. I only wish to contribute whatever I can in my present position to the success of your Administration and, thereby to the welfare of the people of my State and my Country."

Fulbright never had any response from the President.

In the midst of mounting public scorn, Fulbright's wife Betty, on whom he leaned so heavily, suffered a serious heart attack. Soon Fulbright was saying, bitterly, in answer to a question about whether more senators should speak out, "I can't advise them to speak out, because if you do then everyone jumps down your throat. This country has gotten to where you are not supposed to speak out."

It was left to a Republican, Senator Margaret Chase Smith of Maine, the author of the eloquent "Declaration of Conscience" during the McCarthy era, to come to Fulbright's defense.

"I not only defend his right to express his deeply felt views and his sharp dissent; I admire him for speaking his mind and conscience," she said. "I admire him for his courage to run counter to conformity and the overwhelming majority. God forbid that the United States Senate ever becomes so shackled by conformity or dominated by a tyranny of the majority that any senator has to become a mental mute with his voice silenced for fear of being castigated for expressing convictions that do not conform with the overwhelming majority."[9]

For a politician who had engendered so much controversy for so many years, Fulbright displayed a thin skin. He reacted personally—and often petulantly—to criticism. Once Wayne Morse, who glories in public combat, shrewdly commented on the differences between himself and Fulbright. Not long ago he had gone to the White House, Morse recalled, on a routine matter with other senators. When he arrived, Johnson greeted him with the remark: "Wayne, I've never seen you looking so fit. How do you do it?" Morse replied: "Well, Mr. President, I'll tell you. Every time I read in the papers what you're doing about Vietnam, it makes my blood boil. That purges me; it keeps me fit." As for Fulbright, Morse went on, "Bill's a bleeder. He keeps agonizing over it."

Fulbright's moodiness became a familiar trait. He could be caustic, sarcastic, condescending; then, when his words had brought an unusually strong response, he could change abruptly and act offended. At such times he often gave the impression that he had been misinterpreted; that no matter how cutting he had been, he never intended his remarks personally. His actions bewildered those who admired him most, and sometimes disappointed them. To his enemies his behavior was evidence that he was playing the role of Cassandra, and enjoying it. He was accused of taking the easy way, of failing to offer reasonable alternatives, of criticizing for criticism's sake. As his own dissent became more pronounced, it was not unusual to hear important Washington officials privately expressing doubts about Fulbright's psychological make-up. They suspected him of being jealous of those who had the President's ear and frustrated by his own increasing isolation.

The senator was aware of such criticism, and often would refrain from making further public statements or speeches for fear of being regarded a crank. Thus, there were lengthy periods when he withdrew and remained mute, seeming to be brooding in private. His deliberate withdrawal raised a more serious criticism about the nature of his leadership.

By background, taste, training, and personal inclination Fulbright was a figure of the Establishment. For all of his early criticism of the Senate and the seniority system, he enjoyed the privileges of his position; and though he probably would not concede it, he relished the power that came with his office. At the same time he lacked the quality of ruthlessness that had lifted less talented politicians to the top. In fact, viewed solely as a conventional political leader, Fulbright was a failure. Certainly from the standpoint of the peace movement in the United States, Fulbright was far from the hero his supporters wanted him to be. He did not lead his battalions in some glorious—if vain—charge. Indeed, for a long time he stood apart and offered little public encouragement to the cause. Neither was he entirely consistent in his actions. Once having raised an issue, he often failed to offer any solutions. For instance, he spoke out again and again about the administration's Tonkin Gulf resolution—but he always refused to try and repeal it. His reason was calculated and understandable: Congress certainly would support the President in a showdown and in so doing would appear to give Johnson more support than he actually had. But such actions also left his would-be followers feeling he had let them down.

But those who thought of him as a gentle philosophical politician, temperamentally standing a safe distance from the guns, did not know him well. Although clearly he went through inner turmoil over any major issue, once he was convinced he was right he could become inflexible. It was, one of his intimates remarked, "the German strain in him." And, as the administration and the country at last came to understand, when finally committed to a fight, Fulbright never gave up.

For all of his public disputes, Fulbright remained one of the most private men in Washington. Unlike others whose names were household words, one heard no stories about Fulbright's personal life, no juicy gossip to enliven a stultifying cocktail party. From his home, overlooking Rock Creek Park near Embassy Row, to his office on Capitol Hill, Fulbright's life was marked by a quiet that belied his reputation.

The office itself reflected his personality. There, even in the midst of the most searing controversies, one found unusual decorum. His staff was small and devoted to him. Every one was a native of Arkansas; every one had served him for years. And unlike the chambers of other famous men on the Hill, Fulbright's office was remarkably free of those who attached themselves to the great and who intended to rise with them. One could not imagine any diarists scribbling private conversations while working for Senator Fulbright.

On a typical day, the senator arrived on Capitol Hill about 9:30 o'clock after driving alone from his home, and let himself into his private office with a key. Often members of the staff never knew whether he was there or not. The work itself went smoothly and quietly. Once his desk was clear, he customarily traveled alone to the Senate floor in the Senate subway. In the Capitol he had an unpretentious small private office near the Foreign Relations Committee room where he often retired to prepare a speech, study an issue, or draft a series of questions for a witness. He seldom left the Hill during the day. At lunchtime he normally returned to the Senate Office Building to eat in the Senate dining room. By seven or eight o'clock at night he left his office and drove home.

Physically, the senator had changed little in his years in Washington. After a quarter of a century in the Congress, he weighed only five pounds more than he had when he left college. He was a bit grayer; he had a few more lines; but he continued to give an impression of contained vitality that complemented his rather rugged features.

Seeing him in the privacy of his office or at his home, it was hard to imagine him as a cantankerous public figure. Alone or surrounded by family and friends, he was relaxed and disarming. The drawl, the resonant voice, the quizzical manner, the slow smile, the bright blue eyes—all imparted informality and charm. He was colloquial, and in private conversation used a fair amount of damns and hells and occasionally stronger expressions (he seemed surprised, when seeing a transcript of his conversation or hearing a taping of his words, to discover just how frequently he relied on them). When talking about his own career, the senator was detached and candid on every subject but one. On the question of civil rights, his manner changed noticeably. He became defensive, and once remarked, "That's going to be the hardest thing to deal with when you write about me." Otherwise, he obviously enjoyed discussing a wide range of topics at length, and told his stories with a fine sense of humor and timing. He would watch a visitor slyly, his head cocked to the side, to see if he caught the point. Fulbright seemed so easygoing, so diffident and slow, that it always was a surprise to see him leave his desk and dart to a roll call, to a hearing or to a luncheon appointment. He retained the athlete's movements. His staff liked to characterize him by reciting an old saying. The senator, they would say, is fond of old shoes, old cars, old wives. He drove a second-hand Mercedes for twelve years until he bought a more recent model in 1967; once he wore a pair of shoes for fifteen years, and, of course, there was only one woman in his life.

Before her heart attack, Betty Fulbright maintained an active social life. She is an outgoing person, without pretense, and she keeps the Fulbright private life pleasant and as free of stress as possible. After her illness, her heavy social calendar was sharply curtailed. The senator did not seem to miss the engagements. He was not particularly interested in social life anyway, and preferred to spend his time relaxing at home with his wife and a few friends. Betty, in fact, often had to prod him into going out. When they went to his favorite vacation spot in Bermuda, for instance, the senator typically would not go out except to swim and snorkel. Occasionally, he played golf, and whenever he was in Arkansas, he tried to find time to take the baths at Hot Springs.

They are grandparents, now, and take the usual pride in their offspring. Their elder girl, Betsey, married a Washington doctor, John Winnaker, and has two children. Roberta (Bosey) married a young lawyer, Thaddeus Foote III, a cousin of Adlai Stevenson, and lives in St. Louis with their two children. The daughters seldom went to Arkansas; most of their lives were spent in Washington and private Eastern schools.

The senator, though, remains attached to Fayetteville. His older brother, Jack, died in 1968; his older sister, Anna Teasdale, lives in St. Louis near Tad and Bosey. The twin sisters have died. But in Fayetteville, the Fulbright presence is still evident. Roberta Fulbright, the senator's mother, died in 1953 during the McCarthy era, but her newspaper is as strong as ever. Her son-in-law, Hal Douglas, and her nephew, Allan Gilbert, direct the paper (like Roberta, Gilbert writes a daily column). The Fulbrights still control the lumber yard and the Coca-Cola bottling plant, but the family home on Mount Nord was sold years before. Now, from Mount Nord one looks down on the University campus and sees a handsome girls' dormitory named in memory of Roberta Fulbright. In years to come, there undoubtedly will be similar memorials to her son.

In his later years, the senator began to express a certain nostalgia for the past. Reminiscing, however, was a luxury he was seldom permitted after he became President Johnson's most celebrated critic.

Early in December, following his Dominican speech and while the stories continued to make the rounds of Fulbright being cut off the White House's guest list, the senator left the fractious air of Washington as the head of a congressional delegation to a Commonwealth Parliamentarians meeting in New Zealand.

He departed under inauspicious circumstances: his four-engine prop plane took four days to reach Australia; earlier the Air Force had turned down a routine request by Carl Marcy for a jet to transport his delegation. For reading matter, the senator brought along *The Crippled Tree* by the Chinese-Belgian author, Han Suyin. The book contained a vivid and personal account of China's ill-treatment at the hands of the West. Fulbright's thoughts naturally turned to Vietnam and Asia as his plane headed out over the Pacific. The next step in his dissent was inevitable.

5

THE LAND OF THE DOMINOES

TO THE FRENCH, it was *la guerre pourrie*. Americans would share the feeling. It was the rotten war, the most frustrating war, and, on its face, the most unlikely war for Americans.

"How did it happen," Fulbright would ask, "that America, the foremost advocate of colonial liberation after World War II, who set an example by liberating its own Philippine colony in 1946, allowed itself to be drawn into a colonial war and then a civil war in Indochina?"[1]

How, indeed?

The Country:

Like the American West and the Russian East, Vietnam developed in stages. First there were the Viets, fleeing south in 500 B.C. from their Chinese overlords and eventually being overtaken and captured by the river in the valley around the present city of Hanoi. Then came the migration south again, in the tenth century A.D., to the central highlands. Then the move south once more, and the final settling of the delta by 1780. United briefly under Emperor Gia Long, the country was divided again into thirds when the French seized control in 1884. Since 1954, when the Geneva agreement of that year created a Communist state in the north and a non-Communist one in the south, it has been cut in two along the 17th Parallel.

The History:

At the heart of the Vietnam tragedy is a central dilemma. As Fulbright would point out, "the most powerful nationalist movement in that country is one which is also Communist." And the Communist leader of that movement is a genuine nationalist revolutionary. All of the debate would center around these facts, and the questions arising from them.

Ho Chi Minh has personified the ambiguities. Born Nguyen Van Thanh on May 19, 1890, in Annam, in the central highlands, Ho has traveled the world. He stayed in New York and Paris, learned to speak French, English, Russian, German, Czech, Japanese, and several Chinese and Annamese dialects, was active in the '20s and '30s in the clandestine nationalist Vietnamese groups, and was arrested in Hong Kong in the late 1930s. Then he disappeared. During World War II, he emerged in Chungking, the nationalist capital of China. Again he was arrested. Subsequently freed by the Chinese on the condition that he work for them, he was sent to North Vietnam where he conducted espionage and guerrilla operations against the Japanese. There, he also assisted the U. S. Office of Strategic Services (OSS)—the forerunner of the CIA—and helped rescue American pilots. And there, on V-J Day, he proclaimed the independence of all Vietnam. It was Ho, the wispy and unfathomable figure from the north, who led the long and vicious war of liberation against the French, which cost them 174,000 casualties and, after their great defeat at Dienbienphu, their colony.

The United States moved to fill the vacuum of the French defeat of 1954, thus vastly expanding an initial commitment that had begun in the early months of the Korean War. The timing of both actions was crucial to the deep involvement that developed.

The Commitment:

In August, 1950, confronted with an aggressive Communist drive from North Korea, and facing the peak of the cold war, it was easy for American policy makers to view the French fight against Asian Communists as analogous to the Korean conflict. It was equally easy to discount considerations of nationalism and anticolonialism. Thus, the first thirty-five American military advisers, watched sullenly by the French, arrived in Vietnam.

The commitment grew slowly, steadily.

By October 12, 1952, the 200th American ship carrying military aid had arrived in Saigon. By 1954, at the time of Dienbienphu, with a new administration in power, America nearly intervened directly on behalf of the French. Admiral Arthur Radford, the chairman of the Joint Chiefs of Staff, urged such action. General Matthew Ridgway, the hero of Korea and then the Army Chief of Staff, argued that it would be disastrous to commit ground forces there. Two years later, in his memoirs, Ridgway recalled how close the U.S. had come to intervening and wrote:

"In Korea, we had learned that air and naval power alone cannot win a war and that inadequate ground forces cannot win one either. It was incredible to me that we had forgotten that bitter lesson so soon—that we were on the verge of making that same tragic error. That error, thank God, was not repeated."[2]

But the commitment remained; it coincided, unhappily, with the height of the McCarthy era, amid what Fulbright would call "an attitude of fear and hostility toward Communism in all its forms."

President Eisenhower spelled out the American policy in detail at a press conference on April 7, 1954. He was asked to comment on the strategic importance of Indochina to the free world—a question raised, the reporter said, because there has been "some lack of understanding on just what it means to us."

Eisenhower cited what he termed "the falling domino principle."

"You have a row of dominoes set up," he said, "you knock over the first one, and what will happen to the last one is a certainty that it will go over very quickly. So you could have a beginning of a disintegration that would have the most profound influences."

The loss of Indochina would be followed by Burma, Thailand, the Malay peninsula, and Indonesia until "now you are talking really about millions and millions of people." In Eisenhower's view, it would not stop even there: The dominoes would continue to fall until Australia and New Zealand were threatened, until the defensive island chains of Japan, Formosa, and the Philippines were forced to turn toward the South, and until they had only one place to turn—toward the Communist East.

Under Eisenhower and John Foster Dulles, American military and economic aid poured into South Vietnam: nearly two billion dollars worth in eight years. Within five years after the arrival of the first U.S. advisers, the U. S. Military Assistance Advisory Group (MAAG) had taken over the training of the South Vietnamese army.

On July 6, 1956, Vice President Richard M. Nixon, on a visit to South Vietnam, handed a letter from Eisenhower to President Ngo Dinh Diem pledging many years of partnership between the countries. Before the South Vietnamese Constituent Assembly, Nixon declared that "the militant march of Communism has been halted." A year later, Diem visited the U.S., addressed a joint session of Congress, received a twenty-one-gun salute at the White House, and was given a pledge by Eisenhower that any Communist aggression "would be considered as endangering peace and stability" in his land. That fall, the first U.S. military personnel were injured in a guerrilla attack. Over the years, Eisenhower's pledges grew more binding. Less than two weeks before John F. Kennedy was elected President in 1960, Eisenhower assured Diem that "for so long as our strength can be useful, the United States will continue to assist Vietnam in the difficult yet hopeful struggle ahead." Nine days after Kennedy's inauguration, Radio Hanoi was saying the National Front for Liberation of South

Vietnam had pledged itself to the "sacred historical task" of overthrowing the "U.S.-Diem clique" and liberating the south.

On Kennedy would fall the burden of making the preliminary decisions to expand or withdraw the American presence.

The Kennedy Years:

On February 2, 1961, Kennedy was handed a gloomy report about Vietnam written by Colonel Edward Lansdale, the legendary CIA operative and prototype of the fictional hero of *The Ugly American*. Kennedy read it; then he turned to Walt W. Rostow.

"This is the worst yet." He added, "You know, Ike never briefed me about Vietnam."[3]

Kennedy had had more experience with Vietnam than most Americans. In 1951, he had gone there as a young congressman; he had left highly critical of American support for the French. The United States, he said then, should go over the heads of the French and "build strong native non-Communist sentiment within these areas." In 1954, when the question of U.S. intervention was being debated, he spoke out strongly in the Senate against such a move.

"For the United States to intervene unilaterally and to send troops into the most difficult terrain in the world with the Chinese able to pour in unlimited manpower, would mean that we would face a situation which would be far more difficult than even that we encountered in Korea."[4]

He carried his skepticism to the White House.

In the spring of 1961, shortly after the Bay of Pigs, he dispatched Lyndon Johnson to Saigon. When Johnson returned, he reported to Kennedy that "the basic decision in Southeast Asia is here. We must decide whether to help these countries to the best of our ability or throw in the towel in the area and pull back our defenses to San Francisco and a 'Fortress America' concept. More important we would say to the world in this case that we don't live up to our treaties and don't stand by our friends. This is not my concept. I recommend that we move forward promptly with a major effort to help these countries defend themselves."[5]

For Kennedy, the most important moment of decision came in October, 1961. Diem was then calling for increased American military support and declaring "it is no longer a guerrilla war waged by an enemy who attacks us with regular units fully and heavily equipped. . . ." American military leaders were pressing for an expansion of U.S. support.

In a valuable footnote to history, Kennedy's old family friend, Arthur Krock, recalled a private luncheon he had with Kennedy on October 11, 1961, in the White House.

"According to notes I made immediately afterward," Krock said, "the President had just come from a meeting on the problem in Vietnam. He said the Pentagon generally approved a recommendation by the Chiefs of Staff to send 40,000 troops there. The President said he was not favorable to the suggestion at that time and therefore was sending General Maxwell Taylor to investigate and report what should be done. It was a hell of a note, he said, that he had to try to handle the Berlin situation with the Communists encouraging foreign aggressors all over the place.

"The President said he was thinking of writing Khrushchev, urging him to call off these aggressors in Vietnam, Laos, et cetera, and asking Khrushchev how he thought he could negotiate with Kennedy if their positions were reversed. The President still believed, he said, in what he told the Senate several years ago—that United States troops should not be involved on the Asian mainland, especially in a country . . . inhabited by people who didn't care how the East-West dispute as to freedom and self-determination was resolved. Moreover, said the President, the United States couldn't interfere in civil disturbances created by guerrillas, and it was hard to prove that this wasn't largely the situation in Vietnam.

"I asked him what he thought of the 'falling domino' theory—that is, if Laos and Vietnam go Communist, the rest of Southeast Asia will fall to them in orderly succession. The President expressed doubts that this theory had much point anymore because, he remarked, the Chinese Communists were bound to get nuclear weapons in time, and from that moment on the nations of Southeast Asia would seek to be on good terms with Peking."[6] [Two years later, however, Kennedy was saying forcefully and publicly that he believed in the validity of the domino theory.][7]

When Taylor (who had been accompanied by Walt W. Rostow) returned from Vietnam, he recommended bolstering American forces there. In a point of major significance later, Taylor and Rostow for the first time raised the question of bombing North Vietnam. Although Taylor refrained from an outright endorsement of bombing, Rostow, later to become one of Johnson's principal Vietnam strategists, argued vociferously for a bombing plan. He even circulated copies of such a memo to newsmen.

Kennedy reached a decision: He would send additional American military advisers and equipment, but specifically *not* commit American combat forces.

Arthur M. Schlesinger, Jr., recalled Kennedy saying he didn't like a proposal made then to send an American combat team of about 10,000 men.

"They want a force of American troops," Kennedy told him. "They say it's necessary in order to restore confidence and maintain morale. But it will be just like Berlin. The troops will march in; the bands will play; the crowds will cheer; and in four days everyone will have forgotten. Then we will be told we have to send in more troops. It's like taking a drink. The effect wears off, and you have to take another."[8]

Yet even with the additional aid, there were only about 4000 U.S. military personnel in Vietnam by early 1962. And despite all the turmoil of the next year and a half—the building of strategic hamlets, the increasing pressure from the Viet Cong, the eventual overthrow and assassination of Diem, the slow rise in the number of U.S. military advisers to about twenty thousand—Kennedy, in the months before his death, was talking in terms of limited American involvement. In the fall of 1963, for instance, during a television interview with Walter Cronkite, he said of Vietnam: "I don't think that unless a greater effort is made by the [South Vietnamese] government to win popular support that the war can be won out there. In the final analysis, it is their war. They are the ones who have to win or lose it. We can help them, we can give them equipment, we can send our men out there as advisers, but they have to win it—the people of Vietnam —against the Communists." Exactly one week before his murder, the U.S. military spokesman in Saigon was reporting encouraging news: beginning December 3, 1963, he said, 1000 American servicemen would be able to be withdrawn from South Vietnam. The withdrawal never occurred.

The War:

By early spring of 1965, President Johnson had authorized the bombing of targets in North Vietnam and the dispatch—for the first time—of U.S. combat units to South Vietnam. The mission of the troops was limited to protecting U.S. installations. In June the State Department was acknowledging that U.S. forces were seeking out the enemy in defense of these bases—and would assist South Vietnam forces if requested.

From Capitol Hill, came increasing murmurs of dissent. Senator Jacob Javits of New York, certainly no "dove," began warning that the U.S. was moving swiftly toward a massive war without the specific consent of the Congress or the people. By then, the number of American troops had increased to 53,000; more were coming in regularly and the B-52 bombers already had begun their raids from Guam. From Arthur Krock came another criticism: He referred to the official "evasive rhetoric" accompanying such expansion of the U.S. military role.

Once more, Tom Dodd delivered the administration's reply in the Senate. The President's critics, he said, were appeasers and defeatists; the American press was further misleading the public.

In the face of the criticism, Johnson responded defiantly. He already possessed the authority to increase the U.S. commitment to South Vietnam, he said at a news conference. He did not need any further congressional approval. His authority came, he said, from the Tonkin Gulf resolution of August, 1964.

And using this "authority," the President announced a major military escalation. Effective "almost immediately," he said, American forces in Vietnam would increase to 125,000. The draft calls would be raised; the reserves might be activated.

No one assessed the changes of the next six months with more clarity than James Reston of the *New York Times*. Twice, in these months, Reston visited Vietnam.

"I went there in September worried about whether we could really exercise our power all the way across the Pacific Ocean and make it effective," he said, "but after being there for a little while, I saw ships come into Chulai right near the shore, roll out a floating dock, run the bulldozers down and clear off a whole line of fire. This is an enormously impressive thing, these easy-walking American kids moving into a wholly foreign situation. It seemed to me they did it much better than I dreamed they could."

He returned reassured. In December, 1965, he went back to Vietnam.

"By that time we had moved in-country and there you saw the same kids walking in the elephant grass. We had exchanged strategy between August and December. We had gone to a strategy of searching out the enemy and destroying him on his terms, in his country, and that's now my new worry. I think we can do the first better than I thought and I am worried about the second."[9]

Among those who felt the same concern was J. William Fulbright as he headed to New Zealand at the end of 1965. Less than two months after his return he began the hearings which always would be associated with his name.

6

THE ARROGANCE OF POWER

IN JANUARY OF 1966 THERE WERE 180,000 American troops in South Vietnam. Everyone knew more would be needed. How many more, for what period of service, and at what increasing ratio—these were unanswered questions in Washington. On Capitol Hill, sentiment was rising for a full investigation of the war. As always, the Hill mirrored the country: everywhere, Vietnam was stirring new discord and dissension.

Fulbright by then had served in Washington under five presidents and had dealt with eight secretaries of state. Since 1943, he had been involved in every major foreign-policy issue. None was more important than Vietnam; none was as divisive; none held greater implications for the future.

Already, by early '66, there had been fundamental changes in American military and diplomatic policies. The original U.S. aim of keeping South Vietnam non-Communist through a limited counterinsurgency operation had altered. The conflict had become largely an American war. In an effort to save the failing South Vietnamese forces, the U.S. had committed its own army; it was fighting on land, sea, and air across national boundaries and promising, if successful, to provide protection for other non-Communist countries in Asia. Once the area was secure militarily, the U.S. had pledged enormous amounts of economic aid in an attempt to reshape the lives of hundreds of millions of Asians. Did the American people wish to undertake such a venture? Did the Asians desire it?

Fulbright had returned from his trip to New Zealand and Australia with a strong interest in Asian affairs. Along the way to the Far East, he had read—and underlined extensively—*The Crippled Tree,* Han Suyin's account of life in China. As he read, Fulbright would check a point with Hiram Fong, a Republican Senator from Hawaii who accompanied him. "Is this right, Hiram?" Fulbright would ask. "That's right," Fong would reply. It was a form of Asian education. When he came home, Fulbright recommended that book to his friends as an excellent example of why Red China is so hostile to the West.

He also was influenced by Jean Lacouture's *Vietnam: Between Two Truces.* Lacouture stressed the autonomy of the Viet Cong and tended to deprecate the administration's argument that the war was, as Rusk had said, "a war of aggression, mounted in the North against the South."*

The difference of opinion was crucial to one's view of the war. If you believed, as Rusk did, that it was a case of aggression, then Vietnam was a major international war, as vital to American interests as when North Korea invaded South Korea. If you thought, as Fulbright did, that it was a civil war, then the United States should not be involved. Fulbright would take the position that there were no historical analogies involved; that Vietnam was not a classic case of aggression; that there was nothing comparable, say, between appeasing Hitler at Munich and failing to assist South Vietnam thirty years later.

"How the Vietnamese work out their internal problems is not worth a major war or even gives us the right to intervene," Fulbright would say.*

On January 28, 1966, Dean Rusk was scheduled to appear before the Senate Foreign Relations Committee. He was testifying in behalf of S.2793, a bill authorizing an additional $415 million in foreign economic aid for the fiscal year. Most of it was slated for Vietnam. Only three days before he had testified before a friendly Foreign Affairs Committee in the House.

"The heart of the problem in South Vietnam," he told the senators, "is the effort of North Vietnam to impose its will by force. For that purpose, Hanoi has infiltrated into South Vietnam large quantities of arms and tens of thousands of trained and armed men, including units of the North Vietnamese Regular Army. It is that external aggression, which the North has repeatedly escalated, that is responsible for the presence of U.S. combat forces."

* Fulbright's critics say that he is too easily swayed by a single book or argument and does not treat such ideas with sufficient dispassion.

* In the same period, Fulbright was receiving a number of private messages praising him for his dissent on the Dominican crisis and urging him to continue to speak out. One of the most flattering was a letter from Martin Luther King, who praised the senator for his "courageous and prophetic leadership," compared him to the "voice crying in the wilderness," and went on to say "In many respects the destiny of our nation may rest largely in your hands." King implored him not to "let any pressure silence you" and "to continue to speak in a firm, reasoned, objective manner to our nation and to the world."

He continued:

"While assisting the South Vietnamese to repel this aggression, the United States had made persistent efforts to find a peaceful solution. The initiatives for peace undertaken by us and by many other governments during the last five years are almost innumerable. You are familiar with the vigorous and far-reaching peace probes which the United States has made during the past month, which I have had a chance to discuss with the committee in executive session.

"None has brought a positive or encouraging response from Hanoi. . . . The United States has a clear and direct commitment to the security of South Vietnam against external attack. The integrity of our commitments is absolutely essential to the preservation of peace right around the globe. At stake also is the still broader question whether aggression is to be permitted, once again, to succeed. We know from painful experience that aggression feeds on aggression."[1]

When he finished, Fulbright began his dissent on Vietnam.

"Mr. Secretary," he said, "I need not tell you that many of us are deeply troubled about our involvement in Vietnam and it seems to us that since this is the first bill this session dealing with the subject, now is an appropriate opportunity for some examination of our involvement there for the clarification of the people of this country."

He started asking his questions.

The Senator: "How do you foresee the end of this struggle? Do you think we are likely to be there, five, ten, or twenty years?"

The Secretary: "Well, I would hate to try to cast myself in the role of a specific prophet in the development of this particular situation."

The Senator: "I have seen in the press that our approval of these very large requests, not only the one now before this committee, but the one that will come before the Senate in the military field, will be interpreted as a vote of approval of the over-all policy. I think there is a great doubt about whether or not we are on the right track, and these doubts need to be cleared up."

Fulbright then made a lengthy extemporaneous comment that foreshadowed the debates to come.

"You said there had been great discussion in depth about Vietnam. I would submit, in all honesty, that the discussion has been rather superficial. We had a relatively small commitment even as late as the time of the Bay [sic] of Tonkin affair. I personally did not feel at that time that we had undertaken a course of action that could well lead to a world war. . . .

"I believe that one of the reasons for this concern and apprehension is a feeling on the part of some people—including very reputable scholars and others—that we inadvertently, perhaps, for irrelevant reasons, stepped into a colonial war in 1950 on the wrong side. Whether or not we did is one of the questions at issue. It seems to me that something is wrong or there would not be such great dissent, evidenced by teach-ins, articles, and speeches by various responsible people. I do not regard all of the people who have raised these questions as irresponsible.

"I think it is the duty of this committee, the administration, and others to try to clarify the nature of our involvement there, what it is likely to lead to, and whether or not the ultimate objective justifies the enormous sacrifice in lives and treasure.

"I think in all honesty, that is why there is such interest in the matter. It is very difficult to deal with. I have never encountered such a complex situation. It is not clear cut, like Korea, or like the Second World War.

"You state very positively this is aggression by the other side. But this is not quite as convincing under the circumstances as it was in North Korea, for example. There was definite overt aggression in Korea. It is not comparable to the bombing of Pearl Harbor. There was no doubt in those situations. . . . Vietnam is subtle. Perhaps, as you say, this situation is different. But it needs to be understood if we are to approve of it in the sense of voting these very large sums. If we pursue this policy, and resume the bombing [which had been halted at the end of December], then we are committed, and will have passed the Rubicon. I think that is what justifies some discussion of this. . . .

"I am not ready to say at the moment that I am positive that our policies in Vietnam have been wrong, but I am anxious to have greater enlightenment about just what we are about and what our ultimate objective is."

Three days later the bombing raids were resumed on North Vietnam. On Thursday of that week, Fulbright announced that his committee would summon a number of witnesses to testify on the aid appropriation. It was an oblique way of saying that the committee would be investigating Vietnam policies. Obscure though it was to the general public, the administration got the message—and responded.

The next day, President Johnson called a surprise press conference in his office. He had dramatic news: he was leaving within twenty-four hours —on February 5—for Honolulu, with all his chief advisers, to confer with General Nguyen Cao Ky, the head of the Saigon military junta, on the entire range of Vietnam problems. Thus the President, in calling the first of a series of Vietnam "summits," successfully dominated the news as the Foreign Relations Committee's hearings on Vietnam began.

The Honolulu conference resulted in further disquieting news for Fulbright—and the most sweeping commitment yet by the United States.

At its conclusion, Johnson and Ky issued a joint declaration. Out of that came what Vice President Hubert H. Humphrey soon was defining as a "Johnson Doctrine."

Asia, the President said, was "the crucial arena of man's striving for independence and order." Humphrey, in interpreting the remarks, said the Johnson Doctrine meant a "pledge to ourselves and to posterity to defeat aggression, to defeat social misery, to build viable, free political institutions and to achieve peace. . . ." As he acknowledged, these were "great commitments" but ". . . I think there is a tremendous new opening here for realizing the dream of the Great Society in the great area of Asia, not just here at home."[2]

Later, Fulbright would comment wryly that: "All this must come as a big surprise to senators who have not even been informed of these sweeping commitments, much less asked for their advice and consent." And he would say that the Johnson—or Asian—Doctrine represented a "radical departure for American foreign policy in that it is unilateral and virtually unlimited in its effects." If allowed to stand, America would become, in his phrase, "the policeman and provider for all of non-Communist Asia."[3]

At the time, Fulbright had nothing to say about the Honolulu pronouncements. He was already deeply involved in the Vietnam hearings, which, as they continued, were attracting wide public attention. They were carried, live, in color, by the television networks. For a change, foreign affairs took precedence over the daytime quiz and exercise shows and soap operas. Like the Kefauver crime investigations of 1951 and the Army-McCarthy encounters of 1954, the Vietnam hearings, through television, became a part of the average American's daily life.

It was typical of Fulbright that he would consider his committee's Vietnam hearings as an experiment in public education. "All we seek," he said as the hearings opened, "is some information and enlightenment so that our country's judgment, the judgment of our people, of this committee, may be as wise as possible."

Others saw the hearings as high drama, heightened by the war-and-peace stakes involved: Fulbright, leaning forward intently toward the witnesses, his eyes shielded by dark glasses from the glare of the powerful television lights, listening, occasionally interrupting, and engaging in sharp exchanges; the retired general, James M. Gavin, explaining his "enclave" theory by which the U.S. forces would occupy certain coastal areas while allowing the Vietnamese to fight in other areas; the other general, Maxwell Taylor, recently returned from Saigon as ambassador, stoutly defending administration policy as "the best that has been suggested," and clashing with Fulbright (The Senator: "How do you describe the war of 1776? Was that a war of national liberation, or wasn't it?" The General, quoting the Greek philosopher, Polybius: "It is not the purpose of war to annihilate those who provoke it but to cause them to mend their ways"); George Kennan, the author of the "containment" policy that governed U.S. actions toward Russia in the postwar years, saying, "Vietnam is not a region of major military and industrial importance. It is difficult to believe that any decisive developments of the world situation would be determined in normal circumstances by what happened on that territory."

Their appearances set the stage for Dean Rusk's return. By his attitude and his beliefs, Rusk pointed up the differences between Fulbright and the administration.

On the surface the two men seemed to have much in common: both Southerners, both Rhodes Scholars, both versed in foreign affairs. At times Rusk could express the same kind of sentiments one would hear from Fulbright. Thus, on growing up in the South (he was from Cherokee County, Georgia, the son of a Presbyterian preacher and sometime teacher, sometime mail carrier) and witnessing poverty at firsthand, Rusk would say:

"I think if one goes back fifty years, Cherokee County was what we would call an underdeveloped part of the world. There was very little public health. There was only limited medical care and very little advanced agricultural technique. The school was primitive—a one-room school for about seven classes. . . . And I've seen many villages and rural areas in other parts of the world, but it's very seldom you can find one today where typhoid fever is just a part of the environment as it was for us at the beginning there in Cherokee County. . . .

"In other words, I've been able to see in my own lifetime how that boyhood environment has been revolutionized with education, with technology, with county agents, and with electricity—all that helping to take the load off the backs of the people who live there. Now when I can see that this can happen in one lifetime, I disregard those who say that underdeveloped countries need two or three hundred years to develop because I know it isn't true. Because I've seen it with my own eyes."[4]

And, on being aware that people in backward areas did not feel close to their government:

"I don't remember waking up as a boy in Cherokee County and beating my breast and saying, 'What can I do for Woodrow Wilson today?' "[5]

Yet in other respects Rusk and Fulbright were fundamentally different. Rusk had earned his way through college, working in summers, and waiting on tables. Unlike Fulbright, Rusk had a strong interest in the military. Indeed, there were those who believed Rusk had lost his calling; that perhaps his greatest talents lay as a command and staff officer. In high school and at Davidson College in North Carolina, he had compiled the unusual record of having been in the Reserve Officer Training Corps for eight years.

When he was examined by the Rhodes Scholarship Board, he was asked about those eight years in ROTC. Rusk later recalled those questions:

"One of them asked me about my eight years of ROTC and my obvious active interest in ROTC, and I did at that time point out that the American eagle on the great seal has the arrows in one claw and the olive branch in the other and the two have to go together."[6]

At Oxford, where he attended St. John's College in the Class of 1933, Rusk was one of the few pro-military students. As he was to tell the Fulbright committee, he was troubled by the pacifist sentiments expressed by students then.[7]

In 1940, he was called to active duty before the U.S. entered the war. Years later, as Secretary of State, he would often talk of his days as deputy chief of staff in the India-Burma theater and of his adulation for General (and later Secretary of State) George C. Marshall. It was a cliché in Washington to say that Rusk was an enigma, aloof, bland, difficult to fathom. When asked once why he had no cronies in Washington, he answered: "I learned a long time ago from General Marshall that you cannot mix state business with personal friendships. Persons in high office must have ice water flowing through their veins to be able to look at what public interest requires. They must shun personal involvement."[8]

But the emotion was there. Once, he remarked to an intimate, "I have glands, too, you know." And he was known to have wished to resign as Secretary at the end of 1964. He stayed on only at Johnson's persistent requests.

He testified before Fulbright's committee with obvious distaste, clearly convinced that little would be accomplished in such a public framework. But he had to; the President wanted him to.

He began with a familiar statement.

"The situation we face in Southeast Asia is obviously complex, but in my view the underlying issues are relatively simple and are utterly fundamental. . . . We must recognize that what we are seeking to achieve in South Vietnam is part of a process that has continued for a long time—a process of preventing the expansion and extension of Communist domination by the use of force against the weaker nations on the perimeter of Communist power."

And he went on to say, again, the Vietnam war "is clearly an armed attack, cynically and systematically mounted by the Hanoi regime against the people of South Vietnam."

The heart of his encounter with Fulbright was reached in the afternoon session. The senator had said, "Frankly, Mr. Secretary, we are very much more deeply involved in Vietnam, far more than I ever imagined possible and I am very worried about future commitments, as for example to Thailand, made without full discussion and consultation, and I hope, approval by this Congress."

Rusk seemed annoyed. Then he and Fulbright engaged in a running dialogue, the senator saying the U.S. was not being conciliatory enough, the Secretary disagreeing. Finally Rusk said plaintively:

"Senator, do you have any doubts about the good faith and the credibility of the other side in this situation?"

Moments later, the exchange:

Fulbright: "I think there is something wrong with our approach. Let's assume that these people are utter idiots. There must be something wrong with our diplomacy."

Rusk: "Senator, is it just possible that there is something wrong with them?"

Fulbright: "Yes. There is a lot wrong with them. They are very primitive, difficult, poor people who have been fighting for twenty years and I don't understand myself why they can continue to fight, but they do."

Rusk: "And they want to take over South Vietnam by force."

Fulbright: "It is said the liberation front would like to take it over by election. That is what they say."⁹

On that note, the Vietnam hearings ended. The questions had been asked before an audience of millions, the issue had been more fully explored than any in recent times, but the end result was inconclusive.

In less than a month, the Foreign Relations Committee followed up its Vietnam hearings with more "educational hearings" on the question of China.

Had he chosen to remain silent at the end of these hearings, his difficulties with the President might have been smoothed over. Instead, in April, Fulbright delivered his most critical examination of American foreign policy.

Senator Fulbright's dissent was voiced in a series of three Christian A. Herter lectures at Johns Hopkins University. The first, given on April 21, 1966, became known by the senator's phrase "the arrogance of power" and was remembered for his plea to follow "a higher patriotism" rather than uncritically support U.S. foreign policy. America, he said, was in danger of "succumbing to the arrogance of power"—the same malady that had led the Athenians to attack Syracuse, and Napoleon and Hitler to attack Russia.

"Certain pledges must be repeated every day," he said, "lest the whole free world go to rack and ruin—for example, we will never go back on a commitment no matter how unwise; we regard this alliance or that as absolutely 'vital' to the free world; and, of course, we will stand stalwart in Berlin from now until Judgment Day.

"Certain words must never be uttered except in derision—the word 'appeasement,' for example, comes as near as any word can to summarizing everything that is regarded by American policy makers as stupid, wicked, and disastrous."

The word "consensus"—a favorite of the President's—was, in Fulbright's view, only "pernicious and undemocratic" when used to mean "unquestioning support of existing policies."

He reaffirmed his opinion that Congress—and particularly the Senate—had neglected its responsibilities in foreign relations, thus giving the President increasing power. "The result," he said, "has been an unhinging of traditional constitutional relationships; the Senate's constitutional powers of advice and consent have atrophied into what is widely regarded—though never asserted to be—a duty to give prompt consent with a minimum of advice."

As for Vietnam, he questioned whether the American effort was not also "a commitment to American pride."

"The two, I think, have become part of the same package. When we talk about the freedom of South Vietnam, we may be thinking about how disagreeable it would be to accept a solution short of victory; we may be thinking about how our pride would be injured if we settled for less than we set out to achieve; we may be thinking about our reputation as a great power, marking us as a second-rate people with flagging courage and determination."

Beyond that, the war was sowing discord at home, diverting attention away from unmet needs—from poverty, conservation, the alienation of the races, the crisis of American cities, the growing distrust of citizens toward their government. These, too, were by-products of the arrogance of power. America, in short, was at a pivotal stage in its history, a point at which, as he said, "a great nation is in danger of losing its perspective on what exactly is within the realm of its power and what is beyond it." History offered too many examples for Americans to remain complacent: Other great and powerful nations "have aspired to too much, and by overextension of effort have declined and then fallen."

In these lectures, Fulbright spelled out his philosophy of dissent.

Criticizing one's country was "to do it a service and pay it a compliment. It is a service because it may spur the country to do better than it is doing; it is a compliment because it evidences a belief that the country can do better than it is doing."

In a democracy, "dissent is an act of faith. Like medicine, the test of its value is not its taste but its effect, not how it makes people feel at the moment, but how it makes them feel and moves them to act in the long run. Criticism may embarrass the country's leaders in the short run but strengthen their hand in the long run; it may destroy a consensus on policy while expressing a consensus of values."

And, "there is also, or ought to be, such a thing as being too confident to conform, too strong to be silent in the face of apparent error. Criticism, in short, is more than a right; it is an act of patriotism, a higher form of patriotism, I believe, than the familiar rituals of national adulation."

He went on to discuss the *duty* of dissent, and also the *fear* of dissent in America.

"In the abstract we celebrate freedom of opinion as part of our patriotic liturgy; it is only when some Americans exercise it that other Americans are shocked."

Fulbright knew, as he pointed out, that "intolerance of dissent is a well-noted feature of the American national character."

His position as a dissenter would take many forms in the months to come. He would criticize the CIA, domestic policies, the military. Nothing, however, demonstrated his new role better than his feeling toward foreign aid.

From the beginning of his tenure as a professional politician, Fulbright had been solidly in favor of the principle of foreign aid. A large part of his commitment grew out of his experience in Arkansas. Like Rusk with Georgia, he regarded Arkansas in some ways as resembling an underdeveloped country. What the federal government had been able to do in helping Arkansas to grow economically could be achieved through foreign aid for other lands, he believed.

But the senator came to feel that he had misjudged foreign aid. "I thought," he would say, "foreign aid was intended to do just what the federal government had been able to do for us. I didn't recognize the incipient imperialism which accompanies the foreign aid. I think this is a recent development. I don't believe before that anybody had any idea of dominating other countries. That grew. It's one of the instincts of power. So, it's a bitter lesson from this point of view. Another fallout, I might say, from this feeling about Arkansas, is that I understand the resentment of a lot of these little countries to the big countries, including us. The imposition upon them in the past. Their desire for independence."

The senator's arrogance of power lectures laid him open to a new round of criticism. Barry Goldwater sounded the note of opposition by calling on him to resign. "No American has the right or the justification to level such charges against his country," Goldwater said.[10]

The White House had no immediate comment. On May 12, the Democrats gathered for their annual fund-raising dinner at the National Guard Armory in Washington. Normally, the dinner was a festive occasion. This year, something was lacking. Hubert Humphrey, ebullient, signing autographs, valiantly sought to warm up the audience in after-dinner remarks. A group of congressmen, in red-and-white striped coats, dark trousers, hard straw hats, played "Deep in the Heart of Texas." The crowd remained listless. At the head table sat the usual political dignitaries, including J. William Fulbright, puffing a cigarette, drinking water from a gold-rimmed goblet.

At 9:35 P.M., twenty-five minutes early, the President arrived, and immediately began to speak. Noticing Fulbright seated a few paces away from him, the President interpolated and said, with a glance in Fulbright's direction:

"I'm glad to be here among so many friends"—a pause—and then: "and some members of the Foreign Relations Committee."[11]

In the cavernous amphitheater, a roll of nervous laughter from six thousand persons.

A week later, the President spoke at another fund-raising dinner, this time in Chicago. He brought up Vietnam.

"I do not think that those men who are out there fighting for us tonight think that we should enjoy the luxury of fighting each other back home."

Then he said:

"There will be Nervous Nellies and some who become frustrated and bothered and break ranks under the strain and turn on their leaders, their own country, and their own fighting men."[12]

The President never mentioned Fulbright by name, but the senator's staff understood the point. Within weeks the girls in the senator's office were sporting large buttons that read: "I'm a Nervous Nellie."

7

THE NERVOUS NELLIE

LATE ONE AFTERNOON Fulbright completed a typical day of committee hearings and returned to his office. He was tired. The passing months had not improved his state of mind. In Vietnam, the war moved upward relentlessly. No one could foresee its end. At home, the country was passing through a period of unusual violence and dissension. The summer had brought more racial riots; everywhere, it seemed, were signs of a national sickness: in Chicago, a depraved man methodically butchered eight young nurses; in a quiet suburb, Charles Percy's lovely young daughter was stabbed to death in her own bedroom; in New Haven, a Negro calmly walked in a restaurant, suddenly pulled a gun and without a word began shooting until five were dead; in Austin, Texas, a white student climbed to the top of the tallest building and, for no apparent reason, laid seige to the University of Texas campus with a rifle, firing until twelve were killed and thirty-three wounded.

Fulbright himself felt the strain. Publicly, he stood at the center of the greatest controversy of his lifetime, a man praised and defamed. Privately, he continued to worry about his wife's health—and he, also, was concerned about his own physical condition. At that time he was being treated for a "spastic stomach"—aggravated by tension, his doctor said—and was unable to eat normally.

He lay down on a couch in his office that afternoon, placed patches over his eyes, and rested briefly until he was interrupted to fill an appointment with a writer.

The conversation immediately—and naturally—turned to Vietnam. Then, as always with Fulbright while he relaxes and reminisces in the privacy of his office, it evolved into other topics. His words, as recorded and reprinted here, provide an intimate glimpse into the real Fulbright, not the "nervous nellie" that his enemies disparaged or the petulant critic that others saw, but the rational and reflective senator and statesman.

To be sidetracked into this war just does something to me. To me it's an utterly foolish war. When I hear some of the others talking about it, I must say, occasionally I think, 'well, maybe I'm completely cockeyed.' But then, when I read another piece and get back on it, I don't think I am. I only waver occasionally about whether or not this war's justified—whether we really have any important interest involved —any justification for doing what we're doing.

I think it's beginning to destroy all kinds of activities that we had going for us. I think it's affecting our domestic and our foreign relations. It's almost impossible for me to express what I think about the tragedy of getting involved in it.

I think the President has finally made up his mind. I think he was puzzled for a while, but he's taken the bull by the horns and he's going through with it. And now there's no looking back, and so everything that disagrees with this view he just shoves aside. He's almost on a moral crusade, a religious crusade, a belief that we're dealing with this evil that we must eradicate. I think this is a very terrible thing. I utterly disbelieve this being involved at all.

I mean to say, Stalin was a devil, a tyrant—I can agree with that, and I can agree that many of the leaders of this movement are complete devils. But I don't think this is so when you talk about communism. Communism, in many respects, is a more idealistic philosophy of life than ours is. I think it's impractical, and I don't advocate it, but it's not the sort of thing that Rusk seems to talk about. And I think it's a terrible distortion of truth and it's going to lead us to disaster. Not only because we are rich and powerful, and so on, but it just seems such a shame for a country to have reached a point of opportunity where we could do something.

My criticism is not that we're doing anything different from other countries, but that we're doing too much the same as people always have who have had power. I want us not to play the role any better, but to have a new game. And the only way you can get a new game is for a powerful country to initiate it. No little country can do it. They can't; we have to. Now, I know this is asking a lot, and probably more than you'll get—but I don't see any reason why we shouldn't ask it. I think the future of this country might well depend on it, modern weapons being what they are.

What we're doing in Vietnam isn't bad in the light of history. It's the same thing that powerful countries have always done. What I'm trying to get across—and apparently having difficulty getting across —is that I hope this country won't act like other countries always have done. Why can't it do better? And it could do better. The big powerful country ought to take the initiative and show some magnanimity and make some proposal. Our ego shouldn't be out on our sleeve. We ought to have enough assurance to take the initiative to do anything that would settle this business, and then get to what I consider to be our national interest. We ought not to be afflicted, in other words, with these traditional concepts of prestige and national honor.

As I said before, I thought what Johnson calls the Great Society and this program of education, the attack on poverty, Appalachia—all that was good and was a beginning of a reassessment of our priorities. Certainly, I thought so. But then, just as it was getting off the ground, Vietnam comes in and is almost destroying the effectiveness of those programs.

We ought to be doing much more in the field of education, health, pollution, improvement of our cities, and so on. These are things that seem to me so obviously should come before such things as space and these enormous armaments.

That doesn't mean we're a bad country, or that other countries are better. We're a very privileged country and we have tremendous advantages over other countries. You look around the world and there's hardly any with our heritage or our land. Russia has the land area, but she has a terrible heritage of tyranny in her political life.

We inherited the most liberal political institutions of their day and we've benefited. We should have great advantages over a country like Russia, in that sense of having the advantages of the best political and juridical system that had been developed. We're the heir of all Western civilization, going on back to Greece, and also in the cultural field. Of course, the Russians shared the cultural field, too. They're a mixture in a way. I mean, they have had some advantages, since Peter the Great, at least. But they did have, and still have, a terrible political heritage. And it's a big effort to overcome that.

I don't know, I just have a feeling that we ought to do better. I don't mean to say that we're doing worse than, well, look how stupid the French were when they were a powerful people and they went off on these ridiculous ventures with Napoleon I and Napoleon III, and they destroyed much of their power. They didn't make this transition, either.

The British, I always felt, did very well with very little. And it's a small, little old country. And think what a little tiny country it is and what they did. They contributed a great deal. But they suffered—

finally fell—suffered from arrogance, too. They weren't immune to it. I mean, *The Proud Tower* [by Barbara Tuchman], I don't know whether you've seen it or not. It's a magnificent book, describes so vividly and persuasively the conditions that existed in Western Europe at the beginning of World War I. Especially the very first part of it on England, and how really arrogant the British had become due to 100 years of affluence since Napoleon, you know. And old Lord Salisbury—what an arrogant aristocrat he was! And then the concentration of wealth in England. It was incredible. I read a lot of British history, but nobody had ever bothered to really bring it out so well. Practically everything above reasonable subsistence belonged to 2,500 families out of 40 million people. This is a much greater concentration of land ownings and things of this kind and the privileges than I had thought. But this is a prelude, of course, to disaster overtaking them. And the British, however, had, you know, developed the really great institutions of self-government, and economics, industrial revolution, all these contributions—literary, and Shakespeare, and all that goes with it. I mean, a very great civilization they developed.

We should benefit by the moral of this. We are the heir. And I don't mean to say we've done a hell of a poor job. It's much easier to just sit back and say 'well, we're a great people, and forget about it and let's go fishing.' I've always thought it was my duty as a senator to try to bring this kind of discussion before the public.

But I must say, I've been very puzzled here lately by appearing to be so belligerent. Hell, it's a curious thing. I never considered I was particularly antagonistic or belligerent in temperament. But it begins to appear that way. Everyone is beginning to say now, 'the attacks upon so and so,' 'the attacks upon Lyndon Johnson.' I don't consider it attacking. I really must say in all honesty the press, I think, distorts this relationship of criticism into an attack. It seems to me it's quite possible that you'd have a legitimate difference of opinion without it being an attack on somebody. But they won't allow it to remain just a difference of opinion, or an analysis or criticism. It becomes an attack.

I'm not trying to be a maverick or a sorehead. For instance, when they ask you to speak at a university. Well, what are you going to speak about? Seems to me you ought to speak about something worthwhile. It always kind of bored me—these eulogies. Either eulogies of yourself or your country—the self-adulation that, oh, De Tocqueville is talking about. Well, what good does it do? It seems to me you get nowhere by that. If you're a poor, little, and very underdeveloped country and you need something to sort of buck you up and give you the courage to face the next day is another thing. But here's this great country. It all seems a little silly for us to engage in self-adulation all the time. We know we're good. I know we're good. I know we have things, and practically every country in the world is envious. That's all self-evident. I don't see what point there is in going on talking about it all the—but of course I know most of my colleagues don't agree with me on that.

Now if you ask me what sort of impact I've had, or what good it does, I don't know. I don't exercise direct power. I don't cut people's heads off, politically speaking or symbolically speaking. I don't make people do things. However, I think these discussions are like any form of education. It's hard to prove, but I think it's there. And every now and then I notice coincidences between other people, many of whom can write better than I can and express themselves better. It seems to me ideas that you advance begin to develop. Now I can't prove these things. And of course I benefit from their ideas, too. It's an interplay back and forth. I don't mean to say I originate all these, but the fact you're a senator and you say them gives them a little different currency, and in a different area. The Senate, I think, gives it a little different impact.

The Exchange Program. I can't prove it to you—like a balance sheet of a corporation could—but I haven't the slightest doubt that that's been a very great influence in many fields. It's not a panacea. It's relatively small compared to the world, I mean, and the tasks involved. But I think it's been a very good investment and has a lot of influence. I think it's been a great success and it's the kind of thing that is accumulative. It spreads. Even those who haven't actually participated in it have come under the influence of those who have.

I haven't any doubt about it's being a very good program and useful. But I don't know whether the world can be substantially improved or not. There are so many prejudices and bitter hatreds and feelings that people have. How to eradicate them I don't know. My goodness, look what we have here in this country itself. I mean the internal violence that afflicts us.

These are hard things to analyze and say they're making progress. At the moment we seem to me to be going through a period of unusual violence domestically. But there's always been violence, I guess. We have a history of violence in this country. Maybe all do. I don't know. But I mean—our frontier days—the television you look at, you know. This depresses me because such a large part of it is given over to real, outright violence of one kind or another or these chillers or strange, distorted, perverted kinds of human activity.

I don't know what to do. I wish I did know. The only thing, when you don't know anything else, you say, 'well you've got to give more emphasis to education in the hopes that the people themselves will recognize how futile and how stupid and silly it is to waste their time on this sort of thing and demand the better programs.' But the impact of the television is so much greater than anything I can say or do that, my goodness, it looks like an unequal battle.

You know, we have this old idea that government always botches things. I don't know why we're so ambivalent on that. We have that on the one hand, but we also have an unlimited admiration for the military, for example. It's government too. But we think they're perfect. They never make a mistake. There are strange discrepancies in the way we look at these things.

But I don't know whether there's any hope. I don't like to dwell on that too much because whether there is or isn't, it seems to me your duty to try to change it anyway--even if you think the hope is very vague, very faint.

Unless you just think it's utterly hopeless. Which I don't.

EPILOGUE

Assessment

OCCASIONALLY, WHEN THE DAY was right and he was in an introspective mood, Fulbright would look back on his career and indulge in a fanciful what-might-have-been. More than most politicians, it seemed, his life had been governed by unforeseen and unsought opportunities.

Supposing, at the end of the '30s, he had gone into the hotel business in Little Rock with his old friend, Sam Peck? Supposing he had remained a teacher, or a university administrator? Supposing he had become a writer, a journalist, or an essayist? There, he would say, lay one of the surest means of advancing ideas and influencing events.

Looking back on what he had done, and what he had said—all the speeches, all the articles, all the trips—he would express embarrassment just at the thought of the sheer volume of the record. All past, all to what end?

By the beginning of 1968 he had completed a quarter of a century in the Congress. Once again, he was coming up for another election, this time in a presidential year. If he ran and won, he would be nearing seventy by the time his next term expired. That would be enough, he would say.

Perhaps it was too much. His wife thought so. For some time she had been urging him to retire and return to the Ozarks; she even had a site picked out on the crest of a hill overlooking Fayetteville. The idea was attractive, and her health was a factor in his decision. But he has decided to run—and he will probably win—and remain to fight more battles and become involved in new controversies. Clearly, he only recently had reached the peak of prestige as a world figure. His final chapters have not been written.

Within a year after the Vietnam hearings, he had begun referring privately to the war in the past tense. He had continued to speak out, and had traveled the country talking of what he called the "two Americas"— the America of Lincoln and Stevenson and the America of Theodore Roosevelt and the modern superpatriots—with his own preference eloquently expressed; and he had gone through some depressing moments as the war spiraled upward with still no clear end in sight, but the great decisions already had been taken. His own sharp dissent had been recorded. It had not altered the course of the war, but it clearly had changed the direction of American thinking and led eventually to new hope for peace. By the time he held his second public hearing on Vietnam in March, 1968, American public opinion had begun to crystallize and the process of dissent, once thought so noisy and dangerous, had moved into the realm of respectability. Within the Congress, and particularly the Senate, there were increasing reservations about our involvement and a new questioning toward the type of commitments America should be making for the next twenty-five years. Fulbright's own stature had increased, among his colleagues and the public.

There had been a period in Washington when it was popular to say he had waited too long to criticize; that by the time he emerged as the foremost foreign policy critic of the President he had dissipated whatever influence he might have exerted on events. Some of his colleagues, who admired his gifts, viewed him as something of a tragedy. *If only he had been more aggressive, if only he had followed through with more vigor, if only . . .*

Yet his influence had been significant, and possibly historic. Certainly no one could have dreamed that Fulbright's leading the Foreign Relations Committee into open dissent against the administration's foreign policies would culminate two years later in Lyndon Johnson's announcement not to seek another term. Johnson's action was without parallel in American history, and it held forth the promise of an entire review of American policies at home and abroad. Years would pass before all the ramifications of that step became clear, but the central point was evident: the dissenters, few and ignored at first, had helped to fashion a profound change. They themselves would have to be judged for the wisdom of their course and the influence they had exerted on events. Fulbright had asked the great questions; he had helped to marshal opinion; he had acted as a restraining force; and, perhaps most important of all, he had taken the lead in checking the shift of power from the Congress to the White House. One hopeful sign out of the morass of Vietnam was a new spirit of independence on Capitol Hill, coupled with a desire among Democrats and Republicans alike to refuse to play as passive a role in the momentous debates to come.

He was controversial, difficult to place, difficult to evaluate. His detractors pointed to his ambiguities, his false starts, his petulance, his figurative wringing of hands, his lack of appreciation for the dilemmas of attempting to exercise prudent power. And yet at a party one night in Georgetown, long after the Vietnam hearings, another senator would turn to a writer and say, "You know, fifty years from now the only one of us they'll remember will be Fulbright."

At the very least, he is certain to rank among the major political figures of his times. Years before he became involved in the contentious disputes that made him a national issue, Walter Lippmann had said of him: "The role he plays in Washington is an indispensable role. There is no one else who is so powerful, and also so wise and if there were any question of removing him from public life, it would be a national calamity."

The passing time has only served to confirm Lippmann's judgment and to assure its acceptance throughout the country.

In a special sense, Fulbright has been an original political thinker. At his best, he has been a voice of reason—and conscience—in the Senate. The call for higher ethics in public life, the attempt to redefine political values and elevate the stature of the politician, the bold dissents, the memorable speeches, the unheeded advice, the exchange program—these will endure.

Whether quixotic or cautious, Fulbright's career has been marked by one consistent theme. He has been a teacher in public life. Despite his doubt and occasional despair, he has retained his belief that man's best hope lies in education. It has been his central message.

At the end of 1966 he traveled to Stockholm for the Nobel prize ceremonies—a prize for which he had been twice nominated in the peace category, and twice passed over—and there, in a speech before the Swedish Institute for Cultural Relations, he summed up his own philosophy. It was, in a way, his personal political testament. "My theme," he said, "is the contribution of education, particularly international education, toward restraining the competition of nations." He went on to say:

"The hope contained in education is a simple hope for man, a hope that is held not because man is thought to be basically good as the eighteenth century philosophers thought he was, nor because he is thought to be capable of heaven as theologians have believed, but simply because he is man, because he is exactly what he is, neither inherently virtuous nor inherently wicked, predestined so far as we know neither to heaven nor to hell. At its best education aims to bring forth in a man nothing more nor nothing less than the best of his human capacities. It aims to make him knowledgeable without pretending he can be omniscient; it aims to make him wise without pretending he is capable, or ought to be capable, of total selflessness."

What he hoped to achieve was what any educated man sought, the "civilizing and humanizing" of relations between men and nations. That, at least, seemed within the limits of human capacity.

In the end, that desire stands as the sum of all his actions. How well he has succeeded cannot be determined. His has been only one voice raised in a profession too little regarded for wisdom and too long alienated from the public it is supposed to serve—and lead. If that knowledge has made him pessimistic at times, there is solace for him and for all the Fulbrights who are working for that civilizing process.

Henry Adams, whom he resembles in so many respects, expressed the thought—and the potentiality—best. A teacher, Adams said, affects eternity. He never knows where his influence stops.

BIBLIOGRAPHICAL NOTES

The basic source material for this book comes from the complete files of Senator Fulbright, from interviews with him and those who have dealt with —or against—him on issues stretching back more than twenty-five years. In addition, the authors personally have observed a number of the episodes discussed in this book, both in the United States and abroad. We have used, in the natural course of research, a considerable number of secondary books and memoirs dealing with the various periods at hand. Many of these are indicated in the footnotes that follow this bibliographical essay.

We have tried to keep our footnotes to a minimum, and consequently have followed the technique of citing only where the source material is not obviously indicated in the manuscript. In other words, we do not as a rule cite speeches or debates recorded in *The Congressional Record*. These are readily available and clearly indexed. Neither do we cite every newspaper or journal when the date is indicated in the text. Also, whenever direct quotation marks are used without a citation, they indicate interviews by the authors.

The published material about Senator Fulbright is growing rapidly. One biography already has been written. Tristram Coffin's *Senator Fulbright: Portrait of a Public Philosopher* (E. P. Dutton & Co., Inc., 1966) is sketchy and without a critical word. More valuable are the collections of the Senator's own words in his own books. Random House has published *Prospects for the West* (1963), *Old Myths and New Realities and Other Commentaries* (1964), and *The Arrogance of Power* (1966). Essentially, these are collections of the Senator's major addresses of those periods, with some new material added. Random House also has published *The Vietnam*

Hearings, with an introduction by the Senator, providing the complete transcripts of the Foreign Relations Committee's hearings in 1966. An earlier collection of Fulbright speeches, *Fulbright of Arkansas: The Public Positions of a Private Philosopher* (Robert B. Luce, Inc., Washington, 1963) was skillfully edited by Karl E. Meyer. It contains extracts of the Senator's speeches from his university presidency on through 1962. A complete, up-to-date collection is badly needed, however, and even the Meyer book was hampered by space limitation.

At this writing, some of the best treatments of Fulbright's career have appeared in journals and magazines. Those worthy of note are listed here in chronological order.

"Just a Boy From the Ozarks," by Walter Davenport in *Colliers,* Feb. 10, 1945, is the first general sketch. Edgar Kemler's "The Fulbright Fellow" appeared in *The Nation,* Feb. 20, 1954 at the height of the McCarthy era. Charles B. Seib and Alan L. Otten's "Fulbright: Arkansas Paradox" in *Harper's* of June, 1956, is probably the best written of the magazine articles. The May 2, 1959, *Saturday Evening Post* carried Beverly Smith, Jr.'s "Egghead From the Ozarks," an interesting portrait written as Fulbright became chairman of the Foreign Relations Committee. That same year saw Sidney Hyman's "The Advice and Consent of J. William Fulbright," an analysis of the Senator's criticism of the Eisenhower-Dulles policies, in the Sept. 17 issue of *The Reporter.* Ernest K. Lindley gave a more formal portrait of Fulbright at the same time in his "Senator Fulbright, Chairman of the Foreign Relations Committee," *The American Oxonian,* April, 1960. E. W. Kenworthy's "Fulbright Becomes a National Issue" in *The New York Times Magazine* of Oct. 1, 1961, is an important article and an excellent portrayal of Fulbright the man. Less ambitious but interesting is Ian Sclander's gentle essay, "The Quiet Spokesman for Sanity in the U. S. Senate" in *MacLean's Magazine,* Sept. 9, 1961. Don Oberdorfer composed a worthy assessment of the Fulbright Fellowships in his "Common Noun Spelled f-u-l-b-r-i-g-h-t," *The New York Times Magazine,* April 4, 1965. In the same period was Andrew Kopkind's thoughtful "The Speechmaker," in the Oct. 2, 1965, *New Republic.* More recent years have brought an increasing number of assessments. Among them are Philip Carter's "Our Neighbor, Senator Fulbright," a particularly good analysis of Fulbright, the Southerner, in *The Texas Observer* of April 15, 1966. *Life's* "The Roots of the Arkansas Questioner," by Brock Brower (May 13, 1966) is useful but somewhat superficial. More revealing is Eric Sevareid's perceptive interview with Fulbright entitled, "Why Our Foreign Policy is Failing" in that month's *Look.* A more critical view was Henry Fairlie's "Old Realities and New Myths" in *The Reporter,* June 16, 1966. That same month *Ramparts* carried "J. William Fulbright, A Profile in Courage," a slightly exaggerated but effective synthesis of the impact of the Vietnam hearings and Fulbright's evolution as a dissenter. Later that year I. F. Stone produced perhaps the strongest and most searching, albeit friendly, criticism of Fulbright yet written in three successive issues of *The New York Review of Books*.

One more source should be mentioned. The Fulbright files contain virtually every transcript of every radio or television interview given by the Senator during his years in Washington. The spontaneity and timeliness of many of those interviews give them a special value for recreating the mood of a particular moment.

ACKNOWLEDGMENTS

We owe a special debt to many more than we can acknowledge here, but we wish particularly to express our appreciation to the following:

to Lee Williams, Parker Westbrook, Jim Cash, Kitty Johnson, Clara Buchanan, Pallie Sims, and other members of Senator Fulbright's personal staff who put up with us so patiently for so long and who rendered so many invaluable services;

to Seth Tillman and Carl Marcy of the Foreign Relations Committee, who assisted whenever they could;

to Hal Douglas, Allan Gilbert, Fenner Stice, T. C. Carlson, and Robert Leflar who were so helpful in their recollections of the Fulbrights in Fayetteville;

to Jack Pickens, William Darby, Sidney McMath, Orval Faubus, and others in Little Rock who interrupted their schedules to give their views;

to Evelyn P. Metzger, Doubleday's Washington editor, who deserves far more than a passing mention here, and to Samuel S. Vaughan of Doubleday for his help;

to Burt Hoffman, Charles B. Seib, and Emerson Beauchamp, Jr., our colleagues, who offered helpful criticism;

to the members of the stack and reader division of the Library of Congress who performed many useful services for our study room;

and finally to Carol Godsey who once again was the best of secretaries, and Angela Orlen, who delivered splendidly in a last-minute crisis.

NOTES

BOOK ONE: *Student*

CHAPTER 1. "IN THE MAIN, HONEST, TRUSTWORTHY"

1. John Gould Fletcher, *Arkansas,* Chapel Hill: University of North Carolina Press, 1947.
2. Mark Twain, *Life on the Mississippi.* New York: Harper Brothers, 1907, p. 32.
3. Walter Scott McNutt, Olin Eli McKnight, George Allen Hubbell, *A History of Arkansas.* Little Rock: The Arkansas House, 1932, pp. 392–93.
4. Roberta Fulbright's direct quotes are taken from her own newspaper columns "As I See It," in *The Northwest Arkansas Times* from 1932 to 1952. A collection of her writings was published in Fayetteville in December, 1952, and may be seen in the files of the Washington County Historical Society, Fayetteville, Arkansas.

CHAPTER 2. ALL-AMERICAN FROM ARKANSAS

1. From a Fulbright speech, "Scouting and Political Well Being," before the Arkansas Bar Association, Feb. 6, 1940.
2. Fulbright files, newspaper article Dec. 17, 1924, name of paper missing.
3. See profile, "Arkansas Player Railway Magnate," *Arkansas Gazette,* Little Rock, Oct. 23, 1924.
4. Roberta Fulbright column, March 4, 1936. All of her other quotes are also taken from her column in those years.
5. *Arkansas Gazette,* Oct. 23, 1924.
6. The best work on the Rhodes Scholarships is *The First 50 Years of the Rhodes Trust and the Rhodes Scholarships. 1903–53.* Edited by Godfrey Elton Elton. Oxford, 1955. We also used Prosser Gifford, *Oxford and the Rhodes Scholarship.* Swarthmore, Pennsylvania, 1958.

CHAPTER 3. "IF CONVENIENT, SOME KNOWLEDGE"

1. *50 Years of the Rhodes Trusts, op. cit.*
2. *Ibid.*
3. *Ibid.*
4. *Ibid.*
5. "Sunday Postscript," a speech delivered over the British Broadcasting Company, London, April 28, 1944, text, Fulbright files. Hereafter cited as London speech.
6. "Economic Problems of Arkansas," speech, Chamber of Commerce, Little Rock, Oct. 18, 1940. Hereafter cited as "Economic Problems" speech.

CHAPTER 4. THE SQUIRE OF RABBIT'S FOOT LODGE

1. *New York Times,* Aug. 30, 1934. For a further discussion of the Schechter case, and the subsequent Supreme Court ruling, see Henry Steele Commager's *Documents of American History, Fifth Edition, Vol. 2.* New York: Appleton-Century-Crofts, Inc., 1949, pp. 458–63.
2. Authors' interview.
3. "Economic Problems" speech.

CHAPTER 5. "IT HAS BEEN SUGGESTED I AM TOO YOUNG"

1. Authors' interview.
2. *The Daily Oklahoman,* Nov. 26, 1939.
3. From an unpublished manuscript written by Irene Carlisle, circa 1942, and printed in "Flashback," Vol. VI, No. 2 of the Washington County Historical Society, Fayetteville, Arkansas, May, 1966.
4. Notes, in Fulbright's hand, headed "Notes for Remarks Made While President of University of Arkansas."
5. "The Social Function of the University," speech Dec. 10, 1939, Fort Smith, Arkansas, Civic Club.
6. Speech, Feb. 6, 1940.
7. "Economic Problems."
8. *Ibid.*
9. *Congressional Record,* March 6, 1940.
10. "Economic Problems."
11. Draft, Fulbright files, undated, 1939.
12. "Economic Problems."
13. "Financial Problems in Arkansas Education," speech, undated, 1940.
14. Fort Smith speech, Dec. 10, 1939.
15. "The Politician in Society," April 20, 1940, before Fort Smith school teachers.
16. University of Oklahoma address, July, 1940.
17. *Ibid.*
18. *Ibid.*
19. *Ibid.*
20. The phrase appears in typed note cards in Fulbright files, dated only years 1941–42.
21. *Ibid.*
22. Authors' interview.

23. *Northwest Arkansas Times*, files, Roberta Fulbright columns.
24. *Northwest Arkansas Times*, June 10, 1941.

BOOK TWO: *Politician*

CHAPTER 1. A FAMILY AFFAIR

1. Authors' interview.
2. "The Legislator," a speech delivered at the University of Chicago, 1947. An earlier draft was entitled, simply, "A Primer for Congressional Candidates."
3. Authors' interview.
4. *Op. cit.*
5. "Equality: The Objective of the War," speech, State Democratic Convention, Little Rock, Sept. 16, 1942.

CHAPTER 2. THE MAD CAPITAL OF A MAD WORLD

1. *Washington Star*, Jan. 1, 1943.
2. *Ibid.*
3. Gould Lincoln, *Washington Star*, Jan. 18, 1943.
4. *The Public Papers and Addresses of Franklin D. Roosevelt. 1944–45.* Compiled by Samuel I. Rosenman. New York: Harper & Brothers, 1950, pp. 483–506.

CHAPTER 3. "I AM FULLY CONSCIOUS OF MY DEFICIENCIES"

1. *PM*, Feb. 28, 1943.
2. *Ibid.*
3. Fulbright files.
4. *Op. cit. PM.*
5. Hearings were Jan. 29, 1943. See House Foreign Affairs Committee files.
6. "A Creative War," speech, Feb. 1, 1943, George Washington University Law School.
7. The date was May 13, 1943.
8. *Washington Star*, June 15, 1943. Cf., *The Autobiography of Sol Bloom.* New York: G. P. Putnam's, 1948, pp. 264–65. For the complete transcripts see *Hearings Before the Committee on Foreign Affairs, House of Representatives, Executive Session. 78th Congress. 1st Session.* June 8, 11, 15, 1943. Washington: U. S. Government Printing Office.
9. Senator Tom Connally, *My Name Is Tom Connally.* New York: Thomas Y. Crowell Company, 1954, p. 263.
10. *Life*, June 28, 1943.
11. *The Memoirs of Cordell Hull.* New York: The Macmillan Company, 1948, p. 1262.
12. *Ibid.*
13. *Ibid.*, pp. 1259, and 1263.
14. *Chicago Tribune*, Sept. 22, 1943. For an analysis of national and international comment see the unpublished study, "Editorial Opinion on the Fulbright Resolution," prepared by the Legislative Reference Service, Library of Congress, Oct. 19, 1943, Fulbright files.

15. *The New Yorker,* Oct. 2, 1943.
16. *Arkansas Democrat,* Little Rock, Oct. 20, 1943.
17. Associated Press story by Norman Walker, distributed Nov. 21, 1943, Fulbright files.
18. Irving Howe and Lewis Coser, *The American Communist Party.* New York: Praeger, 1962, pp. 431 ff.
19. *Ibid.*
20. "War and Peace," speech before the United Commercial Travelers, Little Rock, Dec. 10, 1943.
21. Allen Drury, *A Senate Journal: 1943–45.* New York: McGraw Hill, 1963, p. 62.

CHAPTER 4. BRITISH BILLY
1. *Arkansas Democrat,* Aug. 10, 1944.
2. The quote is taken from the Fulbright campaign publication, *Victory News,* Fulbright files.
3. *Arkansas Democrat,* Feb. 18, 1944.
4. Department of State Press Release No. 159, May 3, 1944. For a fuller account of the working of the London delegation see, *Foreign Relations of the United States. Diplomatic Papers,* 1944. Vol. I., U. S. Government Printing Office, 1966, pp. 668–69.
5. London speech.
6. *Ibid.*
7. Hull's letter was dated May 16, 1944, Fulbright files.
8. *Pine Bluff Commercial,* July 2, 1944.
9. Undated newspaper clipping, Fulbright files.
10. *Ibid.*
11. The broadside quoted was headed "A Bothered Conscience Needs No Accuser, Mr. Fulbright." See also the Aug. 5, 1944, letter to Fulbright from Price Dickson, a lawyer, speaking on behalf of Fulbright's Local Board A in which Dickson says "There is not a grain of truth in this malicious propaganda." The letter and the broadside are in the Fulbright files.
12. Speech text, no date or heading, Fulbright files.
13. *Ibid.*
14. *Ibid.*
15. *Forrest City* (Arkansas) *Daily Times-Herald,* Aug. 10, 1944. See also the Fulbright speech "Bureaucratic Government Control or Private Enterprise" printed as a brochure and distributed throughout the state.
16. Fulbright files.
17. *Arkansas Gazette,* July 23, 1944.

BOOK THREE: *Senator*

CHAPTER 1. "JUST A BOY FROM THE OZARKS"
1. Drury, Senate Journal, p. 332 ff.
2. *Ibid.*
3. Barkley's letter was dated Feb. 6, 1945, Fulbright files. See also Fulbright's letter to John Gunther, May 24, 1945.

4. *Congressional Record,* March 12, 1945.
5. Untitled clipping, Fulbright files, from article by B. T. Richardson.
6. *Ibid.*
7. Fulbright files.
8. Harry S Truman, *Memoirs.* Vol. 1. New York: Doubleday & Company, Inc., 1955, p. 6.
9. *New York Times,* April 13, 1945.
10. *Washington Star,* undated clipping.
11. Commencement address, Gettysburg College, April 26, 1945.
12. *Arkansas Gazette,* May 29, 1945.
13. Fulbright files.
14. *Arkansas Gazette,* July 8, 1945.
15. *Arkansas Democrat,* June 14, 1945.

CHAPTER 2. "A PROFOUND UNEASINESS HAS SPREAD"
1. *Public Papers of the Presidents, Harry S Truman,* 1945. Washington: U. S. Government Printing Office, p. 505. Hereafter cited as *Truman Papers.*
2. *Ibid.,* pp. 506–8.
3. *Ibid.*
4. The speech was Oct. 20, 1945. See also the account by Raymond P. Brandt, *St. Louis Post-Dispatch,* Oct. 21, 1945.
5. "What About Russia?" delivered over NBC, Nov. 23, 1945. Text, Fulbright files.
6. *Truman Papers,* p. 513.
7. "The Legislator," previously cited.
8. *Ibid.*
9. *Arkansas Gazette,* Jan. 8, 1946.
10. Milwaukee speech, Oct. 14, 1946.
11. *Washington Post,* Nov. 11, 1946.
12. *Washington Times-Herald,* Nov. 9, 1946.

CHAPTER 3. A COMMON NOUN CALLED FULBRIGHT
1. Private letter from Fulbright to a scholar, Fulbright files.
2. Walter Johnson and Francis Colligan, *The Fulbright Program: A History.* University of Chicago Press, 1965. The Kennedy quote comes from a statement by the President Aug. 1, 1961. See *Public Papers of the Presidents. John F. Kennedy.* 1961. U. S. Government Printing Office, 1962, p. 544.
3. *Ibid.*
4. "Education in International Relations," speech, University of Colorado, Aug. 1, 1966.
5. Hoover's letter of Feb. 8, 1946, is included in the *Hearings Before a Subcommittee of the Committee on Military Affairs, United States Senate.* 79th Congress. 2nd Session. Feb. 25, 1946. U. S. Government Printing Office, pp. 5–6.
6. Department of State Press Release No. 532, Aug. 1, 1946.
7. *International Educational Exchange. The Opening Decades, 1946–1966.*

A Report of the Board of Foreign Scholarships, 1966. U. S. Government Printing Office.

8. *The New Yorker,* May 10, 1958.
9. Undated statement, Fulbright files.
10. Fulbright files.
11. Silver's article appeared in *The Clarion-Ledger,* Jackson, Mississippi, Dec. 20, 1949.

CHAPTER 4. THE DETERIORATION OF DEMOCRACY

1. Authors' interview with Dean Rusk.
2. Cited, Eric F. Goldman, *The Crucial Decade—And After. America, 1945–60.* New York: Vintage Books, 1960, p. 147. Hereafter cited as Goldman.
3. *Ibid.,* p. 178.
4. Text of Truman-MacArthur Wake Island Conference, reprinted in Richard H. Rovere and Arthur Schlesinger, Jr., *The MacArthur Controversy.* New York: Farrar, Straus and Giroux, 1965 edition, p. 280.
5. *Ibid.,* p. 275.
6. Rusk spoke May 18, 1951 before the China Institute in America, New York. See account and full text in the *New York Times,* May 19, 1951.
7. Private letter, Feb. 2, 1951, Fulbright files.
8. Miscellaneous clippings, Fulbright files.
9. *Buffalo Evening News,* March 8, 1951.
10. *Washington Post,* March 29, 1951.
11. Charles B. Seib and Alan L. Otten, "Fulbright: The Arkansas Paradox," *Harper's,* June 1956.
12. *Truman Papers,* 1951, pp. 144–46.
13. *Detroit News,* March 15, 1951.
14. Goldman, p. 190.
15. Undated clipping, Fulbright files, March, 1951.
16. *Arkansas Gazette,* May 20, 1952.
17. Draft, Fulbright files.
18. Truman, *Memoirs.* Vol. 2, p. 498.

CHAPTER 5. "SENATOR HALFBRIGHT"

1. Speech on the Bricker Amendment, *Congressional Record,* Feb. 2, 1954.
2. Richard Rovere, *Senator Joe McCarthy,* 1960 paperback edition of the original Harcourt, Brace printing.
3. Richard M. Nixon, *Six Crises* (paperback reprint of the original Doubleday edition), p. 68.
4. Rovere, *op. cit.,* and Eric Goldman, *Crucial Decade, op. cit. cf.,* the statement by Senator Herbert H. Lehman and others in connection with McCarthy and Lustron, *Congressional Record,* Aug. 2, 1954.
5. *Washington Star,* Sept. 20, 1951.
6. *New York Times,* Oct. 19, 1951.
7. Nixon, *Six Crises, op. cit.,* p. 125.
8. Fulbright files.
9. *Washington Star,* July 24–25, 1953.

10. Walter Johnson and Francis J. Colligan, *The Fulbright Program, op. cit.,* pp. 102–3. The testimony is also reprinted on pp. 86–104.
11. The date was Feb. 2, 1954.
12. *Point of Order! A Documentary of the Army-McCarthy Hearings.* Produced by Emile de Antonio and Daniel Talbot. New York: W. W. Norton & Company, Inc., 1964, p. 95.
13. Charles B. Seib and Allan L. Otten, "Arkansas Paradox" *Harper's, op. cit.*
14. *Congressional Record,* Aug. 2, 1954.

CHAPTER 6. "OH, NO, SENATOR, NOT YOU!"

1. "Reinhold Niebuhr, Prisoner of the South," *The New Leader,* April 27, 1964.
2. Roy Reed, *Arkansas Gazette,* Sept. 2, 1962.
3. Authors' confidential interview.
4. Truman, *Memoirs,* Vol. 2, *op. cit.,* p. 494.
5. Fulbright files.
6. Martin Luther King, Jr., *Why We Can't Wait.* New York: Harper & Row, 1964, p. 24.
7. William Faulkner, *Life.*
8. Fulbright files.
9. Senate speech, April 8, 1948.
10. Undated speech, Fulbright files, 1964. For one of the best expositions of Fulbright's personal views toward Negroes, the South, and civil rights see his lengthy exchange with Senator Jacob Javits of New York, *Congressional Record,* April 29, 1964.
11. Fulbright brief, *Amicus Curiae,* filed with the U. S. Supreme Court, Aug. 27, 1958.
12. Undated clipping, Fulbright files.
13. Authors' interview.
14. Fulbright files.
15. Quoted, *New York Times,* Sept. 29, 1957.
16. *Ibid.*
17. *Ibid.*
18. *Arkansas Gazette,* Aug. 23, 1958.
19. Quoted by Philip Carter, "Our Neighbor, Senator Fulbright," *The Texas Observer,* April 15, 1966.

CHAPTER 7. "THE AGE OF THE AMATEUR IS OVER"

1. "The Character of Present-Day American Life, Its Order of Values, and Its Sense of Purpose and Direction," *Congressional Record,* Aug. 21, 1958.
2. Sherman Adams, *Firsthand Report: The Story of the Eisenhower Administration.* New York: Harper & Brothers, 1961, p. 86.
3. *New York Times,* Feb. 1, 1959.
4. See David Wise and Thomas B. Ross, *The Invisible Government.* New York: Random House, 1964. Also Paul W. Blackstone, *The Strategy of Subversion. Manipulating the Politics of Other Nations.* Chicago: Quadrangle Books, 1964.

5. Fulbright files.
6. *Ibid. cf.*, Fulbright Speech, *Congressional Record*, Jan. 23, 1958.
7. Herman Finer, *Dulles Over Suez. The Theory and Practice of His Diplomacy*. Chicago: Quadrangle Books, 1964, p. 46.
8. *Ibid.*, pp. 47–52.
9. Draft, Jan. 24, 1957, Fulbright files.
10. See particularly Fulbright Senate speech, June 20, 1958.
11. Quoted, Edgar Kemler, "The Fulbright Fellow: An Arkansas Traveler," *The Nation*, Feb. 20, 1954.
12. From Transcript of Fulbright interview.
13. *Congressional Record*, March 20, 1958.

BOOK FOUR: *Critic*

CHAPTER 1. JFK: "HE MADE ME PROUD OF MY COUNTRY"

1. Edward Weintal and Charles Bartlett, *Facing the Brink: An Intimate Story of Crisis Diplomacy*. New York: Scribner's, 1963, p. 144.
2. Arthur M. Schlesinger, Jr., *A Thousand Days. John F. Kennedy in the White House*. Boston: Houghton Mifflin Company, 1965, p. 139.
3. *Ibid.*, p. 140.
4. Weintal and Bartlett, *op. cit.*, pp. 224–26.
5. Transcript of Voice of America program, "Press Conference USA," broadcast for overseas audience, Nov. 30, 1963.
6. Fulbright files.
7. Haynes Johnson, *The Bay of Pigs. The Leaders' Story of Brigade 2506*. New York: W. W. Norton & Company, 1964.
8. *Ibid.*, pp. 68–69, 86, 142, 224, *cf.*, Schlesinger account, *A Thousand Days*, pp. 256, 292–97. Also, Theodore C. Sorensen, *Kennedy*. New York: Harper & Row, 1965, p. 302.
9. Schlesinger, *op. cit.*, p. 252.
10. Johnson, *Bay of Pigs*, p. 152.
11. Fulbright files.
12. *Congressional Record*, June 29, 1961.
13. *Ibid.*, July 15, 1961.
14. "Memorandum Submitted to Department of Defense on Propaganda Activities of Military Personnel," printed, *Congressional Record*, Aug. 21, 1961.
15. *Ibid.*
16. *Ibid.*
17. Sorensen, *Kennedy, op. cit.*, pp. 702–3.
18. J. William Fulbright, *The Arrogance of Power*. New York: Random House, 1966, pp. 48–49.
19. Voice of America press conference, *op. cit.*

CHAPTER 2. LBJ: "ON THE VERGE OF THE GOLDEN AGE"

1. Internal staff memorandum, Fulbright files.
2. *Newsweek*, April 13, 1964, p. 19.
3. *Congressional Record*, April 7, 1964.
4. *Washington Star*, July 10, 1964.

5. *Congressional Record,* Aug. 15, 1964.
6. Quoted, Theodore H. White, *The Making of the President, 1964.* New York: Atheneum Publishers, 1965, p. 360.

CHAPTER 3. THE BREAK: PRELUDE

1. *Public Papers of the President, Lyndon B. Johnson. Vol. 2, 1963–64.* Washington: U. S. Government Printing Office, p. 926.
2. *Washington Star,* Aug. 3, 1964.
3. *Johnson Papers, op. cit.*
4. *Ibid.,* p. 928 ff.
5. *Congressional Record,* Aug. 6, 1964.
6. *The Arrogance of Power, op. cit.,* pp. 51–52.
7. Quoted in Philip L. Geyelin, *Lyndon B. Johnson and the World.* New York: Praeger, 1966, p. 195. For other transcripts of Johnson's comments on Vietnam in the campaign, see *Johnson Papers, op. cit.,* pp. 1019 ff., 1126–27 and 1164.
8. Geyelin, *op. cit.,* p. 197.
9. *Ibid.*
10. Roger Hilsman, *To Move a Nation,* New York: Doubleday & Company, Inc., 1967, p. 534.
11. *Ibid.,* p. 527.
12. *New York Times Magazine,* July 4, 1965.
13. *Washington Star,* Jan. 4, 1965.
14. *Ibid.*
15. *Time,* Jan. 25, 1965.
16. Weintal and Bartlett, *op. cit.,* p. 154.
17. *Johnson Papers,* Vol. 3.
18. *Ibid.*
19. *Johnson Papers.*
20. *Washington Star,* April 12, 1965.

CHAPTER 4. THE BREAK: DENOUEMENT

1. Fulbright files.
2. *Johnson Papers.*
3. In addition to confidential and privileged source material, we have relied on John Bartlow Martin, *Overtaken by Events, The Dominican Crisis from the Fall of Trujillo to the Civil War,* New York: Doubleday & Company, Inc., 1967. *Cf., Dominican Action—1965. Intervention or Cooperation?* A study prepared by The Center for Strategic Studies. Georgetown University, Washington, D.C., July 1966, which reprints as-yet declassified cables and gives a complete chronology.
4. John Bartlow Martin, *op. cit.,* p. 661.
5. *The Arrogance of Power,* pp. 59–60.
6. "The Situation in the Dominican Republic," speech, *Congressional Record,* Sept. 15, 1965.
7. *Ibid.,* Sept. 16, 1965.
8. *Washington Post,* Sept. 17, 1965.
9. *Congressional Record.*

CHAPTER 5. THE LAND OF THE DOMINOES

1. *The Arrogance of Power*, p. 115.
2. General Matthew B. Ridgway, *Soldier: The Memoirs of Matthew B. Ridgway*. New York: Harper & Brothers, 1956, p. 277.
3. Schlesinger, *op. cit.*, p. 320.
4. *Congressional Record*, April 6, 1954.
5. *Background Information Relating to Southeast Asia and Vietnam*. (Revised edition), June 16, 1965. Committee on Foreign Relations, United States Senate. Washington: the U. S. Government Printing Office, 1965: This is the best chronological compilation of the American involvement and official statements relating to the U.S. commitment. Hereafter cited as *Committee Background*.
6. Arthur Krock, *In the Nation: 1932–1966*. New York: McGraw-Hill Book Company, 1966, pp. 324–25.
7. *Committee Background, op. cit.*, pp. 100–1. (Transcript of Kennedy TV interview, Sept. 9, 1963.)
8. Schlesinger, *op. cit.*, p. 547.
9. Transcript of National Educational Television program interview "A Conversation with James Reston," Jan. 1966.

CHAPTER 6. THE ARROGANCE OF POWER

1. *Hearings Before the Committee on Foreign Relations, United States Senate, 89th Congress, 2d Session, on S. 2793. Part I*. Washington: U. S. Government Printing Office, 1966, p. 2 ff.
2. Quoted, *The Arrogance of Power*, pp. 52–53. *Cf.*, Philip Geyelin article, "Humphrey Says Meaning of Honolulu Talks Is a Sweeping U.S. Commitment for Asia," *Wall Street Journal*, April 20, 1966.
3. *The Arrogance of Power. Ibid.*
4. Transcript of television interview with Dean Rusk, WST-TV, Atlanta, Georgia, Aug. 11, 1965, reprinted, *Atlanta Magazine*, Oct. 1965.
5. Authors' interview, Rusk.
6. Rusk Atlanta interview, *op. cit.*
7. Vietnam *Hearings, op. cit.*
8. *Newsweek. Cf.*, Weintal and Bartlett, *op. cit.*, pp. 160–61.
9. Vietnam *Hearings*, pp. 661–69.
10. Fulbright files, undated clipping.
11. *Washington Star*, May 13, 1966.
12. *Ibid.*

APPENDIX

(Landmark Fulbright speeches)

On December 10, 1939, only weeks after becoming president of the University of Arkansas, Fulbright delivered his first public address before the Fort Smith (Arkansas) Civic Club. In that speech, entitled "The Social Function of the University," he set out themes which would recur throughout his career. He was then thirty-four years old and the youngest university president in the United States.

I appreciate this opportunity to meet with you. Judge Ragon said that he didn't care what kind of speech I prepared and that I might speak it, sing it, or read it. The main thing was that you all should have an opportunity to see me, and I, an opportunity to meet you. Now that you have seen me, I feel that the greater part of my duty has been discharged. Many remarks have been made about my youth. I really mean no offense by it and I am confident that definite progress is being made every day to correct it.

This is my first public appearance as President of the University of Arkansas. I think it is fitting and proper that it be in Fort Smith because Fort Smith has always been a strong supporter of the University. . . . But further than that, your support of the University indicates that your people are aware of the advantages of a strong university. You understand that in order for your city and our state to prosper our young men and women must receive the best training possible. . . .

One of the primary elements of success, either in a city or a university, is the proper sense of values on the part of those in control. The emphasis must be put in the proper place. This is a proposition easy to state but difficult to elucidate or apply. However, I shall attempt a simple illustration of what I mean by this thought as applied to education.

On Nov. 24th one of our senators made a speech in which he said (quoting the *Arkansas Gazette*):

"These men and women who have devoted their lives to this work (training of youth) are not to be criticized, but the time has arrived when they, as leaders, must use that leadership in the establishment of courses of study and instruction in such a manner as to place *first things first.*" The phrase "first things first" caught my attention. It expresses very well the problem, but the difficult matter is to determine what is the first thing in education.

From the report of his speech I infer that *he* believes the first thing to be taught is how to procure and retain a job. I agree that that *is* one of the important objects of any educational program, but I am not so sure that it should be the principal, or first, object of education.

During the past decade the economic distress of the world in general, and of this country in particular, has given rise to a great deal of criticism of practically all of our institutions. Our government, our banks, our great corporations, our churches, and our schools have been closely scrutinized and some, or all, blamed. On the whole, it is a healthy condition. In our educational system the debate has centered around the question of vocational education versus liberal or cultural education. Those of you who have read President Hutchins' articles in *The Saturday Evening Post* and the reply to his arguments, are familiar with the essence of the problem. It is not an easy one. In my own mind I am unable to accept entirely either view. A thorough discussion of the enormously complicated problem is entirely too much for an occasion of this kind. But there is one thought about the matter that I *would* like to leave with you.

When we look at the causes of our distress, isn't it true that we often arrive at the conclusion that some part of our government is at fault or at least that it can and should remedy the situation? We generally agree that our scientists have done, and are doing, a fine job, our manufacturing companies certainly can produce more than the people can buy, our farmers flood the market with every kind of product, and so on. On the other hand, whenever two people gather in serious conversation they usually find some fault with the conduct of our government. Not all of the criticism is justified, of course. I am convinced that we have the best system of government ever devised by man and I do not believe that all of our officials are incompetent, although some are even worse than incompetent. We have had Huey Long, Tom Pendergast, and Jimmy Hines. The disposition of these men through the courts by an aroused citizenry is one of the chief reasons why I feel sure our system *can* be made to work. When Tom Pendergast was sent to the penitentiary I think every decent citizen felt a warm glow of confidence in the inherent strength of our government.

I wish to emphasize here the fact that I do not intend this observation to be a criticism of any government officials now in office. In fact, we have in Washington County the best administration that we have had in years. Likewise, I believe that our state and national administration are, on the whole, in excellent hands. My point *is* that many people seem to feel that our system of government is threatened as never before by Communism, or fascism, or perhaps both. On the other hand, I personally feel that this awareness of the dangers is the best possible insurance for the preservation of our democratic system.

If it is granted as a premise that the functioning of our government has been and is our weakest point as a nation and society, then it seems to me that our universities should direct their efforts toward the improvement of this weakness. The point of attack is not the legislature directly, but it is the students who will be the voters, and representatives of the voters, in the days that are ahead. In simple language we should train good citizens, citizens able to assume the responsibilities of, and to function in, a democratic society.

What is a good citizen? It is true that a good citizen must be able to earn a living, but that is only a beginning. He must appreciate the importance of a good government. He must be able to realize that business of every description, that literature, art, and the professions can thrive only if an honest, equitable, and stable government exists to protect these activities from oppression. He must realize that his government touches every activity of his life from his birth until his death. He must see that in these days there is absolutely no escape from one's government.

Because *some* of our public servants have been delinquent, many of our citizens have thrown up their hands and have said that politics is a rotten business and that they will have nothing to do with it. The word politics has unfortunately with some people acquired a meaning synonymous with corruption. If it *was* ever justified, it was because of the indifference of our citizens and it is every decent citizen's duty to help bring the word back into good repute. I used to advise my best law students to go into politics and some of them were horrified that I should want them to engage in such a corrupt business. You might have thought I had advised them to be bootleggers. This attitude has kept many of our best minds from politics, and this attitude has been largely created by their parents and teachers. Too many of our older citizens have adopted the attitude that nothing can be done about politics. This defeatist view is, in my opinion, the greatest single threat to the preservation of our democratic form of government. I am certain that something can be done to improve the quality of our politics.

You may ask what can the University do about it? I believe that by the proper emphasis on the right subjects the universities, in the course of time, can make the students realize the importance of a good government, can teach them that politics can be the most honorable of all professions, and can induce the best of them to enter political life as a career. Our efforts should be directed toward the fulfillment of society's greatest need, which is wise and capable statesmen, and wise statesmen can be procured only as the result of intelligent, interested and active citizens. . . . With our government in the hands of our best citizens, the arts, sciences, business, and religion will inevitably flourish.

Five years after the end of World War II, Americans were fighting again. But in the early 1950s the Korean War seemed, to many Americans, secondary to problems at home. It was a time of political corruption, cynicism, and what appeared to be a decline in public and private morality. In such a setting, in the aftermath of his Reconstruction Finance Corporation investigation, Fulbright stood on the Senate floor and spoke on "The Moral Deterioration of American Democracy." The date was March 27, 1951.

Mr. President, when the Subcommittee on the Reconstruction Finance Corporation undertook its study, more than a year ago, I anticipated the development of little more than the usual issues which grow out of an investigation of the executive branch of the Government. I expected just another case study of an agency, with a finding of facts to be made and an orthodox legislative remedy recommended.

Before we had proceeded very far, however, it became evident that we were dealing not simply with a legal or legislative problem but with a moral problem. The first case to which my attention was called was one involving the employment, by a borrower, of an RFC employee who had recommended the granting of the loan. The Board of Directors of the RFC thought this practice quite proper. I thought it improper. So from the beginning we were confronted with a difference in ethical standards. It presents a very difficult problem. It is difficult because the evils to be dealt with are so seldom amenable to the processes of law. When confronted with an evil, we Americans are prone to say, "There ought to be a law." But the law does not and cannot apply effectively over wide fields of men's activities. It cannot reach those evils which are subtle and impalpable. Generally speaking, it reaches only the overt and the blatant acts of the wicked.

EVIL BEYOND THE LAW

Much of the evil of the world is beyond the reach of the law. The law cannot prevent gossip. It cannot prevent men from bearing false witness against their neighbors. It cannot restrain men from avarice and gluttony. It cannot restrain a man from betraying his friends. In short, it cannot prevent much of the evil to which men are, unfortunately, too prone. The law being inadequate, men long ago supplemented the law courts with courts of equity, where the spirit of the law, rather than its letter, is paramount. Underlying the law are the codes of ethics promulgated by the great religions and recognized by all civilized men as being essential to a humane and enlightened existence.

As our study of the RFC progressed, we were confronted more and more with problems of ethical conduct. What should be done about men who do not directly and blatantly sell the favors of their offices for money and so place themselves within the penalties of the law? How do we deal with those who, under the guise of friendship, accept favors which offend the spirit of the law but do not violate its letter?

What of the men outside Government who suborn those inside it? They are careful to see that they not do anything that can be construed as illegal. They operate through lawyers—men who are known as clever lawyers; a cleverness which is like the instinct of the rat that knows how to get the bait without getting caught. Many businessmen, ostensibly reputable businessmen, employ these knavish lawyers to circumvent the law and enrich themselves at Government expense. Too often the law cannot touch them.

WHO IS AT FAULT?

Who is more at fault, the bribed or the bribers? The bribed have been false to their oaths and betrayers of their trust. But they are often relatively simple men—men of small fortune or no fortune at all—and they weaken before the temptations held out to them by the unscrupulous.

Who are the bribers? They are often men who walk the earth lordly and secure; members of good families; respected figures in their communities; graduates of universities. They are, in short, of the privileged minority, and I submit that it is not unreasonable to ask of them that high standard of conduct which their training ought to have engendered. Is it too much to ask of them that they do not use a Government lending agency as a dumping ground for their own mistakes in judgment? Is it too much to ask of them, the favored few of our country, that they behave with simple honesty; with that honesty which looks, not to the letter of the law, but to its spirit?

Mr. President, the essence of what we have been studying in our committee is but a reflection of what may be seen in many other phases of our national life. The Government and its activities are, in a very real sense, a mirror of our national life. The inquiry into the RFC has revealed conditions which unfortunately may be found in other activities of our people.

CYNICISM IN COLLEGES

Let us consider what has developed in our colleges where the characters of our young men and women are being molded. Our colleges, under extreme pressure from the alumni, have become so intent upon winning football and basketball games that they use any means to gain their ends. They hire players who are not bona fide students and thus make a mockery, a farce, of the whole concept of amateur sport for the health and entertainment of our young men. They corrupt not only the hired players, but also the entire student body, who learn from their elders the cynical, immoral doctrine that one must win at all costs.

A by-product of this doctrine, this necessity for big money, led naturally to betting and to the shocking episode of the widespread bribery of basketball players in New York. I find it difficult to blame the players. They are but following a logical sequence of influences, beginning with the corruption of the sport at its source by pressure from the alumni.

This question of the moral strength of our people is not just an internal domestic matter. It has grave implications in our international relations. Without confidence in their Government, the people will not make the sacrifices necessary to oppose Russia successfully. Professor Toynbee, in his well-known historical study, demonstrated clearly how the vast majority of great civilizations have been destroyed, not as a result of external aggression, but as a consequence of domestic corruption. A democracy can recover quickly from physical or economic disaster, but when its moral convictions weaken it becomes easy prey for the demagogue and the charlatan. Tyranny and oppression then become the order of the day.

A TOTALITARIAN CONCEPT

I wonder whether in recent years we have unwittingly come to accept the totalitarian concept that the end justifies the means, a concept which is fundamentally and completely antagonistic to a true domestic society. Democracy is, I believe, more likely to be destroyed by the perversion of, or abandonment of, its true moral principles than by armed attack from Russia. The evil and insidious materialism of the Communists is a greater danger to us than their guns.

One of the most disturbing aspects of this problem of moral conduct is the revelation that among so many influential people, morality has become identical with legality. We are certainly in a tragic plight if the accepted standard by which we measure the integrity of a man in public life is that he keep within the letter of the law.

Mr. President, the growing size and complexity of our Government, as much as we may deplore it, only emphasizes the need for a clarification, a restatement of the moral standards of governmental conduct. When our Government was small, when it took only ten percent of our earnings in taxes, we could afford a certain amount of official boodling. Today, it has become too important. We simply can no longer afford moral obtuseness in our public officials.

CONDONING CORRUPTION

Scandals in our Government are not new phenomena in our history. What seems to be new about these scandals is the moral blindness or callousness which allows those in responsible positions to accept the practices which the facts reveal. It is bad enough for us to have corruption in our midst, but it is worse if it is to be condoned and accepted as inevitable.

Mr. President, is there anything we can do here in Washington to help our country reaffirm or reestablish a higher concept of public conduct?

Some weeks ago, I suggested, informally, that it would be beneficial to have a commission of eminent citizens designated by the Congress, to consider the problem of ethical standards of conduct in public affairs. I renew that suggestion now, and I have a resolution which will be ready for presentation to the Senate tomorrow.

Such a commission should be composed of private citizens of outstanding achievement and character, whose integrity is beyond question. As examples of the type of men who should serve, I suggest the following: former Justice Owen Roberts, of Pennsylvania; former Senator La Follette, of Wisconsin; Judge Learned Hand, of New York; Mr. Walter Reuther, of Detroit; Mr. Paul Hoffman, of the Ford Foundation; Dr. Reinhold Niebuhr, of Union Theological Seminary; Dr. Theodore Greene, of Yale; Dr. Hutchins, of Chicago; President Clinchy, of the Conference of Christians and Jews; Father Parsons, of Catholic University. Such a list could be extended indefinitely, but I think I have adequately indicated the type of person I have in mind.

Such a commission, as I conceive of it, would be a catalytic agent, stimulated by public indignation, to draw forth meaning from the mass of data revealed by the several current investigations. The commission would evaluate the conditions which have been exposed, and drawing upon its combined wisdom would restate again, or formulate anew, principles which, it is to be hoped, would strengthen the faith of all decent men in our democratic society.

PEOPLE OF LITTLE FAITH

Too many people in our Nation do not believe anything with conviction. They question the precepts of God or of man, indiscriminately. The values of life which were clear to the Pilgrims and the founding fathers have become dim and fuzzy in outline. False propaganda and the "big lie" of demagogues have created doubt in the minds of men. Professional political hucksters, imported from afar, without local responsibility or restraint, corrupt our free elections and poison democracy at its source. The principal objective of the study I suggest is the restoration of the faith of our people in the validity of the traditional precepts of our democratic society. It is not a job for politicians; it is not a job for the inexperienced; it is a job for the wisest of our citizens under a mandate from the Nation.

Mr. President, in making this suggestion, I am quite prepared to be dubbed naïve. It will not be the first time. As I look back upon our history or upon my own experience, nearly every progressive or fruitful move, especially if it was novel, has been considered naïve. To expect, or even hope, for an improvement in the moral climate of Washington, is, in the eyes of the boys who know, I am sure, thoroughly utopian.

I confess that I do not know what should be done. If I knew, I would not call upon the wisest men of our country. I would suggest it myself. But, Mr. President, I am unwilling to accept the view that nothing can be done, that the moral deterioration, which is so evident to all, must continue, to its logical conclusion, which is the destruction of our free democratic system. Mr. President, I think something can be done. This may not be the right thing; but, if anyone has a better suggestion, let him step forward.

I submit, Mr. President, that further investigations, as instructive as they may be, are not nearly as important as an understanding of what has already been exposed and action to remedy the situation.

The Cold War brought its reaction, as well as its burden, to Americans unaccustomed to shouldering world leadership and responsibility. One of the immediate reactions was a desire by many to withdraw from the struggle. The proposed Bricker constitutional amendment was intended to accomplish that. On Feb. 2, 1954, Fulbright spoke against it and took a long look at the American form of government and the forces threatening to change it radically.

Mr. President, the American Constitution is one of the miracles of man's history. It was hammered out initially by great men in a series of great debates. Then it was subjected to the most searching examination in another series of debates carried on throughout the Thirteen States before it was finally adopted.

Generation after generation of Americans has turned to the Federalist debates for enlightenment, not only as to the foundations of the Constitution but also for enlightenment upon the philosophy of democratic government in the United States. The Constitution is our most brilliant, as it is our most enduring, political success. It has been a pre-eminently workable document adaptable to the incalculable social and political changes that have occurred upon this continent and in the world since it was written nearly two centuries ago. Under it this Nation has successively weathered the mightiest civil war of all time and three world wars stretching from the days of Napoleon to those of Kaiser Wilhelm II, Hitler, and Mussolini. Nor is this all. Under it also the American people have achieved more happiness and prosperity for a longer time and over a wider area than any other system ever erected by men.

The reader of the constitutional debates feels, again, a solemn pride in his country. The debaters were gifted men. They constituted, indeed, such a brilliant company as has rarely been found anywhere, and whose like we have not had since their passing. Widely and deeply educated, they drew upon all the legal-philosophical sources of the ancient and contemporary world. Themselves learned, they respected both learning and the learned. They were free of that swinish blight so common in our time—the blight of anti-intellectualism. I should like to remind you, if I may, that this blight, hitherto alien to our democracy, was endemic in Fascist Italy and Germany as it is endemic today in Soviet Russia.

The Founding Fathers were children of the age of enlightenment. They believed in reason. They sought to convince other men by persuasion rather than to try to bludgeon them into submission by force. They were serene in the belief that reason, applied to human affairs, could bring men to a better way of life and living. They had an immense contempt for the debater who descended to the low level of personalities. They detested the use of slogans and epithets, for their use is the last refuge of the mentally insecure and the intellectually bankrupt. They appealed to men's minds; not to their passions. In short, they were reasonable men seeking to establish a new state upon a rational foundation so firm that it could withstand the stress of change in decades to follow.

And here, if I may divert for a moment, I should like to say that I am tired of name calling directed at anyone who does not agree with the other fellow. I am prepared to debate the principles in which I believe. I am not, however, prepared to indulge in any contest of name calling, for not only is this repulsive but it is also, as I see it, an offense to manners that govern the conduct of decent men, and it is antidemocratic in the operation of a democratic society.

The Founding Fathers pursued rationality in their acts and in their debates for another reason. They believed that our democratic society presupposes the code of the gentleman. It does not expect saintly conduct of men. It does, however, expect that they should conduct themselves with a decent respect for the opinions of mankind. But when they do not do so, when public men indulge themselves in abuse, when they deny others a fair trial, when they resort to innuendo and insinuation, to libel, scandal, and suspicion, then our democratic society is outraged, and democracy is baffled. It has no apparatus to deal with the boor, the liar, the lout, and the antidemocrat in general.

Under the Constitution, the United States has gone from weakness to strength, from strength to greater strength, from isolation to world leadership, until now we are a people having an unparalleled prosperity at home and an unprecedented power abroad.

The Founding Fathers were, I repeat, eminently successful in their efforts. Only once was their work violently challenged. And we paid a stupendous price for that challenge in blood, treasure, and heartbreak. At that time, as you know, there were fanatics in Boston and there were other fanatics in Charleston. Men hurled epithets at one another, they refused to listen to reason, faith gave way to fanaticism, and, as Americans venomously distrusted one another, we came to a bloody civil war.

It is then no small thing to drastically alter the Constitution by an amendment that in effect throttles the President of the United States in his conduct of foreign relations. It is indeed bewildering to see the Constitution, which for so long has been the bulwark of our liberties and the primary source of our political strength, come under such violent attack as we have not witnessed since the 1850s. It is even more bewildering when one considers that, so far from being a "loophole" in our Constitution as is now claimed, the treatymaking power was perhaps the most urgent reason for calling the Constitutional Convention. Treaties made under the Articles of Confederation were not enforceable as internal law. The debates of the Convention and the Federalist papers show the extreme care taken in the formulation of this power, and the system of checks and balances applicable to it.

But today I am less concerned with the Bricker amendment in its direct constitutional sense than I am with it as evidence of a disturbing phase of present-day thinking common to many men.

The essence of their malady, as I see it, is this: It is an attempt to escape the world. As troubles and problems, many of them apparently insoluble, pile one upon the other, an irresistible desire to escape it all wells up in their consciousness. Political scientists call this tendency to withdraw from the struggle and to pretend it does not concern us "isolationism." The psychologists tell us that it is a very natural yearning of a deeply troubled adult to return to the peace and quiet of prenatal security.

Whatever the instinct or the motive we know that such retreat from the world is impossible. Our salvation, if we are to be saved, will come from looking the facts in the face and following wise policies based upon those facts.

We often talk about adopting a tough policy in foreign affairs. I suggest that loose talk about being tough is evidence more of weakness than strength, for a strong man who really believes in himself does not try to impress the other fellow by being tough. We need, not toughness, but toughmindedness; that is, the willingness and ability to look facts in the face, however bitter they may be, to appraise them at their true worth and then to act calmly, judiciously, and determinedly.

I shall not attempt here even to state, much less appraise, the facts of the perilous, troubled world in which we live; a world perhaps teetering to destruction even as we sit here.

Senators are well acquainted with the events of recent years. Suffice it to say that the world order of the last 300 years, under which we developed great wealth and power, has been destroyed. Europe, the predominant influence in that period, is stricken and unable to direct the course of events.

The spread of modern technology into hitherto backward lands has created opportunities and possibilities for peaceful or warlike developments heretofore unimagined.

In a word, the destruction of the old established pattern of world power has left us in a period of inevitable and unpredictable change. These are the facts of life, and not idle speculation. We will not be able to go back to the halcyon days of 1900, but must, on the contrary, continually face unforeseeable perils. This being true, we shall not triumph by any device, whether isolation, neutrality, or the Bricker amendment, whose underlying objective is a retreat from the world.

One reason of course that we should like to retreat from the world is that struggle—constant, unremitting, blood-and-sweat struggle—is the primitive law of all life on this planet. Struggle successfully, and you survive. Fail to struggle enough, and you perish. The record of mankind is replete with illustrations of tribes and nations long vanished from the face of the earth because they were unable to meet ·the conditions of struggle imposed upon them either by their environment or by human enemies. History records their passing but nature does not weep for them.

Nature—pitiless in a pitiless universe—is certainly not concerned with the survival of Americans or, for that matter, of any of the two billion people now inhabiting this earth. Hence, our destiny, with the aid of God, remains in our own hands.

Mr. President, we have been given at times to adopting methods that seem strange to a civilized and enlightened people. For these methods, in essence, are those of the witch doctor in a primitive African village. He attempts to drive away the evil spirit by beating drums or by chanting cabalistic incantations. We who are brought up in the tradition of science are saddened by this spectacle, knowing how fruitless it is. But incantations can be chanted in more ways than one, and when we do it by assuming that we can banish the evil spirits of an evil world by turning our backs upon it through such concepts as neutrality or the Bricker amendment, we are merely denying our intelligence, turning our backs upon our knowledge, retreating from the facts of life, and placing our faith in methods that all history and all experience have demonstrated to be futile.

Our enemy is not the President of the United States, whether the incumbent, his successor to come, or his predecessors. Indeed, so far as President Eisenhower is concerned, it is an unbelievable spectacle to see Members of the Senate—particularly members of his own party—trying to hamstring him in the exercise of perhaps the most solemn and far-reaching obligations of his office —namely, the conduct of our foreign relations—when not long ago this Nation gave its life into his hands by making him the supreme commander of our military forces. And one's amazement becomes greater in the face of this spectacle seeing that recently the American people, believing not only in his high qualities as a man but also in his high abilities as a diplomat trained in the hard school of experience, elected him President of the United States at a period when the successful or unsuccessful conduct of our foreign relations may mean the life or death of this Nation.

Mr. President, the Constitution charges the President with the duty of conducting our foreign relations by and with the advice of the Senate. It makes him the leading actor; not a spectator and a mere witness. And this role has been discharged by successive Presidents of the United States throughout the nearly two centuries duration of the Constitution. It was never intended by the Founding Fathers that the President of the United States should be a ventriloquist dummy sitting on the lap of the Congress.

I do not share the fears of an ignorant or willful President or Senate, and this faith on my part is not merely an innocent trust in individuals, present and future. It is a faith in the form of government which we have known for 165 years, in the traditions and history of the institutions of the Presidency, the Senate, and the Supreme Court, and in the ability of our people, present and future, to regulate those institutions through the processes of government, as they have in the past.

Yet we have come to this constitutional crisis—not, I believe, because Members of this Senate, whether Democrat or Republican, have little faith in President Eisenhower's wisdom and patriotism. We have come to it, I think, because in our desperation to escape the world that we can never escape, we are seeking some device of magic that would enable us to accomplish an impossible end.

Many years ago I read an old-fashioned oration on George Washington by Edward Everett. Everett said that "common sense was eminently a characteristic of George Washington." I could not have been more disappointed and disillusioned than by this appraisal of one of my heroes. For as a boy I naturally thought of Washington as a dashing figure on a horse leading his troops into battle, or crossing the ice-caked Delaware to strike the Hessians at night. It was years later that I realized the significance of Edward Everett's words and understood that without George Washington's common sense it might have been impossible to establish this democracy. Washington has been dead now some 150 odd years. But common sense is as valuable now as it was in his day, even if it is apparently becoming rarer. I suggest that we could return to it with the greatest benefit to us all.

Presidents come and go. Some are wise; some are less wise. Some are strong; some are less strong. Some are gifted; some are less gifted. This is true, too, of all the men who have sat in Congress since the founding of this Nation. But all our Presidents, our Congresses, and the members of our Supreme Court proceeding with such wisdom as was given them, and operating under the checks and balances of our constitutional system, erected here a system of government without parallel among civilized men.

In so doing they were aware of the wisdom of George Washington when he said in his farewell address:

Toward the preservation of your Government and the permanency of your present happy state, it is requisite, not only that you steadily discountenance irregular opposition to its acknowledged authority, but also that you resist with care the spirit of innovation upon its principles; however specious the pretext. One method of assault may be to effect, in the forms of the Constitution, alterations which will impair the energy of the system; and thus to undermine what cannot be directly overthrown. In all the changes to which you may be involved, remember that time and habit are at least as necessary to fix the true character of governments, as of other human institutions—that experience is the surest standard by which to test the real tendency of the existing constitution of a country—that facility in changes, upon the credit of mere hypothesis and opinion, exposes to perpetual change from the endless variety of hypothesis and opinion; and remember, especially, that for the efficient management of your common interests in a country so extensive as ours, a government of as much vigor as is consistent with the perfect security of liberty is indispensable. Liberty itself will find in such a government, with powers properly distributed and adjusted, its surest guardian.

Mr. President, I am opposed to the Bricker amendment and urge the Senate to reject it.

One year later Fulbright, who had taken the lead in opposing Senator Joseph R. McCarthy, spoke up in behalf of dissent at the annual National Book Award dinner in New York on Jan. 25, 1955. His speech, "The Mummification of Opinion," was an epitaph for McCarthyism, and a warning for the future.

May I at the outset express my appreciation for the invitation to share in these ceremonies. I feel a close tie with all of you who know that works of the mind should be honored no less than works of the hand.

Elsewhere today, it seems at times that a man can be arrested for unlawful assembly when he merely collects his thoughts. Elsewhere, too, we see that action for action's sake, divorced from thought, is offered as a supreme proof of patriotism. For myself, I often feel that if men in public life read and thought a little more, and talked and acted a little less, we would the better know what to do and how to do it.

Beyond the personal honor you pay me through your invitation, I know that its larger motive is the recognition you mean to give to the exchange of persons program with which I have been identified. Its objective, like that of the writer, is to improve human understanding. By the end of this year, twenty thousand participants from many countries will have shared in the program. I deeply appreciate your past support of it. I know I can count on your support of it in the future.

As for this meeting, I wavered between alternative topics I might talk about. I could not tell you how to write a book, or criticize it, or sell it. But among the many questions in which you and I as citizens of the Republic have a mutual interest, one in particular towered above the others in its special significance to you as writers and to me as a public official. That question is the degree to which freedom of opinion and expression has been curtailed in our country, and the meaning this has for all of us.

As far back as the 1830s, *freedom* of discussion and the influence of the *majority opinion* thereon was a matter of real concern to thoughtful people. Alexis de Tocqueville put it well, I think:

"I know of no country," he wrote, "in which there is so little independence of mind and real freedom of discussion as in America." "The will of man," he said of the *majority* opinion, "is not shattered, but softened, bent, and guided; men are seldom forced by it to act, but they are constantly restrained from acting. Such a power does not destroy, but it prevents existence; it does not tyrannize, but it compresses, enervates, extinguishes, and stupifies a people. . . . The majority," continued De Tocqueville, "no longer says: 'You shall think as I do or you shall die'; but it says: 'You are free to think differently from me and to retain your life, your property, and all that you possess; but you are henceforth a stranger among your people. You may retain your civil rights, but they will be useless to you, for you will never be chosen by your fellow citizens if you solicit their votes; and they will affect to scorn you if you ask for their esteem.

" 'You will remain among men, but you will be deprived of the rights of mankind. Your fellow creatures will shun you like an impure being; and even those who believe in your innocence will abandon you, lest they should be shunned in their turn. Go in peace! I have given you your life, but it is an existence worse than death.' "

The sharp edge of that prophecy cuts deeply into us today, not alone because of the Senator from Wisconsin and not alone because of the driving pressure of his avowed followers. Restrictions on freedom of expression come from many sources—some of them, very respectable—and in some cases, for reasons unrelated to the ambitions of the Wisconsin revolutionary.

There is, for example, the narrowing effect inherent in the concentration of managerial control of the press, the radio, the movies—and, in the foreseeable future, television.

Within the last forty years, according to Morris Ernst, one-third of our daily newspapers have disappeared, and more than three thousand weeklies, have ceased publication. As of a recent date, ten of our states did not have a single city with competing papers, and in the whole of America, there are only a few more than one hundred cities where one can find daily papers in competition. The pattern of concentration extends elsewhere. In radio, one-fifth of the stations are interlocked with newspapers. Four networks dominate national radio, while less than two dozen advertisers account for fifty percent of network income. And in the film industry, five big companies exercise a dominant influence upon the industry.

Let me make one thing plain. I am not saying that what brought this to pass was in all cases the hand of monopoly grabbing for bigness as an end in itself. In some cases, *cost*-account sheets *compelled* owners and managers to seek their survival by enlarging themselves through mergers. And it is to the credit of some of these, that when they found themselves in a monopolistic position, they tried to run the communications property as if it were a responsible public utility. But men of this outlook are, unfortunately, in the minority.

The general effect of what approaches monopoly control is that people hear, see, watch, read, and listen to only one side of public questions. And this in turn can adversely affect the public man to whom the guidance of public affairs is entrusted. He may know the truth and want to speak it. Yet he doubts whether his views, as transmitted to his constituents by those who control communication channels, will be fairly presented, or presented at all. So there often follows from this a chain reaction of cynicism leading to corruption. This public man, to achieve anything at all, will not use the open road, but will crowd himself into the path of low intrigue. He will not boldly scout what lies ahead for the nation. He will bend the weight of his energies to the end of having everything stand still. He will voice no prophecies of what ought to be. He will speak only the sterile dogmas of the street, and only those bits of rumor which bear the general sanction of the lords of communication.

And what of the end result to all this? It can be a society shaped in imitation of an Egyptian mummy; a society where the embalmer holds the highest place of honor; a society of fixed, painted, and hard shells; a society feeding on its dry rot, until the fateful hour when a probing finger striking the shell from without makes it collapse on the empty center.

This vision of the future is not drawn from the thin air or from a fevered imagination. It came after reading the report on tax-exempt foundations issued recently by the Reece Committee of the House of Representatives. There, in one sentence, Chairman Reece put himself on the side of all the Pharaohs from Rameses the First to the gentleman whose solar ship was uncovered recently. "The trustees of the tax-exempt foundations" said the Reece report, "should . . . be very chary of promoting ideas, concepts, and opinion-forming material which run contrary to what the public currently *wishes, approves,* and *likes.*"

I said a moment ago that, in addition to Senator McCarthy, restrictions on freedom of expression have been imposed by the most respectable sources. Recently, for example, our military academies banned all student debate on the question of the recognition of Red China. The cadets at West Point and the midshipmen at Annapolis, who are destined to be our military chiefs, presumably could discuss how many angels can sit on the point of a needle, or any other celestially remote matter. But it was officially decreed that they should hold to the public posture of being blind, deaf, and dumb to the most tortured issue of the moment; an issue whose correct handling can determine whether the students themselves as well as the rest of us will live or will die.

I am indebted to the *Princeton Alumni Weekly* for another example in the same vein. The *Weekly*—scarcely a radical publication—took notice of undergraduate apathy toward political and social questions. And in listing some of the underlying causes for a phenomenon common to other colleges, it included the pressures to conform exerted by our great industrial corporations on students. To illustrate, the *Weekly* then cited from a personnel pamphlet issued by the powerful Socony Vacuum Oil Company advising students how they should behave in college if they wished to be employed on graduation. The order of the day reads, and I quote from the pamphlet: "Personal views can cause a lot of trouble. The 'isms' are out. Business being what it is, it naturally looks with disfavor on the wild-eyed radical or even the moderate pink."

Consider the implications of this text. With one hand, it gags the breath of student curiosity. With the other hand, it dangles bread before his mouth as a reward for silence, unbroken even by a moderate gurgle. It says to the student: "You will be saved only if you consider yourself a beast of burden or a beast of prey." It says to him: "Production and not the producer is the object of life on earth." It says to him: "We ourselves are the judge and the jury of what a wild-eyed radical and a moderate pink is. And if you ask us what it is, in the act of asking you become the very thing we don't want." And it says to him: "If you must find some way to spend your energies as an undergraduate before we take complete charge of you, there are football games, movies, and now television spectacles of magnificent dimensions which you may attend provided they have been screened for security and do not cause you to think."

How should those of us here bear ourselves in a climate where the pressures to conform are so remorseless?

To the politician who means to be faithful to his oath of office, the answer is plain. It is to draw closer still to the letter and spirit of the Constitution. For in the degree to which he does this, he can better follow the guidelines staked out by the Founders.

They were not prepared to lodge the rule of our society in the majority opinion. They knew it to be a quick and volatile thing; knew that it required a frame of law to study it and bring it into creative focus. Neither did they say that the frame of law was itself limitless in what it could cover. They said the law itself should be limited to enumerated topics which are a proper concern of Caesar. All else—the dreams and speculations of artists, or any other manner of activity involving a connection between a man and his God—were not to be invaded by the law.

Beyond this, the Founders were under no illusions about the nature of power. "Give all power to the many," they said, "and they will oppress the few. Give all power to the few, they will oppress the many. Both, therefore, ought to have power that each may defend itself against the other." And with this in mind, the organ of government they framed was a balanced arrangement for unity and diversity, authority and liberty, security and freedom, continuity and new birth. Elsewhere, other societies have divorced these coupled terms, saying that they were incompatible, and that one could survive only if the other was eliminated. And elsewhere, too, the effect of such a divorce has led directly to the dissolution of the society that was meant to prosper.

If the American politician draws close to the letter and spirit of the Constitution, he will not only gain strength and direction from what the Founders first explored. He will be further reinforced when he grasps the keystone fact that the Constitution is superior to any majority or minority. In consequence of this, his oath of office does not require him to swing with every breeze. The oath requires of him that he should reflect the *deliberate* sense of the community. And this in turn means that he ought to consider himself a teacher, offering by precept and example a style and method of deliberation that can be imitated by the community at large as it seeks on its own to know, and then to do the good. It also means, as is often the case with teachers, that he must be prepared to accept banishment or destruction at the hands of the people because he has aroused their anger in the very act of serving them well.

And finally what of the writer? You have a unique responsibility to the political community of which you are a part. That responsibility arises from your talent, from your capacity to enlighten, to civilize, those citizens to whose hands is entrusted the ultimate power in our society. The writer is the natural teacher of the people.

In this hurried mechanical age, the artist and intellectual are among the few who have the serenity and sense of perspective which may help us to find a way out of the fevered confusion which presently afflicts us.

Through you, the political community needs to be taught how and what to laugh at; how and what to scorn or to pity; needs to be taught continuously that honor is not the same as fame or notoriety; that physical bravery is not the only form of courage. It needs to be taught the proper objects of anger or of love. It needs to be taught the nature of justice. And above all, through you, the political community needs to be taught that the capacity of the human mind has yet to be explored, that there can be new possibilities for men themselves.

After his celebrated speech calling on Americans to turn away from old myths and face new realities, Fulbright expanded his theme to encompass the era of the cold war and what it was doing to the American character. His title: "The Cold War in American Life." His place: the University of North Carolina. The date: April 7, 1964.

The Constitution of the United States, in the words of its preamble, was established, among other reasons, in order to "provide for the common defense, promote the general welfare, and secure the blessings of liberty." In the past generation the emphasis of our public policy has been heavily weighted on measures for the common defense to the considerable neglect of programs for promoting the liberty and welfare of our people. The reason for this, of course, has been the exacting demands of two world wars and an intractable cold war, which have wrought vast changes in the character of American life.

Of all the changes in American life wrought by the cold war, the most important by far, in my opinion, has been the massive diversion of energy and resources from the creative pursuits of civilized society to the conduct of a costly and interminable struggle for world power. We have been compelled, or have felt ourselves compelled, to reverse the traditional order of our national priorities, relegating individual and community life to places on the scale below the enormously expensive military and space activities that constitute our program of national security.

This, of course, is not the only change in American life brought about by the cold war. There have been many others, some most welcome and constructive. Directly or indirectly, the world struggle with Communism has stimulated economic and industrial expansion, accelerated the pace of intellectual inquiry and scientific discovery, broken the shell of American isolation and greatly increased public knowledge and awareness of the world outside the United States. At the same time, the continuing world conflict has cast a shadow on the tone of American life by introducing a strain of apprehension and tension into a national style which has traditionally been one of buoyant optimism. The continuing and inconclusive struggle, new in American experience, has in Walt Rostow's words, "imposed a sense of limitation on the Nation's old image of itself, a limitation which has been accepted with greater or less maturity and which has touched the Nation's domestic life at many points with elements of escapism, with a tendency to search for scapegoats, with simple worry, and with much thoughtful, responsive effort as well."

Overriding all these changes, however, good and bad, has been the massive diversion of wealth and talent from individual and community life to the increasingly complex and costly effort to maintain a minimum level of national security in a world in which no nation can be immune from the threat of sudden catastrophe. We have had to turn away from our hopes in order to concentrate on our fears and the result has been accumulating neglect of those things which bring happiness and beauty and fulfillment into our lives. The "public happiness," in August Heckscher's term, has become a luxury to be postponed to some distant day when the dangers that now beset us will have disappeared.

This, I think, is the real meaning of the cold war in American life. It has consumed money and time and talent that could otherwise be used to build schools and homes and hospitals, to remove the blight of ugliness that is spreading over the cities and highways of America, and to overcome the poverty and hopelessness that afflict the lives of one-fifth of the people in an otherwise affluent society. It has put a high premium on avoiding innovation at home because new programs involve controversy as well as expense and it is felt that we cannot afford domestic divisions at a time when external challenges require us to maintain the highest possible degree of national unity. Far more pervasively than the United Nations or the "Atlantic community" could ever do, the cold war has encroached upon our sovereignty; it has given the Russians the major voice in determining what proportion of our Federal budget must be allocated to the military and what proportion, therefore, cannot be made available for domestic social and economic projects. This is the price that we have been paying for the cold war and it has been a high price indeed.

At least as striking as the inversion of priorities which the cold war has enforced upon American life is the readiness with which the American people have consented to defer programs for their welfare and happiness in favor of costly military and space programs. Indeed, if the Congress accurately reflects the temper of the country, then the American people are not only willing, they are eager, to sacrifice education and urban renewal and public health programs—to say nothing of foreign aid—to the requirements of the Armed Forces and the space agency. There is indeed a most striking paradox in the fact that military budgets of over $50 billion are adopted by the Congress after only perfunctory debate, while domestic education and welfare programs involving sums which are mere fractions of the military budget are painstakingly examined and then either considerably reduced or rejected outright. I sometimes suspect that in its zeal for armaments at the expense of education and welfare the Congress tends to overrepresent those of our citizens who are extraordinarily agitated about national security and extraordinarily vigorous about making their agitation known.

It may be that the people and their representatives are making a carefully reasoned sacrifice of welfare to security. It may be, but I doubt it. The sacrifice is made so eagerly as to cause one to suspect that it is fairly painless, that indeed the American people prefer military rockets to public schools and flights to the moon to urban renewal. In a perverse way, we have grown rather attached to the cold war. It occupies us with a stirring and seemingly clear and simple challenge from outside and diverts us from problems here at home which many Americans would rather not try to solve, some because they find domestic problems tedious and pedestrian, others because they genuinely believe these problems to be personal rather than public, others because they are unwilling to be drawn into an abrasive national debate as to whether poverty, unemployment, and inadequate education are in fact national rather than local or individual concerns.

The cold war, it seems clear, is an excuse as well as a genuine cause for the diversion of our energies from domestic well-being to external security. We have been preoccupied with foreign affairs for twenty-five years, and while striking progress has been made in certain areas of our national life, the agenda of neglect has grown steadily longer. We can no longer afford to defer problems of slums and crime and poverty and inadequate education until some more tranquil time in the future. These problems have become urgent if not intolerable in an affluent society. It is entirely reasonable to defer domestic programs in time of an all-out national effort such as World War II, but in the present cold war it is not reasonable to defer our domestic needs until more tranquil times, for the simple reason that there may be no more tranquil times in this generation or in this century.

In the long run, the solution of our domestic problems has as vital a bearing on the success of our foreign policies as on the public happiness at home. We must therefore reassess the priorities of our public policy, with a view to redressing the disproportion between our military and space efforts on the one hand and our education and human welfare programs on the other. We must distinguish between necessity and preference in our preoccupation with national security, judging our military needs by a standard which takes due account of the fact that armaments are only one aspect of national security, that military power, as Kenneth Thompson has written, "is like the fist whose force depends on the health and vitality of the body politic and the whole society."

The single-minded dedication with which we Americans have committed ourselves to the struggle with Communism is a manifestation of a national tendency to interpret problems in moral and absolutist terms. We are, as Louis Hartz has pointed out, a Nation which was "born free." Having experienced almost none of the anguished conflict between radicalism and reaction that has characterized European politics, we have been virtually unanimous in our adherence to the basic values of liberal democracy. We have come to identify these values with the institutional forms which they take in American society and have regarded both as having moral validity not only for ourselves but for the entire world. We have therefore been greatly shocked since our emergence as a world power to find ourselves confronted with revolutionary ideologies which reject the faith in individual liberty and limited government that has served our own society so well.

Because of these predilections, the cold war has seemed to represent a profound challenge to our moral principles as well as to our security and other national interests. We have responded by treating Communist ideology itself, as distinguished from the physical power and expansionist policies of Communist states, as a grave threat to the free world. The cold war, as a result, has been a more dangerous, costly, and irreconcilable conflict than it would be if we and the Communist states confined it to those issues that involve the security and vital interests of the rival power blocs.

The ideological element in the cold war, reinforced by the moralist tendencies of the American people, has also had the effect of making the world conflict a much more disruptive element in American life than it would be if it were regarded primarily in terms of its effect on our national security. To an extent, the issue between the Communist and the free worlds is moral and ideological, but ideas and principles in themselves threaten no nation's vital interests except insofar as they are implemented in national policies. It is the latter, therefore, that are our proper concern. To the extent that we are able to remove the crusading spirit and the passions of ideology from the cold war, we can reduce its danger and intensity and relax its powerful hold on the minds and hearts of our people.

The fears and passions of ideological conflict have diverted the minds and energies of our people from the constructive tasks of a free society to a morbid preoccupation with the dangers of Communist aggression abroad and subversion and disloyalty at home. The problem did not end with the McCarthy era of a decade ago nor is it confined to the neurotic fantasies of today's radical right. The cold war malady affects a much broader spectrum of American society. It affects millions of sensible and intelligent citizens whose genuine concern with national security has persuaded them that the prosecution of the cold war is our only truly essential national responsibility, that missiles and nuclear armaments and space flights are so vital to the safety of the Nation that it is almost unpatriotic to question their cost and their proliferation, and that in the face of these necessities the internal requirements of the country—with respect to its schools and cities and public services—must be left for action at some remote time in the future—as if these requirements were not themselves vital to the national security, and as if, indeed, our generation is likely to know more tranquil days.

In the 1830s Alexis de Tocqueville saw America as a nation with a passion for peace, one in which the "principle of equality," which made it possible for a man to improve his status rapidly in civilian life, made it most unlikely that many Americans would ever be drawn to form a professional military caste. In 1961, President Eisenhower warned the Nation of the pervasive and growing power of a "military-industrial complex." Tocqueville was quite right in his judgment that the United States was unlikely to become a militarist society. We have, however, as a result of worldwide involvements and responsibilities, become a great military power, with a vast military establishment that absorbs over half of our Federal budget, profoundly influences the Nation's economy, and exercises a gradually expanding influence on public attitudes and policies.

Without becoming militarist in the sense of committing themselves to the military virtues as standards of personal behavior, the American people have nonetheless come to place great—and, in my opinion, excessive—faith in military solutions to political problems. Many Americans have come to regard our defense establishment as the heart and soul of our foreign policy, rather than as one of a number of instruments of foreign policy whose effectiveness depends not only on its size and variety but also on the skill, and restraint, with which it is used.

Our faith in the military is akin to our faith in technology. We are a people more comfortable with machines than with intellectual abstractions. The Military Establishment is a vast and enormously complex machine, a tribute to the technological genius of the American people; foreign policy is an abstract and esoteric art, widely regarded as a highly specialized occupation of eastern intellectuals, but not truly an American occupation. Our easy reliance on the Military Establishment as the foundation of our foreign policy is not unlike the reliance which we place on automobiles, televisions, and refrigerators: they work in a predictable and controllable manner, and on the rare occasions when they break down, any good mechanic can put them back in working order.

The trouble with the American technological bias is that it can conceal but not eliminate the ultimate importance of human judgment. Like any other piece of machinery, our Military Establishment can be no better than the judgment of those who control it. In a democracy, control is intended to be exercised by the people and their elected representatives. To a very considerable extent the American people are not now exercising effective control over the Armed Forces; nor indeed is the Congress, despite its primary constitutional responsibility in this field. Partly because of anxieties about the cold war, partly because of our natural technological bias, which leads us to place extraordinary faith in the ability of technicians to deal with matters that we ourselves find incomprehensible, and partly because of the vested interests of the military-industrial complex, we are permitting the vast Military Establishment largely to run itself, to determine its own needs, and to tell us what sacrifices are expected of us to sustain the national arsenal of weapons.

David Lloyd George once declared that "there is no greater fatuity than a political judgment dressed in a military uniform." To the extent that the American people and the Congress shrink from questioning the size and cost of our Defense Establishment, they are permitting military men, with their highly specialized viewpoints, to make political judgments of the greatest importance regarding the priorities of public policy and the allocation of public funds.

The abnegation of responsibility by the Congress in this field is strikingly illustrated by its debates or, more accurately, nondebates, on the defense budget. When, for example, Senator McGovern, of South Dakota, suggested last September that Defense spending might be reduced by five percent, the Senate, with virtually no discussion, voted the McGovern amendment down by a vote of 70 to 2 and proceeded, after an afternoon of desultory discussion, to enact the whole Defense appropriation bill. When, later in the fall, I had the dubious honor of managing the foreign aid bill on the Senate floor through three weeks of extremely contentious debate, I could not help noting how astonishingly the forces of economy had picked up strength between the debate on the $50 billion Defense appropriation and the $4 billion foreign aid bill.

Again this year, the Congress is speeding the enactment of the Defense budget with splendid indifference to its size and content. By the end of February both Houses had enacted a military procurement authorization bill of over $17 billion. The only controversial item in the bill was an amendment authorizing $52 million for development of a new strategic manned bomber, which was adopted by both Houses despite the firm opposition of the Secretary of Defense. In the course of this debate, Senator Nelson, of Wisconsin, posed a most pertinent question. "I am questioning," he said, "what is apparently an established tradition—perhaps a national attitude—which holds that a bill to spend billions of dollars for the machinery of war must be rushed through the House and the Senate in a matter of hours, while a treaty to advance the cause of peace, or a program to help the underdeveloped nations of the world, or a bill to guarantee the rights of all our citizens, or a bill to advance the interests of the poor, must be scrutinized and debated and amended and thrashed over for weeks and perhaps months."

"Like most other Americans," writes Julius Duscha of the *Washington Post,* "Members of Congress believe that the bigger the defense budget, the safer the country. And in today's world there is no question that the United States must spend billions to keep up its defenses. But record-breaking budgets year after year do not necessarily mean a stronger Nation. The bigger any Government program gets, the greater are the dangers that funds will be wasted and that the goals of the program will become entangled in a morass of vested interests, venal political considerations, and the rivalries that inevitably evolve from them. And there is no better catharsis for huge government expenditures than informed, skeptical, and continued questioning of them."

The ease with which defense budgets are enacted by Congress, as Mr. Duscha points out, is in no small degree due to the enormous importance of defense spending for the economy. Defense contractors and great numbers of workers all over the country have a vested interest in a high level of defense spending. It is the beneficiaries of the jobs and profits that defense spending creates, along with the generals and admirals, who constitute the formidable military-industrial complex. And because of the jobs and profits stimulated by defense, Members of Congress have taken a benign attitude toward waste and duplication in the defense budget that is nothing less than amazing by contrast with the deeply held convictions about economy that influence their attitudes toward education, urban renewal, or foreign aid.

The truly astonishing thing about the uncritical support which the American people and their representatives give the Military Establishment is the apparent enthusiasm with which the sacrifice of personal and community interests is made. Goldsworthy Lowes Dickinson was, if anything, understating the matter when he wrote that "Nations are quite capable of starving every other side of life—education, sanitation, housing, public health, everything that contributes to life, physical, intellectual, moral, and spiritual, in order to maintain their armaments."

Many Americans may regard huge military and space programs as the only truly urgent requirements on our national agenda, but it is difficult to believe that this enthusiasm is shared by the 4.2 million Americans who are unemployed or by the 30 million Americans who have incomes of less than $3000 a year.

While the cold war and our enormously costly national security programs pre-empt so much of our time and attention and national wealth, the most important resources of our country—its human resources—are being extravagantly wasted and neglected. As the President's recently issued Manpower report points out, unemployment in 1963 increased to 5.7 percent of the labor force despite major advances in production and employment; unemployment of young workers, between the ages of sixteen and nineteen, reached seventeen percent in 1963 while unemployment among nonwhite Americans stood at eleven percent; despite an unemployment rate twice as high for school dropouts as for high school graduates, thirty percent of all young people continue to end their education before completing high school; despite the decline in unskilled jobs and the expanding demand for professional, technical, clerical, and service workers—for workers, that is, with at least high school education and specialized training—nearly a million young people are leaving school every year without having completed elementary or secondary school.

These are only a few of the statistics of hopelessness and deprivation that afflicts the lives of millions of Americans. Unless the present trend is reversed, 7½ million of the 26 million young people between sixteen and twenty-four who will enter the labor force during the present decade will be school dropouts. These undereducated young men and women are for the most part the children of poverty. The basic fact to be contended with, as President Johnson pointed out in his message to the Congress on poverty, is that "there are millions of Americans—one-fifth of our people—who have not shared in the abundance which has been granted to most of us, and on whom the gates of opportunity have been closed." It is one of the tragedies, and one of the great failures, of our national life that in the years between 1936 and 1964, while the total wealth and productivity of the Nation grew tremendously, the number of ill-housed, ill-clothed, and ill-fed Americans dropped only from one-third to one-fifth of our population.

The statistics of poverty, though striking, are antiseptic compared to the actual misery and hopelessness of being poor. The real meaning of poverty is not just losses of learning and productivity, but thousands of angry and dispossessed teenagers who make our city streets dangerous for "respectable" citizens; 350,000 youngsters across the Nation who form what the Secretary of Labor has described as an "outlaw pack" because they have stopped looking for work, are unemployed today, and will remain so for the rest of their lives; children in a blighted mining town in eastern Kentucky who are potbellied and anemic from lack of food; sharecroppers, white as well as black, living in squalid shacks and working for a few dollars a day—when they can find work at all—anywhere in a crescent of rural poverty that extends from southern Virginia along the Coastal Plain across Georgia and Alabama into the Mississippi Delta and the Ozarks.

Poverty in America has a radically different moral connotation from poverty in underdeveloped nations. The poor countries of the world have the excuse, for what it is worth, that the means of feeding, housing, and educating their people simply do not exist. In America the means do exist; the failure is essentially one of distribution. The children who go to bed hungry in a Harlem slum or a West Virginia mining town are not being deprived because no food can be found to give them; they are going to bed hungry because, despite all our miracles of invention and production, we have not yet found a way to make the necessities of life available to all of our citizens—including those whose failure is not a lack of personal industry or initiative but only an unwise choice of parents.

What is to be done? In his poverty message to the Congress, the President made proposals for a constructive start—although only a start—toward meeting the problem of poverty in America. Under the proposed Economic Opportunity Act, a National Job Corps would undertake the social rehabilitation, through basic education, job training, and work experience, of 100,000 young men "whose background, health, and education makes them least fit for useful work;" a work-training program would provide vocation education and part-time jobs for 200,000 young men and women in projects to be developed by State and local governments and nonprofit agencies; a national work-study program would provide Federal funds for part-time jobs for 140,000 young Americans who, though qualified, would otherwise be unable to afford to go to college. In addition, the President's program would encourage and help finance local antipoverty programs, would enlist volunteers in the war against poverty, and would undertake other financial and educational programs all to be coordinated under a new Office of Economic Opportunity.

President Johnson's program can serve as a point of departure for a full-scale national program to eliminate poverty and unemployment from American life. Such a program must be mounted through government fiscal policy, public works, and expansive economic policies, but primarily through programs of education and training. Education is not the whole solution but it is, by all available evidence, the keystone of the arch. As John Kenneth Galbraith recently wrote, "To the best of knowledge there is no place in the world where a well-educated population is really poor."

Building on this premise, Professor Galbraith proposes that the hundred lowest income communities in the country be designated as "special educational districts" to be equipped with primary and secondary schools and recreational and transportation facilities of the highest quality. The schools would be staffed by an elite corps of highly qualified, highly trained, and well-paid teachers. Grants would be provided for food and clothing for the pupils when needed as well as counseling and medical and psychiatric services.

After one year, the program would be extended to another 150 or 200 areas and eventually to cover all areas of great need. As income rises in the recipient school districts, the schools would be turned back to the localities.

The Galbraith plan is an excellent one and I, for one, would welcome the submission of such a plan to the Congress, although there can be no doubt that it would generate great controversy. I think that we must face up to the need for major new legislation in the field of education regardless of the partisan divisions which it may provoke. We must do so if we truly mean to alleviate the scourge of poverty in American life. And although it is clear that there is no simple dollar-for-dollar relationship between savings in the defense and space budgets and congressional willingness to appropriate money for education, it seems to me quite possible that the elimination of superfluous defense and space funds would in fact help overcome the reluctance to support education legislation of certain Members of Congress whose concern with economy is genuine and strong.

As a result of the rapidly spreading automation of the American economy, the traditional mechanism of distributing purchasing power through employment and income is breaking down. In essence, our ability to generate economic demand is falling steadily behind our ability to increase the supply of purchasable goods and services. It may be that the growing disequilibrium is so profound as to be irreversible by government policies designed to stimulate economic growth and full employment. If so, we shall eventually have to devise new ways of providing income to those who cannot be put to gainful work.

Whether truly radical measures will be required or not, there is no question that if our national war on poverty is to come anywhere near the goal of total victory proclaimed by President Johnson, it will require enormous public effort and a great deal of public money. To those who shrink from such a commitment in the name of economy, I would emphasize that the elimination of poverty and inadequate education are at least as important to the security of our country in the long run as the maintenance of a strong defense establishment and a good deal more important than a voyage to the moon. I commend to them the words of Edmund Burke, that "economy is a distributive virtue, and consists not in saving but in selection. Parsimony requires no providence, no sagacity, no powers of combination, no comparison, no judgment."

The cold war has diverted us from problems both quantitative and qualitative. The quantitative problem is essentially to devise ways of elevating the one-fifth of our people who live in poverty to the level of the four-fifths who live in greater material abundance than any other society in human history. The qualitative problem is to find ways of bringing meaning and purpose and standards of excellence into the lives of a people who, because of their material affluence, are free, as no people have ever been before, to shape a spiritual and intellectual environment of their own choice.

While the attention and energy of our public policy have been focused through these postwar years on crises in Berlin and Cuba and the Far East, America, almost behind our backs, has been more and more taking on the physical appearance, and the cultural atmosphere, of a honky-tonk of continental proportions. This is not to suggest that the quest for intellectual, artistic, and scientific excellence has been abandoned in our country. On the contrary, it is being pursued by more people with more energy and more striking results than at any time in our history. But the pursuit of excellence and creativity remains the occupation of an elite segment of our society, a large and brilliant elite, to be sure, but one which is still largely isolated from the nation as a whole. The creative elements of American society are probably growing larger and are constantly reaching new levels of achievement, but they are not yet successfully communicating their standards to the generality of their countrymen.

I do not think we can avoid the conclusion that despite a broadening interest in the arts, the level of popular taste in America remains far below what it can be and ought to be.

The evidences are all around us: in the mindless trivia that fill the television channels and occupy the leisure hours of tens of millions of Americans; in the paperback pornography that has become a major national industry; in the gaudy and chaotic architecture that clutters the central areas of our great cities from Manhattan to Miami and Los Angeles and in the festering slums that surround them.

It can be pointed out, and rightly, that all this is mitigated by the growing popularity of good music and good art, of the serious theater and of quality films. But this, I fear, is confined to the "other America," to the large but isolated elite who are supposed to set, or at least suggest, popular standards of taste and style but who somehow are failing to do so.

Nowhere is the vulgarization of standards more conspicuous than in the artifacts of urban America. It is difficult to judge what is the most depressing sight in New York City: the jungle of antiseptic glass towers that have taken order and humanity out of the midtown area, the sprawling slums that are never far away, or the dreary acres of identical brick housing, devoid of any charm or individuality, that constitute urban renewal. It is equally difficult to understand how Washington, the Nation's beautiful, monumental city, the living symbol of what is valued and emulated in America, should have permitted itself to be marred by stark, prisonlike new Federal office buildings that suggest arid dehumanized activities within them, or by the elephantine Rayburn

House Office Building, built in what has been described as the early Mussolini style of architecture, a building so ugly that one can only regard it as the product of an organized effort in tastelessness and vulgarity.

I feel certain that this debasement of standards is not inevitable in contemporary America. About a half mile from the new prisonlike office buildings in Washington stands the new National Geographic building, an elegant example of contemporary architecture, a structure of grace and dignity and human warmth. A half mile in another direction stands the Old Senate Office Building, a model of dignity and beauty in the classic style. This contrast symbolizes the polarization of standards between "two Americas" that constitutes a growing problem of our national life. Somehow we must strive to bring the two, alienated cultures of our country together again, to make the quest for beauty and excellence a truly national endeavor.

In a recently published book of incisive text and brilliant photographs illustrating "the planned deterioration of America's landscape," Peter Blake offers the following bleak prognosis for America's cities:

"With a very, very few exceptions, our cities seem to be headed for a grim future indeed—unless we determine to make some radical changes. That future looks something like this: first, our cities will be inhabited solely by the very poor (generally colored) and the very rich (generally white)—plus a few divisions of police to protect the latter from the former. Second, they will become primarily places to work in—places for office buildings and for light industry. Third, they will become totally ghettofied—not merely in terms of racial segregation, but also in terms of usage: there will be office ghettos, industrial ghettos, apartment ghettos, amusement or culture ghettos (like Manhattan's gold-plated Rockefeller ghetto, Lincoln Center), bureaucratic ghettos, shopping ghettos, medical-center ghettos. In other words, there will be virtually no mixed uses of streets or of neighborhoods, so that most areas of the city will be alive for mere fractions of each day or week, and as deserted as Wall Street on a weekend for the rest of the time."

One can hope that it will not come to this, that before our cities are lost to glass palaces and slums, the suburbs to housing projects and automobile junkyards, the highways to gaudy motels, and the countryside to a solid wall of billboards, the vulgarizing trend will be arrested and reversed. If it is to be reversed, we must begin by recognizing that private property rights cannot extend to the debauching of America's landscape. An ugly city is not like a bad painting, which can be shut up in a museum out of the sight of anyone who does not wish to see it. Our cities and highways and countryside are part of our common legacy. They either enrich or impoverish our lives and it cannot be left to the sole discretion of promoters and developers to determine which it will be.

There is so much in the American environment that is good, so much that is both beautiful and efficient, that the widespread prevalence of disorder and decay is beyond excuse or understanding.

Obviously, we cannot impose high standards by force, as in certain respects the Russians have—by the simple, puritanical expedient of withdrawing from their people those forms of art and recreation that are deemed to be vulgar and decadent. Only by very limited—though still important—means can we use the law to combat ugliness and bad taste: by establishing and enforcing high architectural standards for urban construction and urban renewal; by restricting the placement of billboards on our highways; by preserving our shrinking areas of natural beauty in national parks; by revising the practice of rewarding slum landlords who allow their property to deteriorate with low tax assessments; by imposing some order on the planning of schools and housing and parks and expressways.

Beyond these limited measures of community action we must strive as individuals to bring together the two Americas, to restore the lines of communication between the minority that value excellence and the majority that settle for mediocrity. I do not know how this is to be accomplished, but I think there is a clue in what seems to me to be one of the major sources of the postwar vulgarization of American life: the combination of widespread affluence with the intense anxieties generated by the cold war, resulting both in a fixation on foreign problems and in an almost compulsive search for release from anxiety through trivial and tasteless, but convenient and diverting, channels of popular amusement. The cold war, writes David Riesman, "is a distraction from serious thought about man's condition on the planet."

If there is any validity in this analysis, then it follows that the first thing we must do toward raising the quality of American life is to turn some part of our thoughts and our creative energies away from the cold war that has engaged them for so long back in on America itself. If we do this, and then let nature take its course, we may find that the most vital resources of our Nation, for its public happiness and its security as well, remain locked within our own frontiers, in our cities and in our countryside, in our work and in our leisure, in the hearts and minds of our people.

In Stockholm, at the annual meeting of the Swedish Institute for Cultural Relations, Dec. 5, 1966, Fulbright expressed the hopes and needs of "Education for a New Kind of International Relations."

The hope contained in education is a simple hope for man—a hope that is held not because man is thought to be basically good as the eighteenth century philosophers thought he was, nor because he is thought to be capable of heaven as theologians have believed, but simply because he is man, because he is exactly what he is, neither inherently virtuous nor inherently wicked, predestined so far as we know neither to heaven nor to hell. At its best, education aims to bring forth in a man nothing more but nothing less than the best of his *human* capacities. It aims to make him knowledgeable without pretending he can be omniscient; it aims to make him wise without pretending he can be infallible; it aims to make him compassionate without pretending he is capable, or ought to be capable, of total selflessness.

In the field of international relations the purpose of education is the civilizing and humanizing of relations between nations in ways which are within the limits of human capacity. The question above all others that must concern us is whether that capacity is great enough to meet the needs and to overcome the dangers of our time. There can be no answer to this question at present but we do not really need one in order to know what we must do. Even if it should turn out, as it may, that man's capacity is not great enough to eliminate the danger of nuclear war, to feed an overcrowded world, and to elevate the human majority from the degradation of poverty, it is better for us not to know in advance that we are going to fail. Our own human nature does not allow us to give up the game in advance, to reconcile ourselves to hopelessness or to death in a nuclear war. Our own human nature requires of us a certain faith in ourselves, an optimism which, unjustified though it may be, nonetheless must lead us to do what we can to feed the hungry, to cure the sick, to live in dignity and to try to civilize the unrestrained competition of nations which threatens us with nuclear destruction.

My theme is the contribution of education, particularly international education, toward restraining the competition of nations. My question is whether, in this era in which man has become capable for the first time of destroying his species, we can close the gap between our needs and our traditional forms of behavior, whether, to put it another way, we can change the nature of international relations, not merely by improving our traditional way of doing things but by devising new techniques and new attitudes, techniques and attitudes which one may hope will be within our capacity but adequate to our needs. The question may be answered with catastrophic suddenness or it may never be answered; what is called for, however, is not an answer but an effort, an effort rooted in acceptance of our own humanity, in hope for our future, and in a certain, perhaps not entirely justified, faith in ourselves.

New concepts are required, not only as applied to international relations but for the nation itself and the purposes it is meant to advance. It is a curious thing when you think of it that we refer to nations as "powers," as if the exercise of power in foreign relations rather than the government of people, the administration of territory, and the organization of societies were the principal reason for their existence. The new concept that is required is simple but fundamental: We must try to think of the nation as more nearly a *society* than a *power,* as a political arrangement whose primary business is the regulation of internal rivalries and the advancement of the welfare and happiness of its citizens.

It is in a way a mystery that, instead of demanding that their governments give primary attention to their own needs and aspirations, most of the citizens of *big* countries—those, that is, that have the status of being "powers" in the world—readily, even eagerly, accept the primacy which is given to foreign and military concerns. Far from being self-centered and materialistic as they are commonly credited with being, the ordinary citizen and his elected representative all too often turn out to be romantics, ready and eager to sacrifice programs of health, education, and welfare for the power and pride of the nation.

Power and pride are not cheaply bought. The great nations of the world feel obliged to spend an enormous portion of their total public expenditures each year on armaments—amounting in the case of my own country to the fantastic sum of $60 billion a year. Neither the Soviet Union nor the United States has yet become a paradise of prosperity and happiness but both feel obliged to expend additional vast sums of money and effort on space exploration in order to avoid what seems to each to be the unspeakable humiliation of allowing the other to be the first to land a man on the moon.

Aside from the fact that two great nations engage in so costly and wasteful a competition, the truly astonishing thing is the apparent acquiescence of their respective populations in the prodigality which gives national pride so much higher a priority than the welfare of the people. What this means is that the Russian people apparently are willing to live with many fewer of the material comforts than their economy is capable of providing and the American people are willing to tolerate slums, poverty, and pollution in order to finance an endless struggle for primacy in the world.

This, we are told, is political "realism." But if realism has anything to do with the satisfactions of human life, then, far from being realistic, the preoccupation with power and pride is strikingly romantic. What after all are their rewards? The Romans were able to glory for a while in their domination of the Mediterranean world and to swell with pride in the knowledge of being Roman citizens, but eventually their empire decayed and fell apart. The British were able for a few decades to survey an empire over which the sun never set but that did not make Liverpool a beautiful place to live in, nor did it make the children of Welsh coalminers healthy and strong; on the contrary, it consumed resources that might have gone for these purposes, and then after all the sun did set on the British Empire. I see no important difference between this kind of "realism" and the "realism" of Mr. Cassius Clay, who proclaims, "I am the greatest!"—as indeed he is, for the moment—but someday there will be a new heavyweight champion of the world and what will Mr. Cassius Clay have to boast about then?

I do not suggest that self-esteem is not important for a nation; it is indeed indispensable. But dignity has nothing to do with domination nor is self-respect the same thing as arrogance. A nation can take pride in its accomplishments without taking on a missionary role in the world; it can be full of self-confidence and self-respect without being disrespectful to other societies which may be less successful or less fortunate or simply inclined to do things in a different way.

There must be something more substantial for a nation to seek, something more durable and rewarding than the primacy of its power. The alternative that seems so obvious, so desirable and yet so elusive is the pursuit of public happiness. For reasons that I must confess an almost total inability to understand, large nations seem to be driven by a sense of imperial destiny, as if it would be craven to forego adventure and to concentrate on the intelligent government of a society. And yet, what is the greater legacy that any generation of leaders can bequeath: a temporary primacy consisting of the ability to push other people around or a well-run society consisting of cities without violence or slums, of productive farms, and of education and opportunity for all of the country's citizens?

I have the impression that big countries like the United States have something to learn in this respect from the example of small countries like Sweden. Lacking the power for pretensions to global responsibility, a small country is left free if it wishes to concentrate its resources on the good government of its people. Some small countries, of course, prefer to squander their resources on small imperial ventures or on flashy weapons that they cannot afford and do not need; others, among whom Sweden is a notable example, have preferred to make their societies into models of prosperity and good government.

Power is a dubious blessing and the absence or loss of it can have surprising rewards. Japan, for example, having lost her bid for the domination of Asia, has been left to build one of the world's most productive and fastest growing economies. Japanese social services are efficient and well-developed; the Japanese literacy rate is higher than that in the United States and a higher percentage of Japanese young people have higher education than is the case in most or all the countries of Western Europe. The Japanese, however, are said to be feeling a growing anxiety about their failure to play a role in the world proportionate to their importance. Having been brought to grief by their past militarism, and as the only country on which nuclear bombs have exploded, the Japanese emphatically reject a military role for themselves, but they do seem to be moving toward the acceptance of major responsibilities in providing economic, technological, and educational assistance to the less developed countries of Asia. In addition, just as she was once an inspiration for the nationalist movements of Asia, Japan is emerging as a model and an inspiration for Asian societies which aspire to both democracy and modernization.

The Japanese example is doubly instructive. In the first place, it suggests that a rich and successful nation has an instinct and an obligation to play a part in the world outside its frontiers. Secondly, it suggests that in the age of nuclear weapons there are, and indeed must be, other ways for a great nation to play a major role in the world besides the traditional way of armies and empires.

The latter is an extremely important point, pertaining to a matter currently under discussion in my own country. Some Americans and some friends of America abroad have expressed concern about the danger of a "neo-isolationism," about the possible withdrawal of America from world responsibilities. It is true that some Americans—I am one of them—believe that the United States has made some excessive and unwise commitments of its power, but even more important than the extent of a great nation's foreign responsibilities is the kind of responsibilities that are undertaken and the means that are used to discharge them. A great nation cannot escape important commitments in the world; the real question is the appropriateness of traditional methods of meeting those commitments and the availability of new ones in this age in which the use of military power by a great nation, on however limited a scale, contains the risk of a catastrophe for the whole human race.

There is nothing new about the irrational inversion of priorities as between human and national needs. Nations have always tended to give primacy to their role as "powers" while neglecting their responsibilities as "societies." What is new is the danger of universal catastrophe in a nuclear war. The irrationality of unrestrained national rivalries makes it desirable to develop new concepts of the nation and of international relations; the danger of universal destruction makes it absolutely essential.

Twice in this century honest, hopeful but thus far unsuccessful efforts have been made to bring unrestrained national rivalries under the civilized rules of an international community. These two efforts, the League of Nations and the United Nations, were born of the breakdown of traditional techniques of international relations in the two world wars. It is sometimes said that the League failed and the United Nations falters because they were excessively visionary and idealistic—as if they had been undertaken in a recklessly unhistoric spirit, in wholesale disregard for the tried and true methods of the past. In fact they were undertaken only when the traditional techniques collapsed in cataclysms that destroyed tens of millions of human lives. In proportion to the failure of the old techniques of power politics and in proportion to the needs of the human race, the League and the United Nations were far from excessively idealistic; both represented very modest efforts indeed to lay the foundations of an international community in a world of anarchy and violence.

It is not our *needs* but our *capacities* that have been exceeded by the modest experiments in international organization which have been undertaken in this century. The central question about the United Nations—more exactly about the international security community envisioned in the United Nations Charter—is not whether we need it but whether we are capable of making it work. We are caught in this respect in the dilemma to which I referred at the beginning of my remarks: Can we devise a course of action toward the building of an international community which is both bold enough to eliminate or reduce the danger of nuclear war and modest enough to be within the limits of tolerance imposed by prevailing fears and prejudices?

As I have said, there is no ready answer to this dilemma but there is hope, and that hope consists primarily in the promise of education for narrowing the gap between our needs and our capacities. There is nothing we can do to reduce our needs: We cannot put the atomic genie back into its bottle, and as long as it is out, the life of every human being on earth will be precarious indeed in the absence of an international community which is capable of making and enforcing civilized rules of international conduct, enforcible upon great nations as well as small ones. What we can do, through the creative power of education, is to expand the boundaries of human wisdom, sympathy and perception. Education is a slow-moving but a powerful force. It may not be fast enough or strong enough to save us from catastrophe but it is the strongest force available for that purpose, and its proper place, therefore, is not at the periphery but at the center of international relations.

Before developing this proposition I should like to say a further word about the comparative responsibilities of small countries and big countries in the effort to build a world community.

Generally, I have the impression that the large countries dominate world affairs to a degree which is disproportionate to their actual size and power, while the small countries exercise a disproportionately small influence on the course of events. Power begets itself a bonus; small countries, aware of their smallness, tend to underestimate the power they do have, thus by default handing it over to the big countries, who, tending in any case to exaggerate their own power—or "responsibilities" as they prefer to say—accept the gratuity from the small countries as their rightful due.

The result is an unhealthy distortion. The large countries, with all their pride, pretensions, rivalries, and sense of mission, dominate events to an even greater degree than is necessary—or desirable—while the smaller countries, some of whose leaders are among the most experienced, talented and objective statesmen in the world, fail to exercise the constructive influence of which they are capable. The pre-eminence of the large countries is probably inevitable but their absolute domination of things is not. The Latin American countries, for example, could not have prevented the United States from intervening in the Dominican Republic in April of 1965, but they could have prevented the United States from obtaining the formal approval of the Organization of American States after the event by withholding their votes in that organization.

Representatives of small countries often object that they cannot act independently because of the sanctions—political, economic, or unknown—that they believe will surely be taken against them if they do. In many instances the large country concerned does not even have to make a threat; the very fact that it might take some hostile action wins the tame compliance of some small neighbor, and in such a way that the big country comes under the illusion that others are following it out of simple good sense or even affection.

I do not have much sympathy with this attitude on the part of small countries. Aside from the fact that it is not very brave, it is not really very accurate either. In recent years those small countries which have followed their own course, or have actually defied the great powers, have had an impressive record of getting away with it; I am thinking, for example, of Mexico, Yugoslavia, Rumania, Cuba, and Cambodia.

It is not, however, by defying the big countries—although that can have its uses—but by bringing to bear the benign and objective influence of which those who are free of great pretensions are capable that a relatively small country like Sweden can play a constructive role in world affairs. It can do so in a number of ways. It can help to breathe vitality into such international organizations as the United Nations and the World Bank by acting through these organizations, speaking out through their forums, and providing them with the leadership which the great powers, by reason of their rivalry, are precluded from providing. Sweden has set a constructive example in this respect, notably through the distinguished person of the late Secretary General Dag Hammarskjold and through her support of the International Development Association. A few other countries have also made noteworthy contributions to the United Nations and other international organizations but there remain great opportunities for the smaller countries to lead in the strengthening of international organizations.

Another way in which the small countries can exert a greater influence in world affairs is simply by speaking out, by pressing unsolicited advice on the big countries—in much the same way that members of legislative bodies sometimes provide unsolicited advice to their executives. Disinterested, knowledgeable, and experienced as they often are, the leaders and scholars of small countries can exercise a moral authority which is convertible into greater political influence than they may realize.

Finally, the world's smaller nations can exercise an important, long-term influence through educational and cultural exchange. As you do not need to be reminded, many of those who participate in exchange programs become leaders in their countries, and almost all are destined to be among the more articulate and influential members of their societies. Educational exchange is a way in which all countries, small as well as large, can plant the seeds of ideas and influence in each other's societies. One cannot tell in advance what the precise rewards are going to be, nor can one necessarily identify them when they come, but one can be certain that nearly every educational exchange to one degree or another will advance its own proper purpose, which, as defined by Mr. Charles Frankel, my country's distinguished Assistant Secretary of State for Educational and Cultural Affairs, is "not to affect the individual's behavior for just this moment but over a long period of time, and with regard to a variety of situations that cannot be foreseen."[1]

Small countries can contribute to the building of a world community by overcoming their sense of impotence; big countries can contribute to the same end by overcoming their arrogance. The latter must recognize the enormous and often unintended impact they have on other societies, an impact which comes of their sheer size and weight aside even from their actions, from the simple fact that they take up so much space in the world, occupy so much of its attention, shape so many of its values and styles and generate so many of its anxieties, profoundly influencing the lives of others even when they are not trying to do so. Most of all they must recognize the impact of their rivalries on the smaller nations of the world, the fear that small countries have of being caught up in those conflicts and, what is probably worse, the sense of helplessness to do anything to escape it.

Power confuses itself with virtue. Powerful countries habitually assume that more than luck, circumstance and human ingenuity were responsible for the acquisition of their power. Just as seventeenth century Calvinists judged that wealth was a sign of God's favor and poverty a sign of deserved damnation, powerful nations tend to see themselves as the chosen instruments if not of God

---

[1] Charles Frankel, *The Neglected Aspect of Foreign Affairs*. Washington, D.C.: The Brookings Institution, 1966, p. 70.

then of "Nature," or of some deified force of "History." They become, in the well-chosen words of Herbert Butterfield, "giant organized systems of self-righteousness."[2]

I do not know whether it is possible to expect the great nations of the world, including my own, to forbear from chronic interference in the affairs—including the revolutions—of societies whose problems they do not understand and which in any case have no direct effect on their own interests. I do not know whether the leaders of the great powers are capable of the wisdom of Winston Churchill, who once, when asked to comment on an American Presidential election, replied, "I find the politics of my own country confusing enough without getting involved in the politics of any other." Nor do I know whether the world's great nations are capable of what would surely be unprecedented forbearance in the use of power as their necessary contribution to the building of a world community.

There is at present no indication that the great powers—or the less than great powers—are prepared to vest positive and effective authority in an international security organization. It may be that an awareness of the unprecedented dangers of the nuclear age will lead the great nations to an unprecedented act of forbearance, but danger alone has seldom, if ever, been an inducement to intelligent restraint. Wisdom is the product of perspective rather than of peril, and these in turn are products of education. We come back, therefore, again to the power and importance of learning as the crucible—the only crucible—in which a new kind of international relations can be shaped.

What we must all try to acquire through education and especially through international education is some degree of perception and perspective about the world, both as to the varieties of preference and aspiration in different societies and as to the common humanity which unites all societies. In a word, we must seek through education to develop *empathy*, that rare and wonderful ability to perceive the world as others see it. Or, as Charles Frankel has put it, "A primary purpose of education and cultural exchange is to become aware of others' cultural codes and of our own—to bring to the surface the context of unspoken facts and assumptions within which their words and actions, and ours, can be correctly interpreted."[3]

"The lack of objectivity, as far as foreign nations are concerned," writes Erich Fromm, "is notorious. From one day to another, another nation is made out to be utterly depraved and fiendish, while one's own nation stands for everything that is good and noble. Every action of the enemy is judged by one standard—every action of oneself by another. Even good deeds by the enemy are considered a sign of particular devilishness, meant to deceive us and the world, while our bad deeds are necessary and justified by our noble goals which they serve. Indeed, if one examines the relationship between nations, as well as between individuals, one comes to the conclusion that objectivity is

[2] Herbert Butterfield, *Christianity, Diplomacy and War.* New York: Abingdon-Cokesbury, 1953, p. 43.
[3] Charles Frankel, *The Neglected Aspect of Foreign Affairs.* Washington, D.C.: The Brookings Institution, 1966, p. 104.

the exception, and a greater or lesser degree of narcissistic distortion is the rule."[4]

Education is the best means—probably the only means—by which nations can cultivate a degree of objectivity about each other's behavior and intentions. It is the means by which Russians and Americans can come to understand each other's common aspirations for peace and for the satisfactions of everyday life. It is the means by which Americans may come to understand why many Europeans regard the war in Vietnam as an American imperialist war and also the means by which Europeans may come to understand why Americans believe themselves to be fighting for freedom in South Vietnam and for the security of the free world. And education is the means by which, some day, China may be drawn out of her isolation and brought into mutually respectful relations with other nations—including, I very much hope, my own.

Educational exchange can turn *nations* into *people*, contributing as no other form of communication can to the humanizing of international relations. Man's capacity for decent behavior seems to vary directly with his perception of others as individual humans with human motives and feelings, whereas his capacity for barbarism seems related to his perception of an adversary in abstract terms, as the embodiment, that is, of some evil design or ideology. China and the United States, for example, seem to think of each other as abstractions: to the Chinese America is not a society of individual people but the embodiment of an evil idea, the idea of "imperialist capitalism;" and to many Americans China represents not a people who have suffered greatly at the hands of the West and who are now going through an extremely difficult period of revolution but rather appears as an evil and frightening idea, the idea of "aggressive Communism."

Perhaps the greatest power of educational exchange is the power to convert nations into peoples and to translate ideologies into human aspirations. I do not think educational exchange is certain to produce affection between peoples, nor indeed do I think that is one of its necessary purposes; it is quite enough if it contributes to the feeling of a common humanity, to an emotional awareness that other countries are populated not by doctrines that we fear but by individual people—people with the same capacity for pleasure and pain, for cruelty and kindness, as the people we were brought up with in our own countries.

If international education is to advance these aims—of perception and perspective, of empathy and the humanizing of international relations—it cannot be treated as a conventional instrument of a nation's foreign policy. Most emphatically, it cannot be treated as a propaganda program designed to "improve the image" of a country or to cast its current policies in a favorable light. Nor can its primary purpose be regarded as simply the cultivation of "good will," which may come as a by-product of serious educational activities but cannot be regarded as their direct objective. Nor can educational exchange properly be treated as an instrument of foreign policy in anything like the sense that diplomacy is such an instrument; it is indeed a corruption of the educational process—and one that is likely to fail besides—to try to use educational exchange as a means of advancing current political, economic, or military projects. Edu-

[4] Erich Fromm, *The Art of Loving*. New York: Harper & Brothers, Inc., 1956, p. 120.

cation can be regarded as an instrument of foreign policy only in the sense
that the cultivation of international perception and perspective are—or ought
to be—important long-term objectives of a country's foreign policy.

The purpose of international education transcends the conventional aims of
foreign policy. This purpose is nothing less than an effort to expand the scope
of human moral and intellectual capacity to the extent necessary to close the
fateful gap between human needs and human capacity in the nuclear age. We
must try, therefore, through education, to realize something new in the world,
an aim that will inspire us and challenge us to use our talents and material
wealth in a new way, by persuasion rather than force, cooperatively rather
than competitively, not for the purpose of gaining dominance for a nation or
ideology but for the purpose of allowing every society to develop its own concepts of public decency and individual fulfillment. Far therefore from being a
means of gaining national advantage in the traditional game of power politics,
international education should try to change the nature of the game, to civilize
and humanize it in this nuclear age.

By the summer of 1967, Fulbright had broken with the Johnson administration's Vietnam policies and become the nation's leading dissenter. In his strongest criticism, he said Lyndon Johnson's "Great Society" had turned into the "Sick Society," and asked whether America was not in danger of losing her soul. His "The Price of Empire" speech was given Aug. 8, 1967, at an American Bar Association meeting in Honolulu.

Standing in the smoke and rubble of Detroit, a Negro veteran said: "I just got back from Vietnam a few months ago, but you know, I think the war is here."

There are in fact two wars going on. One is the war of power politics which our soldiers are fighting in the jungles of Southeast Asia. The other is a war for America's soul which is being fought in the streets of Newark and Detroit and in the halls of Congress, in churches and protest meetings and on college campuses, and in the hearts and minds of silent Americans from Maine to Hawaii. I believe that the two wars have something to do with each other, not in the direct, tangibly causal way that bureaucrats require as proof of a connection between two things, but in a subtler, moral and qualitative way that is no less real for being intangible. Each of these wars might well be going on in the absence of the other, but neither, I suspect, standing alone, would seem so hopeless and demoralizing.

The connection between Vietnam and Detroit is in their conflicting and incompatible demands upon traditional American values. The one demands that they be set aside, the other that they be fulfilled. The one demands the acceptance by America of an imperial role in the world, or of what our policy makers like to call the "responsibilities of power," or of what I have called the "arrogance of power." The other demands freedom and social justice at home, an end to poverty, the fulfillment of our flawed democracy, and an effort to create a role for ourselves in the world which is compatible with our traditional values. The question, it should be emphasized, is not whether it is *possible* to engage in traditional power politics abroad and at the same time to perfect democracy at home, but whether it is possible for *us Americans,* with our particular history and national character, to combine morally incompatible roles.

Administration officials tell us that we can indeed afford both Vietnam and the Great Society, and they produce impressive statistics of the gross national product to prove it. The statistics show financial capacity but they do not show moral and psychological capacity. They do not show how a President preoccupied with bombing missions over North and South Vietnam can provide strong and consistent leadership for the renewal of our cities. They do not show how a Congress burdened with war costs and war measures, with emergency briefings and an endless series of dramatic appeals, with anxious constituents and a mounting anxiety of their own, can tend to the workaday business of studying social problems and legislating programs to meet them. Nor do the statistics tell how an anxious and puzzled people, bombarded by press and television with the bad news of American deaths in Vietnam, the "good news" of enemy deaths—and with vividly horrifying pictures to illustrate them—can be expected to support neighborhood anti-poverty projects and national programs for urban renewal, employment and education. Anxiety about war does not breed compassion for one's neighbors; nor do constant reminders of the cheapness of life abroad strengthen our faith in its sanctity at home. In these ways the war in Vietnam is poisoning and brutalizing our domestic life. Psychological incompatibility has proven to be more controlling than financial feasibility; and the Great Society has become a sick society.

I. IMPERIAL DESTINY AND THE AMERICAN DREAM

When he visited America a hundred years ago, Thomas Huxley wrote: "I cannot say that I am in the slightest degree impressed by your bigness, or your material resources, as such. Size is not grandeur, and territory does not make a nation. The great issue, about which hangs the terror of overhanging fate, is what are you going to do with all these things?"

The question is still with us and we seem to have come to a time of historical crisis when its answer can no longer be deferred. Before the Second World War our world role was a *potential* role; we were important in the world for what we *could* do with our power, for the leadership we *might* provide, for the example we *might* set. Now the choices are almost gone: we are *almost* the world's self-appointed policeman; we are *almost* the world defender of the *status quo*. We are well on our way to becoming a traditional great power—an imperial nation if you will—engaged in the exercise of power for its own sake, exercising it to the limit of our capacity and beyond, filling every vacuum and extending the American "presence" to the farthest reaches of the earth. And, as with the great empires of the past, as the power grows, it is becoming an end in itself, separated except by ritual incantation from its initial motives, governed, it would seem, by its own mystique, power without philosophy or purpose.

That describes what we have *almost* become, but we have not become a traditional empire yet. The old values remain—the populism and the optimism, the individualism and the rough-hewn equality, the friendliness and the good humor, the inventiveness and the zest for life, the caring about people and the sympathy for the underdog, and the idea, which goes back to the American Revolution, that maybe—just maybe—we can set an example of democracy and human dignity for the world.

That is something which none of the great empires of the past has ever done—or tried to do—or wanted to do—but we were bold enough—or presumptuous enough—to think that we might be able to do it. And there are a great many Americans who still think we can do it—or at least they want to try.

That, I believe, is what all the hue and cry is about—the dissent in the Senate and the protest marches in the cities, the letters to the President from student leaders and former Peace Corps volunteers, the lonely searching of conscience by a student facing the draft and the letter to a senator from a soldier in the field who can no longer accept the official explanations of why he has been sent to fight in the jungles of Vietnam. All believe that their country was cut out for something more ennobling than an imperial destiny. Our youth are showing that they still believe in the American dream, and their protests attest to its continuing vitality.

There appeared in a recent issue of the journal *Foreign Affairs* a curious little article complaining about the failure of many American intellectuals to support what the author regards as America's unavoidable "imperial role" in the world. The article took my attention because it seems a faithful statement of the governing philosophy of American foreign policy while also suggesting how little the makers of that policy appreciate the significance of the issue between themselves and their critics. It is taken for granted—not set forth as an hypothesis to be proved—that, any great power, in the author's words, "is entangled in a web of responsibilities from which there is no hope of escape," and that "there is no way the United States, as the world's mightiest power, can avoid such an imperial role. . . ." The author's displeasure with the "intellectuals"—he uses the word more or less to describe people who disagree with the Administration's policy—is that, in the face of this alleged historical inevitability, they are putting up a disruptive, irritating and futile resistance. They are doing this, he believes, because they are believers in "ideology"—the better word would be "values" or "ideals"—and this causes their thinking to be "irrelevant" to foreign policy.

Here, inadvertently, the writer puts his finger on the nub of the current crisis. The students and churchmen and professors who are protesting the Vietnam war do not accept the notion that foreign policy is a matter of expedients to which values are irrelevant. They reject this notion because they understand, as some of our policy makers do not understand, that it is ultimately self-defeating to "fight fire with fire," that you cannot defend your values in a manner that does violence to those values without destroying the very thing you are trying to defend. They understand, as our policy makers do not, that when American soldiers are sent, in the name of freedom, to sustain corrupt dictators in a civil war, that when the CIA subverts student organizations to engage in propaganda activities abroad, or when the Export-Import Bank is used by the Pentagon to finance secret arms sales abroad, damage—perhaps irreparable damage—is being done to the very values that are meant to be defended. The critics understand, as our policy makers do not, that, through the undemocratic expedients we have adopted for the defense of American democracy, we are weakening it to a degree that is beyond the resources of our bitterest enemies.

Nor do the dissenters accept the romantic view that a nation is powerless to choose the role it will play in the world, that some mystic force of history or destiny requires a powerful nation to be an imperial nation, dedicated to what Paul Goodman calls the "empty system of power," to the pursuit of power without purpose, philosophy, or compassion. They do not accept the Hegelian concept of history as something out of control, as something that happens to us rather than something that we make. They do not accept the view that, because other great nations have pursued power for its own sake—a pursuit which invariably has ended in decline or disaster—America must do the same. They think we have some choice about our own future and that the best basis for exercising that choice is the values on which this republic was founded.

The critics of our current course also challenge the contention that the traditional methods of foreign policy are safe and prudent and realistic. They are understandably skeptical of their wise and experienced elders who, in the name of prudence, caution against any departure from the tried and true methods that have led in this century to Sarajevo, Munich, and Dienbienphu. They think that the methods of the past have been tried and found wanting, and two world wars attest powerfully to their belief. Most of all, they think that, in this first era of human history in which man has acquired weapons which threaten his entire species with destruction, safety and prudence and realism require us to change the rules of a dangerous and discredited game, to try as we have never tried before to civilize and humanize international relations, not only for the sake of civilization and humanity but for the sake of survival.

Even the most ardent advocates of an imperial role for the United States would probably agree that the proper objective of our foreign policy is the fostering of a world environment in which we can, with reasonable security, devote our main energies to the realization of the values of our own society. This does not require the adoption or imposition of these values on anybody, but it does require us so to conduct ourselves that our society does not seem hateful and repugnant to others.

At present much of the world is repelled by America and what America seems to stand for in the world. Both in our foreign affairs and in our domestic life we convey an image of violence; I do not care very much about images as distinguished from the things they reflect, but this image is rooted in reality. Abroad we are engaged in a savage and unsuccessful war against poor people in a small and backward nation. At home—largely because of the neglect resulting from twenty-five years of preoccupation with foreign involvements— our cities are exploding in violent protest against generations of social injustice. America, which only a few years ago seemed to the world to be a model of democracy and social justice, has become a symbol of violence and undisciplined power.

". . . It is excellent," wrote Shakespeare, "to have a giant's strength; but it is tyrannous to use it like a giant." By using our power like a giant we are fostering a world environment which is, to put it mildly, uncongenial to our society. By our undisciplined use of physical power we have divested ourselves of a greater power: the power of example. How, for example, can we commend peaceful compromise to the Arabs and the Israelis when we are unwilling to suspend our relentless bombing of North Vietnam? How can we commend democratic social reform to Latin America when Newark, Detroit, and Milwaukee are providing explosive evidence of our own inadequate efforts at democratic social reform? How can we commend the free enterprise system to Asians and Africans when in our own country it has produced vast, chaotic, noisy, dangerous, and dirty urban complexes while poisoning the very air and land and water? There may come a time when Americans will again be able to commend their country as an example to the world and, more in hope than confidence, I retain my faith that there will; but to do so right at this moment would take more gall than I have.

Far from building a safe world environment for American values, our war in Vietnam and the domestic deterioration which it has aggravated are creating a most uncongenial world atmosphere for American ideas and values. The world has no need, in this age of nationalism and nuclear weapons, for a new imperial power, but there is a great need of moral leadership—by which I mean the leadership of decent example. That role could be ours but we have vacated the field, and all that has kept the Russians from filling it is their own lack of imagination.

At the same time, as we have noted, and of even greater fundamental importance, our purposeless and undisciplined use of power is causing a profound controversy in our own society. This in a way is something to be proud of. We have sickened but not succumbed and just as a healthy body fights disease, we are fighting the alien concept which is being thrust upon us, not by history but by our policy makers in the Department of State and the Pentagon. We are proving the strength of the American dream by resisting the dream of an imperial destiny. We are demonstrating the validity of our traditional values by the difficulty we are having in betraying them.

The principal defenders of these values are our remarkable younger generation, something of whose spirit is expressed in a letter which I received from an American soldier in Vietnam. Speaking of the phony propaganda on both sides, and then of the savagery of the war, or the people he describes as the "real casualties"—"the farmers and their families in the Delta mangled by air strikes, and the villagers here killed and burned out by our friendly Korean mercenaries"—this young soldier then asks ". . . whatever has become of our dream? Where is that America that opposed tyrannies at every turn, without inquiring first whether some particular forms of tyranny might be of use to us? Of the three rights which men have, the first, as I recall, was the right to life. How then have we come to be killing so many in such a dubious cause?"

II. THE SICK SOCIETY

While the death toll mounts in Vietnam, it is mounting too in the war at home. During a single week of July 1967, 164 Americans were killed and 1442 wounded in Vietnam, while 65 Americans were killed and 2100 were wounded in city riots in the United States. We are truly fighting a two-front war and doing badly in both. Each war feeds on the other and, although the President assures us that we have the resources to win both wars, in fact we are not winning either.

Together the two wars have set in motion a process of deterioration in American society and there is no question that each of the two crises is heightened by the impact of the other. Not only does the Vietnam war divert human and material resources from our festering cities; not only does it foster the conviction on the part of slum Negroes that their country is indifferent to their plight: In addition the war feeds the idea of violence as a way of solving problems. If, as Mr. Rusk tells us, only the rain of bombs can bring Ho Chi Minh to reason, why should not the same principle apply at home? Why should not riots and snipers' bullets bring the white man to an awareness of the Negro's plight when peaceful programs for housing and jobs and training have been more rhetoric than reality? Ugly and shocking thoughts are in the American air and they were forged in the Vietnam crucible. Black power extremists talk of "wars of liberation" in the urban ghettoes of America. A cartoon in a London newspaper showed two Negro soldiers in battle in Vietnam with one saying to the other: "This is going to be great training for civilian life."

The effect of domestic violence on the chances for peace in Vietnam may turn out to be no less damaging than the impact of the war on events at home. With their limited knowledge of the United States, the Vietcong and the North Vietnamese may regard the urban riots as a harbinger of impending breakdown and eventual American withdrawal from Vietnam, warranting stepped up warfare and an uncompromising position on negotiations. It is possible that the several opportunities to negotiate which our government has let pass, most recently last winter, could not now be retrieved. Some eighteen months ago General Maxwell Taylor said in testimony before the Senate Foreign Relations Committee that the war was being prolonged by domestic dissent. That dissent was based in part on apprehension as to the effects of the war on our domestic life. Now the war is being prolonged by the domestic deterioration which has in fact occurred and it is doubtful that all of the dissenters in America, even if they wanted to, as they certainly do not, could give the enemy a fraction of the aid and comfort that has been given him by Newark, Detroit, and Milwaukee.

An unnecessary and immoral war deserves in its own right to be liquidated; when its effect in addition is the aggravation of grave problems and the corrosion of values in our own society, its liquidation under terms of reasonable and honorable compromise is doubly imperative. Our country is being weakened by a grotesque inversion of priorities, the effects of which are becoming clear to more and more Americans—in the Congress, in the press and in the country at large. Even the *Washington Post*, a newspaper which has obsequiously supported the Administration's policy in Vietnam, took note in a recent editorial of the "ugly image of a world policeman incapable of policing itself" as against the "absolute necessity of a sound domestic base for an effective foreign policy," and then commented: "We are confronted simultaneously with an urgent domestic crisis and an urgent foreign crisis and our commitments to both are clear. We should deal with both with all the energy and time and resources that may be required. But if the moment ever arises when we cannot deal adequately and effectively with both, there is no shame—and some considerable logic—in making it plain beyond a doubt that our first consideration and our first priority rests with the security of the stockade."

Commenting on the same problem of priorities, Mayor Cavanaugh of Detroit said:

"What will it profit this country if we, say, put our man on the moon by 1970 and at the same time you can't walk down Woodward Avenue in this city without some fear of violence?

"And we may be able to pacify every village in Vietnam, over a period of years, but what good does it do if we can't pacify the American cities?

"What I am saying . . . is that our priorities in this country are all out of balance . . . Maybe Detroit was a watershed this week in American history and it might well be that out of the ashes of this city comes the national resolve to do far more than anything we have done in the past."

Priorities are reflected in the things we spend money on. Far from being a dry accounting of bookkeepers, a nation's budget is full of moral implications; it tells what a society cares about and what it does not care about; it tells what its values are.

Here are a few statistics on America's values: Since 1946 we have spent over $1,578 billion through our regular national budget. Of this amount over $904 billion, or 57.29 percent of the total, have gone for military power. By contrast, less than $96 billion, or 6.08 percent, were spent on "social functions" including education, health, labor, and welfare programs, housing and community development. The Administration's budget for fiscal year 1968 calls for almost $76 billion to be spent on the military and only $15 billion for "social functions."

I would not say that we have shown ourselves to value weapons five or ten times as much as we value domestic social needs, as the figures suggest; certainly much of our military spending has been necessitated by genuine requirements of national security. I think, however, that we have embraced the necessity with excessive enthusiasm, that the Congress has been all too willing to provide unlimited sums for the military and not really very reluctant at all to offset these costs to a very small degree by cutting away funds for the poverty program and urban renewal, for rent supplements for the poor and even for a program to help protect slum children from being bitten by rats. Twenty million dollars a year to eliminate rats—about one one-hundredth of the monthly cost of the war in Vietnam—would not eliminate slum riots but, as Tom Wicker has written, "It would only suggest that somebody cared." The discrepancy of attitudes tells at least as much about our national values as the discrepancy of dollars.

III. THE REGENERATIVE POWER OF YOUTH

While the country sickens for lack of moral leadership, a most remarkable younger generation has taken up the standard of American idealism. Unlike so many of their elders, they have perceived the fraud and sham in American life and are unequivocally rejecting it. Some, the hippies, have simply withdrawn, and while we may regret the loss of their energies and their sense of decency, we can hardly gainsay their evaluation of the state of society. Others of our youth are sardonic and skeptical, not, I think, because they do not want ideals but because they want the genuine article and will not tolerate fraud. Others—students who wrestle with their consciences about the draft, soldiers who wrestle with their consciences about the war, Peace Corps volunteers who strive to light the spark of human dignity among the poor of India or Brazil, and VISTA volunteers who try to do the same for our own poor in Harlem or Appalachia—are striving to keep alive the traditional values of American democracy.

They are not really radical, these young idealists, no more radical, that is, than Jefferson's idea of freedom, Lincoln's idea of equality, or Wilson's idea of a peaceful community of nations. Some of them, it is true, are taking what many regard as radical action, but they are doing it in defense of traditional values and in protest against the radical departure from those values embodied in the idea of an imperial destiny for America.

The focus of their protest is the war in Vietnam and the measure of their integrity is the fortitude with which they refused to be deceived about it. By striking contrast with the young Germans who accepted the Nazi evil because the values of their society had distintegrated and they had no normal frame of reference, these young Americans are demonstrating the vitality of American values. They are demonstrating that, while their country is capable of acting falsely to itself, it cannot do so without internal disruption, without calling forth the regenerative counterforce of protest from Americans who are willing to act in defense of the principles they were brought up to believe in.

The spirit of this regenerative generation has been richly demonstrated to me in letters from student leaders, from former Peace Corps volunteers and from soldiers fighting in Vietnam. I quoted from one earlier in my remarks. Another letter that is both striking and representative was written by an officer still in Vietnam. He wrote:

"For eleven years I was, before this war, a Regular commissioned officer—a professional military man in name and spirit; now—in name only. To fight well (as do the VC), a soldier must believe in his leadership. I, and many I have met, have lost faith in ours. Since I hold that duty to conscience is higher than duty to the administration (not 'country' as cry the nationalists), I declined a promotion and have resigned my commission. I am to be discharged on my return, at which time I hope to contribute in some way to the search for peace in Vietnam."

Some years ago Archibald MacLeish characterized the American people as follows:

"Races didn't bother the Americans. They were something a lot better than any race. They were a People. They were the first self-constituted, self-declared, self-created People in the history of the world. And their manners were their own business. And so were their politics. And so, but ten times so, were their souls."

Now the possession of their souls is being challenged by the false and dangerous dream of an imperial destiny. It may be that the challenge will succeed, that America will succumb to becoming a traditional empire and will reign for a time over what must surely be a moral if not a physical wasteland, and then, like the great empires of the past, will decline or fall. Or it may be that the effort to create so grotesque an anachronism will go up in flames of nuclear holocaust. But if I had to bet my money on what is going to happen, I would bet on this younger generation—this generation who reject the inhumanity of war in a poor and distant land, who reject the poverty and sham in their own country, this generation who are telling their elders what their elders ought to have known, that the price of empire is America's soul and that price is too high.

INDEX